5/22/98 - Ta⁻ ... ...
5/23/98 - Tr⁻ ...

S0-AWG-306

HARBIN
— HOT —
SPRINGS

HEALING WATERS
SACRED LAND

Ellen Klages

Harbin Springs Publishing
Middletown, CA

PHOTO CREDITS

p. *113*, photo courtesy of the Sharpsteen Museum photo collection,
Calistoga; p. *152*, photo courtesy of the collection of Gary Phillips;
p. *159*, photo courtesy of the California State Library collections;
p. *167*, top photo courtesy of the Lake County Historical Society;
pp. *208* and *229*, photos courtesy of the collection of Irl Rickabaugh;
pp. *198, 217, 223, 230, 233* and *240*, photos courtesy of Pam Booth;
p. *297*, original art by Even Eve; p. *293*, photo by Matthew Scherer;
p. 287 and *332*, photos courtesy of Jane Hartley.

© 1991 Harbin Springs Publishing

All rights reserved. No part of this publication may be
reproduced, stored in a retrieval system, or transmitted, in any
form or by any means, electronic, mechnical, photocopying or
otherwise without the prior written permission of
Harbin Springs Publishing.

ISBN# 0-944202-01-2

Library of Congress Cataloging-in-Publication Data

Klages, Ellen, 1954-
    Harbin Hot Springs : healing waters, sacred land / Ellen Klages.
      p. cm.
    Includes bibliographical references and index.
    ISBN 0-944202-01-2 : $11.95
    1. Harbin Springs (Calif.)—History. 2. Lake County (Calif.)—
History. I. Title.
F869.H38K55 1991
979.4'17—dc20

                        91-2092 CIP

TO ROBERT HARTLEY,
WITHOUT WHOSE VISION
HARBIN WOULD BE NOTHING
BUT HISTORY.

Morning at Harbin Springs

❖   ❖

Like morning incense to the skies
    From Harbin's fountains far and near,
I see the curling steam arise;
    And sounds of welcome greet my ear.
The throng, with mingled hope and fear,
    Here turn from Art to Nature's cure,
And drink within an arbor near
    The water bubbling bright and pure.

Some seek alone relief from care,
    And coming hope to leave behind,
Within the city's stifling air,
    The troubles that oppress the mind.
Here age, now leaning on his cane,
    Hopes to prolong its lease awhile;
And joyous youth still free from pain,
    With festive sports the hours beguile.

— *Anonymous guest, circa 1885*

ACKNOWLEDGMENTS

THIS BOOK HAS BEEN MORE THAN THREE YEARS IN THE making, and is the result of many, many people, scattered all over Northern California (and beyond) who were generous enough to share their knowledge and memories with me.

For her seminal work on the Lake Miwoks, and for her thoughtful reading and comments on the manuscript of Chapter Two, I want to thank Catherine Callaghan. I also want to thank Bill Toney for his information about aboriginal sites at Harbin, and Don Grimm for helping me get a feel for the Lake Miwok's daily life through his collection of artifacts. The volunteers and staffs of the Genealogical Societies and Historical Societies of Napa, Solano, Sonoma, Yolo and Yuba Counties were invaluable in helping me track down old deeds, census records, marriage certificates and the like on the trail of the elusive Messrs. Harbin, and their cronies. I am indebted to the Bancroft Library, the California Historical Society Library and the California State Library for the use of their collections of rare and hard-to-find materials, and of their photographic collections.

I spent a lot of the last three years in the sometimes dusty and musty back shelves of libraries—which I considered a great adventure. Local libraries in all of the above-mentioned counties were a delightful source of pamphlets, newspapers and other materials. I am especially grateful for the collections in the California Room of the Santa Rosa Public Library, and the amazing local resources of the Lake County Library. The Lake County Historical Society provided me with wonderful photographs and many informative meetings, especially Norm Lehrman's talk about Lake County geology at a meeting in Middletown. Barbara Neelands and the Sharpsteen Museum in Calistoga were extremely helpful in filling in some visual and factual gaps about Richard Williams and his business.

I knew nothing at all about boxing history and had no idea where to begin when I found Gary Phillip's business card in my mailbox. Over the next few months he shared his collection of letters, newspaper clippings and photographs, along with his own vast store of knowledge, which helped make Jim Jeffries come to life for me and made Chapter Five possible.

Irl Rickabaugh invited me to his home to browse through his wonderful collection of Lake County postcards, and generously allowed me to photograph a few dozen Harbin cards; some of the images appear in Chapters Four and Six. The editorial staff of the Middletown *Times-Star* was kind enough to let me sit in their back offices on Thursdays and Fridays, reading old newspapers to my heart's content, which provided me with the needed local perspective on the events of Chapter Seven.

Facts and photographs alone make for accurate, but impersonal history, and I am grateful to the people who allowed me to interview them about their experiences and memories of Harbin's past. Lucille Goodwin was a waitress at Harbin in 1922; her stories about working and playing here vividly recreated life at the Booth's resort. Pam Booth shared an afternoon of stories about her family and their lives, and let me rummage with her through a box of old photos to find the perfect pictures to illustrate them. Earle Wreiden's knowledge of the ins and outs of Lake County, Harbin and Stuparich in the '20s and '30s was invaluable, as was the information Bob Kies shared with me about the '60s.

Art Blum took time out of his busy schedule to reminisce about his brief span as the owner of the Golden Spa, and Don Brown and John Paul filled me in on the adventures of the Golden Toad and their days at Harbinger University. Michael Horowitz (and his unparalleled library of drug and counterculture material) helped me discover a wealth of information about Don Hamrick and the Frontiers of Science, and tracked down an actual copy of *The Changes* for me to read.

I owe a deep debt of gratitude to Donna Howard, curator of the Lake County Museum, who not only allowed me access to all its collections, but took me into the back rooms and let me browse, and even stayed late a few times so I could finish reading one more year of the Lake County *Bee*, or copy the last of the documents from the Jim Hays probate file. She listened to my questions, helped me find answers and shared my enthusiasm for arcane bits of Harbin trivia.

Thanks, too, to all the Harbin residents and guests who shared what they knew, or whom they knew. Thanks to the anonymous guest who gave me a copy of the 1968 *Harbinger*, and to the unknown friend who mailed me a 1918 Harbin brochure. This is truly a community effort.

As the research turned into writing, I was fortunate enough to have four of the best readers an author could ever want. Libby Baltrusch found every typo, each inconsistency, and is a better grammar monitor than I am. Really. Thanks, Lib. Neil Murphy is not only a stickler for proper usage, his marginal notes were entertaining, interesting, and, well, enlightening. Julie Adams was sparing with her comments and abundant with her support for the book from its inception. Sandra Pungor's sense of humor kept me going, and her insights improved the style and narrative flow of the work ten-fold. Thank you all; this couldn't have happened without you.

I want to thank Ish and Carol O'Shea and the Board for believing, three years ago, that I could be a writer and a historian and giving me the go-ahead for this project. And Becky Weed for keeping me on track and on time and even a little sane through the months of proofing, indexing and production.

Finally, I want to thank Julie and Khan, for their love and their support, for listening to all the historical trivia I brought home with me and not yawning (at least in front of me), for helping me to believe in myself and in this book, and for being my sisters. I love you both.

Ellen Klages
Harbin Hot Springs
February, 1991

PREFACE

HARBIN HOT SPRINGS IS A RETREAT CENTER AND intentional community in Northern California. About 120 people live year-round on its 1200 acres, which makes this a fairly large book about a fairly small place.

Why write a book about it? Harbin Hot Springs was the first resort to open in Lake County, about 125 years ago. That in itself might be worthy of a little bit of a history, certainly more than just a footnote somewhere. But what's remarkable about Harbin is that after all these years, it's still here, still welcoming guests to come and soak in its healing waters.

What's important is not so much what Harbin *was* as much as what it has become, and just *how* it became what it is today. A thousand years ago, and more, a people lived on this land who respected and honored it; a few weeks ago, I watched as once again a Native American elder called upon his spirit guides to bless and protect this land. We have come full circle, completed a cycle, from ancient times to the present, and it is time to tell the story of that journey.

❖   ❖

MANY PEOPLE THINK HISTORY IS PRETTY BORING. (PERSONALLY, I find it rather exciting, but then that's why I wrote this.) It's certainly presented as dull stuff, more often than not—obligatory facts and dates that seem to be completely irrelevant to anything happening now. Take the ubiquitous "George Washington slept here." Yawn. So what? I used to think that the point was the (boring) fact that *he* slept someplace, like history was just a list of beds, but I don't think that's it. For me it's the idea that everything from the past is built up in layers, and the top one is the present. Finding places that still exist, places where one of the older layers is still at the surface—George Washington's bed, the Shiatsu Building at Harbin—is a way of stepping back in time.

There are a lot of different layers of the past at Harbin, going as far back as a few thousand years. There are pieces of arrowheads, obsidian arrowheads, just lying in the dirt up in the hills. I can pick one up, and hold it in my hand, and know that before my great-great grandfather was even born the last person to hold it was already gone. But the point still exists, right where he dropped it.

It's a mistake to confuse history with the past, as a friend of mine kept reminding me while I wrote this book. The past is what happened (and history is what was written about it), but a good history can serve as a kind of guidebook for armchair touring through the past.

❖   ❖

I CAN'T TRAVEL BACK IN TIME. I OFTEN WISH I COULD. I WOULD like to meet Mat Harbin (I think). I'd like to see the Stuparich Resort, about 1924, all lit up for a Saturday night dance. I want to walk through the lobby of Harbin's Main Hotel, buy a pack of Lifesavers, put a nickel in the slot machine and then sit in a rocking chair on the porch, with a frosty glass of iced tea in my hand. I'd like to play croquet with Jim and Maggie Hays on a still summer evening.

But I've been lucky, because even if I couldn't actually go back to the past, I could look at all the photographs of what Harbin used to be and walk to the same place (now) where the photograph was taken (then)—a spot marooned in time—and go imagining. And now it's time to share these photographs, and what I've learned about the people and the buildings they depict, so that others can go imagining too.

Many of the people who will read this book will pick it up because they have been fortunate enough to visit Harbin in person. Not only will most of the geographic references (Azalea, the Meadow) be familiar to them, but they can also use this book as a guide for actually touring the remains of its past.

There are few written records of any of the activities of the Lake Miwok people, but the land that they held sacred is still here. (Most places in America were, at one time, Indian settlements, but I find it hard to imagine aboriginal life on a site that is now downtown Oakland.) One of the things that makes

Harbin such a remarkable place is that if you go back up into the hills, nothing much has changed in the last few thousand years. What you see around you is exactly what a Lake Miwok would have seen—same sky, same hillsides, same kind of deer.

In a lot of ways it's easier to visualize the world of the Lake Miwok than that of later Harbin inhabitants, because everything but the land *has* changed. Azalea and Walnut and Stonefront are remnants from the 1920s, and the Shiatsu Building has been here since the "original" resort was built (although it has been repainted and repaired). And there's a stone wall, up by the baths, that Richard Williams and his crew built just after the Civil War. You can put your hand on any of them, and imagine.

One night when I was in the midst of writing Chapter Four, I needed to get far enough away from 1989 to see 1889 in my mind's eye, so I walked up the hill to the Bird House, where a friend was living. The night was pitch dark, there was no moon, and it was only when I got within a hundred feet of the building that I could see the light of the lantern in her window, shining through the trees. And I thought—this is what it was like, before there was electricity in the world. This is how it looked outside of every cabin back then. At that moment, everything looked like the past, felt like the past, and there was nothing I could perceive (except my clothes and my decidedly twentieth century attitudes) that disturbed the illusion. When I went home to write, I tried to combine that experience with the facts and dates I'd accumulated, and make them live.

❖   ❖

THE RESEARCH FOR THIS BOOK ACTUALLY BEGAN WHEN I FOUND out about the Old Stagecoach Inn, which (as it turned out) never existed.

About four years ago, on one of my first visits to Harbin, I went hiking up into the hills and, about two miles from the main area, came upon an old rock wall. Not just a wall, but the remains of the foundations of a building of some sort, hearth, chimney and all. I wondered what it had been—a barn? a house?—and who had lived there, and when.

At dinner I asked a friend if he knew what it might be. "Oh," he said, "that's the Old Stagecoach Inn." Harbin had been a resort for a long time, he said, and in the olden days, people came here by stagecoach, and sometimes stayed at the inn on their way to or from Harbin. I have a passion for history—things that have been misplaced by time, and old, odd facts—and I asked a lot of questions about when and who, and pressed him for details. But there weren't any, just the tail end of a kind of legend he believed to be fact.

A few weeks later, in the Bancroft Library, on the trail of some other mystery, I decided to try and track down the old inn, maybe even find a picture of it in its heyday. I imagined this treasure...a postcard of a stagecoach and a team of horses standing in front of the broad stone entranceway to Stunkard's Inn or the Mountain House or whatever it had really been called. I shopped in the card catalog computer, looking up Lake County, and Harbin, and stagecoaches and inns; I found a few interesting references to Harbin's early days, but no Stagecoach Inn.

I knew a man who dealt in antique postcards and other paper memorabilia, and the next time I was in his shop, even more anxious for a picture of the elusive inn, I asked if he had any Lake County cards. Again there were a few views of Harbin, but no inn.

Not finding treasure is more addictive than finding it; I had to keep looking. After six months I'd found exactly nothing about the inn, but had a file of old postcards and xeroxes and notes about the past hundred years at Harbin.

That file changed my life. I ended up moving to Harbin to work on the history, only to find someone else was planning to write it. He got a "real job" and moved, and I got the project after all. A month later, in San Francisco, my car was broken into and all my research and postcards—every last one of them—were stolen.

I started over.

Nothing much in the way of old records still existed at Harbin itself because anything paper had been burned or tossed out years before, so I had to go out into the world to find what I was looking for. The world is very far from Harbin (the county seat is a 70-mile round trip, the Bancroft or the State libraries about 200); I drove a lot. I spent hours (and hours, and hours) in innumerable County Recorder's offices, tracing the ownership of the land backwards from the present. I read ledger after ledger in florid 19th century handwriting, looking for the familiar names of the people I was beginning to feel as if I knew—J. Harbin, J. Hays, R. Williams—and was overjoyed when I reached the turn of the century (when the typewriter began to be used by civil servants) and the indexes became legible. I copied the information from a hundred deeds, mortgages, death certificates and probate files, until I had a clear trail of ownership, from 1988 back through the beginning of record-keeping in California, around 1850. (No argument here, that sort of information really *is* boring, but like the concrete foundation of a house, it supports all the (metaphorical) gingerbread and stained glass that makes history interesting.)

The more I discovered, the more confused I became. The older the original source, the more limited his perspective and access to information. In the age of computerized indexes, databases and cross-referencing, even though I was at a great distance from the events themselves, I had gathered enough certain facts for the ambiguities and the contradictions to become puzzling.

The geology and the Miwoks were fairly straightforward, but when I got into Chapter Three, I came up against the Harbins. There was no doubt in anyone's mind that James Harbin had something to do with the hot springs, because it had his name on it, and because he was fairly well-documented in the pages of old histories. Maybe a little too well-documented. He had the most interesting, and the most contradictory, life I'd ever come across. In one of those rare "ah ha!" moments (in this case a small newspaper article discussing his death, and his age at death), I realized that no matter how clever he was, he couldn't, flat-out couldn't, have been born in 1822 and die 55 years later at the age of 81.

With one impossibility firmly in hand, I began to sift back through all the other information I had about him, and try to make sense of it. He'd done enough in one lifetime for two men. As it turned out, he *was* two men. Or, rather, two men (father and son, with the same name) had been routinely and mistakenly assumed to be the same person by previous historians.

What other information that I was taking as fact was going to turn out to be a little off? One account talked glowingly about the courage of Richard Williams, struggling to rebuild Harbin after the fire of 1894, even though he was old and in poor health. According to legal records, he'd also been dead for twelve years. Little things like that kept me digging, in the hopes of one day being able to present something close to the truth about Harbin's history.

Truth isn't usually as much fun as legend. I liked the romantic image of the Old Stagecoach Inn on the mountain better, but the stones up by the Gulch House turned out to be part of a sawmill—Brookin's Sawmill—built about 1905. (I'm 99% certain. I never did find a photograph, of the inn or the mill.) By the time I finally stumbled across a map with the mill on it—in the exact geographic position where the ruins of the "inn" are—I had already written half this book. It seemed silly to stop just because there was no inn; I'd found so much more.

❖   ❖

I'VE SPENT MORE THAN THREE YEARS WALKING AROUND HARBIN, looking intently at old buildings that no one else could still see. A part of me wrote this book so that when I look at the Volleyball Court and see a majestic white hotel, I won't be alone.

Harbin is my home, and I love it. I couldn't have spent this much time or energy on its story if I didn't. Through this book I want people to discover it, to come and visit, to grow to love it too, so that its land and its water will continue to be treasured. I want people to love it just as it is, but I also want to share the wonder of everything it's been and how beautiful it was.

Come now. Turn the page and take a stroll with me through a Harbin that lies just beyond the veil of the present. There are words and maps and photographs to guide you on the journey. If I've done my job well, you'll be able to visit any time you want.

CONTENTS

HARBIN HOT SPRINGS
1991

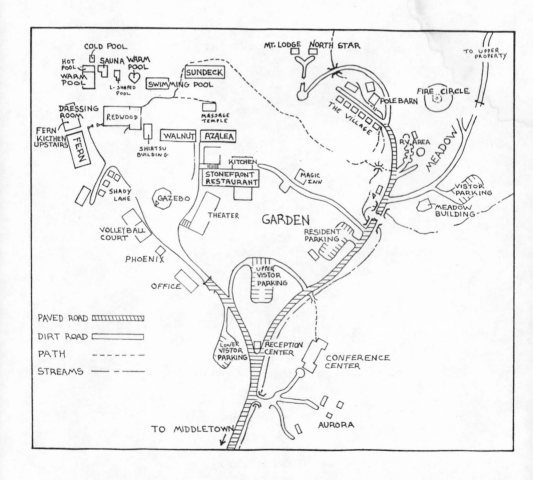

HARBIN
HOT
SPRINGS

Healing Waters,
Sacred Land

CHAPTER ONE

The Land Itself

HIGHWAY 29 THREADS ITS WAY UP CALIFORNIA'S NAPA Valley, through picturesque towns and vineyards flanked by rolling hills. When it reaches Calistoga, it leaves the gentle tranquility of the valley and begins to climb the steep slopes of Mt. St. Helena.

Grapevines quickly give way to scrub oaks and oaks to deep forest as the road twists and turns its way up the mountain. As it climbs higher, vistas open up on either side—broad panoramas of the valley far below; a line of cliffs, solitary and remote against a deepening blue sky.

By the time the road enters Lake County (less than 15 miles from the head of the Napa Valley) it has journeyed into another land—a land of mountains and towering pines, deep lakes, geysers and hot springs. It passes through the small village of Middletown, forming its main street, and continues on to resort towns beyond.

In the center of Middletown, across from the grocery store, another road turns west, into the hills. It rises gradually, through fields and into woods, until it turns again to enter the canyon formed by Harbin Creek. Four miles outside of Middletown, California, in a secluded, wooded canyon, is a retreat center and community on the site of an old resort, which was itself on the site of an aboriginal settlement called *eetawyomi*—the hot place.

For thousands of years, people have traveled over the mountain to the land that we now call Harbin Hot Springs. They have come to heal, to celebrate and to relax. In looking at the history of this place, the land has been as important as the

1

people. It is the land itself that has drawn people to come *here*. More specifically, it is the water than runs underneath and through the land that forms the basis for the rest of Harbin's history. For without the water, there would be no people, no settlements, no resort, and no need for a history.

What makes this place special, different from other places on the earth and the nearby countryside? Here, on a wooded hillside, hot water comes out of the ground.

❖   ❖

TWO MILLION YEARS AGO, THE AREA THAT IS NOW LAKE COUNTY was still ocean, an inland sea between the Coast Range and the Sierras. Fossil squids have been found that are believed to be 135 million years old. There is speculation that this sea was also the home of plesiosaurs and other aquatic dinosaurs, but no fossil remains have yet been discovered.

As the Coast Range was formed, internal pressures in the young mountains caused great cracks to form, and volcanic activity began. The cracks were leaks in the plumbing system of the earth, from which molten rock—magma—escaped. Volcanos rose from the weakest spots in the earth's crust—the places most likely to spring a leak. As they emerged, some of the water of the sea evaporated with the intense heat, and some of it poured through the cracks in the surface and filtered down into the earth for miles and miles until it reached an impermeable bottom.

After many periods of volcanic collapse and reformation, the area stabilized, more or less. Lake County is still an active volcanic area. Volcanic action has a cycle of 500,000 years—"on" for 300,000 and "off" for 200,000. Right now Lake County is about 100,000 years into a 300,000-year active period. Mt. Konocti, a volcano constructed on sediments formed when Clear Lake (the oldest lake in North America) was young, is dormant at the present time, but is believed to be a "live" volcano. There is also a large magma chamber centered about four miles underneath Mt. Hannah (about 12 miles north of Harbin), a sphere of molten rock about 13 miles in diameter.

Harbin Hot Springs is part of this volcanic system, as are The Geysers and other hot springs in the county. Hot springs only occur when there is a magma chamber relatively close to the surface of the earth. They are the final stages of thermal activity in volcanic regions, lingering on for eons as visible proof of the unseen fires below.

❖ ❖

IN GEOLOGIC TERMS, HOT SPRINGS CONSIST OF CIRCULATING ground water, heated and augmented by steam rising from the underlying magma through deep cracks in the earth's crust. In the place where the springs emerge, thermal activity has not only brought water to the surface, but transformed the very structure of the rocks in the process.

> In the vicinity of Harbin Hot Springs...there are broken fragments of granite to be found in the hillsides. They do not assume the shapes of boulders, nor seem to have ever come into contact with running water at all, but rather to have been exposed to the action of fire, and the outer crusts of the fragments are so charred that their identity is almost destroyed and even upon breaking them in twain all characteristics of granite are seen to have disappeared in many of them, except the peculiar form of crystallization.[1]

Two separate sources combine to form the water that comes out of the pipe in the Hot Pool at Harbin. First, there is *ground water*, which is water that falls to earth as rain or snow. Much of it runs off in streams and rivers; the rest sinks into the ground, percolating through porous places and crevices wherever it can find a way, until it reaches bedrock or a layer of clay and can go no deeper. It collects in underground chambers and in the porous layers of the aquifer.

The second type of water that comprises Harbin's springs is called *juvenile water*. This is water that has never been to the surface of the earth. Despite its name, it is ancient water, the remains of the inland sea. It is water that has been trapped

---

1   In order to interrupt the flow of the story as little as possible, sources for quotes in this and following chapters are listed at the end of the book, beginning on page 348.

3

miles beneath the earth for 100 million years—water that dinosaurs once swam in.

Every drop of water that comes out of the hillside and into the Hot and Warm Pools at Harbin contains some of this juvenile water, making its first journey to the surface of the earth, and its first contact with human beings.

The juvenile water is "stored" at a level of solid rock, deep in the earth, often miles away from the mouth of the springs. After a rain, the ground water seeps through the aquifer until it reaches an impermeable level, and flows into a similar storage area. Beneath this solid layer (approximately four miles beneath the surface, in this area) is a magma chamber of molten rock at extreme temperatures. The magma boils the water, turning it to steam and forcing it back upward into a layer of permeable rock. Above this porous layer is a thicker layer that prevents the steam from escaping. Small fissures in that layer form channels for the steam to rise to the surface; as it nears the earth's surface and cools, it changes back into water. The ends of these channels, the places where the water reaches the surface of the earth, are what we call hot springs.

There are countless tiny springs all over the hills of Harbin; the main spring and bath area consists of seven major springs: two hot springs—one sulphur, one iron; four cold soda springs; and one warm arsenic spring. The hot springs are currently combined to flow into the Hot and Warm Pools. Three of the cold springs feed into the Cold Pool, and one into the water fountain by the Warm Pool. The arsenic spring flows into a tiny footbath beside the Warm Pool.

At Harbin, as in many other volcanic regions, hot and cold springs exist side by side. Although they appear to emerge from the ground next to each other, the water of the cold springs and of the hot springs actually comes from storage areas in different strata of the rocks—varying depths which cause the variations in temperature. The original source for some of the cold springs is several miles away from the opening on the hillside above the pools.

In the early stages of recorded Harbin history, a magnesia spring of slight flow is mentioned, but it seems to have diminished over time. The birth or death of a spring can be due to many factors: the eventual clogging of the channel by deposited minerals; the depletion of subterranean water storage; mild earthquake activity which shifts the rock strata, causing new channels to open or old ones to close; and the opening of new channels when a last barrier of rock is dissolved by the acids present in the super-heated water. In September of 1988, a new cold spring appeared at Harbin in previously dry and unbroken ground; it is not unlikely that appearances and disappearances of this sort have been happening periodically for ages.

From a comparison of modern and historic records, it appears that the flow from the springs has changed somewhat over the last hundred years. The combined flow of the sulphur and iron springs today is about 800 gallons per hour; an 1888 analysis of Harbin's water by Dr. Winslow Anderson (a nineteenth century physician and water analyst) lists it over 1500 gallons per hour. Today the hot iron spring flows at a temperature of 120°F, the sulphur at 112°F, and the arsenic at about 113°F. The same 1888 analysis shows temperatures of 120°F, 116°F and 90°F, respectively. It's difficult to know, when dealing with a spring whose approximate age is over one million years, whether or not these hundred-year fluctuations are significant, or merely incidental and temporary changes.

❖   ❖

DR. ANDERSON DEFINED A MINERAL SPRING AS "ONE YIELDING water impregnated to a greater or lesser extent with substances rendering it suitable for medicinal purposes."[2] Most springs are referred to by their dominant mineral content—Iron, Sulphur, Magnesium.

The mineral composition of a spring depends entirely on the rocks through which the water percolates. Mineral waters contain high levels of dissolved solids and gasses—gasses from underground volcanic emanations and solids from the materials leached from the surrounding earth.

---

2   Medicinal claims for Harbin's water are discussed in detail in Chapter Four.

As ground water seeps down through the soil, it comes in contact with decaying vegetation, from which it absorbs small quantities of organic acids and carbonic acid (from the carbon in the plant matter). Large quantities of carbonic acid are also given off beneath the surface of volcanic regions,[3] and are rapidly absorbed by the heated water. Both the ground water and the juvenile water, one coming down into the earth and the other percolating up through it, absorb carbonic acid and sulphuric acid, which is created when the water combines with sulphur in the earth.

These acids increase the solvent powers of the water, enabling it to slowly but effectively dissolve the surrounding rock. With an increase in temperature and pressure miles below the surface, the water is able to dissolve and hold in suspension a remarkably higher level of minerals than the same water at a cooler temperature.

By the time the water reaches the surface of the earth, it has cooled off considerably, often more than 100°F, and the pressure it is under has also lessened dramatically. As the temperature and pressure drop, the water cannot hold the volume of minerals it has absorbed, and deposits them in the channel through which it flows, and in the surrounding earth.

One of the characteristics of a hot spring is the deposits of various minerals around its "mouth." The hole in the ground from which the water comes is fascinating; it is both literally and figuratively a window into ancient and subterranean depths, the primordial underworld. The rock walls of the opening are warm and slimy with deposited minerals; around the edges are soft ropes of material in transition from solution to solid—they have the look and feel of snails. As the water flows over the rocks and into the air, layer after layer of these lithic snails are deposited on the surrounding rocks, hardening over time. Depending on the minerals through which the water flows, these deposits can eventually create fantastic

---

3   Carbonic acid is a result of the combination of super-heated water and molten quartz coming into contact with the subterranean limestone and other carbon-based rocks.

formations—natural art that combines the softness and flowing forms of water with the permanence of stone.

Often the most noticeable of these mineral deposits is sulphur. The sulphurous smell of many hot springs (including Harbin's Hot Pool, very close to the outlet pipe) is a result of the sulphuric acid in the water being released as hydrogen sulfide (a colorless gas that smells distinctly like rotten eggs) as it cools. Sulphuric acid also dissolves gold; while the super-heated water is traveling up from the aquifer, it digests the gold in the earth it passes through.[4] As it cools, the gold precipitates and is deposited along the channel. Over a period of millions of years, enough gold and other mineral deposits line the sides of the channel to restrict the flow of water and, eventually, to block it completely. Many, if not most, gold-producing veins are the shining results and remains of ancient hot springs.

Gold and sulphur are not the only minerals that Harbin spring water carries. According to Dr. Anderson's analysis, Harbin's waters contain Sodium, Potassium, Lithium, Calcium, Magnesium, Iron, Aluminum, Manganese, Sulphates, Chloride, Carbonates, Metaborates, Arsenates and Silica.

In areas of volcanic activity, when molten rock and vapor are forced out of the magma chamber into the air or into the surrounding rock structures, they crystallize as they cool. (An exception to this is obsidian, a volcanic glass that cools so rapidly that it does not crystallize at all, and has no discernible atomic structure.) Many factors influence the formation of the crystals: quartz crystallizes into different forms depending on temperature; the longer the cooling period, the bigger the crystals. Lake County diamonds, for example, are formed from molten quartz (silica) which melts at a temperature of 600°F, and cools over a period of 200 years or so. Other minerals present in the silica when it cools influence the final crystal—amethysts, carnelians and even opals are all quartz crystals of varying mineral content.

---

4 There is over one ton of gold in an average cubic mile of earth.

Of the 600 simple minerals which have been discovered on the earth's surface, only nine form any considerable portion of it. Of these, quartz or silica is the most abundant of all, comprising at least three-quarters of all the crust of the earth....In Lake County the very waysides are strewn with gems in the shapes of quartz crystals. The more highly esteemed variations being amethyst, rose quartz, smoky and milky quartz, chalcedony, carnelian, agate, onyx, jasper and bloodstone. Most all of these variations occur in greater or lesser amounts throughout the county.

Harbin's spring water percolates through layers of earth, minerals and crystals. In the New Age movement, with its emphasis on the healing and psychic power of crystals, it might be said that the minerals release their energy into the water, imbuing it with healing qualities. In the 1800s, the curative powers of Harbin water were ascribed to the medicinal virtues (scientifically) inherent in each of the minerals they contained. The aboriginal peoples of the area believed that the waters of Harbin's springs had great healing power because they came from the underworld, the spirit realm of the shaman's visions.

Whatever the era, and for whatever the reason, it has been recognized for countless centuries that the water of Harbin's hot springs is quite extraordinary.

❖   ❖

A HOT SPRING IS A CLOSED SYSTEM OF FIRE AND AIR, WATER AND earth that is continually evolving and changing, and yet stays the same. The water coming out of the hillside at Harbin is ancient and constant. When zebras and mammoths and giant sloths roamed this land, the water was flowing, as it had flowed for ages, as it was flowing when the first humans discovered it and adapted it to their own use.

CHAPTER TWO

The First People

T HE FIRST INHABITANTS OF THE LAND NOW CALLED Harbin Hot Springs were members of a Native American tribe known as the Lake Miwok. They lived in this area for thousands of years. Relatively little is known about them.

These aboriginal people had no written language, and most of the oral history that was recorded in their legends and memorized stories has been lost. Any records of their culture come as part of the documentary record of European exploration, with its built-in biases.

Although a few Jesuit and Franciscan fathers did attempt to study and record the languages and cultures of various tribes, the majority of priests and soldiers viewed them as ignorant and stupid savages, and were not particularly interested in recording the "heathenish customs" of the Lake Miwok and other natives, only in using them as labor.

By the time serious ethnographers and anthropologists began to record any data about the tribes of California, the native culture had been changed beyond recognition. Contact with whites, slavery and exposure to previously unknown diseases had decimated the native population in the state, from an estimated 300,000 in 1769 to less than 100,000 by 1850. Twenty years later, this figure had been halved again.[1]

---

1   Ethnographer Stephen Powers, in his 1877 book, *The Tribes of California,* erroneously
     reported that the Lake Miwok were "now extinct." Since Powers' work was relied on as
     a primary source by later ethnographers, this assertion was taken as fact; early
     ethnographers did not attempt to study the Lake Miwok because they believed the
     tribe no longer existed.

When A. L. Kroeber of the University of California began his classic and systematic study of the California Indians around 1900, he was observing cultures whose customs and languages had been influenced and changed by long exposure to the Spanish, and later to the Americans. Speakers of a pre-contact native language were extremely rare; dress, food and rituals had become Europeanized and/or mixed with the languages and customs of other tribes. Fortunately, there were still a few elders who had knowledge of the old ways and language, who had been born before the main thrust of the Spanish conquest.

What is known about the Lake Miwok comes from Kroeber's interviews with these elders, and from the mid-twentieth century work of Catherine A. Callaghan, who has done the only in-depth study of the language and culture of this small tribe. The Lake Miwok, at their zenith, are estimated to have been a society of about 500 people. By 1905 there were only 41. (Today there are a handful of Lake Miwok people in Lake County, but only one man still speaks the language.)

Callaghan's information came from a small group of Lake Miwok people still alive in the 1950s, most of them elderly, and their reminiscences of their childhoods and stories that their grandmothers and grandfathers had told them. But their world was not the world of their grandparents. The dictionary of the Lake Miwok language that she compiled includes a word for "Camel cigarette" (*p^hum'ele luumakayaw*—literally, "hunchback tobacco"), and a word for "atomic bomb" (*'u'kasan hattuk*—"something monstrous explodes") which were obviously not part of the language in aboriginal times.[2]

This history of Harbin Hot Springs begins with the Lake Miwok, but their portion isn't really a history in the usual sense of a chronological record of people and events. In the story of the Lake Miwok at Harbin there are only guesses at a beginning —sadly, the ending is known. In between, because there were

---

2   Lake Miwok was never a written language, and many of its sounds are not adequately
    represented by the English alphabet. For pronunciation of the Lake Miwok words in
    the text, see Appendix I: A Brief English - Lake Miwok Dictionary, on page 335.

no written documents, there just isn't any framework of names and dates to anchor what is known about their culture.

For a period of about three thousand years, the Lake Miwok people lived in the area now called Harbin Springs. The names of their leaders and any significant events in the history of their people are completely unknown. Instead of a time-frame for their lives there is only a place-frame. We do know *where* the story takes place.

❖ ❖

THE STORY OF THE LAKE MIWOK, CURIOUSLY ENOUGH, PROBABLY began in northwest Siberia, along the mighty Ob River, where the Voguls and the Ostyaks (collectively, the Ob-Ugrians) and the Samoyeds live.

Physical anthropologists have theorized for a long time that the native people of North America migrated from Asia over the Bering Strait more than 12,000 years ago,[3] a theory supported by archaeological evidence and similarities in social structure.

The Ob-Ugrians, the Hungarians and the Finns all stem from one Siberian group, which separated and dispersed throughout Northern Europe. A possibly related group from the same area crossed over into North America, entering Central California from the ocean at Bodega, San Francisco and Monterey Bays.

The arctic hunters and fishermen, their wives, children and dogs, left Siberia and crossed into North America at what is now the Bering Strait. They dressed in the furs of animals they killed with bows and flint knives. Their utensils were made of wood, bark, and skin. These materials were not only lighter to carry than those made of pottery or stone, but they were also

---

3 Even this part is more definite in its geography than its time. Some anthropologists estimate the migrations began as far back as 30,000 years. Recently, Dr. Otto von Sadovsky has proposed a theory which linguistically links the Miwok (and four other Central California groups) to the Ob-Ugrians, but dates the migration of these tribes as being much more recent, only about 3,000 years ago. His theory is disputed by many linguists and anthropologists. Migration dating back 12,000 years seems to be the majority opinion.

more resistant to cold and made of materials that were readily available during the course of the migration. The nomads also carried their shelters with them, in the form of poles and rolls of bark and skins that made a tipi-like structure.

These nomads would later be known as the Costanoans (who settled in San Francisco), the Miwok (including the Coast, Lake, Bodega and Sierra branches), the Wintun, Maidu and Yokut (inland Northern and Central California). Together they form the Penutian language family, related to each other, but often living next to tribes whose languages shared no similar characteristics.[4]

Because they lived in close contact with many other tribes, the Lake Miwok language evolved over time, incorporating words from other native languages, especially Patwin, much as English contains "borrowed" words such as *alligator* and *bureau*, which are of Spanish and French derivation, respectively. (As in any area in which many languages are spoken, one language was used for formal inter-tribal communication. Patwin was the language of culture among the Central California tribes, much as French is in Europe.)

The Miwok dispersed over a large part of California. Anthropologists believe that the homeland of the proto-Miwok was in Northern Napa County. The tribes spread out from there to the coast, into Lake County and down the Central Valley to the Sierras. It is thought that at one time Miwok territory was continuous, but that intervention from other tribes in the Central Valley caused the groups to be split geographically. Over time the languages and customs of each Miwok group became different and distinct from the others.

---

4 Any linguistic linkage between the Penutians and Asian/European language groups is tenuous, at best. The comparison of languages is interesting, but not conclusive. The Lake Miwok word for "trout" is *huul*; the Vogul word for "fish" is *hul*; the Hungarian word for fish is *hal*. There are hundreds of these comparisons of the Lake Miwok language with its Siberian "cousins": *nomu*—rabbit (Samoyed) and *nomeh*—cottontail rabbit (Lake Miwok); *pu*— fish eggs (Samoyed) and *puu*— fish eggs (Lake Miwok); *kolo*—track, foot (Ostyak) and *kolo*—track, foot (Lake Miwok). Oddly enough, many of the tribes in the Penutian family also had words for intense cold and blizzards, which are much more common in Siberia than in Central California.

At the time of contact, the people we now call the Lake Miwok were settled in a very small area between Mt. St. Helena and the south arm of Clear Lake. No settlements were on the lake itself, but rather on the drainages of several creeks and stream valleys, primarily Cache Creek and Putah Creek.

The area in which the Lake Miwok settled was populated by members of the Hokan language group, primarily the Pomo. The more-recently arrived Lake Miwok, surrounded by a populous and prosperous people, naturally absorbed much of the culture from the larger Pomo tribe. It is not known whether any territorial disputes which arose were settled peacefully, or whether the arrival of the Lake Miwok was seen as an invasion of the Pomo territory. There is no indication that there was ever conflict between the two groups. As far as anyone knows they traded openly and peacefully, joined in ceremonial dances, and traveled freely through each other's territories.

Pomo territory lay to the west and north of the Lake Miwok. Other neighboring tribes were the Wappo to the South (including most of present-day Middletown) and the Wintun to the east. (See map, page 14.)

❖   ❖

LIKE THEIR NEIGHBORS, THE LAKE MIWOK WERE A SMALL, DARK, muscular people, the men averaging about 5'4" in height, and the women proportionally smaller. From descriptions, it seems they were built very much like wrestlers; they have been described as "stout and strong," with the women having large breasts and wide hips. The men were extremely broad shouldered, generally beardless, and could carry large loads for very long distances. Their skin tone and eyes were both dark, almost black, and their faces were round, with low foreheads, prominent cheekbones, very dark bushy eyebrows and dark, straight hair.[5]   Narrow noses and thin lips were considered

---

5   Both men and women wore their hair braided, if long, or cut it in a short, blunt style, by either burning it off with a glowing stick of wood, or cutting it with an obsidian flake. Hair was combed with twigs or fronds from sharp-stalked plants.

FIGURE 1:

Lake Miwok Territory in Lake County

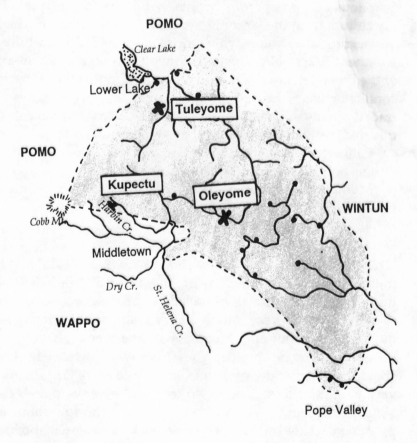

handsome by the culture, although many descriptions of individuals note "large mouths with thick, prominent lips."

(These descriptions come, again, from early European explorers, whose cultural ideals of beauty were quite different. By European standards even the most handsome of the Lake Miwoks were considered far from attractive. Descriptions were often quite derogatory, but since there are few, if any, photographs of pre-contact Lake Miwoks, judicious excerpts of these accounts will have to suffice. Most photographs of "Lake Miwok" people have turned out to be of Pomos [whom they resemble], or have been of much later Lake Miwoks whose forebears had intermarried with people of other tribes, or with whites. Native peoples living in Lake County today are almost all of Pomo or mixed ancestry, and are considerably taller and lighter-skinned than the aboriginal Lake Miwoks are believed to have been.)

It is often difficult for a person raised in Western culture to fully understand the Oriental way of thinking. It is a quantum leap of difficulty for a twentieth-century American to even begin to comprehend the way of life of the Lake Miwok. In the thousands of years between their migration from Siberia and their first contact with Europeans, the culture of the Lake Miwok, although constantly evolving, had materially changed very little. During the time that Europe went through the Iron Age, the Bronze Age, the Dark Ages, the Renaissance and into the Industrial Revolution, the Lake Miwoks remained a Stone Age culture.

What does that mean? It means that, until contact with Europeans in the early 1800s, they had no metal tools, no farming, no domestic animals, no horses, no written language, and no idea that any of those existed. They produced, by hand, literally everything they owned or wore or ate, all from the land around them.[6]

---

6   The Lake Miwok are among the tribes of natives later known by the epithet "diggers" or
     Digger Indians, (by which the Spanish lumped dozens of tribes into one amorphous
     group of "savages") because of their use of roots for both baskets and food.

It is an awesome experience to walk the land of Harbin trying to see with a Lake Miwok's eye. What is visible is all that was available to provide food, clothing, shelter, utensils and art —hillsides, animals, plants and rocks.

The Spanish, when they arrived, called the Miwok tribes savage; anthropologists would call them primitive. It may be a European bias to classify a people by what they lacked; perhaps it is more fruitful to view these geographic ancestors by what they *had*—the intelligence and the ingenuity to cope with their environment and to treat it with reverence and respect.

Europeans (and Americans) considered themselves more civilized than the Lake Miwok and their neighbors. But if civilization involves being able to coexist in comparative peace with little or no war or crime, without abusing or destroying the environment, and with a close kinship and understanding between members of a community, the Lake Miwok were far superior in their brand of civilization.

In any of the accounts or legends of this people, there is no mention of major conflicts with other tribes. There were some feuds between tribes, usually over poaching, and occasional ambushes and deliberate killings, but there was no war, no large-scale or organized discord in their realm until the European explorers came.

Their skill in the craft of basket-making was unsurpassed, equalled only by the neighboring Pomo. Although their materials and techniques were simple, the results were far from crude or primitive. It would be judgmental and romantic to claim that they were happy in their simplicity. Maybe they were. No one knows. They knew of no other life.

❖   ❖

THE PRIMITIVE MATERIAL CULTURE OF THE LAKE MIWOK WAS sustained by a rich and elaborate mythology whose main character was *'oleenawa*, Old Man Coyote, a hero and trickster who was one of the First People. The First People were a race of beings, materially different from humans, who had inhabited the earth before them. Old Man Coyote, through his great magic, created men and women out of sticks and clay and feathers. He was helped in this endeavor by *Peteeli*, the lizard,

16

whose contribution to the newly-created people was the gift of five fingers because, having five himself, he understood their value.

The belief in the creation of man from feathers was extremely strong with the Lake Miwok, which accounts for the fact that feathers were treated with great respect and also with fear, because the failure to handle them properly and observe the rituals in connection with feathers on ceremonial objects could be followed by illness or disaster. The red feathers of birds, notably the hummingbird and the woodpecker, were believed to have been in contact with the fire which was stolen.

Like most creation myths, the Lake Miwok tales relate a source of primordial heat and light (called fire, sun or morning) which existed some great distance from their territory, and relate the theft of this most valued of phenomena from its keepers. In Lake Miwok myths it is *Wek-wek*, the Bullet Hawk, grandson of Old Man Coyote, who is their Prometheus, causing fire to be stolen from the "gods" and bringing it to man. In connection with the theft of fire there is also a flood story, in which the world is threatened, but saved by "divine" intervention. (See Appendix II: Lake Miwok Creation Myths.)

After Old Man Coyote created people from feathers and sticks, the First People transformed themselves into animals and other natural objects. Animals, trees, rocks, stars, even the hail and the rain were thought to be First People. They retained their personalities throughout the transformation, so that *Kule*, who was fond of acorns, was still fond of them once she became *kule*, the grizzly bear. The names of the individuals among the First People were carried on to the animals, objects or forces which they became at the time of transformation. In the myths, however, it is the First People, not the animals, who are the characters. Thus *wekwek*, the Miwok word for a specific kind of hawk, refers in daily life to the actual bird and in myth to *Wek-Wek*, grandson of Old Man Coyote , a being of great supernatural powers.

Because all the plants and animals and rocks and such had once been First People, they were treated with a kind of respect more often associated with people than with objects. In daily life, the Lake Miwok spoke of animals and objects as being inhabited by spirits, to whom they sang and prayed. To them everything was sacred. Everything had a spirit; everything was a First Person, an ancestor.

There was a definite hierarchy to the non-human realm, though. *Wek-wek* and *peteeli* are more revered than *kaluk*, the skunk (who is seen as greedy and oppressive) or *huyuuma*, the meadowlark (who is uncomplimentary).

The personalities of the First People fostered some interesting beliefs among the Lake Miwok about their animal counterparts, although the stories behind most of them are not known. The meadowlark was thought to speak some Lake Miwok, and to imitate him would cause sore feet or other misfortune. Bothering porcupines was believed to cause rheumatism, a nosebleed or a headache. It was bad luck to call a wood rat by its right name (*yullu*), so they called him *tumay kook*, "wood tail." Water spiders were allowed to bite pregnant women so their breasts would not grow too large. Certain women were able to stop the wind by prying open the mouth of a lizard, pointing it into the wind and talking to it. It was bad luck to keep a quail as a pet.

The First People and their various personality traits also served as lessons, much as the animals in Aesop's fables do. Through the device of detailing the experiences of the pre-human race, they established, in the mythic past, the order of all things to be followed in the human present. These tales not only explained natural phenomena and told how customs were different in the time before humans, but also illustrated what was considered socially acceptable behavior within the tribe, as in this short Lake Miwok myth, "Wild-Oats Man and the Thunder."

> The Thunder eats people. He catches them with his hands and eats them. He lives in the North. When he comes down to hunt people, that's when there are black clouds and lightning. When he goes back, the sky clears again.
>
> It was Wild-Oats man who killed him. Wild-Oats was a great fighter. He had his arrows always ready, pointing in every direction. He could shoot as many as twenty men at one draw. He went to meet Thunder and shot him with his arrows. That's the way he killed him.

After that Wild-Oats was different. He began to hunt people. He killed them and ate them, just like Thunder.

His sister was worried. She felt bad about her brother. Then she came to see him. She said: "That's not good what you are doing. You must stop. You mus'n't kill people like that!"

He quit. He didn't kill any more people after that.

❖　　❖

SOCIAL REGULATION WAS NOT A MATTER TO BE LEFT SOLELY UP to myths. Each tribelet or village had leaders who served the functions of the police, courts, churches and "government" of our society. Political organization didn't really exist above the village level. Each village was autonomous; the leaders of various villages undoubtedly met together to discuss broader regional problems, and villages frequently camped, hunted and danced together, but they didn't function as a larger political unit.

(Although we refer to the Lake Miwok as a "tribe", they might not have described themselves that way. They were a group of people living in close proximity who shared a common language, but affiliations were based more on villages than on the body of people as a whole. They called themselves *koocako*, which meant "people" or "family" and also meant "living things." It wasn't until the Spanish came that all the people who spoke the Lake Miwok language referred to themselves by a given name. Before then there had been no need to assert that kind of identity; neighboring tribes could tell each other apart by dress and by language.)

There were two permanent and primary villages in the Lake Miwok territory. The oldest settlement, *Tuuleyomi* ("deep place"), was about four miles south of Lower Lake. It was the principal village of the Northern area of Lake Miwok territory, also known as Old Man Coyote's Home, and the site of many Lake Miwok creation myths. (Tuleyome[7] was also the word

---

7　In the rest of this text, the English-language spelling "Tuleyome" will be used in referring to the village or tribe.

used to describe all Lake Miwok domains, similar to "Sonoma" being the name of both a city and a county. Many early ethnographers referred to the "tribe" itself as the Tuleyome, or the Tuleyome Miwok, to distinguish them from the Sierra or coastal branches.)

The second, more recent, settlement was called *'oleeyomi* (Oleyome: "coyote place"). It was located in the Coyote Valley, along the banks of Putah Creek, near where the Guenoc Winery is now located, and was the principal village of the southern section. (See map, p. 14). There are believed to have been about 24 Lake Miwok village sites altogether, containing a total tribal population of about 500. With the exception of Tuleyome and Oleyome, most were not permanent settlements, but temporary, seasonal camps.

At least these two main villages, and possibly some of the other larger ones, had their own leaders. The secular head of the village was a man called the *hoypu*, who was the equivalent of "mayor" or "chief" of the village. It was primarily a hereditary position, passed down from father to son, but if a man didn't prove to be a good leader (evidenced by courage under pressure, wisdom in handling other people, upright conduct), he could be forced by social pressure to forfeit the position.

The hoypu had very little direct power, unless there was an emergency; his main duties were to help bring peace between quarrelling families or individuals, to organize food-gathering or trading expeditions, and to influence people to lead cooperative and productive lives. Primarily a diplomat and an orator, he gave lectures in the dance house (the main public gathering place of the village) to the men who were assembled there, telling them how they should behave, and what tasks needed to be done for the village and its people. The hoypu was assisted by a man called the *malle*, whose job it was to help enforce these administrative harangues, and to assume the duties of the hoypu if he was away from the village.

Villages consisted of three different kinds of structures: multi-family dwellings (*weeyi*), a sweat lodge (*lamma*) and a dance house (*lakihniweyi*). The houses were round (often as large as 40 feet in diameter) and built over a shallow excavation.

The men erected a frame of lashed poles with a large center pole as support; a hole in the center of the roof let out smoke, and a hole in the side formed a door. Brush, leaves and tules[8] were gathered by the women, placed over the framework and covered with dirt. This provided insulation so that the houses were relatively cool in the summer and warm in the winter.

Several families lived in each weeyi, sleeping on tule or fur mats around the perimeter, and leaving the center open as a communal cooking area. They sometimes dug out small depressions to sleep in, and lined them with tule or fur. Tule was also used as a light blanket; in the winter deerhide was used, or blankets were woven of rabbit fur and hemp. The Lake Miwok slept naked; in large dwellings they slept with their feet close to the center fire, and their heads out, but in smaller houses they slept curled around the fire, their uncovered backs inward.

The sweat lodge was an extremely important part of the village. Smaller than the family houses, it was similarly constructed, except that the excavation pit was deeper, usually a foot or more, and there was a much smaller roof hole. Only men were allowed in the sweat lodge (except for a very occasional older woman, often a shaman, for ritual purposes), and they used it daily. Besides being a place for ceremony, it was often a men's dormitory in the winter months, and used as a sort of clubhouse for the discussion of men's business.

Men went to sweat once or twice a day. A large fire was built with many rocks in it, similar to a dry Swedish sauna. When the fire was hot, the men gathered in the sweat lodge and closed the door, remaining inside until they could no longer bear the heat, at which point they rushed outside and jumped in the nearest available cold water.

Competitive sweating involved two teams of men, one on either side of the lodge, each with a deer hide tied to a stick. They wafted the hot air over to the other team until one side

---

8   Tule is a kind of bulrush grown on the shores of Clear Lake and some streams and used for practically everything. The Lake Miwok made baskets, houses, cradles, sandals and plates out of tules. Shredded tules were even used as diapers.

had to leave because of the extreme heat. The losers were jeered by the winners and then everyone went swimming.

In the lodge, the men danced and sang, rapidly, raucously, as the intensity of the heat swelled. Dancing in the sweat lodge was used for initiations into various rites and also used for healing, with the dry heat and perspiration drawing the toxins out of the sick person's body. Certain herbs were sometimes added to the fire; breathing the fumes helped with the cure. Men generally smoked carved stone or wooden pipes in the sweat lodge, each man offering a song or a prayer and then passing the pipe along. Primarily a social interaction, two or three puffs of their extremely strong tobacco could also cause dizziness or sleep, and enhance the effect of the stupefying heat.[9]

❖   ❖

THE OTHER PRINCIPAL STRUCTURE OF ANY VILLAGE WAS THE dance house, where most of the rituals and ceremonies took place. Dance houses were built in much the same fashion as sweat lodges, but were very large—as much as 70 feet in diameter—and had a tunnel entranceway with two doors. On the interior, the fire pit was in the center of the circle and leaves and branches were spread around the perimeter for spectators to sit on.

---

9   Early white explorers were not enamored of the charms of the sweat lodge, as indicated in this excerpt from a late 19th century account of one man's experience: "Round about the roaring fire the Indians go capering, jumping and screaming, with the perspiration starting from every pore....The air grows thick and heavy, and a sense of oppressing suffocation overcomes one; when a rush is made at the door, for self-protection, judge their astonishment, terror and dismay to find it fastened securely...there is no alternative but to sit down in hopes that the troop of naked fiends will soon cease, from sheer exhaustion. Vain expectation!...Was ever the human body thrown into such convulsions before?...The heat is equal to that of a bake oven. Temperature 500 degrees, pressure of steam 1000 pounds per square inch. The reeking atmosphere has become almost palpable, and the audience is absolutely gasping for life....Death shows his visage, not more than five minutes distant...then the Indians vanish through the open aperture, and the victims dash through it like an arrow and in a moment more are drawing in buckets of cold, frosty air, every inhalation of which cuts like a knife and thrills the system like an electric shock."

There were dances for every type of ceremonial occasion. At the end of a festival, the Old Time Dance was held, in which both men and women took part. The women wore feather coats and headpieces and danced in place in a circle nearest the fire while the men, also in feather coats, danced counter-clockwise around them. The Coyote Dance celebrated the recovery of a sick person. His family invited the hoypu, who contacted dancers and singers to come and participate. The family paid expenses, decorated the dance house and donated food for the feast table after the dance. Dances were also held to celebrate the departure for, or the return from, long journeys.

One of the dances whose details have been recorded is the *Bole Maru*, or Big Head dance, the primary ceremony of the Kuksu cult (see page 27). The main dancer, the Big Head, impersonated Kuksu, and wore an elaborate headdress of innumerable feathered sticks, which created the effect of a giant ball around his head. Major performances were held at the dance house in the main village of Tuleyome, and the people of other villages (and from some neighboring tribes as well) were invited. Dancing began at sundown and lasted until sunrise on four consecutive nights. It was considered a great honor to be one of the dancers, and the people involved in the dance itself fasted for the entire period of the festival.

The leader of the dance was the dreamer (*huuni*), who dreamed the dance songs and then released them with his rattle. Before the ceremony began, he chanted his dream song as he circled the principal dancer's head with the Big Head feathers, and then placed them on the headdress. In a very large dance there might be as many as four Big Head dancers. Dancers dressed and prepared for the dance in a roofless room outside the dance house. (In rainy weather the back of the dance house itself was partitioned off.)

Besides the dreamer and the dancers, the men involved in the dance were: the caretaker (*mallele*), who kept order using his foot drum and rattles, throwing those who misbehaved into the fire, and praying to his spirits to protect the dancers on their way home after the dance; the timekeeper (*helama*) who signalled the dancers to enter the dance house and cued them when to dance, slow down or stop; and the director (*mece*), who tended the fire and collected any feathers which may have dropped on the floor during the dance. (It was considered dangerous to touch the feathers from a dancer's head; the director collected the fallen feathers and gave them to the leader who returned them to the dressing room.)

At sundown the leader shouted four times in the voice of the cougar, as a signal for the spectators (men and women) to enter, and then delivered a speech. The timekeeper then signalled the dancers, who entered the dance house, announcing themselves at the front door by whistling and shaking their rattles. The leader and the Big Head dancer entered and circled the fire once, the leader going clockwise and the other in the opposite direction. The dance step was mainly an alternate raising of the knees with a violent foot-stomp. As the timekeeper signalled them, they danced four times on the right side of the building, then four times on the left, with the Big Head dancer returning to the front door after each dance. As they danced, their families and friends tossed shell and bead money to them, which the director collected. The dancers repeated their circuit four more times, changing directions, and then the Big Head backed out the door and returned to the dressing room, where his assistants took his feathers.

Once the main dancers were finished, spectators could dance as well. The dreamer gave his rattle to an old man (or woman) who sang once, sitting with his back to the fire, and then sang again, louder, while standing up. If a singer was called upon to sing and refused, he had to pay the caretaker. The dancing lasted until sunrise, and began again at sundown the next evening. There was feasting during the daytime for everyone except the ceremonial officials and dancers, who were fasting.

Dance houses and sweatlodges were also used for initiation ceremonies. There were probably puberty rites for young boys before or after their first hunt, but little information is available about those rituals. One initiation ceremony that is well-documented is the "ghost initiation" in which ghosts and Kuksu shamans put young boys through ordeals and instructed them in proper ritual behavior. During the initiation, a young boy was tossed back and forth over the fire and treated roughly, had burning coals placed on his hands or neck, and finally was thrown out the smoke hole. He lay belly down over the hole and a small arrow was shot into his navel. He was then rolled down and his parents bathed him in cold water. At the end of the initiation period, a general feast was held in the dance house. [10]

Each village probably had its own sweat lodge, and many of the smaller villages most likely used the structure as a combination sweat lodge and dance house, as only the larger villages had permanent dance houses. These dance houses served not only as a gathering place for their own village, but also as a location for dances and ceremonies to which people of the neighboring, smaller villages were invited.

❖   ❖

THE SOCIAL STRUCTURE OF THE LAKE MIWOK INCLUDED SOME very definite gender distinctions, among them the taboo against women being in the dance house, except on high ceremonial occasions, when they might be allowed in. Since the women could not be instructed by the hoypu, (except when he made public speeches, often from the roof of the dance house) there was also a female leader, the *maayen*, who performed a similar function, and was often the wife of the hoypu.[11] It is also likely that the men were expected to instruct their wives in the lessons of the hoypu.

Under the leadership of the hoypu and the maayen, most members of the village had specific occupations.[12] Both women

---

10 From the descriptions, it seems unlikely that these initiations were entirely secret, but were probably private, closed to the general public. An analogy might be that major dances were held by the local church, and these initiations by the native version of the Masons or Elk's Club.

11 A linguistic note: the word "maayen" also meant "queen" and, probably used sarcastically, "girl who sits around and refuses to work."

12 Gender distinctions in accounts of Lake Miwok culture are unclear. The society itself was definitely structured as a patriarchy; within that, some areas are definitely male or female, and the rest seem to have been shared equally. The third person pronoun, which in English indicates gender (he, she) is neutral in their language—"*iti*"—referring to either men or women.

and men could be medicine people or basket-makers. A large village had a time-keeper, who kept count of the months, seasons and years using beads and sticks of graduated size, and who acted as a kind of historian, relating events with the aid of his markers. Women in the village were responsible for most of the basket-making, and the cooking, childcare, and gathering of seeds, roots and herbs. Some women fished, but most dried the fish or game and tanned the skins from the animals the hunters killed. Fishing and hunting were mostly the province of the men, who provided food for their individual families. Men also made some of the more coarsely woven baskets, nets, arrows, bows and other hunting implements.

Every tribe had specialists (basket-makers; arrow, spear and point knappers; especially skilled hunters) who concentrated their efforts on one or two specific tasks. Rather than hunting to provide food for themselves and their families, these individuals were generally paid for their services with shell beads, food or other barter items. Because of the mild climate and abundant wildlife and vegetation, the Lake Miwok only had to "work" a few hours a day in order to provide themselves with the necessities of life. The rest of their time was spent making baskets and musical instruments, praying, singing, dancing, gambling and enjoying other, more leisurely activities.

The true head of the village was not the hoypu, but the *yomta*, the shaman, (medicine man) who was the religious and ceremonial leader of the community, as well as the doctor. There were two different types of shamans: the *huuni yomta*, the "power" or "singing" doctor; and the *luubak yomta*, the sucking doctor.

The sucking doctor sucked or brushed the affected area during a ritual dance and extracted the foreign bodies— feathers, stones, obsidian flakes—which had "caused" the disease. Sometimes he made an incision with a piece of obsidian and actually sucked blood out of the area, spitting it into a small vessel of ashes.

The singing doctor used only his magical powers (and native healing herbs) in his work, singing and dancing to diagnose and cure the sick. He had a fetish sack in which he kept tobacco (which he smoked before beginning the ritual), obsidian, feathers, herbs and other power objects. During the curing ritual, he sang and prayed to his familiar spirit, Noble Person. While he was actively doctoring, a yomta fasted for four days and nights and slept very little. If a shaman became ill himself, his wife or assistant rubbed his body with white feathers tied to an elderberry stick, asking Noble Person to return the disease he had drawn out of the sick person to its original source.

There were both male and female shamans, although little is known about the distinctions between them. A novice acquired power individually, by dreaming, or by learning curing techniques from an older shaman. Dreams were the most important "tools" a shaman had. Dreaming a doctor's song was considered a call to shamanism and, if ignored, was thought to result in death or disability. (If a person dreamed a song that would cure another person, but refused to sing it, the punishment was believed to be even more severe.) The shaman's songs usually remained his exclusive property; if he chose to pass them on both he and his apprentice had to fast during the instruction. A shaman also dreamed what feathers belonged on his rattle, and was visited by animal guardian spirits in dreams, who informed him what methods could cure a particular illness.[13]

The shamans of the Lake Miwok were probably also members of the Kuksu "religion", a Central California cult based on a male secret society, whose membership was limited to those who had been initiated. Rituals involved elaborate paint and feather disguises, and dances impersonating various characters and animals, including Kuksu, from whom the cult got its name. In the Lake Miwok language, *Kuksu* is translated as "a feather-covered ceremonial character who dismembers

---

13 Some of the power of the shaman may have come from his/her knowledge of herbal remedies for ailments, such as: pepperwood tea for colds; wormwood for diarrhea; yerba santa for severe illness; soaproot powder to counteract the effects of poison oak; willow bark, chewed or in tea, for headaches. Because they were the primary herb gatherers, and because, as wives and mothers, they were the primary caregivers, it is possible that the women, particularly the female shamans, were also the primary herbalists within the tribe.

young boys, piles up their extremities in the sweathouse, and puts them back together after pleas from older people."

The Kuksu cult seems similar in structure to many modern societies, with initiations occurring around puberty, and adult members proceeding through 12 "degrees", each preceded by instruction, and leading to knowledge of a new impersonation. Members of the secret society were considered socially, politically and economically superior to those in the tribe who were not initiates, and membership was often used to form inter-village or even inter-tribal alliances.

Kuksu societies, although almost universal throughout Central California, were as autonomous as the villages their members lived in; the Tuleyome members were not a branch of the parent organization, but were just men who lived at Tuleyome and practiced rituals they shared with most of their neighboring tribes.[14] Kuksu rites were predominantly held in winter, when the dance house offered both warmth and shelter. The dance house and the winter rites are about the only characteristics that all the tribes who practised Kuksu have in common; everything else seems to vary not only from tribe to tribe but from village to village within a single tribe.

There were also societies that existed outside the regular social structure of the village. Although the Lake Miwok were basically a peaceful people, they were not perfect and did have some of what we would call crime or evil. As in any society, the outlaws served, in a way, to strengthen the fabric of community by being a counterpoint to the existing moral and social order. They were examples of what not to do, and opposition to them

---

14 Little is written about the specific religious or social customs of the Lake Miwok because they were such a small tribe, and because they were virtually disintegrated as a separate entity by the time studies were conducted. For the most part they are thought to have been quite similar to the Clear Lake Pomo in their beliefs and practices. If this is true, then the status of Lake Miwok women was probably quite high: there was some matrilineal descent, especially among female shamans or medicine women; some women chiefs (rare, but some); and some female secret societies. The wife of an important man of the tribe gained status because of her marriage, but it seems possible, if not likely, that there were also women of the tribe whose status was based on their own power. Female shamans were forbidden from practicing during their menstrual periods, and a male shaman could not perform rituals during his wife's period.

brought a spiritual strength and cultural unity to the rest of the group. Bullies, thieves and others who operated outside the moral structure were the "sinners" the hoypu lectured against. Individual acts against the larger group were dealt with by peer pressure, and by the hoypu or by the yomta, but there were also people who practiced "black magic" to deal with problems.

Two kinds of people used their magic to harm, not to heal— bear shamans and poisoners. According to a Coast Miwok informant, the bear shamans who practiced in this area were members of a secret society who dressed in bearskins with armored breastplates. In other tribes the bear society was a private, but legitimate, shamanistic religion. In both the Pomo and Lake Miwok cultures, however, the "bear doctors" were members of a renegade cult whose "powers" came only from owning the bearskin suit, not from a belief in the bear as a guardian spirit. A novice proved his worthiness by stopping a large rock that was rolling downhill; once initiated, they were thought to have invulnerability and to be able to travel long distances at superhuman speed. They were considered dangerous, carried knives and were likely to kill anyone they encountered, or to use the fear that they inspired to make others do their bidding. They were opposed by the hoypu and yomta, which is one of the reasons their society was secret.

The second type of non-healing shaman was the 'amaayomi (the "enemy" or the "Night Man"), the poisoner, and information about them is understandably sparse. Poisoners were people, predominantly men, who knew the techniques for producing illness or death, and would do so for a price. Sometimes they did this by actually introducing noxious herbs into a person's food; often they relied on the power of suggestion and made the victim think he was being poisoned, by placing power objects (like snakeskins) in or near his home, or using personal objects (nail parings, hair) from the victim in rituals. The fear of the poisoner was sometimes enough to cause death, certainly illness. The family of the victim tried to counteract the poisoner's charms and rituals by calling in the yomta and praying and chanting to the victim's guiding spirits to save him.

Poisoners that operated for hire were tolerated, grudgingly, and actually worked as part of the society (sort of like an executioner) for they were often the only recourse for serious grievances.[15] In case of unjust bewitching, the yomta could reverse the poisoner's magic, and turn it back on the amaayomi. The *wallipo* was another matter, a poisoner who was totally dysfunctional and outside the social structure. He dressed in owl feathers, hooting and running everywhere at high speeds. Naturally, he was avoided, and often the men of the tribe ambushed such outlaws and killed them for the good of the village.

❖　❖

LIKE ALL NATIVE TRIBES, THE LAKE MIWOK LIVED ENTIRELY OFF the land, and what the land provided them changed with the seasons. Throughout the year they traveled to different campsites, depending on what plants were ripe, or what game was plentiful at that time. The people who had seasonal camps at Harbin had a permanent "home base" just north of Middletown (the center of the village was at the present site of the south goalpost of the high school football field), and traveled to their other camps for extended periods. (This permanent village had an estimated population of 90 in 1850, and 9 by 1880. Perhaps half to two-thirds of the original number populated sections of Harbin seasonally.)

Maps of Lake Miwok territory (see page 14) show a small village, Kupetcu, ("Koo-pay-chu") on the edge of Wappo territory, about four miles north of Middletown, on the land drained by *'eetawwuwe* ("hot creek"), a small branch of Putah Creek now known as Harbin Creek.

Although only one site is shown on the maps, there was actually no permanent village on Harbin property, but rather many seasonal camps on the land; Kupetcu may have been the

---

15　Poisoners also had a beneficial, if unintended, environmental influence. The Lake Miwok washed daily and cleaned up garbage and debris with great care, because if any of that material were to be found by a poisoner, he could use it to cause great harm. An interesting, if severe, anti-littering campaign.

largest of these. According to Bill Toney, a former Harbin resident and a resource for Lake County Indian lore, on the approximately 1200 acres of modern Harbin, besides the springs themselves, there were once three separate campsites and several other sites used for various sacred activities by the hunters and their families whose main villages were elsewhere.

Hunters traveled with their entire families, while older members of the tribe, those unable to hunt, those with specialized occupations and, possibly the shaman and other leaders, remained in the main village. Each family had its own favorite sites, and several families camped together for the months of the fishing or hunting seasons, creating their own small temporary villages.

In February and March, when the streams were swollen with the winter rains, fishing camps were established along the creeks. Harbin Creek was once home to two and three pound trout, and there was a sizeable fishing camp on the hill between the Village and the Fire Circle (see map, page 33), which may well have been Kupetcu. A great many obsidian shards and artifacts have been found at that location.

Fishing was done by both men and women. Some men learned to catch the fish in their bare hands; usually basket traps and nets were used. Obsidian fishhooks have been found at some sites, and spearing was another common method for catching fish. In order to maximize the catch during heavy runs of fish, slow-moving streams were sometimes dammed, and soaproot or poisonous dove weed was thrown into the pools that were formed, which stupefied the fish and made them easy to catch, without rendering them inedible. Some fish were eaten fresh; others were preserved by drying them on wooden frames or slowly baking them.

At the end of fishing season the camps were broken down (some hut frames were left up year-round and some of the heavier utensils were buried for the next year's use, rather than being carried back and forth) and the families returned to the main village. There they stored the dried fish they had prepared, reunited with the other members of the tribe, feasted, danced, and generally caught up on what had happened in the village and the tribe in the months they had been gone.

In early spring, when the flowers bloomed, the First Fruits Dance was held to celebrate the return of the growing season. (Among the Coast Miwok this dance was called the First Salmon Dance.) Under the supervision of the yomta, everyone in the tribe—men, women and children—danced with flowers in their hands and in their hair. Some male dancers handled rattlesnakes as part of the performance. Participants observed a four-day taboo against eating meat or fish following the ceremony; first time participants (presumably adolescents) abstained from meat and fish for a year.

After a month or two in the main village many of the tribe traveled to their Spring camp in the Meadow where they hunted birds, gathered grass seeds, picked berries and flowers and collected materials for baskets. Archaeologists have found artifacts and evidence of old campfires which indicate that the Spring camp at Harbin was used in May and June and stretched from a grove of oaks at the lower end of the Meadow (near the fork of the creek) up to the edge of the hill by the Fire Circle.

Both edible and non-edible plants and roots were harvested in the spring, for food and for baskets. Grass seeds were toasted and eaten, or ground in mortars and used as flour. The nuts of the California Bay tree, plentiful along the creeks of Harbin, were gathered and roasted, then pulverized and stored for the winter months. Edible roots were dug in the spring; cow parsnip was boiled into soup, while squawroot was washed, trampled, washed again and cooked like potatoes.

Plants that couldn't be eaten were used to make baskets, an essential and integral part of Lake Miwok life. Both the Pomo and the Lake Miwok are considered the finest basket-makers in North America, from an artistic and utilitarian viewpoint. Since the Lake Miwok had no pottery or metalwork, virtually all of their carrying, cooking and storage vessels were woven; baskets were used for almost everything.

Most of the basketry was made by the women; men made some net sacks, fishing baskets and carrying baskets. Women and girls gathered the basket materials in the spring and the fall, choosing warm sunny days for their expeditions down the creeks and rivers, looking for sedge roots, bulrushes, and willows. The women laughed and sang and talked as they

FIGURE 2

Lake Miwok Seasonal Camps and Sacred Spots on Harbin Land

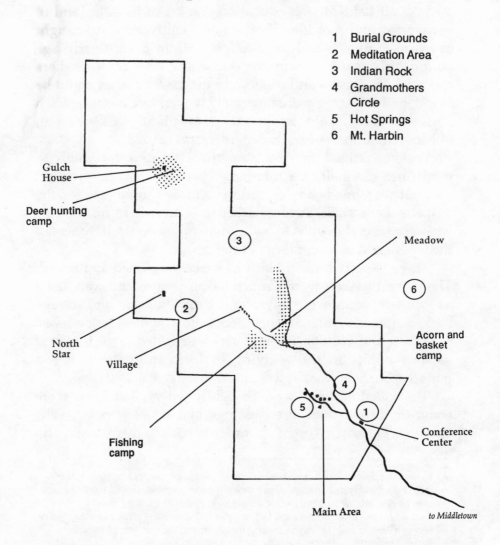

1   Burial Grounds
2   Meditation Area
3   Indian Rock
4   Grandmothers Circle
5   Hot Springs
6   Mt. Harbin

Gulch House

Deer hunting camp

North Star

Village

Fishing camp

Meadow

Acorn and basket camp

Conference Center

Main Area

to Middletown

found and cut the plant materials and dug the roots, using hardwood digging sticks with sharpened tips. The materials were cut and sorted, then hung up to dry for a year, while baskets made from the last spring's gathering were begun. Younger children usually helped with the foraging until they got bored, then played in the meadows and the creeks until it was time to return to camp.

Like all Lake Miwok education, the art of basketry and of herb, grass and root identification and cultivation was taught by word-of-mouth and by example. From a very early age young girls learned from their mothers and grandmothers about which grasses and roots were used, where they could be found, and how they were intricately woven into baskets. Each object in the Lake Miwok universe—plant, rock, animal, hillside, streambed—had its own identity and use.

Baskets ranged in size from three or four feet high to miniatures as small as a thimble. The latter had no practical use, but were made as decorations and as showpieces for the basketmaker's skill. A fine basket took anywhere from a few weeks to several months to make, depending on the tightness of the weave and the complexity of the design.

There were two main kinds of baskets—twined and coiled. The twined baskets were a much looser weave, and were used as strainers, winnowing trays, large carrying packs and storage baskets. Basket materials included willow withes, sedge roots, pine roots and grasses. Redbud bark was added to the basket at various points in the weaving to form intricate dark red patterns; burnt bulrushes were used to make black designs.

The coiled baskets[16] were so tightly woven that many were water-tight, and were used as jugs and cooking pots. (The baskets were not fire-proof. In order to cook in them, water and

---

16 To begin a single stick coiled basket, two roots of sedge grass were knotted together, then one willow branch was added at a time. The sedge root was coiled tightly around each piece of willow so that when the basket was finished the willow was completely hidden. An awl made from a deer horn or a piece of obsidian was used to force a space between the root and the willow, making it easier to coil the root around the willow withe. The top of the basket was often finished off with a circle of willow, wrapped in sedge root.

grain, vegetables, meat or fish were placed in the baskets. The water swelled the basket materials, tightening the seal. Stones were heated on the fire until almost red hot, then picked up with tongs made of looped willow, and put in the filled baskets. The stones heated the water almost to boiling, and the food cooked. Dense dishes required a second batch of rocks. The cooled stones were removed before serving.)

From birth, every aspect of a Lake Miwok's life was full of baskets. Like the Eskimos and their myriad words for snow, their language contains dozens of words for basket, each succinctly identifying a different form. Babies were placed in woven cradles which were carried in the mother's arms or on her back using a forehead band. A similar band enabled the men and women to carry very large baskets on their backs when traveling. It was not unusual for a strong young man to walk many miles carrying a hundred pound basket this way. Seeds were gathered into tightly-woven, conical baskets. Large baskets holding dried fish, acorns, berries and roots were placed on the floors of homes or hung from the ceilings and walls of the dwelling to keep mice and other vermin out.

Very large baskets were used to store ceremonial regalia for dances. They were made from dried tule stalks (similar to cattails), and were rather flimsy for their size; the material stored in them was light and they were left in one location and rarely moved. Smaller ceremonial baskets were decorated with abalone shells, beads and colorful bird feathers as well as bark. These baskets were prestige items, stored in dry pepperwood (bay laurel) leaves as a protection against moths, and were burned when their owner died. Other ceremonial baskets were presented as gifts to the leader or the shaman, or were considered family heirlooms and passed on to successive generations.

While the women collected basket-making materials and food, the men at the spring encampment went bird hunting. Many species of birds were hunted for food, including quail, waterfowl and woodpeckers. Woodpeckers were carefully trapped. A conical trap of loosely woven twigs, about 18" long, was placed with the open end over a woodpecker's hole, and tied to the tree with hemp. The woodpecker, not known for its caution, darted out of its hole into the narrow end of the cone, where it stuck tight, its feathers undamaged.

Beyond their mythical association with fire, woodpeckers were especially prized because of their dramatically bright red, black and white feathers. The Lake Miwok culture was essentially monochromatic; most everything was some shade of brown. Baskets were made from dried leaves and grasses, clothing and housing from tules and deer skins. The sky was blue and the leaves were green, red, and orange, but the people had no way to represent these colors on anything they made.

Redbud bark and bulrushes woven into the baskets provided some color, and various plant dyes were used to decorate animal skins, but even these materials were in the range of muted earth tones. Other than the flowers in the spring, which were quite ephemeral, the only source of usable bright colors was bird feathers, which were, naturally, eagerly sought and treasured, and used almost exclusively to decorate ceremonial objects. It is probably because of their colorful similarities that the Lake Miwok used the same word for "flower" and "feather"—*pakah*.

Because their feathers were not as desirable, quail and waterfowl were rarely trapped, but were more often hunted with blunt arrows, which had the effect of stunning the small birds and knocking them out of the air, rather than piercing them or ripping their flesh. This spring game was generally roasted whole, and provided a welcome change from the dried foods of the winter months.

❖   ❖

ONCE OR TWICE A YEAR THE LAKE MIWOK JOURNEYED ACROSS the mountains to the ocean, where they traded with their "cousins", the Coast Miwok, primarily the *Olamentko* at Bodega Bay. Given the extremely hot, dry climate of Lake County in the summer months, it is likely that they went to the much cooler seacoast during July and August.

They traveled in groups, single-file and barefoot, carrying pack-baskets that weighed over a hundred pounds. Those who carried baskets, mainly the women who were not carrying children, walked and trotted along in a stooped position; men armed with bows and arrows guarded the front and rear. Usually the whole village went on this expedition, except those who, due to age or illness, were unable to travel. It was an exciting event for everyone, especially the young children, whose known universe expanded with every new ridge.

The trails were always well-maintained, free of brush or sharp rocks—anything that might injure a foot or cause a twisted ankle was removed. As they walked along, each member of the party snapped off any protruding branches or twigs, and picked up any debris that might have fallen along the trail since it was last used. This practice not only kept them from minor physical harm along the way, but also insured that their sturdy, but delicately-woven, baskets were not vulnerable to a stray, sharp twig.

When a large expedition was planned into or through the territory of another tribe, runners were sent ahead as messengers to the area's leaders. Swift young men who could cover incredible distances, sometimes running as much as a hundred miles in a single day, the runners carried with them the message that they would be passing through or, in the case of the Olamentko, that they were coming for their annual visit. Runners carried a bundle of sticks to give to the other tribe, signifying the date of their arrival. The host leader threw away one stick each day, and when there were no sticks left, the visitors were expected to arrive.

The probable trail that the Lake Miwok took to Bodega Bay took them through Wappo and Pomo territory before they entered into Coast Miwok lands. Trails followed ridges where there were canyons, and river or creek beds in the valleys. They may have gone down Mt. St. Helena to (what is now) Healdsburg, connecting with a main Pomo trail there, and continuing on to the coast. Another route involved going down Mt. St. Helena to Calistoga, over to Santa Rosa and then to the sea. Either way, it was a journey of several days to a week.

Besides escaping the oppressive summer heat of the high country, travel to the ocean provided the Lake Miwok with supplies that were not available in their own area. They gathered seaweed (*haskuula*) on the coast, which they dried on rocks in the sun and took home to store, later baking it into cakes. Kelp was often eaten fresh, baked in hot ashes. They fished for crabs, mussels and oysters (roasted and eaten fresh) and saltwater fish, which they dried and stored. They also hunted otters and seals, for their warm and waterproof pelts. Even more importantly, they collected salt from the seaweed and by evaporating sea water. This extremely precious commodity was not available inland (except for a few isolated salt licks) and a year's supply was gathered and prepared during the few weeks of their seaside stay.

Other than salt, the most precious commodity garnered from this annual trek was clams (*kaay*) whose shells were used to make money. A species of large clam was abundant at Bodega Bay, and all the tribes of this area traded with the Olamentko for their shells.

The Lake Miwok and their brethren were primarily hunters and gatherers, who bartered for goods they could not produce locally. The clamshell money was a kind of bartering shorthand —its value was based on what it could buy—but the money itself, the actual clamshell beads, also had value as objects, much as feathers did. A man with a lot of money was, in their culture as well as ours, able to acquire both goods and status that a man without it could not, but amassing it doesn't seem to have been as much of a compulsion.

Clamshell money was not marked; it was not the currency of one tribe, different from that of another (although anthropologists can usually tell which area beads came from by the type of workmanship, color of the clamshell, and minerals used in the preparation). Almost all the tribes in California accepted the same beads and cylinders as legal tender; some have been found in Washington State and as far away as the Great Lakes Region.

Clamshells were broken into small fragments of varying sizes, and given a crude round shape using a piece of sandstone, then each shell was drilled. A man sat, holding the piece of shell with his big toe; with his hands he twirled a stick whose tip had been imbedded with a sharp rock or piece of obsidian, keeping a steady, firm pressure on the center of the piece of shell, until a round hole was formed. A skilled worker might go through 20 such drill tips in a single day. It was tedious and time-consuming work.

Once the shell disks had holes, they were strung on two leaves of wire grass, until a strand was four inches long. These strings of crudely shaped beads were rolled on a flat stone with a little water, rolled and rolled for about eight hours, until the whole strand was nearly perfectly round. A standard negotiable string of money contained about two hundred round beads, and measured from the tip of the fingers of one outstretched arm to the opposite nipple (about three feet). One measure was worth a deer or a basket of fish; two bought a bow and arrow and quiver; a man with four strands of beads could acquire a dugout canoe.

There were "denominations", or differing values, according to the size or thickness of the disks or their age. Old strings of beads were especially prized; years of handling gave them a deep, rich patina that was unattainable using any other method. Long, cylindrical clamshell beads, (luppahuya) made from the thickest part of the shell, were each worth 20-40 disk beads.

Another form of money used, which was to clamshell beads as gold is to silver, was magnesite cylinders (awaahuya); one finished cylinder was worth 20 feet of shell beads.[17] Magnesite was quarried from a ridge just east of Clear Lake, in Pomo territory, and trading for quarrying rights or for the mineral itself provided a portion of Pomo income. The mineral is a dull white, sometimes with gray streaks, and is relatively soft when dug out of the ground, making it easy to work with.

Cylinders one to three inches long were formed by grinding, then drilled, using a method similar to creating clamshell beads. When the shaping was finished, the cylinders were baked in a fire of manzanita, an extremely hot-burning wood. The magnesite hardened and changed color as it baked, turning a

---

17 Figuring 200 shell beads to a strand, one cylinder was worth about 1400 beads or 35-70 clamshell cylinders or 6-2/3 deer or a canoe and a half. Another source claims magnesite cylinders were worth 2000-4000 beads each; value depended on who was trading with whom. Tribes closest to the seacoast valued the clamshell cylinders and disks much lower than tribes farther inland, a difference that can be attributed to distribution and transportation costs.

deep brownish red. The baked cylinders were polished using powdered stone and a lot of hand rubbing.

In the baskets the Lake Miwok carried with them over the St. Helena trails were the items they brought to trade with the Olamentko. They offered dried freshwater fish, deer and rabbit skins, acorns and baskets in trade for mussels, seaweed, seal and otter skins, salt, and abalone shells (whose pearly interiors would be formed into earrings,[18] pendants, beads and disks to decorate ceremonial clothing and baskets) and clamshells.

The Lake Miwok also brought magnesite beads, ore and obsidian from the Pomo around Clear Lake, and bearskins and sinew-backed bows from the northern Yuki tribe—results of other trading expeditions. Later they would trade some of the coastal products with the Pomo, Wintun, Yuki, and other inland tribes, to complete the native economic cycle.

Trading, hunting and gathering were the primary reasons for the journey to the sea, but not the only focus. During the weeks that they were at the shore, they socialized with the other tribes staying there, dancing and singing, feasting and gaming, and even arranging some marriages between eligible young men and women, which strengthened the alliances between the tribes involved.

At the end of an extended stay, the tribes often held a dance, a kind of going away party. The dance house was most likely a small, temporary structure, unless the visit had been to one of the main villages. Dances often went on for days, with trading, feasting, gambling and other game-playing going on as well. Singing provided the main music, accompanied by a wide variety of instruments, many of which were decorated with bright feathers.

Men played drums of hollow logs, using their feet to keep the beat. Bull roarers, strips of wood whirled at the end of a cord, made a whirring sound as the dancers circled the fire. High pitched sounds came from whistles made of pieces of

---

18 The Pomo are known to have pierced both their ears and noses in order to wear plugs of abalone shell. The Lake Miwok shared most of Pomo material culture, probably including this form of personal adornment.

clam shells or acorn tops, and flutes from elder shoots. Cocoons filled with tiny pebbles and tied to a stick, or fir cones hollowed and filled with stones, were used as rattles for amusement and to keep time.

Another kind of rattle was used by the women. An elderberry stick (or sometimes an elk rib) was split from the top to about three inches above the base. It was bound with bark at the bottom, and bounced off the hands as a clapper stick. Both men and women sang, but usually only the men danced; the women clapped their sticks and hands, hummed and swayed to the music, but rarely were active participants.

After visiting for a few weeks, perhaps a month or more, the Lake Miwok traveled back to their own territory, baskets re-laden with new treasures.

❖   ❖

IN THE EARLY FALL, FAMILIES AGAIN CAMPED AT THE FOOT OF the Meadow at Harbin, to gather acorns, pine nuts, and other seeds and wild grains. The acorn (*waya*) was the primary staple of almost all of the aboriginal people of California—what corn was to other North American Indians, rice to Asian cultures, or wheat to our culture, acorns were to the Lake Miwok.[19]

The transformation of a virtually inedible nut into "daily bread" was a lengthy, though simple, process. In late September and early October, men, women and children used large, conical baskets to gather the acorns from the black oak, tanbark oak and live oak trees that grew on Harbin's woodland hills. Much of the crop was stored in other large baskets inside their dwellings, for later preparation and use. The rest was ground into meal.

Before grinding, the acorns had to be shelled, and the yellowish-white meats dried. The nuts were hulled on a flat slab of rock, with a smooth, fist-sized rock held in the hand and

---

19 The Lake Miwok dictionary lists no fewer than 16 entries under "acorn", delineating not only the fruits of different types of oaks, but also acorn bread, sweet acorn bread, acorn flour, coarse acorn flour, acorn meal, acorn mush, thick acorn mush, cracked acorns, acorn soup, etc. etc. The word for autumn itself is *waya-wali*, "acorn season."

rubbed gently over them, cracking the shells without crushing the nuts. The contents of the slab was scooped into a shallow winnowing basket and tossed carefully; the wind and the tossing action separated the light hulls from the nutmeats, which were then dried in the sun on shallow basket-trays.

In villages or frequently-used campsites, a depression was painstakingly ground out of a large rock to be used as a permanent mortar (*tamih*). Smaller stones, six to eight inches in diameter, were similarly ground to be portable mortars (*tukulli*) for expeditions away from the main camp. These were frequently ground on the site, and left there for future use (and to avoid having to carry the heavy stones back to the main village). A smaller, rounded stone, carefully shaped and smoothed, was used as a hand-held pestle, considered a household item, and carried from place to place.

The dried acorn meat was placed in the mortar and ground into a coarse meal. Baskets whose bottoms had worn through from extended use were placed over the mortar hole to keep the acorn particles from flying out during the grinding and pounding process.

The meal was still not edible; acorns are full of bitter tannic acid, which must be leached out of them before they can be eaten. Pits in the tops of cones of sand, resembling miniature volcanos, were filled with the meal; cold water was continually poured over them for several hours, leaching all the acid into the filtering sand. After sifting the sand out, using baskets whose weave was sized for this purpose, the meal was ready to be used.

Acorn meal was cooked in a water-tight basket with hot stones, creating a mush, or with greens and bits of meat, for soup. The meal could be further ground into flour, mixed with water and *'awaayowa*, (a kind of red soil known later as "Indian baking powder," which leavened the resulting dough slightly, and which counteracted any remaining acid in the flour) and baked into lumps of dense "bread". Acorn flour mixed with some acorn kernels and water was wrapped in black oak leaves, placed on hot stones, covered with dirt and cooked overnight. The next morning the Lake Miwoks enjoyed a very dark, somewhat sweet cake.

Unlike many tribes in other areas of the country who were dependent upon one primary crop or animal (corn, buffalo) for subsistence, and who, if that crop failed, were threatened with starvation, the Lake Miwok and other California natives had a variety of abundant food sources. An oak blight one year might cause hardship, but never starvation. This diversity was especially important because they had no agriculture, no planned crops, no planting. The same person was, depending on the season, a gatherer or a hunter. They harvested what was naturally available each year, and adapted to the changes in their environment, rather than trying to change it to suit their own needs.

The techniques they used for securing food were inter-related; few of the processes involved required high skill, danger or very strenuous effort. Patience, simplicity and adaptability allowed them to modify a process and use it on other kinds of food, as needed. The same techniques used for preparing acorns were also used for other nuts, berries and "variety foods." Buckeyes were made into flour after a leaching process of several days.[20] Manzanita berries were gathered in the summer, dried, ground into flour, dampened, rolled into balls, and eaten as candy.

One of the more striking and seemingly bizarre examples of this adaptability was the use of insects as food. Gathering insects is actually quite similar to gathering plants: a woman's digging stick turns up worms as easily as roots; grasshoppers and caterpillars are like acorns—they appear seasonally and can be gathered in large numbers. Dietary requirements for humans haven't changed much over the years—we need carbohydrates, protein and fats. All of these were abundant and available to the Lake Miwok on the land, but some were found in sources most modern Americans never considered.

It's a stretch for the Western mind, but grasshoppers and yellow-jackets, tossed quickly in a basket with hot coals to roast

---

20 The hulled buckeyes were put in a closed, but permeable, basket in a stream, where the water continually flowed through them, leaching out the acids. An alternate method was to bury them in mud.

them, were considered delicacies—small, crunchy foods, like popcorn and peanuts. Other insects were dried and ground, just like acorns or pine-nuts, and used as "flour" for protein-rich cakes. "Certain large, fat, reddish spotted worms" were used as shortening for bread; if cultural repulsion can be overcome, this is a remarkable source of oil. There were few local plants or nuts which produced oil that was easily processed, and most of the animals that were hunted were lean, and yielded little renderable fat.

The Lake Miwok were not vegetarians by any means, but their diet consisted more of plants and gathered food than of hunted meat. In addition to nuts, berries and insects, they boiled the leaves of some plants and ate others raw, such as mustard greens and miner's lettuce. Roots and tubers were dug up and baked like potatoes, or peeled and boiled into soup. Seaweed was used as a vegetable and salty flavoring; honey and the sap from the sugar pine were used as sweeteners.

During the growing season (late spring to early fall), much of their food was eaten fresh, but a lot of their work consisted of drying, processing and storing food for the more dormant months. Almost everything could be dried for storage—fish, acorns, deer meat, seaweed, berries—to be eaten later, as is, or reconstituted with water. Foods were gathered and harvested when they were ripe and available; consumption and preparation were spread throughout the year.

❖   ❖

HUNTING WAS ALSO A YEAR-ROUND ACTIVITY. SMALL GAME WAS plentiful; rabbits, ducks, wood rats and squirrels provided most of the meat that was consumed throughout the seasons. Although deer were also hunted year-round, the major deer hunts took place in the late fall.

There appear to have been two deer-hunting camps at Harbin: a small one at the same site in the lower Meadow used for spring root gathering and early fall acorning; and a second, main camp in a walnut orchard about a mile NNW of the springs, near the Gulch House. (See map, page 33. This may also have been the "village" called *Kupetcu* on the maps of Lake Miwok territory. No one currently alive knows the exact location; one source thought that the fishing camp near the RV area was *Kupetcu*, but another source felt that *Kupetcu* referred to this hunting camp up the hill.) Large areas of blackened soil, indicating fire circles of repeated use, discovered here during a survey conducted in 1982, led archaeologist John Parker to conclude that the site "appears to be a significant seasonal habitation area." The Lake Miwok probably occupied the camp for six to eight weeks in the late fall.

This site has yielded the most identifiable artifacts of any area on Harbin property, including obsidian flakes and tools, and some ground stone slabs, but no mortars. One of the reasons for the abundance of artifacts, besides the fact that it was a main camp, is that it was a hunting camp; the tools used for hunting expeditions were small, numerous and frequently abandoned after one use. Arrows that hit their mark were often chipped or broken and discarded; shafts that missed were frequently lost in the woods. Knappers apparently sat away from the orchard to work, choosing an odd promontory overlooking the valley, and a tremendous number of points and shards have been found in that location.

All of the Lake Miwok's tools were made of bone, horn, obsidian, stone or wood, in various combinations. In general, pounding and grinding tools were stone; striking tools were bone, horn or smaller stones; drills, handles and stirring implements were wood; cutting tools were made of obsidian. There were some bone knives, sharpened on one side, the other side held in the hand, that were used for eating and carving cooked meat. The women of the tribe made their own cooking utensils and food processing tools, shaping spoons, ladles and digging sticks out of a variety of woods, and mortars and pestles from stone. A skilled woman might also make the knives and scrapers used in skinning and cooking; the rest of the tools, especially obsidian ones, were primarily made by the men.

Obsidian (*cicca*, which also meant "quartz," "flint" or "arrowhead" or *takse luppu*, which meant "glittering rock") is the result of a volcanic explosion; it is molten lava that cooled very rapidly, so rapidly that it had no time to crystallize, forming glass instead of rock. Because of this non-crystalline structure, it is very brittle, breaking easily under pressure or percussion, but it has an advantage for forming tools that minerals lack.[21] Minerals can only fracture parallel to the crystal structure— they will only break in certain directions. Obsidian, lacking that structure, can break in any direction, can hold an extraordinarily sharp edge,[22] and can be shaped for any use.

There were two local sources for the volcanic glass: Mt. Konocti (near Bottle Rock Road), in Pomo territory; and Glass Mountain (off the Silverado Trail in Napa County), controlled by the Wappo. The Miwok mostly traded with the Pomo for the obsidian they needed.

Although many people in a village or campsite probably had some skill in making tools, the obsidian knapper was usually a specialized craftsman. A skilled knapper could choose his nodules by judging, from the dull outside of the piece, whether there were likely to be any internal cracks or flaws that would spoil the final product. His own tools— hammerstone, horn hammers, anvil—were very carefully selected and, after years of use and handling, shaped to his hands. Like any modern artisan, his tools were his prized possessions, and he carried them wrapped in a pouch of soft deerskin when not in use.

Once his piece of obsidian was selected, the knapper might have begun to form the rough chunk into a hand-axe. He used his hammerstone, a smooth rock slightly smaller than his hand, to break through the dusty outer layer and expose the shiny black interior. The hammerstone struck repeatedly, flaking off deep rippled pieces of glass until the rough shape of the tool was formed. At this point he abandoned the stone hammer for a softer hammer of deer or elk horn, which sheared off longer,

---

21 Flint is an exception, having a very minimal structure; it also fractures in any direction, is a very common mineral in the U.S. and was used by tribes in other areas in exactly the same way as the Lake Miwok used obsidian.

22 Although the transition from the Stone Age to the Iron Age is characterized by the use of metal tools, obsidian is not just a primitive material. Modern-day surgeons, especially those who work in very small or delicate areas, such as eye surgeons, have been using small obsidian knives in their work in place of steel—the glass can be flaked to a much sharper and thinner edge, down to a thickness of one molecule.

thinner flakes, creating sharp, flat edges that the hammerstone would have crushed. He flaked steadily, forming a thick tool with thin edges, shaped to a point with a sharp, straight cutting edge and a blunt, smooth side that fit into the palm of the hand. Other axes were formed similarly, but with a notched butt that could be attached to a wooden handle with a deerhide thong or sinew.

For arrowheads, spearpoints and knives, a slightly different technique was used. The knapper selected an oval piece that was about the width and length he wanted the finished object to be, and placed it on a tree-stump anvil. He struck off the top of the nodule, leaving an egg with a flat top, and then made a small v-shaped wedge on one end of the flat area, using his horn hammer. Inserting the tip of his hammer into the wedge at a slight angle to the surface, he struck sharply and precisely, flaking off a thin oval "slice" of glass. Another wedge at the opposite end of the flat area and another strike created a second slice. Using this method, he could get five or six slices from the same size nodule used to make one hand-axe. Each slice was finished with a smaller bone hammer according to its final use —hand-held knives were sharpened on one edge, blunted on the other; knives with handles were sharpened to a fine edge on both sides; arrowheads and spearpoints had bases notched for shafts.

Deer hunting involved the use of all these tools, and others which were crafted using different methods. Soon after setting up camp in late October, men went into the wooded hills, found the deer trails, and set up snare nets woven of hemp fibers. Deer who were not snared in the nets were flushed out of the woods by men with slings and clay pellets. The deer were pursued on foot until they were exhausted, then speared or shot with a bow and arrow.

Bows (koonu) were made from hazel, oak or dogwood, and strung with hemp strengthened with beeswax. Arrow shafts were fashioned out of straightened elder or willow branches, the arrowheads attached to the shafts with sinew from previous hunts. Quivers were commonly made of deerskin, but wildcat or bear cub fur quivers were made for ceremonial hunts and/or for hunters with special status. Sometimes the arrows (kiwwa) were dipped in a poison made by drying and powdering the sacs from black widow spiders; this stunned the animal and prevented it from running away. [23]

Deer meat was as much of a staple food as acorns; in fact, the Lake Miwok word for deer, *sukki*, is also their generic word for "meat." It was eaten fresh, roasted over a fire, or dried and made into jerky for storage. Bones were broken, and the marrow inside used to flavor soups. One "recipe" calls for ground rabbit bones and deer blood to be collected in watertight baskets, allowed to clot, and then baked between leaves on hot coals. The resulting pudding is said to have had the texture of cottage cheese.

No part of the animal was wasted. Deer were perhaps even more valuable than acorns, because they provided not only a large amount of meat, but also sinew, horn, bones and hide. A single animal provided food, tools and clothing for the hunter and his family.

❖   ❖

THE LAKE MIWOK WERE, BY MODERN STANDARDS, RATHER unconcerned about clothing, going without any the better part of the year. Men and children were almost always naked, men occasionally wearing a deerskin breech cloth. Women wore only a string belt around their waists, from which front and rear aprons hung; adolescent girls often extended a third flap upward to cover their breasts. The aprons were made of shredded tules, shredded redwood bark or tules woven with rabbit fur.

In colder weather women draped rabbit skin blankets around their shoulders, or wore cloaks of tule that covered them from neck to feet, thrusting their hands out between the tule fibers. Men wore similar winter cloaks, woven rabbit skin and twine blankets that were tied at the waist or deerskin

---

23 On arrows used for hunting animals, the arrowhead was attached parallel to the notch at the end of the shaft; on arrows used for defense, the head was perpendicular. This is because a good shot is into the heart, between the ribs—in their respective and characteristic postures, the ribs on men are horizontal, on animals vertical.

blankets wrapped around their hips. A few hoypus, yomtas or wealthy men might wear cloaks of otter or seal skins in the winter. Shoes were never worn except in snow or the bitter cold, at which time everyone wrapped their feet in rabbit fur.

Any enthusiasm they may have lacked for everyday garments was made up in their ceremonial clothing and jewelry; they decorated their bodies with shells, feathers, tattoos and paint. Unlike some tribes whose members shared a structured system of tattooing, the Lake Miwok appear to have left this art up to the individual. Those who chose to have permanent tattoos pricked their skin with a sharpened bone, and smeared the area with the juice of green oak galls for a blue-black tone, soaproot for a green design, and baked soaproot or poison oak sap mixed with charcoal for black patterns.[24]

Temporary body decoration—for dances, festivals or initiations—was provided by powdering various plants and minerals and mixing them with water to form paints. Red came from powdered cinnabar, white from clay, purple from soot mixed with wild violet juice, and black from soaproot and charcoal. In addition to the elaborate cloaks and headdresses crafted of feathers, paint transformed ordinary men into fantastic and colorful creatures during dances. The paint was easily removed after the festivities by jumping into the nearest body of water.

The wheel of the year was celebrated with such dancing and ritual; as winter turned into spring, summer into fall, the cycle of renewal and decline was acknowledged. The wheel of life turned more slowly, but the changes in its cycle—birth, puberty, marriage, death—had their own rituals and celebrations as well.

Women gave birth in a special grass hut, and were confined to the hut until the baby's umbilical cord fell off. One of the parents disposed of the cord carefully, throwing it away in a

---

24 The poison oak was baked for more than three days and nights to achieve the desired coloration and eliminate the irritating oils.

specified direction, but not watching where it landed. During labor and for a few weeks after the birth, the mother was forbidden to eat meat, engage in strenuous labor, or travel beyond the village; the father was similarly forbidden to leave his house until the baby was four days old, and could not hunt for two or three months.

Babies were named for people on either side of the family, or for long-dead relatives. A string of beads was placed around the baby's neck to begin the naming ceremony; a male infant was taken to the sweathouse where the *mallele* sucked the side of its head and called upon the spirits to make it strong. Some people's names had meaning within the language (they were named after birds or animals or characteristics), and some did not. Most people in the tribe had two names—a public name and a private name. The public name was most often used, because it was safe; private names could be used by poisoners to cause harm, in the same way that personal objects could be used. Because of this, nothing is known about private names, other than that they existed, because the informants wouldn't share them with the ethnographers.

A baby spent the first year of its life wearing tule diapers, lying in a rabbit fur-lined basket-cradle, which was either strapped to its mother's back, or put on the ground near where she was working. A piece of soapstone was tied to the foot end of the cradle. The mother scraped a little bit off with a knife when she was changing the baby's diaper, using it as baby powder. Its hands, feet and body were tied in for the first few months (tiny hands were freed as they began to grasp things and beads and pieces of wood were strung on an arch of willow at the head end for the baby to play with). By the end of a year the baby was sitting up in the basket, a kind of tiny playpen.

Children were treated like small adults, eating the same foods, helping with the gathering and other simple tasks, spinning acorn tops and playing tag. When they reached adolescence both boys and girls fasted for the first time, and then abstained from any meat other than turtle or fish for some period of time. Boys fasted to ensure the success of their first hunt; girls for the health of their children.

With the beginning of her first menstrual period, a Lake Miwok woman began a life filled with complex taboos about her body and her sexuality.[25] She was confined to the house for eight days during her first period, during which she was not allowed to eat any flesh or wash herself, and had to scratch herself with a special wooden stick. At the end of this time, she was bathed by other women in the tribe and given new clothes. After this initiation, she was considered a marriageable woman, and had to observe a four-day seclusion each month in a special hut where any women who were "on their moon" could go and be secluded together, away from the rest of the tribe and from day-to-day tasks. A menstruating woman was not allowed to drink water after sundown, eat with other people in the tribe, or touch anyone else's food. Once a woman was married, many of these taboos extended to her husband, who was not allowed to hunt during his wife's period.

Marriages were generally arranged for children by their parents, with an exchange of gifts—shell beads and baskets. Intermarriage with other tribes, including non-Miwok-speaking groups, was common and often used as a political move, strengthening the ties between the two groups and cementing trading agreements. The young couple lived with each set of parents for a while, until the woman became pregnant, at which time the marriage was considered final, and they began their own home.

There was no legal marriage, as such. Courtship and sexual relations took place at the same time, and were just considered a love affair, easily discontinued. When the first child was born, it was thought to be a real marriage. (In the case of inter-tribal marriages, this may not have been true; the woman went to live with the man's tribe, unless she came from a larger tribe or more prestigious family.)

---

25 The reasoning behind sexual taboos and blood taboos is often murky. Many were for sanitary reasons; most were based on the belief that a woman was supernaturally powerful during this time, and was therefore dangerous until she returned to her normal state.

The customs of the tribe the couple lived with prevailed. A new bride in a Lake Miwok household refrained from eating woodpecker, salmon or cantaloupe (because her baby would cry a lot, get sores on its head, or get a general rash, respectively), eating woodrat (its sharp nest might appear on the baby's head at birth), or playing with poppies (her breasts would go dry when the baby was born).

Once they had children, a man and a woman were, almost always, married for life. If one of the couple died, the surviving spouse was free to remarry, often to the husband's brother or wife's sister. If the wife died before the baby was weaned, it was buried with her, according to some accounts. Others state that if the mother died, the infant was raised by the maternal grandmother, or the closest matrilineal relative.

The dead were either buried or cremated; no reference has been found as to the circumstances under which one method was preferred over the other.[26] Cremations were ceremonies attended by the family of the deceased and his friends, in some cases most of the village. A six-foot pile of dry wood was built, and the body was placed on top of it, face-down, with the head pointing south, so that the soul could easily travel in that direction. The belongings of the dead person—clamshell beads, baskets, personal possessions—were thrown onto the pyre by mourners. (In the case of burial, these objects were interred with the deceased.)

The reason for the disposal of the deceased's belongings along with the body was twofold: one, it was believed that the dead person might need his personal possessions, especially tools or hunting implements, in order to live well on the other side; the second reason was that if his relatives kept the items, it might be thought that they cared more for the objects than for the departed one.

---

26 Grave robbers, who wore coyote skins and made coyote noises while they were digging, were known to dig up burial treasures. (Perhaps that was a point in the favor of cremation). These ghouls were people with no close relatives, as it was believed that they were cursed and would die hard deaths.

Funerals were times of mourning for all close relatives; according to one informant, it was the only time Lake Miwok adults cried. Very close relatives cut their hair short when in mourning, and men refrained from sweating for several days after the death. A widow burnt off all her hair, and rubbed a mixture of white clay and pitch into the stubble; when her hair grew back the period of mourning was over.

One year after the funeral of a prominent person, a second ceremony was held. The cremated remains were reburned along with material offerings. The final ashes were buried so that enemies of the family could not find them and use them in harmful ways. At the base of the hill behind the Conference Center (see map, page 33) is a site believed to have been the burial spot for persons of high rank—shamans and chiefs—of the Lake Miwok in this vicinity. It was not a general burying ground, but rather the circle at which the initial cremation ceremony and the anniversary ritual and burning for a very select few were held.

Death was thought to be a natural part of the wheel of life, and accepted. Infant mortality and death in childbirth was high, by today's standards, and any injuries or illnesses that went beyond the scope of herbal cures resulted in death. One source, in a listing of ailments and their cures among the natives says, bluntly, "Rattlesnake bite: no cure. Death generally followed." If a person lived to old age (a relative term; in a culture where childbirth routinely occurred at 15 or earlier, a man was often a great-grandfather by the age of 45), he or she was revered as an elder, and offered respect by everyone in the community. After menopause, "crone" women rose in status, were allowed into the sweatlodge with the men, and had some influence in political matters.

A person who knew that death was near, whether from age or from illness, went (or was taken) to a sacred area to prepare for death. About two-thirds of the way up the road to North Star (see map, page 33), at the base of the hill, is a flat circle near what was once a waterfall. It was to this circle that Lake Miwok men and women went to pray to their familiar spirits to guide them into the spirit world, the world beyond this world. Another meditation area, below the great stone formation known as "Indian Rock," may also have been an area where ailing or elderly people went to make their peace. It was definitely a power spot, a place where shamans went to meditate and talk to the spirits, visiting the spirit world through secret passageways—the many cracks and fissures in the rock's surface.

The Lake Miwok believed that after death the spirit traveled to the Land of the Dead, which was across the ocean. There they would meet their dead relatives and ancestors, in a place that was pretty much like this world, but more pleasant.[27]

❖ ❖

THE MOST SACRED SPOT ON HARBIN LAND HAD NOTHING TO DO with death. It was, as now, a place of meditation, of peace, and of communication with the material world of the land, the spirit world, and the world of other people—the hot springs.

There is no way of knowing when the Lake Miwok people discovered the springs and began to bathe in them. Pools had been dug by the time the Spanish arrived, but those pools may have been dug ten, a hundred or a thousand years before.

Perhaps the steam coming up from the ground attracted a hunter's attention, and he climbed up the hill from the creek to investigate. Perhaps a young Lake Miwok man was stalking game in the wooded hills on the left side of the canyon. As he walked silently through the oak and laurel, he may have stepped aside to avoid *'ittum*, poison oak, and suddenly found his foot was covered with hot water. "*Haah! Eetaw-kik!?*" ("What! Hot water!?") he may have yelled, and in that way discovered the springs.

To a shaman, the waters of a hot spring were an entrance way to the underworld. In a trance state, induced by meditating on such a point of entrance—a natural tunnel, rock crevasse or

---

27 When the Catholic fathers arrived, they taught all the local people about the Christian heaven and hell, and these concepts have been integrated with the belief structures that existed previous to contact with the Europeans. The Lake Miwok words for heaven— *liilewali* (sky, heaven, "high world"); hell -- *weyaawali* (hell, "bottom world"); and God— *liilewali kootsa* ("sky person"), are all more than likely post-contact vocabulary.

spring—the shaman could travel from the material world to the spirit realm. There he could talk to the spirits and do healing work which, when returning to a non-trance state, he brought back to the people of his tribe. Since these natural openings to the spirit world are rare, the springs were considered to be a very special and sacred point in the already sacred material world.

The men of the tribe built dams of earth, wood and stone to direct the water on the hillside into pools they had dug. At about the location of today's Hot Pool, they formed a pool deep enough to bathe in, and set up a small camp on the site of Shady Lane. Another camp was down by the creek, where the Harbin residents' parking lot is today. These camps were quite separate, perhaps a 10-minute walk, as the land where the central area of Harbin is now was neither cleared nor leveled; from the creek to the springs the hillside was an unbroken, thickly wooded slope.

These camps, and the entire area surrounding the springs, were part of Lake Miwok territory, but were open to all tribes. The Lake Miwok called them, collectively, *'eetawyomi*—"hot place". Men and women who were sick were brought to the springs for its curative powers; Pomos, Wappos and Wintuns camped there routinely; and any tribes traveling through from the coast to the inland valleys were also welcomed. It was a place of peace, neutral territory; all the various tribes respected its sacred nature.

Each tribe established its own camp, with sleeping, cooking and working areas. The camps were far enough apart to be quite separate, but near enough for visiting. There was a sacred circle or power spot, used for shamanic meditations, ritual gatherings, and dances, on the bank of the creek. Known as the Grandmother's Circle, it is bounded by a great tree and a waterfall, where the hill meets the creek (see map, page 33). It may have been the gathering place for the women, especially the medicine women, of all the tribes.

It is not known whether the tribes shared the springs at the same time, if each tribe bathed with its own people, or if men and women bathed separately, whatever tribal affiliations were observed.

Then, as now, the springs area was both a sacred place for healing and a kind of resort, a place for people of the various tribes to gather. During the day the men hunted and fished together and the women wove baskets and cooked. In the evening there were often communal dinners and feasts with each tribe contributing meat and cakes. After the meal the men smoked, talked and gambled, telling both ancient legends and stories of recent happenings, and catching up on the events of the world beyond their own tribal boundaries.[28]

The area served as a kind of temporary marketplace, where tribes from various areas traded with each other. Furs and skins from animals not available locally were prized, as were baskets woven by women from tribes whose techniques were slightly different, or who used dyes and materials the Lake Miwok women didn't have. Dried meats and fish were bought and traded; knives, spears and arrows made by the craftsmen of each tribe were also sought. Much of the trade was done by bartering, some by the exchange of shell and bead money.

Trading activities were often accompanied by dances held in a temporary dance house structure. When each cycle of dancing was finished, the dancers took off whatever clothing they had been wearing for the dance, and jumped into the creek to swim and cool off or into the Hot Pool to relax. Once refreshed, there was feasting and then more dancing.

The springs area was probably used year-round, and the pool of hot water was undoubtedly very popular during the cold, rainy winter months, when warmth of any sort was at a

---

28 Gambling was a favorite pastime. Women played a dice game called *mulli*, played with pieces of wood 4" wide and 9" long. One side was burnt, the other plain, and three dice were tossed; all three burnt sides facing the same direction, and the person's team got a point. One side tossed until no point was made, then it was the other team's turn. Game was 20 points. They gambled for clothes and beads. The men played *kosi*, the grass game. Two willow sticks wrapped in grass, one with a piece of bark tied around it, or two rabbit bones, one with a piece of string tied around it, were used. Teams consisted of two men per side. A man hid a stick in each hand, shifting them back and forth while dancing and singing to distract the other players. The object of the game was to guess which hand held the marked stick. Each correct guess got a point (indicated by moving one stick from a pile of sticks). Men frequently gambled for everything they owned.

premium. The tribes camped communally for anywhere from a few days to a few months, the population changing as one group left for another camp or returned to its own villages, and another group arrived. In a world where all travel was on foot and all communication was done face-to-face, this "international" area was an extremely important place for inter-tribal exchange of information as well as material goods.

What would eventually become Harbin Springs was an area where all the people could come together, from any tribe, with any beliefs and customs, as long as the peace of the springs was respected. It was a custom that prevailed for thousands of years, uniting the unlimited spirit world with the finite material world, which for the Lake Miwok stretched from Clear Lake to the shores of Bodega Bay. Beyond that was a formless vastness known as "beyond the beyond."

From that vastness, another people would come to the springs. They had different customs, different language, different spirits. And they would destroy, forever, the world of the Lake Miwok.

CHAPTER THREE

Settling the Wilderness

O N NOVEMBER 6, 1821, 67 LEATHER-JACKETED SPANISH soldiers, armed with broadswords, muskets and bullhide shields, rode their horses into the unexplored wilderness of what would become Lake County,[1] and into Tuleyome territory. The contingent, led by Luis Arguello, invaded several villages, including Oleyome, "recruiting" Lake Miwok men to serve as guides. According to Arguello's account, the Indians escaped when the party entered Wappo territory.

The Lake Miwok had never seen horses before. Or swords, or muskets. And the men who rode the horses and carried the mysterious objects were not *kooca*, not Indian people.[2] The tall, bearded strangers had come from another world. Resistance to their conquest was impossible; a naked man on foot is a poor opponent for a leather-garbed soldier on horseback, and even the sharpest, most carefully crafted spearpoint is no match for a musket.

The moment at which Arguello's soldiers and the people of Oleyome saw each other was the moment at which the Lake Miwok began to disappear as a culture. The soldiers had much

---

1   References to geographic areas are made in terms of modern California. Lake County, as a political entity, did not exist until much later. The term is used as a convenience.

2   It is likely that the first Europeans the Lake Miwok were aware of were Russian, not Spanish. The Russians had a settlement on the coast as early as 1808, and traded extensively with the Coast Miwok. The largest collection of Miwok artifacts in the world (much of which is not duplicated in any North American collection) is in the Ethnographic Museum in Leningrad.

experience with Indians,[3] and made no distinction between a Lake Miwok, a Pomo or a Wappo. They were all Indians, all Diggers. From that time on, they were all subject to the laws of the Spanish king as, under the conquistadores, all American natives had been for centuries.

❖   ❖

AFTER CONQUERING THE GREAT CIVILIZATIONS OF THE INCAS and the Aztecs, plundering their cities and their gold, the Spanish believed that the great unknown land to the north of New Spain (Mexico) must also contain "islands of pearls and mountains of gold." They sought to find and conquer the legendary Amazon Island, a land inhabited only by women riding mythical griffins and using tools made of pure gold, ruled by Queen Califia. When Hernando Cortez discovered what he thought was that island (actually the Baja Peninsula), he named it after her—California.

Many Spanish ships sailed up the coast of California, reaching as far north as Eureka by 1603. But the coast was rugged and rocky, with few places to land, and no signs of gold, pearls or fabulous cities. The captains sailed back to Baja California, reporting to the governing officials of New Spain that there was nothing of interest on the 800 miles of coastline to the north.

Because of this lack of interest, it wasn't until 1769 that the Spanish attempted an interior exploration of Alta (upper) California. Aided by a fleet of ships sailing from New Spain to the harbor of San Diego, Captain Gaspar Portola and Father Junipero Serra led a party overland. Between May and November of 1769, they explored the coastal regions by land, establishing settlements at San Diego, Los Angeles, Monterey and San Francisco.

All of the Spanish explorations were led jointly by soldiers and priests, each under the control of the King of Spain. In

---

3   The Europeans lumped all the aboriginal peoples of the area together as "Indians"; I use the term in that cultural context.

effect, the Spanish king ruled the Church in the New World in exchange for financial support and the spreading of Catholicism to the "heathen" peoples of the new lands. There was very little separation of church and state.

The Spanish had found this to be a very workable arrangement for conquering the New World. The priests felt that it was their divine mission to enslave the Indians in this life to save their souls in the next, and were intense and fervent about the value and necessity of their work on the frontier. Spanish viceroys and governors found that the priests were extraordinarily successful in subduing potentially hostile natives with a minimum of expense and bloodshed.

The key to the priests' success in settling an area was the establishment of a mission. Possession of an area was not a matter of buying or selling property, just occupying and settling it. Colonies slowly developed around the mission churches, whose first buildings were crude huts of sticks, plastered with mud or clay and roofed with tule. The only differences between the first missions and the *wayas* of the Lake Miwok were in the rough wooden altars and the gilded crucifixes that adorned the mission chapels.

Priests who explored Alta California were accompanied by soldiers and supplied with provisions by the army. Their first task was to locate suitable sites for missions—places with good soil, a good water supply, and a sizable local Indian population. Their second task was to recruit a labor force from this population, save their souls, and secure their allegiance to Spain. In the first days of settlement, many Indians came of their own free will, out of curiosity and a desire to trade for the exotic goods the Spanish brought with them. The Indians provided all the labor for building the mission and clearing and cultivating the surrounding area; as soon as the mission was self-supporting, the soldiers withdrew, leaving the priests in control.

Between 1769 and 1823, the Franciscans established 21 missions in California, from San Diego to Sonoma, giving the priests possession of most of the choicest land in the province. By 1812, Spanish soldiers were rounding up "free Indians," taking whole villages and sending them to the missions to become diligent, hard-working Christians. This system had a two-fold purpose: it opened the land to unopposed Spanish settlement and provided a work force for the missions, which were the primary economic centers of the empire.[4] Trade ships with provisions from New Spain took weeks or months to reach the northern parts of Alta California; everything else was grown and raised by the Indians at the missions.

The missionaries wrenched the hunter-gatherers from their land, took them to distant and previously unknown realms, and taught them an agricultural, Christian way of life. It is probably true that most of the brown-robed priests sincerely believed that they were saving, or at least helping, the Indians by introducing them to "civilization." Civilizing the Indians meant taking them from their homes, and forcing them to live with people from other tribes, with whom they shared no common tongue. In many cases, members of various tribes who had been enemies weeks or months before found themselves living together in a new kind of "village." All Indians were forced to accept a new language—Spanish—and a new culture, with its very alien moral and social codes. Even those people who had come to the mission freely soon learned that, unlike paying a visit to a neighboring tribe, they were not allowed to leave, nor were their customs, language or ceremonies respected.

Although the missionaries claimed that they tried not to break up families, they refused to recognize Indian marriages; couples were separated unless they agreed to be baptized and remarried in the Church. Intermarriage between Spanish men and Indian women was tolerated, and in some cases encouraged, to further the allegiance of all the people in Alta California to Spain. Children were frequently taken from their parents and raised and educated by the priests who taught in the mission schools. Unmarried women lived in dormitories, which effectively separated them from the Indian men, but less

---

4   Under Spanish law, all lands under Spanish rule became the personal property of the King; under his aegis the Spanish governors of California had the right to give land to whomever they chose—missionary, soldier or farmer. That the land had previously been divided into territories and tribal boundaries meant nothing to them.

effectively from the Spanish soldiers. Without the emphasis on religious instruction, the missions would simply have been slave plantations; as in the American South of the same period, the Spanish economy was overwhelmingly dependent on a readily available and unpaid labor force.

Contact with the Spanish brought an abrupt end to the way of life of the tribes in central and coastal California. Most of the Spanish priests viewed their charges paternally, as if they were children who needed to be taught right from wrong. But the soldiers, whose journals and reports provide much of what we know about this era, wrote that the Indians were less than human, "a connecting link between men and brutes." Although the Spanish king had granted natives of the New World admission to the human race, "equal to Spaniards in the eyes of God and the King," and provided a form of civil rights protection for them under Spanish law, the laws weren't upheld in California.

By 1800, there were more than 13,000 "converts" living in and around 18 missions.[5] In addition to being taught the Spanish language and the Catholic religion, the Indians were also trained to farm and to tend livestock. Indian men were also trained as blacksmiths, stonecutters, carpenters and bricklayers; women were taught tailoring and dressmaking, with the less-skilled workers grinding meal and weaving cloth.

Indian laborers gradually replaced the first mud huts with adobe-brick and stone buildings. Both earthquakes and fire destroyed many early architectural attempts; later missions were massive, imposing structures constructed with red tile roofs and courtyards surrounded by thick walls. Although this offered protection against fire and other "acts of God," it made the lives of men miserable, especially men who had been used to living outdoors, and in harmony with nature. The thick walls and minimal windows made the missions dark and damp, and living conditions for the Indians were squalid.

5　By 1810 there were 19,000; by 1833, 30,000. Kroeber estimates the pre-contact native population of the state to have been about 150,000.

By Spanish standards, however, the Indians prospered. They were "properly" clothed and fed, they were learning to speak a "civilized" tongue, they were developing useful skills, and they were being brought into the fold of Christian life. The Spanish viewed the Indians as lazy, because they didn't appear to like to work; what was more accurate was that, culturally, the men and women of various tribes were used to their own rhythms of working. They labored seasonally, working hard during acorn season, then relaxing. In the missions, they saw no reason to change either their working habits or their customs. The Spanish disagreed.

> If, as not infrequently happens, any of the captured Indians showed a repugnance to conversion, it is the practice to imprison them for a few days, and then allow them to breathe a little fresh air in a walk around the missions to observe the happy mode of life of their converted countrymen; after which they are again shut up until they declare their readiness to renounce the religion of their forefathers.

There were conflicts between the two cultures in every facet of life, and it appears that the Indians were much more tolerant and respectful of the rites and customs of the Spanish than vice versa. The differences were not limited to language and religion; the extremely conservative, strait-laced Spanish were horrified by the more open sexuality of the Indians, and by the fact that they went without clothing, with no visible concern for climate or morality.[6]

From the point of view of the Spanish, the Indians dressed wrong, ate wrong, spoke wrong, prayed wrong and lived wrong.

Naturally, many of the Indians ran away from the missions. Some left because they were physically mistreated. Others left because, given a choice between the "comforts of civilization"

---

6   A Digger, perfectly naked, once met General Vallejo on a very cold morning in Sonoma.
"Are you not cold?" asked the General.
"No," replied the Indian. "Is your face cold?"
"No," replied the General.
"Well," replied the Indian, "I am all face!"

and freedom, they chose freedom. But they were, in most cases, far away from their homes, their people, or their land, in territories held by the Spanish, surrounded by lands belonging to unfamiliar tribes. Most runaways were caught and punished. The few that did escape to outlying villages were more than likely to be conscripted in the next Spanish raid.

During the mission years, the native population of the state dropped dramatically. While some of that drop can be attributed to actual murders by the Spanish, most of the deaths were the results of the toll of mission life.[7] Many people were literally worked to death; many others simply lost the will to live in a hostile and alien culture. Separated from the rites and ceremonies and attendants that had accompanied birth, and living in extremely unsanitary conditions, many women died in childbirth. Infanticide rose sharply, as women refused to submit their children to a life of slavery, or as Spanish fathers demanded the death of an illegitimate heir.[8]

But the biggest factor in the decline of the Indian population was disease. The Europeans brought malaria, cholera, typhoid, syphilis, and a host of other illnesses to the new land, and the Indians had no resistance to these alien germs. According to mission records, by 1815 there were three deaths for every two births. In 1833, a cholera epidemic swept the state, depleting the missions and wiping out entire villages. Some anthropologists have estimated that more than 50,000 Indians may have died in the mid-1830s. Even those tribes who had no direct contact with the Spanish suffered great losses as the contagious diseases spread to them through trading parties.

---

7 There is a commonly-held belief that a massacre occurred on Harbin land, involving the murder of thousands of Indians, many or most of them women and children. It has no basis in fact. The Stone and Kelsey massacre (see p. 69) is the only recorded wholesale slaughter of native people in this area.

8 Except for the native women, the population of early California was primarily male. The priests needed the soldiers on the rugged frontier, but could not control them, and so a double standard developed: priests urged Christian morality; soldiers encouraged, and supported, prostitution. Until the pueblos were well-established, and a normal family life was possible on the frontier, the few non-Indian women in California were wives of governors or military officers.

The missions needed a constant supply of labor in order to survive; the high death rate among the mission Indians led soldiers to journey farther and farther inland to gather converts. Easily accessible central valleys were the first to be plundered, but by the 1820s the missions were in such a decline that the Spanish ventured into previously unexplored territories, such as Lake County.

❖   ❖

IT WAS PROBABLY FOR ONE OF THESE LABOR ACQUISITIONS, AS well as an exploration to see what resources were available, that Luis Arguello entered this area in 1821. His expedition was the first to fully explore the lands north of San Francisco; the party traveled by boat from San Francisco Bay into the Sacramento Delta, going inland at Suisun, and then into Yolo County. They entered Lake County from the east, through the sheer canyon of Cache Creek. The region that is now Lake County was unknown to the Spanish because it was virtually inaccessible. It was a wilderness, entirely ringed by steep mountains, and traversed only by the trading paths of the native peoples.

Arguello "discovered" vast expanses of land for the Spanish crown, and recruited a number of Indian converts. Mission records from San Rafael and Sonoma indicate that Lake Miwok people were obtained during this period of forced conversion. Although the Indians used their "public names" on the registers (if they gave their right names at all), many names and places of origin are recognizable as Lake Miwok. Mission records of San Jose reveal that some people from this area were transported more than 150 miles to serve the Spanish.

In addition to being a landmark year in the history of the Lake Miwok, 1821 was also a turning point for the Spanish. Many of the areas that had been colonized over centuries of exploration, including Mexico, had developed into nations that wanted to be independent from the Spanish crown. Mexico had been settled for over 300 years. From the original Spanish settlements, an independent culture had evolved. Nearly all of the "Spanish" soldiers and priests were Mexican natives (of Spanish and Spanish-Indian origin) who had never seen Spain and felt more loyal to their land than to a distant king. Between

1808 and 1820, Spain's colonies, one by one, revolted. When news of Mexican independence reached the distant province of California in 1821, it was greeted with disbelief. Far from the center of the struggle, California had become part of the revolution with none of the battles or bloodletting. Luis Arguello was the first popularly elected governor of California in 1822, under the new Mexican flag.

The province's change in status brought about a period of unrest and of further change, especially in the area of land rights and the missions. The Spanish had made very few grants of land to private individuals; most land was granted to the missions, presidios and pueblos of the Spanish colonial organization. Wealthy citizens who wanted to acquire land found that the choicest parcels were in the hands of the mission priests, and were not for sale.

But the new government was less interested in religious conversions than in land and cattle, which were more profitable. The purpose of the missions—settling the frontier and supplying food and labor—had been accomplished. The California coast was full of small, but thriving towns, and foreign trading ships were calling on its ports with greater and greater frequency. What they brought to trade were manufactured goods from the United States and Europe; what they took back with them were the hides and tallow from the Californios'[9] cattle.

Cattle raising was, by the 1820s, the mainstay of California economy, and it required vast areas of land for grazing—land which was, by Spanish law, under the control of the mission fathers. So the laws were changed. In 1824, the Mexican government passed the Colonization Act, opening land to Mexican settlers (and any foreigner who would embrace Catholicism and become a Mexican citizen). Beginning in 1828, the government also began the process of secularizing the

---

9 Californios were people of Hispanic descent who were born or settled in California territory under Spanish or Mexican rule.

missions. Under the secularization laws, land which belonged to the missions was to be equally divided between private Mexican citizens and Indian Christians. Although alienation of the Indians' right to the land was expressly forbidden, these laws were actually the means by which the *gente de razon*[10] acquired land for their ranchos, and almost always acquired Indian laborers as part of the bargain. The once-wealthy missions soon began their inexorable decline into physical and social ruin because of the "robbery of the Mexican government."

In 1833, Governor Jose Figeroa issued orders allowing any Indians who wanted to return to their homelands to do so. Few responded. Some were too far away from their tribes or village sites (if either still existed); many had been born and raised at the mission and knew no other home. The missions had only prepared them for life at the mission, not for living independently in a European-based society. Most mission Indians opted for the Hobson's choice of working for the new rancheros. By 1836, the ranchos had replaced the missions as the economic centers of California life, as well as the centers of what culture, civilization and hospitality were to be found.

The treatment of the Indians under the Spanish priests looks quite humane when compared with that of the Mexican rancheros. Between 1833 and 1846 more than 600 ranchos were granted to individuals; a four or five league rancho was considered small.[11] The larger ranchos required hundreds of Indian laborers, and former mission populations soon proved inadequate to supply this need. Free from any altruistic, spiritual motives, the men who owned the ranchos raided Indian villages, conscripting their inhabitants solely for labor, and beating them for any infraction.

Skilled Indian men, especially those who spoke Spanish, became vaqueros (cowboys), excellent horsemen who tended the cattle for relatively good pay ($15 a month). Others worked as servants, menial laborers and farmhands, with wages often

---

10   "The people of reason," a term used to distinguish Mexican citizens and foreign traders from the Indians.

11   A league is equal to approximately 2500 acres.

consisting of as little as some food and a bandana handkerchief. Although slavery was abolished in Mexico in 1829, the law was rarely, if ever, enforced in California; wealthy landowners were free to hire hunters to corral entire villages and drive the Indians back to the rancho.

❖　❖

THE FIRST DECADE OF MEXICAN RULE IN CALIFORNIA WAS A governmental muddle—between 1821 and 1835 there were no less than seven governors; in 1836 alone, six men held that post. That year Juan Batista Alvarado, with the backing of several former governors and the assistance of 75 American sailors and frontiersmen, led a revolt against the Mexican government. In November of 1836, the free and sovereign state of California was declared, with Alvarado's uncle, 28-year old Mariano Guadalupe Vallejo as its Commandante General. What followed was a period of near-anarchy, with mission land and cattle being given away to friends and relatives at the whim of the man in power at the time.

From his headquarters in Sonoma, General Vallejo assigned his brother, Captain Salvador Vallejo, to head an expedition into the Clear Lake area. The captain's report on the region indicated that it had a great potential for cattle raising, but that the area was heavily populated by Indians,[12] and that "grizzly bears and panthers are numerous and resent intruders."

Little else is known about this expedition, except that it was deemed a success "as the Indians of that section were ever afterwards very tractable and especially so towards the Spaniards." Having beaten the Indians into submission, and despite the threat of resentful predators, Salvador Vallejo began an extensive ranching operation. He asked for a grant of 16 leagues for himself and his brother, Antonio; the Laguna de Lupi-Yomi grant was conveyed to him by the Mexican government, and encompassed Clear Lake and the lands

---

12 Pre-contact native population of Lake County is estimated to have been 4000-5000. By the 1880 census there were 765.

around it. By 1840, Salvador Vallejo completely controlled this isolated area. The center of his empire was a log house and a corral near the present site of Kelseyville, although he was never actually a resident of the area.

Salvador Vallejo was a very rich man. Not at all unwilling to take advantage of his brother's position, he "owned", by law or by possession, hundreds of thousands of acres of land in Napa, Sonoma and Lake Counties. Some of his land was granted by the various Mexican governors; much of it was his because he knew it was there before anyone else did, and because the cattle that roamed the open fields bore his brand. By all accounts he and his brother were amazingly wealthy, in a time when currency was just arbitrary paper and wealth was measured only in terms of gold or real estate.[13]

By those same accounts he was not a nice man. In 1843 he set out with a large party of citizens to attack Lake Miwok settlements in retaliation for the supposed theft of a cow near Sonoma, and also to secure a labor force to harvest his wheat crop. The Indians who were kidnapped for him were beaten, whipped and mistreated at his orders. (His brother, the General, was perhaps even wealthier, but seems to have been more reasonable. In an attempt to keep the peace, and perhaps to save his brother from any retaliatory attempts, as well as to "legitimize" occupation of Indian land, M. G. Vallejo signed a treaty with 11 Indian chiefs, including some Lake Miwok *hoypus*. See Appendix III, Vallejo's Treaty.)

Land was the primary motivator in Mexican California. Especially after the short-lived republic, the bonds that connected California to Mexico were even looser than those to Spain had been. The distance and difficulty in direct or current communication with Mexico, combined with a strong sense of

---

13 In 1847, Salvador Vallejo sold his stock and some of the land to an American, Andy Kelsey and his partner, Stone. Their mistreatment of their Indian laborers would result, in 1849 and 1850, in the only Indian massacre to take place in Lake County. For a detailed account of the Stone and Kelsey massacre, see Robert F. Heizer's *Collected Documents on the Cause and Events in the Bloody Island Massacre in 1850*, Department of Anthropology, UC Berkeley.

pride, allied Californios to California rather than to the ever-changing Mexican government.

A paucity of government and an excess of land is an appealing combination, and foreigners began flocking to California in greater and greater numbers. Trading ships stopping in California ports carried home glowing reports of the pastoral, golden land which lay in abundant, rolling hills, and was free for the taking—which helped to popularize the province.[14]

John Sutter, a Swiss-born "dreamer with a golden tongue," who spoke fluent Spanish, arrived in California in 1839. He petitioned then-governor Alvarado for a virtually unexplored tract of land near the junction of two rivers, to provide a buffer against both the Indians and the trappers and frontiersmen coming over the mountains from the United States. The 50,000 acre plot, which would become the city of Sacramento, was granted, and Sutter was given Mexican citizenship. In 1840 he began construction of a fort 150 feet long and 100 feet wide, with adobe walls 18 feet high and three feet thick, which he named "New Helvetia," in honor of his homeland.

Once he became a Mexican citizen, Sutter took steps to control the area of his domain, preventing robberies, repressing Indian hostilities, and checking illegal trapping. But he had a friendly weakness for Americans coming into California over the Sierra passes, which irritated the Mexican government.[15] Within a few years Sutter had established an almost feudal state, located on the main line of overland immigration, and New Helvetia became recognized not only as the primary trade center of the interior, but also as the main rendezvous and orientation point for newcomers winding down the trails from the mountains.

---

14 Although it stretches the imagination a bit, Americans were foreigners. California was an independent republic and the United States was a large, prosperous, but entirely separate, country, more than 1500 miles to the east.

15 The only other way to come to California was by ship. Immigration at the ports was controlled by the Mexican government; people coming overland were untraceable, and outside the law, if they chose to be.

The first organized emigration from the United States was led by John Bidwell in 1841; within a few years thousands of people came west to California by various overland routes. Word of mouth, pamphlets and newspapers extolling the untapped glory of the land to the west coaxed immigrants to embarcation points, the most popular of which was Independence, Missouri. It was from this crude, but cosmopolitan outpost, "the line that divides savage life and civilization," full of people from every walk of life and every part of the world, that Elisha Stevens would leave in May of 1844, leading a party of 50 men, women and children, including 22-year old James Madison Harbin, across the unending plains and prairies and into the mountains of the Golden Land.

❖   ❖

THE SAME YEAR THAT YOUNG HARBIN TRAVELED ACROSS THE continent, James Polk was elected President of the United States, on a campaign promise to re-annex Texas. Texas, which, like California, had declared itself independent of Mexico in 1836, was admitted to the Union in 1845, at which point Mexico broke diplomatic relations with the U.S. The war that followed lasted more than two years, with battles fought on both the Texas and California fronts. Although there were several mini-revolutions during the war, notably the Bear Flag Revolt, Americans did not gain control of California until June of 1847, when the war on that front ended with a treaty. From then until the news of the Treaty of Guadalupe Hidalgo (which ended the war with Mexico in February) reached California in August of 1848, the area was in limbo. Mexican law was still in effect, but the Americans were in control.

The war years, especially those between the two treaties, were unbelievably chaotic. California officials were representatives of neither the United States nor Mexico. For all intents and purposes, there were no laws. Land grants had been frequent, squatters were numerous, and legal ownership of property was an extremely grey area. The transition from a Mexican province to an American state would have been more gradual, and the various irregularities in land rights ironed out more simply, except for one thing: gold.

The discovery of gold in 1848, almost simultaneous with the end of the war, brought more than 100,000 English-speaking people into the state in a matter of a few months. Most of the Americans felt that the land had been won along with the war, and weren't about to let some foreign regulations and grants stand in their way. Mexican land grants had carried rights that were revokable by the government at its convenience. Americans wanted fee-simple titles ("you pay your money and you get your land") so that they would *own* the land on which they would farm or pan for gold. Most of the Americans also wanted the forfeiture of Mexican titles so that they could get the choicest land and develop it without interference from its existing residents—much as the Spanish and Mexicans had done to the Indians.

One of the Americans who profited from the chaos of the waning days of the Mexican Republic was Archibald A. Ritchie, a sea captain from Delaware who arrived in California just as the war was ending in 1848. By 1854, Ritchie had built a large house in the fashionable South Park district (a neighborhood where "people of wealth and quality" lived) in the fledgling boom-town of San Francisco and operated a business at 66 California Street, in the Financial District. In those same six years he had also acquired nearly 50,000 acres of former Mexican land grant property, 29,000 acres of it in Lake County.

Only three land grants were ever made for Lake County land, and only two of those were upheld by the United States Land Commission in its 1851-56 hearings. The Guenoc grant was made by Governor Pio Pico in August of 1845, giving George Rock six square leagues (approximately 21,220 acres) of land (see map, page 75). Rock had been acting as an agent for Jacob Leese, the alcalde of San Francisco (and Mariano Vallejo's brother-in-law), and sold the land to Leese in October of 1845. Leese also acquired the 8,241-acre Callayomi grant (see map) in 1849, purchasing it from Robert Ridley, who had been granted it by Governor Micheltoreno in 1845. Leese sold both grants to Ritchie and his partner, Paul Forbes, for $14,000 in American gold. A great deal of Ritchie's subsequent wealth came from the profits of his Lake County cattle ranching.

In addition to his Lake County grants, Ritchie also owned numerous tracts in Solano and Napa Counties; Napa County records show land transactions between Ritchie and both Vallejo brothers. Ritchie was instrumental in acquiring a large area of what is now Calistoga, in a deed that very specifically requires the survey lines to "make an elbow so as to include all the warm springs."

Perhaps Ritchie had a penchant for warm springs, or perhaps he was a developer with an eye for unusual property. According to every history of Lake County, Ritchie was the first white man to "discover" the Lake Miwok's sacred *eetawyomi* springs. An 1881 account says:

> The old Indians of this section used to be familiar with the medicinal virtues of these waters, and in former times visited them in vast numbers. In this way, Capt. Ritchie came to know about them at a very early day. He obtained possession of the springs, by location or otherwise, and retained them for six years, and then disposed of them to James Harbin....

An even earlier history recounts that:

> The waters of the springs were used by the Indians long before the settlement of the country by whites, on account of the cures affected. The springs were discovered in 1852 by Messrs. Ritchie and Harbin. The land belonged to the United States and was entered by them.

How did Ritchie "discover" the springs?

The northwestern boundary of the Guenoc grant comes within a quarter mile of the springs, although it is unlikely that Ritchie could have just stumbled upon the few acres of geo-thermal land out of the thousands of acres that he owned, none of which had ever been explored, mapped, or cleared.

He owned a lot of land, and a lot of cattle, and so he had a lot of Indians working for him, many of them local Lake Miwok men. It is more than likely that one of his Spanish- or English-speaking vacqueros told him about the hot springs that the people of his village had used. (It is also possible that some of the "free" Indians of the area were still using the springs, although the Lake Miwok camps in the vicinity had been long-abandoned by the early 1850s.[16] He may have simply followed them.)

Another possibility is that he was told about the springs by one of his Mexican foremen who had previously worked in the area for Salvador Vallejo, or from Vallejo himself, who had been ranching in that part of the country for twenty years. In a desolate wilderness, any place as welcome as a hot springs was bound to be common knowledge, passed from Indian to Mexican to Ritchie.

In any event, he "discovered" that the springs existed, and presumed ownership. The springs were very close to, but not legally part of either of his grants, and he never filed any papers establishing his claim to them. Fewer than a dozen non-Indians lived in Lake County, and there was only one wagon track leading into the area, so the competition for the huge acreage of Lake County land in the early 1850s was minimal. Ritchie was simply the only man who owned land near the springs and, as land and property laws were still being established in the infant state of California, that was all he needed.

There is no record of Ritchie improving the property, clearing the land, or widening the trail to the springs. He seems only to have "discovered" and possessed them, and then disposed of them (some sources say "sold") to a Mr. Harbin in 1856.

A. A. Ritchie and James Harbin were both part of an early "good ol' boys" network which included Salvador and Mariano Vallejo, and other landowners in northern California—men who would later be called Founding Fathers. Some of them were Mexican, others American, and what they all had in common was land: lots and parcels and tracts and acres and leagues of land.

These men traded employees and pieces of land with each other in a giant game of California Monopoly. In the early 1850s, both Harbin and Ritchie owned land in the Pueblo de

---

16 Ritchie is credited with the discovery of the springs (with and without Harbin's assistance) in 1850, 1851 and 1852. 1851 seems to be the mostly commonly used date.

FIGURE 3

A. A. Ritchie's Mexican Land Grants in Relation to Harbin Springs

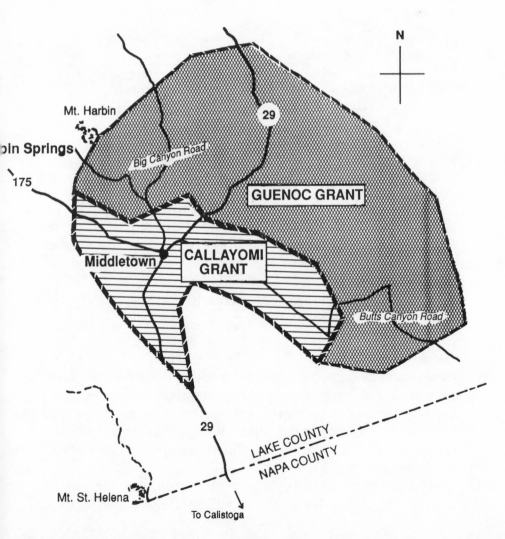

Salvador area near Napa and were involved in land deals with the Vallejos, Nathan Coombs, and other Napa county pioneers. They traveled in the same circles, which in the pioneer days of the state were very small, elite circles indeed.

But Mr. Ritchie never sold any land to Mr. Harbin, at least officially. It is unlikely that any money or documents passed from one to the other in any 1856 transaction, or that Ritchie ever "sold" Harbin the springs that would bear his name.

What the historians of record don't appear to have known is that on July 8, 1856, at about 7:00 pm, Archibald A. Ritchie was found dead on the road between the cities of Napa and Sonoma.

> He was lying upon his face....his horse and carriage were found about 100 yards from him, and his carriage was upset....The probability is that he was thrown [from the carriage] by the conduct of the horse, and was instantly killed. It is supposed that he died of an apoplectic fit [stroke], of which he had been apprehensive for some time, in consequence of the unusual mental agitation produced by a multiplicity of business affairs. It is well known that he had been greatly annoyed by the settlers and other matters pertaining to his valuable ranch.

He was 50 years old, and had died suddenly, without a will. His business affairs were so complicated that a special act of the California State Legislature was approved in 1857, six months after his death, in order to deal with his estate. He was buried in Lone Mountain Cemetery in San Francisco.

And James Harbin assumed ownership of the springs.

❖   ❖

HARBIN NEVER BOUGHT THE SPRINGS, AND DOESN'T APPEAR TO have legally owned them, any more than Ritchie had. Perhaps he was one of the settlers that had annoyed Ritchie to death. However he reached it, there is no doubt that James Harbin was the first man to occupy this land and to build a cabin here: he left his name. This place is Harbin Springs, not Ritchie Springs or Miwok Springs.

Geographical identity is a curious thing. In the period between 1856 and 1866, when Harbin "owned" the springs,

Lake County began to be settled.[17] As more and more people moved into the area, they developed a common vocabulary for what to call the hills and creeks and springs. In all probability, no one actually named it "Harbin Springs." Everyone simply called it that, because it was where Mr. Harbin's cabin was.

So Mr. Harbin *had* to have been there. But Mr. Harbin himself is something of an enigma.

According to various histories, newspaper articles and other sources, James M. Harbin came to California in 1844, was an early Yolo County pioneer, founded the hot springs that bear his name, and then wandered into Mexico and was never heard of again.

At the same time, according to other histories, he came to California in 1846, settled in Napa County, founded the hot springs that bear his name, and died in Solano County.

The story of James M. Harbin is similar to the exploits of the blind men and the elephant. Each contemporary chronicler recorded the facts as he knew them. It is only 150 years later that historical perspective (and access to a cross-reference of a wide variety of sources) is possible, and the seemingly self-contradictory life of James Harbin begins to fall into place.

The key to the puzzle is that there were two men, father and son, both named James M. Harbin.

Unfortunately, because early historians assumed that they were the same man, it is difficult, if not impossible, to separate them at this late date. Following the trail of the two Mr. Harbins through time, they are distinct and separate for awhile, only to blur together again at crucial moments. Because of a lack of concrete records regarding the "Harbin Hot Springs" property, it is unlikely that anyone will ever know, with

---

17 This area was a township of Napa County from 1855 until 1861, when it became Lake County. Although there are some records in the Napa County offices dating back to the formation of the township, the area was so vast and so remote that most land ownership was by possession, not paper. All Lake County land transactions between 1861 and 1867 were lost forever when the Lake County courthouse burned in 1867.

absolute certainty, which James Harbin is *the* Harbin of Harbin Hot Springs.

❖ ❖

JAMES HARBIN (THE ELDER)[18] WAS BORN IN NORTH CAROLINA IN 1796. As a young man, he moved to Tennessee and married a woman named Sarah, who was a year younger than he was. While in Tennessee, the Harbins had two sons: James Carroll Harbin, known as Cal, born in 1820; and James Madison Harbin, known as Mat, born in 1822.[19] The family left Tennessee in 1829 and moved to Missouri, where daughters Clementine and Josephine were born, along with a third son, Joshua.[20]

In 1846, James, Sarah, Joshua and the two girls traveled overland from Missouri into California, stopping at Sutter's New Helvetia. By 1850, they were listed on the census records as residents of Napa, where James was listed as a farmer with real estate holdings valued at $10,000. In 1848 he had purchased Edward Bale's saw mill (just north of what is now St. Helena), and erected the first Napa Hotel in either 1849 (the year the city of Napa was founded) or 1851, selling it in 1856 to the partnership of Gilmore and Taylor.

Between 1849 and 1858 he was a very successful businessman, buying and selling large parcels of land in and around Napa City, almost always at a substantial profit. He is cited, along with Archibald A. Ritchie and many others, as a

---

18 For ease of recognition, I'll refer to the father as James Harbin. He appears in various records as James, James M. and J.M. Harbin.

19 Some of this is unclear. That Mat Harbin was James Harbin's son is certain. Cal Harbin is listed on the census records as part of the family, but his age varies. He is sometimes as much as 13 years older than Mat, or as little as seven years younger, depending on the source. Why a family would name two sons "James" is a mystery.

20 Joshua's existence is more substantiated. Bancroft's history (although it confuses the two James M. Harbins in some places), cites a Joshua Harbin in the same overland party as James, Sr. The boy is then recorded as enlisting in the Mexican-American War in 1846. DePue's Yolo County history recounts the incident of Joshua Harbin's 1851 death by drowning (he fell off his horse crossing a swift river), during a party hosted by Mat, referring to the dead young man as "the brother of our host." There is no official death record, which was not unusual for that year.

claimant for part of Salvador Vallejo's Napa land grant; he subdivided and resold his 688 acres over a period of years. Harbin and other Napa pioneers (John Grigsby, Nathan Coombs, Archer Jesse and George Yount) bought and sold property from each other as the city of Napa grew and the agricultural paradise of the Napa Valley flourished.

One of the things that makes tracing the elusive Messrs. Harbin difficult is that, although they both engaged in numerous land transactions, they are frequently referred to in the long, complex, hand-written documents only by their first initials: J.M. In the decade between 1848 and 1857, in Napa County alone, nearly 40 deeds involve someone named J. M. Harbin, including several in which James Harbin sells property to James M. Harbin. There are few clues as to which man was doing what.

It is difficult to trace James Harbin from year to year with any precision; the census is one of the few existing records for the period, and was only taken every ten years. In 1850 he was in Napa with his wife and daughters; by 1860 he and his wife are listed as residents of the Clearlake Township of Napa County, an area that would, within the year, be known as Lake County.

This is the strongest indicator that he is *the* founding Harbin—he's in the right place at the right time. But he is credited with not only owning the springs, but also clearing some of the land, building a cabin, and widening the trail up the canyon.

In the tumultuous period after California became a state, many previous land titles, granted under the Mexican government, were invalidated by the United States, turning the disputed properties into "public land." Any settler could claim a portion of public land, his claim being the strongest if he could prove that he had actually occupied and settled the area. Squatters on Mexican land could be patient, knowing that when their cases were tried, they would be before an American judge. A squatter established future rights to questionable claims by building a cabin on the property and perhaps even living in it for a time, which may have been Harbin's plan.

An 1871 account (which mixes the facts) says that:

Two or three years after the discovery of the springs, [Harbin and Ritchie] built a small house near them which was occupied by Mr. Harbin as a dwelling place. He soon after bought out Mr. Ritchie's interest, and in 1860 built a new house with five bath-rooms in the lower part, immediately over the springs.

The forest was dense then, and clearing and building anything was a matter of hard work and brute force. At the time he "bought" the springs, James Harbin would have been 60 years old, and 70 by the time he sold it. It is possible that a man that age would choose to clear a wilderness area and live in it, but it's even more likely for a man in his mid-30s, James M. Harbin, to attempt.

❖   ❖

JAMES MADISON HARBIN (HEREAFTER CALLED MAT)[21] MOVED with his family to Missouri, but left for California in 1844 at the age of 22, two years before the rest of the family. He traveled with the Stevens party, one of two to cross the continent that year. Harbin says of the trip:[22]

> We started for the West May 4, 1844 and trailed the sunset for six months. We had eleven wagons loaded with bacon and flour and drawn by oxen. I was the guide. When we got to the head of the Humboldt River I left the party and struck off alone to find a path through the mountains. I found what I was looking for, and we crossed two miles north of the present [railroad] line of the Central Pacific...to the Truckee River [where] I gave the name which still clings to it.

---

21 Mat Harbin's "real name" was J. M. Harbin, James M. Harbin, James Madison Harbin, Madison J. Harbin, J. Madison Harbin, J. Matt. Harbin or Matthew J. Harbin, depending on which record, census, history or narrative is being consulted. (In one source he is identified as John Madison Harbin. That's the only place I've run across that variation, and I assume it's just an 1897 typo.)

22 This and subsequent quotes from Mat Harbin are taken from an 1897 autobiographical piece published in the *San Francisco Examiner*. Harbin was 75 when he wrote it (or was interviewed by the ghost writer), and it would appear that his accounts of the past, especially of his role in the history of California, may have been somewhat embellished, or have grown greater with the passing of time.

Mat Harbin named the Truckee River in 1844. Although the details of the story vary, the salient points are that Harbin had known a Frenchman in Missouri, whom he called "Truckee." (Maybe the man's name was something like Trouquet; we'll never know.) As the overland party approached the eastern slopes of the Sierras, they acquired an Indian guide, who reminded Harbin of the Frenchman; he called the Indian "Truckee."

Truckee assured them that they would soon come to a river, a welcome sight after weeks in the Nevada desert. Day after day the wagons inched forth, but no river. The men in the party, believing that the Indian was lying, began referring to it, sarcastically, as "Truckee's River." When they finally reached the banks, Harbin named the river after the Indian who had guided them to it.

The party reached Summit Valley in September, with 18 inches of snow on the ground. At what is now Donner Lake they built a cabin "because we weren't sure we could make our way down the mountains, and we had a prejudice against dying in the snow."[23] In February of 1845 they succeeded in getting to the Yuba River, where they left the wagons in the ever-deepening snow. Three families, including a pregnant woman called "Aunt Mary," stayed at a camp at the Yuba while the men pressed on to Sutter's Fort. Sutter provided them with mules; they rescued the people at the camp, including the new, three-week old baby ("Aunt Mary had some real grit in her," says Harbin), and led the entire party back to the Fort. They were the first overland party to complete the trip over the Sierras *with* their wagons.

Mat Harbin enlisted in the California Army under Governor Micheltoreno, serving with him four months and then going down the coast to the pueblo of Los Angeles on an exploring expedition. From there he wandered around California, hunting and panning in a minor gold strike until the Mexican

---

23 Two years later, several members of the infamous Donner party would die in that same cabin.

War was declared, enlisting on the American side under Commodore Stockton.

> [I] was with the army until peace was established. I commanded the soldiers at the Battle of Chino, forty miles east of Los Angeles, in September, 1846. The fighting lasted two days. The second day a bullet grazed my left ear, and the last ball fired ripped the middle finger of my left hand, leaving it a wreck. I put up a pretty game fight, I reckon, but I was taken prisoner and put in the next five months as a captive in Los Angeles....
>
> While I was in prison, my mother and her family[24] arrived in California and settled in Napa County. This moved me to what was a heroic effort, my temperament considered: I wrote my mother the first letter of my life. When she read it, she and my young brother [Joshua] held a council of war and my brother shouldered a gun and started for the front, intent on rescuing me from the Mexicans. To this end he joined the forces of Fremont. Good stuff in that brother of mine...

Mustered out of the army in April of 1847, Mat Harbin returned north, "taking with me 4,650 head of as fine cattle as ever trod the earth, and 700 horses." He married the daughter of a Yolo County rancher in June of 1850, one of the first weddings recorded in Napa County. To confuse historians even further he, like his father, married a woman named Sarah. In 1897 he said of his marriage:

> Sarah Adams and I liked each other. Then we liked a little better. Then we loved. Then we married. My love lives on, and should, for I have found little in this world worth clinging to save the memory of that good woman.

His wandering days over, at least for a while, Harbin settled down to domestic life in a household with his 18-year old bride, her father, several of her brothers and sisters, his own brother Cal, a few farmhands, a blacksmith and two vacqueros. "I concluded that it was high time for me to settle down and behave myself," he writes, "so I bought the Thomas Hardy

---

24 Curiously, he doesn't ever mention his father, the "other" James Harbin.

Mexican land grant at Woodland....It touched the Sacramento River and measured about seventeen miles in length by four miles in width. It was something of a bit of land."

It certainly was. The Thomas Hardy grant was a 26,000-acre piece of riverfront property in eastern Yolo County known as the Rancho de Jesus Maria. Governor Micheltoreno had granted it to an Englishman named Thomas Hardy in October of 1843. After Hardy died in 1848, the land was offered for sale at a public auction, and was purchased by Mat Harbin, James Estell, and George Taylor.

The auction wasn't on the level. One of Harbin's friends, another Missouri man named Stephen Cooper, was the administrator of the estate, and arranged for the auction to be held. George Taylor (who sold his share of the property to Harbin immediately after the auction) was the deputy sheriff of the county.

According to contemporary witnesses, when the auction began, Harbin and several other men were bidding for the land. The deputy, and a few other friends of Mat Harbin, told the other bidders to "beat it,"[25] and advised them that if they were foolish enough to continue bidding, they would soon find their lands occupied by squatters.

By the end of the auction, Harbin was the sole bidder, buying the Rancho de Jesus Maria for $6,500. The property had been appraised at $33,300. A Yolo county history says that:

The howl that went up in Yolo County over this piece of skullduggery was heard all over the state...Yolo County had a no more precious crew of villains than Gen. James Estell, Maj. Stephen Cooper, James Madison Harbin, George Taylor and John G. Parrish....[They] left a local impression: Harbin as a defaulter who wandered into Mexico to spend his declining years....

---

25 Legal documents, in referring to this incident, say: "Besides the said confederates, there was one other person present who bid upon said land. That thereupon the land sale was suspended, and the said bidder was taken aside by some of the said confederates and such inducements were offered, or measures taken by them, as inhibited the said person from further bidding." (Yolo County historian William Russell preferred the more succinct "beat it".)

A court case, *The People of the State of California vs. Matt. Harbin, et. al.* (1853), accused Cooper of "preventing, in collusion with the other four conspirators, a large number of people present at the sale from bidding on the estate. Thus was the largest ranch in the county and one of the largest in the entire West passed into the hands of the speculators."

Harbin may have been a scoundrel, but he was successful at it. In his own account, he says he raised cattle on the Jesus Maria land until 1858, clearing $100,000 to $150,000 a year on his ranching operation.[26] He claimed to have been worth over three million dollars by 1858 but, even if it were true, the records show his luck soon ran out. The U.S. government surveyed and approved the original Jesus Maria land grant in 1858, but disputes over Harbin's ownership of the land arose around the same time.[27] Taking advantage of an opportunity to sell the land while it was still legally his, he quickly disposed of most of his acreage to Charles Coit and left Yolo County.

Where did he go?

Russell's history of Yolo County states that Mat Harbin left the county in 1858 to open Harbin Springs in Lake County. Another account says that he and his brother Cal were living in Sol Getz's Hotel in the (soon-abandoned) town of Guenoc, and founded Harbin Springs together. The census records list Mat

---

26 His figures may be slightly exaggerated. A Yolo County commerce directory does list him as "J.M. Harbin, cattleman for the California market," but a bill of sale from the period cites an 1851 sale to Charles Coit of: 1500 Spanish cattle at $18 per head ($27,000) and 200 saddle horses at $40 each ($8,000). It would take five such large sales in a year to net him $150,000.

27 The claim dragged on for years, culminating in a U.S. Supreme Court case in 1871, in which alleged descendants of Thomas Hardy asserted that they had been defrauded of their inheritance. The bulk of the 300-page court document deals with establishing Hardy's identity as a relative of the claimants (and therefore the validity of their claims), and touches only briefly on the manner in which Harbin acquired the land. Although his name appears on the records as the first defendant, Harbin himself was not called upon to testify in the case, the land having passed out of his hands long before.

as an 1860 resident of the Suisun Township of Solano County (living on a portion of what had been A. A. Ritchie's 17,000-acre Suisun Rancho) with his 25-year old wife and three small children (daughters Nora and Dora, and a son, Popo).[28]

There's really no accurate record of where either of the James Harbins were living after 1858. Perhaps Mat and his children (and maybe even his brother and *his* family) lived for a few years in a cabin near an as-yet undeveloped hot springs. Perhaps his father was there too and all three generations were living together, beginning to clear the land and develop the potential of the waters. Perhaps not.

In a very small area there is a Harbin Creek, Harbin Springs, Harbin Mountain and Harbin Flat on the map. It stands to reason that someone named Harbin must have lived in the vicinity at one time. But the name is the only certainty, and the only legacy that remains.

❖   ❖

HARBIN'S OWN ACCOUNT OF HIS LIFE AFTER YOLO COUNTY sounds a bit far-fetched: he claims to have "bought the Mosquito Kingdom in Central America [for $100,000] and planned to fix it up for the Mormons." He says that he set out for Utah, having mortgaged his rancho for $45,000, intending to be gone two months. The two stretched into nine, and since "I didn't tell anyone at home where I was trotting or why...they lost track of me and the report gained acceptance that I was dead." The holders of his note foreclosed on the mortgage, and that's how, he contends, he lost the rancho and all his property.

From there he writes that he moved to Virginia City to supply lumber to the gold mines, making $150,000 and then losing it. In 1864 he says he went to Los Angeles again, ending up, in 1865, "in old Pat Dunn's Hotel at San Luis Obispo the night President Lincoln was shot."

---

28 The 1860 census records, which list Nora as age 6, Dora as age 4 and Popo as age 3, were hand-written in a very florid script, which is often difficult to decipher. But the name was very clearly Popo (in the 1870 census it is transcibed as "Popi"). Another Harbin mystery.

Even if Mat Harbin's account is true, he leaves out some important events. In April of 1864, after a brief and serious illness his wife, Sarah Harbin, died at the age of 32. Her obituary states that she had left Green Valley, Solano County, in November of 1863, and was living in Washoe County, Nevada Territory (now Reno), at the time of her death. Harbin had her body returned to California, and she was buried in Rockville Cemetery, near Green Valley.

She died without a will; the probate file cites her equity in a portion of Solano County land whose mortgage was going unpaid. Her heirs are listed as her husband, J. M. Harbin, and her children, Nora, Dora, "Popi" and Clay, who "are at present residents of Napa County in the State."

In 1864, Mat Harbin claims he was in Los Angeles; Sarah was dying in Nevada; the children (all under the age of ten) were in Napa, presumably living with their grandparents. None of them seem to have been in Lake County. Mat makes no mention of Solano County, his property, his wife, or his children in his memoir. Nor does he mention any hot springs. Was it because he wasn't the founder? Or because it was a minor bit of property to him, just a cabin in an unexplored woods, not worth mentioning?

Historical accounts and Mat Harbin's reminiscences come together again, briefly, when he mentions that "from '65 to '71 I followed the lumber business on Cobb Mountain, Lake County, working more than was good for me and making some money." Sure enough, he was registered to vote in the Cobb Valley precinct in 1867, and the 1870 census shows a 48-year old laborer named Mat Harbin (worth $300 in personal property, but no real estate) living in Lower Lake township with his four children.

Although his dates vary a bit with the records, Mat Harbin unquestionably built a sawmill (called, variously, the Callayomi Mill or Harbin's Mill) on the side of Cobb Mountain in 1873, selling it a few years later. A local observer had this to say about it:

> Had there been timber in proportion to the capacity of the mill
> and the excellence of the machinery, it would have provided a

fortune to its proprietor, instead of a 'humbug' as it is generally denominated by the citizens. There was never much lumber sawed by it, and it is going to ruin. So much for misdirected energy and misapplied capital.

Five years before he built the mill, Mat's mother, Sarah Harbin, died in August of 1868, at the age of 69, and was buried in the cemetery in Yountville.[29] His father died at the age of 81 in 1877 in Green Valley, Solano County, the same locality in which both Mat and Cal and their families had lived, a decade before.[30] It's difficult to tell (in several counties) whether they all lived together, lived in the same place sequentially, or merely lived near each other with great frequency.

There is no death certificate or official mention of James Harbin's death; the only record is a small notice in the *Lake County Bee* on May 24, 1877, saying that he was a pioneer of the county, had owned the hot springs, and had a son named Mat.

The year his father died, or thereabouts, Mat Harbin took off for Mexico, in a thwarted search for yet another fortune, this one in gold. He stayed 20 years, living as a hermit in the mountains.[31]

When I felt lonely, I turned to the stars or the flowers or the waters and was comforted. There's a heap of company in a star if you know how to get on speaking terms with it, and the brooks tell stories and the flowers are full of history, and the birds are honest friends.

---

29 The inscription on her gravestone notes that she was "a member of the Presbyterian Church for 40 years." She is buried next to her daughter Clementine, who died at the age of 23.

30 Just to confuse matters even further Cal, the third James Harbin, also shows up in Lake County on the 1870 census, with his wife and their ten children. In a 1961 article on local pioneers in the Middletown *Times-Star*, Mat and Cal are credited with *jointly* founding Harbin Hot Springs around 1852. Cal was a claimant for 160 acres of public land just over the ridge from the springs, near the site of his brother's mill.

31 At least one of his children stayed in this area. Nora was married in 1870, and moved to Yolo County. But, according to an unidentified source, "the Harbin living on Young Street (Middletown) near the river's edge was known for all those years only as "Plunk" Harbin, son of Mat Harbin." (I like to think it was Popo.)

Although he suffered a stroke around 1890, Mat Harbin stayed in Mexico until 1897, when he returned to the United States, staying with one of his daughters in Pine Ridge, near Fresno.

> Here I am content to spend the few remaining years. I have sounded the deeps and shallows of fortune, and I look out upon the world with something of sadness and nothing of fear or anger. It has not used me well, but then it's such a crude world yet, and I reckon it doesn't know any better.

Perhaps not as content in Pine Ridge as he thought, 78-year old Mat Harbin traveled north one last time, dying on June 8, 1900, near the town of Manton, in Shasta County.

❖   ❖

THE PERIOD THAT JAMES HARBIN IS SAID, IN PREVIOUS HISTORIES, to have "owned" the springs (1856 to 1865 or 1866) may not be accurate at all.   1856, as we've seen, is merely the year of Ritchie's death; 1865 is the year that Hughes and Williams—the first documented owners—bought the property.   Harbin's possession of the property is what occurs between Ritchie and Williams; historians, armed perhaps with only those two dates, attributed the entire period in between to Harbin's ownership. It stands to reason, then, that sometime in those 10 years, but not necessarily for all of them, James Harbin was at the springs.

So.   Which James Harbin was it?   It's unlikely we'll ever know. Within that timespan, both father and son are known to have been in the area.   Both are frequently credited with the founding of the resort. James is more consistently cited as the founder, but Mat is mentioned almost as often.

Although he was in his sixties at the time involved, James Harbin was a wealthy man, and could afford to hire the labor to build the cabin that would secure his claim. If it is true that he attempted to generate revenue from the springs as a primitive spa, it is in character; he had built the Napa Hotel less than a decade before. He may have thought of the untamed area as a retirement spot, far away from the hubbub of Napa City.

He seems more likely to have been a peer of Ritchie and Vallejo, being closer in age and more of a "solid citizen," and

*James Madison
("Mat") Harbin, age 77.*

*Illustration originally
appeared in the
San Francisco Examiner,
June 27, 1897.*

hence more likely to be privy to what lay just beyond the Guenoc grantline. And in 1865, approaching 70, with a wife in ill health, it is more than reasonable that he might relinquish the land, sell off his claim, and live out his last years somewhere more civilized.

Mat Harbin was in his mid-30's in the late 1850s. He was young, he had a family, and he had good reason to leave Yolo County and hide out in the unknown, unsurveyed wilds of Lake County for a while. He had built cabins, cleared land and ranched on the frontier before. He may have built his squatter's cabin here and lived elsewhere for a time, settling at the Springs for a year after his wife died.

He may have had just a shack on the property, or he may have tried to make a little money by building five bath-rooms near the springs and cultivating what local trade there was. He may, at first, have liked the adventure and then, like everything else in his life, tired of it and sold out when he could.

The most solid piece of evidence in Mat's favor is from a "Pioneer Record" archived by the Native Daughters of the Golden West, submitted by his daughter, Nora Harbin Gray, of

Placerville. Besides being the sole mention of the date and place of his death, this document also lists his places of residence in the state as "Yolo, Solano, Lake Co. What is now the city of Woodland (the Rancho de Jesus Maria). Harbin Springs." This is the only account which establishes with certainty that he was at "Harbin Hot Springs." But it gives no clue as to when.

Each of the two J. M. Harbins was probably at the Springs at one point or another. But my hunch is that *the* Harbin, the man who followed Ritchie on the historical timeline and whose residence fostered the Springs' identity, was most likely a bit of a scoundrel named James Madison Harbin, commonly known as Mat.

❖　❖

IN 1865 OR 1866, ACCORDING TO MOST ACCOUNTS, JAMES HARBIN sold his hot springs land to a Mr. Hughes and a Mr. Williams for $3000, for which they received "the property with its one log cabin on it, and no road leading to it."

Unless there were records to the contrary that burned in the courthouse fire in 1867, Harbin never did legally own the property, and the $3000 that he supposedly "sold" it for is perplexing. Given the status of land rights, squatters and public land at the time, for their $3000, Williams and Hughes probably bought a cabin and a promise from Harbin that he wouldn't interfere with their government land claim.

Whether or not any money was exchanged, Williams and Hughes became the first men on record as owners of the property. But when they opened their resort, they would call it *Harbin* Springs.

CHAPTER FOUR

Taking the Waters

Everything north of the Napa Valley is guesswork....All the region through to Clear Lake is a *very* rough country, of which there are as yet no maps anywhere near correct.

JUST AFTER THE CIVIL WAR, A 31-YEAR OLD WELSHMAN named Richard Williams came to this rough country from Camptonville, a small mining town in the northern Sierras.

Although the main Gold Rush was in 1849 and 1850, deposits of the mineral continued to be discovered and create small bonanzas for several years after, as miners moved into unclaimed territories. Camptonville was originally called "Gold Ridge," because of a massive vein found near there in 1852. It quickly became a major stage stop on the only road that led from the San Francisco and Sacramento areas to the northern mines.

Twelve-year old Richard Williams had come to America from Wales in 1846 as part of the same westward migration that brought the Harbin family across the plains. He worked his way across the country to California's gold fields, and in 1854, he and two partners arrived in the boom-town of Camptonville and bought a lot on the south side of the main street, to build and operate a hotel. Eight years later, a successful Williams purchased the saloon across the street from his hotel. The northern Sierra mines brought a wealth of travelers to the area, and the next year Williams bought another lot in town, presumably to expand his business. He also purchased some land, a house and a gold mining claim in an area called Depot

Hill about five miles northeast of town, to try and cash in on a little of the boom for himself.

He was a fairly wealthy young businessman, catering not only to miners and travelers, but to Camptonville's sizeable Welsh community (one of the town's two churches conducted its services entirely in that tongue). He had married a Welsh woman, and they had two children, a boy named William and a girl named Margaret. Richard Williams was well established in Camptonville, and seemed destined to remain there and become one of its pioneer founding fathers.

But sometime in 1863 or 1864, his wife Mary became ill. As the owner of the hotel and the saloon, Williams was in contact with most of the people traveling through the area on the stage, which was the primary source of news from the rest of the state. Somehow, he heard that there was a mineral spring in Lake County that was known for its healing properties. He discovered that it was on public land, and so in 1865[1] he abandoned the gold country and relocated his small family to the land known as Harbin Springs, in the hopes that it might benefit his wife's health.

Although Harbin Springs' water would soon become famous for its miraculous cures of "female complaints," it was not enough to help Mary Williams. She died in September of 1866, three weeks after the birth of their third child, who did not survive. Richard Williams remained at Harbin with his six-year old son and four-year old daughter, to build a resort around the springs. In 1867, he and a fellow native of Wales, Hugh Hughes, each applied for a grant of public land under the Homestead Act of 1862.

Public lands in newly annexed territories, such as California, were property not already in private possession. The government owned the land, but held it open for future sale

---

1 The date that Williams bought the land varies, from 1865 to 1867, depending on the source. An article in the *Alta Californian*, dated June 27, 1866 states that "The Harbin Springs are said to possess good medicinal virtues. The new proprietors there, I am told, are fitting up the place in good order for invalids and others." 1865 would seem to be the correct date for Williams' acquisition, if he was already building by June of 1866.

and settlement. Any citizen of the United States over the age of 21 could pay $10 to register a claim for not more than 160 acres of surveyed public land. After five years of "residence or cultivation," the settler could receive a patent granting him ownership of the land, for a payment of $1.25 per acre. This homesteading allowed people with small amounts of money to occupy land and work on it to provide income, securing the privilege of buying it without fear that someone else with ready cash could come along and take it.[2]

Because of the restriction limiting each settler's acreage, Williams and Hughes each filed a claim for 160 acres of land surrounding Harbin Springs.[3] (See map, page 128.) In April of 1867, Williams sold half of his holdings to Hughes, and Hughes sold half of *his* land to Williams, in order for each man to protect his interest, and to prevent either from selling his portion to a third party. The two sections of property thus legally and fully intertwined, Williams and Hughes began in earnest to build a resort.

One of their primary tasks was to build a road to the springs. Lake County was known as "the Walled-In County" and "The Land Which Was Hid of Old in the West," because of its isolation and formidable natural boundaries. The first road in the county that was wider than a horse trail or a footpath was made by soldiers in 1850, to transport their artillery wagons up from Napa in order to assist in the "Bloody Island" Indian massacre. The road was crude, rough, crooked, steep and generally in poor condition, impassable during the rainy season. Nevertheless, for more than sixteen years, it was the only road that led into the southern part of the county.

---

2   Although both Williams and Hughes were born in Wales, each had become a naturalized U.S. citizen—Williams in Downieville, Sierra County, September 1860; Hughes in San Francisco, February 1867.

3   Land within the county is divided into townships: 36 sections that are one square mile each. Each section contains 640 acres; 160 acres is a quarter of a section. Williams, in the technical geography of land patents, purchased the Southeast quarter of Section 20, Township 11 North Range 7 West; Hughes bought the West half of the Northeast quarter and the East half of the Northwest quarter of Section 20.

In 1866, John Lawley, Henry Boggs and a Mr. Patterson received a franchise from the State Legislature to build a toll road over the steep grade of Mt. St. Helena, from Calistoga. Construction began in 1867; a notation on the 1870 census for Lake County lists "one hundred Chinamen employed by H. C. Boggs in road-making." The 18-mile road was barely five feet wide, clinging precariously to the sides of the mountain as it twisted and climbed. But it was a real road, and a traveler in June of 1868 exulted that:

> ...the road is a very good one....and it commands a multitude of beautiful views, for the sake of enjoying which our party got out of the stage and went up afoot, keeping ahead of the stage all the way.

By the end of 1868 there were regular stagecoach runs from Calistoga to the springs area.

The franchise did not include a route from the Lawley toll road to Harbin, but that same year Williams and Hughes widened the trail up the canyon into a wagon road that came within 500 yards of the springs.[4] Construction was slow and tedious. Most building materials were brought in by wagons, but the wagon road could not reach the building sites until the excavation of the steep hillside was completed. During the winter months all work had to stop because the wagons became mired in the muddy road, and landslides hindered construction.

Perhaps the hindrances proved a bit much for Mr. Hughes. In September of 1868 (right before the winter rainy season began), Hughes sold his portion of the land to Williams for $12,000 in gold, "together with the buildings and improvements upon said premises and being known as the Harbin Springs property." Considering that each man had paid the government $200 for his 160 acres, Mr. Hughes made a rather tidy profit. He

---

4   In 1869, the Board of Supervisors voted to include the wagon road—"the road from Harbin Springs to the most feasible point joining the St. Helena Mountain road"—as part of Lake County's road system.

seems to have taken it and then disappeared completely from the pages of history.

When Williams and Hughes bought the property (according to most sources), it consisted of a rough log cabin, built near a hot springs on the side of a steep ravine, two miles up a densely wooded canyon. With no road, the property was accessible only on foot or horseback, and was several hours' ride from the nearest town. Despite its seclusion, Williams saw the possibilities in using the natural hot springs as the basis for a health resort.

Natural resources had brought the Spanish and the gold miners to California, but in the late 1850s, an appreciation for the land itself, not just its utilitarian use, arose. Historian Kevin Starr commented:

> Helping to offset the work ethic of the gold rush and early frontier, tourists sought out and shaped what there was to enjoy. Up and down the state, they visited geysers, hot springs, rivers, lakes, underground caverns, big trees, mountains and beaches. Hotels and resorts sprang up, crude at first, [but later] such elaborate affairs....California did not abruptly soften, but it ceased being a uniformly harsh frontier.

The work of transforming the harshness of this particular frontier, clearing and excavating the land around the springs, was awesome. Williams immediately tore down the crude cabin, replacing it with a more substantial structure. Initially, lumber had to be dragged along the trail a few pieces at a time, and equipment and other provisions brought in on horseback. Once the wagon road was built, supplies and materials could be brought in more easily, but all labor was done manually. There were no tractors, bulldozers or backhoes; trees were sawed down by hand and stumps and rocks were pulled with a lot of sweat, grit and mule-power. Men armed with picks and shovels slowly and laboriously excavated level sites from the sheer hillsides.

None of the land on the left side of the canyon, from the springs down to the creek, was level; it all had to be dug out, cleared and flattened before any building could begin. The land was rocky, and the soil was hard, except around the springs themselves, where the natural groundwater proved another deterrent to digging solid foundations. The first timbers brought onto the property were used to shore up the sides of the excavations against mudslides from groundwater seepage and the winter rains.

It was a long hard process, but Williams was not clearing the land single-handedly. The 1870 census lists the 36-year old hotelkeeper as the head of a "household" of 16 people, including: his son, William; his daughter, Margaret; a 34-year old English housekeeper, "Widow" Patton and her daughter, Harriet; a Welsh teamster; a Welsh bookkeeper; a Canadian blacksmith; a carpenter from Vermont; three laborers (one English, one German, and one from Rhode Island); an Irish cook, a Chinese cook, and a waiter from New York.

Woodcut of the Harbin Springs Health and Pleasure Resort, circa 1873. Main Hotel (with pillars) is at center, gardens in foreground.

Little by little the work of excavation turned to building, the building to carpentry, and the carpentry to furnishing and decorating. The area around the springs was built up with natural rock walls surrounding the pools, bath houses and dressing rooms.[5] Stables and barns were erected for the horses and other livestock, and woodworking and blacksmithing shops and other outbuildings were constructed. Cottages and a three-story rooming house were built and furnished simply with beds and dressers. A large, white-pillared hotel stood against the hillside, opposite the vegetable and flower gardens. Walkways and paths were laid out across the grounds, with decorative flowerbeds and judiciously distributed shade trees to delight the eye, and shield the invalids from the summer's sun. Guests began to arrive as soon as the buildings were ready, a few one season, more the next.

❖   ❖

IN LESS THAN FIVE YEARS, WILLIAMS AND HIS ECLECTIC STAFF, with the assistance of local laborers not living on the property, had turned the raw, undeveloped land into cultivated gardens, with springs walled and piped into pools, and an imposing hotel that cost more than $12,000 to erect. The Harbin Hot Springs Health and Pleasure Resort was the first resort in Lake County, and "the first resort of any consequence in Northern California." By 1873 a book about the area noted:

> This is fast becoming one of the most pleasant and best patronized watering places on the coast. It is located about 4 miles from Middletown...a small town situated in the Loconoma Valley [which] gets its importance from the travel passing through to the various springs....[Harbin Springs] is well provided with all the conveniences for making guests comfortable. Not only are there suitable hotel accommodations, but also a plat of ground set aside and always kept clean for those who prefer coming in their own wagons and camping out....

---

5   It is difficult to judge the age of rock walls built using indigenous stone—an 1870 wall looks pretty much like a 1920 wall. But I believe that much, if not all, of the stonework that surrounds the baths (and the base of the Fern Building) today dates from Richard Williams' initial construction.

[Mr. Williams] has built several cozy little cottages and a commodious hotel capable of accommodating about 130 persons comfortably. There are quite a number of springs of different temperatures, most of them highly impregnated with iron, magnesia and sulphur. The waters are much liked for drinking and afford delightful baths. The climate about the springs is mild and pleasant.... The evenings are always cool and refreshing. Last summer [1872] more than 1000 people visited this resort.

Perhaps the profitable summer of 1872 reassured Williams that his hope of making a success in the resort business was more than just a dream. It was a banner year for him in more ways than one. On December 4, 1872, he remarried, taking his housekeeper, Annie Patton, as his bride.

In that same summer, more than 10,000 people came to Lake County, nearly all of them staying at the various mineral springs resorts. By 1880 more than 30 lakes and springs had been located and developed, ranging from establishments with a few cabins and a spring of cold water to elaborate pleasure palaces catering to the health-seeker's every need.[6] Harbin Springs was the first and, for a while, the largest of the county's resorts.

Mineral spring resorts were, by far, the most important industry in Lake County before the turn of the century. Besides bringing myriad visitors to the area, they also provided employment for local residents. Many people actually worked at the resorts; still others provided construction materials, horses, food and liquor for the growing tourist business. Even the location of towns was influenced by the springs trade.

By the time travelers had completed the trip up the mountain from Calistoga to the hamlet of Middletown (which was laid out in 1871 and 1872), many travelers were too tired to

---

6 Adams, Allen, Anderson, Baker, Bartlett, Blue Lakes, Bonanza, Castle, Complexion, Dinsmore, Dollar, England (or Elliot), Epson, Gifford, Glen Alpine, Gordon, Harbin, Hazel, Highland, Hough, Howard, Lyons, Morton, Newman, Quigley, Roaring, Royal, Saratoga, Seigler, Soda Bay, Spring Hill and Witter were the major resorts that the 19th century tourist could choose for a Lake County vacation. One hundred years later, as of 1990, Harbin Hot Springs is the only one on this list that still exists and welcomes guests.

continue on for the hour or more it would take to reach Harbin. By 1874, Middletown, named for its location on the stage route between Calistoga and Lower Lake, had a population of about 200. Its business section consisted of three stores, three blacksmith shops, several saloons and one hotel, which was patronized almost exclusively by weary travelers to and from the springs.[7] Lake County historian Henry Mauldin notes that "Harbin Springs was liberally patronized as early as 1870, which was an added reason for the town starting."

Even with new hotels and saloons springing up along the route, travel to Lake County wasn't easy. From San Francisco it was an exhausting nine-hour journey involving several boats, trains and stagecoach changes. Yet in 1872, more than 10,000 people rushed eagerly to the new resorts, and were willing to tolerate any number of inconveniences. All to "take the waters."

❖   ❖

RITUAL OR THERAPEUTIC BATHING HAS BEEN PRACTICED IN every major civilization to some extent, but it wasn't until the end of the 18th century that physicians began to study the effects of water using the relatively new scientific method. Spas were opened by doctors who treated the entire spectrum of human ailments—with varying degrees of success. The water cure was the refuge of the wealthy invalid, and a moderately-known and moderately-effective form of therapy for many ailing European nobles.

In the mid-1830s, Vincent Preissnitz, the son of an Austrian farmer, developed his theories of the relationship between disease and water treatments, based on his own observations. He believed that Man ought to live more naturally, and follow the example of animals by drinking water frequently and bathing in it regularly. He systematized and popularized water

---

7   The small town of Guenoc (about 3 miles southeast of Middletown) had been abandoned, and most of its businesses had relocated to the new townsite. An 1871 travel guide short-sightedly described the fledgling community of Middletown as: "An embryo city, consisting of stables, a saloon and a few houses, without much in the visible surroundings to excite great hopes for the future."

cures, establishing a spa in his home town of Grafenberg, and establishing himself as the father of modern hydrotherapy.

Preissnitz treated, and claimed to cure, a wide variety of afflictions, from hysteria and consumption to dropsy and syphilis. No disease, whatever its cause, he believed, could fail to be vanquished by the healing powers of water. The public seemed to agree.

Despite opposition from the local medical profession, the reputation of his spa grew, and people flocked from all over Europe and America for "the cure." Preissnitz's treatment consisted of applications of water in various forms, usually cold; water was put to almost every use imaginable—patients bathed in it, drank it, sat in it, had it poured over them and squirted at them.[8]

Part of the reason for the success of the Preissnitz water cure, and its sudden and overwhelming popularity throughout Europe in the mid-1800s, was the Victorian obsession with health. Three waves of British and European epidemics[9] had brought disease into nearly every home. The topic of the day was health, as people began to pay more attention to their bodies, and to the precarious balance between life and death.

> No topic more occupied the Victorian mind than Health....In the name of Health, Victorians flocked to the seaside, dieted, took pills, sweated themselves in Turkish baths....Victorians worshipped the goddess Hygeia, sought out her laws, and disciplined themselves to obey her.

It was also a boom-time for quacks. An army of physicians and pseudo-physicians appeared with an arsenal of patent medicines,[10] to cure any ailment for which a Victorian lady or gentleman was likely to be suffering, and then some.

---

8 His regime included wet compresses, wet sheet wraps, douches of cold water applied to every part of the body, sitz baths, head baths and foot baths, in addition to the consumption of copious quantities of the *aqua pura*.

9 Influenza and cholera—1831-1833; flu, smallpox, scarlet and typhoid fevers—1836-1842; and typhoid and cholera—1846-1849.

10 Most of these medicines contained opium or alcohol—ingredients guaranteed to make the patient feel better, at least until the "medicine" ran out.

Fortunately this led more respectable medical practitioners to reform the healing methods being used, with an emphasis, in some quarters, on natural therapies.

In the midst of this movement toward natural, drugless remedies, the water cure caught on like a flash. As a medicine, water was unique. It was universally available, natural, and virtually free. In addition, unlike drugs or surgery, it had very few negative side effects; treatment was painless and palatable. And it worked.

Much of the efficacy of hydrotherapy[11] may have had more to do with hygiene than with pathology; bathing was infrequent in European and American households at the time. Many "miracle cures," especially in cases of skin disease, were probably brought about simply by having the patient wash regularly. Americans not only didn't bathe in water, they didn't drink it either—internal use of water ranked far below beer, wine, cider and tea.

In addition to baths and draughts of cool spring water, most spas insisted their patients follow a regimen that included a plain, balanced and wholesome diet; moderate exercise; plenty of fresh air and sunshine; and regular sleeping habits. Hydrotherapy as practiced in the spas was a rest cure as much as a water cure. The people who frequented the spas were, for the most part, city dwellers, and credit for a few more of the wondrous cures can be given to the clean, non-urban environment of the spa itself.

Along with this change of pace and a virtually stress-free environment, spas allowed the health-conscious, but rigidly moral Victorians to balance the physical pleasures of feeling well, enjoying themselves and soothing their bodies, with the ethical pleasures of self-improvement and behaving properly—all for their own good. Play and relaxation, if ordered by a physician, became a moral duty to which Victorians applied themselves with characteristic diligence.

---

11 The principle of using water as a treatment for illness was called hydrotherapy or "water cure" by some schools and balneology (from the Latin *balneum*, bath: the science of using baths in a therapeutic way) by others.

Victorian lady "taking the waters" at the sulphur spring basin.
(The wall at her back is a holding tank for the Hot Pool;
a cold plunge is now on the site.)

The beauty of the situation...together with the valetudinarian attractions of the mineral springs, soon drew large numbers of visitors: any puritan conscience uneasy at the thought of taking a holiday could presumably be quelled by the assurance that the spring water did you good and, moreover, tasted faintly unpleasant.

Americans were eager to imitate their European counterparts in combining health and pleasure; spas, springs and resorts were established in the eastern United States by mid-century. Saratoga Springs and The Homestead at Hot Springs, Arkansas became two of the best known watering places for Americans with the wealth and leisure to enjoy them. Although water cures could be taken at places boasting no more than a lake or a river, sites with natural mineral springs, either hot or cold, were most popular.

Europe was the arbiter of style and taste for most of the world, whether that style was in art, music, fashion or social customs. Wealthy Americans could afford to have goods shipped over from Europe, or to travel overseas to furnish their homes and clothe themselves. It was a mark of some pride to do something as it was done "on the Continent." But as the United States approached its centennial, American goods were touted, with patriotic excess, as being the equal of anything available in Europe—including the waters:

> When our California springs become more generally known, and their similarity to the famous European spas is better understood, our invalids may not find it necessary to undertake the long, tedious, expensive, and in many cases hazardous journey, when they can find right here in California, at their very doors, as it were, almost the identical waters, with all the conveniences and luxurious accommodations found abroad, and with the additions of a variety of food products and a pure, dry and balmy atmosphere, and an invigorating and stimulating climate unequalled in any other country in the world.

Lake County capitalized on the attraction of things European, advertising itself as "the Switzerland of America," for its mountains, lakes and spas, claiming that within its boundaries lay more mineral springs of a greater variety than in all of Europe.[12] Harbin Springs' water was spoken of as being "similar to that of the famous spring in the south of France called La Malou, where some of the most remarkable cures have been effected."

❖   ❖

WHETHER OR NOT THE PUBLIC WAS ACTUALLY SWAYED BY THIS therapeutic jingoism, Harbin and the other resorts of the county were extremely well patronized. The combination of health and recreation was appealing. Although the healing properties of the waters were far more stressed in advertising, organized leisure was a large part of any summer resort's attraction; it was, after all, a resort and not a hospital. Because of the length and difficulty of the journey to the springs, most people stayed

---

12 One brochure, published by the county, waxed even more poetic, extolling Lake County as "The Switzerland for Scenery, The Germany for Mineral Springs and A Garden of Eden for the Diversity of Crops."

for several weeks or "for the season," and the most popular resorts offered a variety of diversions, making certain that their guests were entertained as well as healed.

Leisure activities were subdued, though, as was fitting for an invalid population.

A Harbin Springs' brochure offered walking "over five miles of beautiful trails leading to charming little nooks and bowers in the mountains" as an activity for its guests, along with horseback riding, carriage drives and other pedestrian exercises. For those inclined to even more leisure, there were hammocks, swings and easy chairs, to wile away the hours between the morning bath and luncheon.

The same brochure enticed gentlemen who fished to come to the springs and "by these running streams, with rod and line...whip the peaceful hours away and return with well-filled creel," and hunters to come and enjoy the chase of a fall buck over the breezy hills. After supper, these same gentlemen might avail themselves of the pleasures of the wine room, adjacent to the dining room, where the bar and billiard table could be found.

The balmy summer evenings were filled with sing-alongs, often with long-gowned women playing the piano in the soft lamplight of the front room of the hotel, and festive dances were held in the pavilion on weekends.

Some gentlemen, and a few of the more robust ladies, spent their afternoons engaged in a spirited (but not overly tiring) game of croquet, one of the most popular games of that century.[13]

---

13 I'm not certain where the croquet ground described on the next page was. From the description, it seems to have been [in modern Harbin geography], on the top of a rise overlooking the swimming pool. The "Bath Path" leads from Shady Lane around the hillside and down again to the pool area. At its highest point, across the path from the cement foundations of an old water tank, is a small, leveled-off area that is now someone's campsite. There is a remnant of what could have been a flagpole, and the area is circular and level. If this is the right location, maybe the croquet court itself was surrounded by wooden curbs; otherwise any stray shot would have sent the wooden balls tumbling 50 or 60 yards down through the thickets on the bluff.

Immediately in back of, or up the canyon from the springs is an elevation of ground extending nearly across the canyon, lessening the size of the latter to little more than a ravine. This elevation of ground rises, perhaps, one hundred feet above the springs, and the top of it has been leveled off, and a flag-pole raised upon it, and seats provided for guests, and a croquet ground staked out. Winding paths lead up to it in a most romantic way...

Although few guests would have enjoyed their stay at Harbin Springs without these activities to keep them occupied, recreation was not what they came for. The main attraction and primary focus of life at the resort was the springs; it was the water and its remarkable properties that thousands of people came each summer to experience, some seeking pleasure and relaxation, but most hoping for a miracle cure to put an end to their suffering.

Winslow Anderson, M.D., whose tome, *Mineral Springs of California* was one of the bibles of the heyday of the mineral springs resorts, hedged his bets, warning that:

Mineral springs are not cure-alls. As a rule, too much is claimed for them. The many miraculous cures cited and the many improbable and ridiculous statements seen on printed circulars do more harm than good....On the other hand, it would be quite as flagrant an error to suppose that all the reported beneficial effects of mineral waters were only the result of extravagant or interested imaginings.

Much was written about the wonders of water cures, and all the springs made great and elaborate use of any healing claims or testimonials from patients, especially those substantiated, at least in print, by a physician. Doctors prescribed a stay at a spa for any number of ailments; the larger resorts had doctors on staff to advise patrons which mineral water would be the most beneficial for their real or imagined diseases. Harbin Springs offered its patrons four different kinds of spring water: Hot Sulphur, Chalybeate (Iron), Magnesia and Arsenic, each with its own healing specialty, according to the literature of the time.

Mineral waters, so the theory goes, are absorbed by the body and change the consistency and composition of the bodily fluids. They release the medicinal materials which they hold in solution, in a process very similar to the geologic percolation of hot springs water in the earth.

> They reach and search the most minute ramifications of the capillaries, and remove the morbid condition of these vessels which are so frequently the primary seats of disease....They communicate an energy to the muscle fiber and to the animal tissues generally, which is not witnessed from the administration of ordinary remedies.
>
> Mineral waters also dissolve many pathological and moribific materials which are more readily eliminated from the body. They act on the nervous system, regulating and stimulating important blood-forming centers whose abnormal action is often the primary cause of deleterious changes in the blood itself.
>
> The waters also serve as simple dilutents, washing out the gastro-intestinal tract, diluting the different fluids of the body, and serving as vehicles of waste products, besides having their own tonic action.[14]

The main source of tonic mineral water at Harbin Springs was the hot sulphur spring (one of the springs that now flows into the Hot Pool), which flowed from the ground at the rate of 1500 gallons per hour (flow rates and temperatures are from Anderson's 1889 analysis of Harbin Springs' waters). It was recommended for both drinking and bathing; taking it internally was suggested for cutaneous afflictions (skin diseases), as well as torpidity (sluggishness) of the intestines, dyspepsia (indigestion), kidney troubles and glandular dysfunction. Prolonged and frequent soaking in the hot sulphur

---

14   This is a typically exaggerated 19th century claim, but much of the basis of it, the chemical and therapeutic reaction of mineral waters on the human body, has been borne out by modern medical research.

water was thought to be beneficial for those suffering from old gunshot wounds, rheumatism, gout or joint diseases such as arthritis.[15]

> The visitors this season [1876] average about 80. Most of them are invalids and some are utterly helpless from rheumatism, gout and nervous disorders. The water most used is sulphur-water having a temperature of 122°. The sufferers, after drinking it copiously for 10 or 20 days and bathing in it once a day for the same time, usually experience relief from even the most desperate cases of rheumatism, and many who came here two weeks ago so helpless they had to be carried to the bath, are now able to walk without crutches.

The other hot spring that now feeds the Hot Pool once flowed into a separate tub. The hot iron spring (which Anderson refers to as the "light chalybeate-carbonated spring") at 116° was slightly cooler than the sulphur spring, and its flow was considerably less at only 60 gallons per hour. Anderson notes that the clear and sparkling water had a pleasant taste and was to be used by patients who suffered from anemia or chlorosis,[16] scrofula, rickets, malaria or any other chronic wasting disease, because of the effect of the iron in building up the red corpuscles in the bloodstream. It, too was advised for patrons with dyspepsia. Presumably the hot iron water was used primarily for drinking; its minimal flow would have made bathing in it a long and tedious process.

The magnesia spring has greatly diminished in the last 100 years.[17] It was a cold spring, slightly carbonated, and was not as popular with the guests as the hot waters. For those who suffered from intestinal distress, drinking it was yet another

---

15 In many "cures" especially in the cases of rheumatism and arthritis, relief was due not only to the sulphur content of the water but also to the naturally soothing and relaxing benefits of heat and moisture.

16 Chlorosis is another form of anemia—"iron-poor blood"—characterized by an (unattractive) yellow-green complexion.

17 There is a very small trickle on the hillside whose water tastes faintly like Milk of Magnesia—a chalky sort of aftertaste. This is probably what remains of the old magnesia spring, and is used (with other springs water) to fill the L-shaped cold plunge.

cure for dyspepsia, as well as colic or flatulence, as it rendered stomach acids more alkaline and promoted the expulsion of gas. Magnesia water was also endorsed for people with kidney or bladder troubles, or for those in need of a gentle, but effective, purgative and laxative. It was also touted as an excellent remedy for those with a "too-familiar friendship with Bacchus."

> The best paying properties in Lake County are mineral springs. All the roads lead to them; all the travel is to or from them. They have placed whiskey at a frightful discount, for whoever drinks of these waters has not the least taste for the ardent. The bars are deserted and even lager goes a' begging.... In every direction "the springs" are the Delphian oracles of the sick.

Many intemperate sufferers joined the throngs of the sick and weary making the journey to Harbin Springs; its waters were thought to have beneficial effects on those addicted to the use of alcoholic drinks. For some the stressless atmosphere, away from their business and other worries that had led them to the refuge of the bottle, proved a wonder cure. But for others, the restful surroundings and medicinal waters were no match for the habits of a lifetime. In the mid-1870s, an unknown journalist reported:

> About 4 weeks ago a man named Seimers, a person of some wealth, who was engaged in business on the San Mateo road, near San Francisco, came to Harbin's Springs to recuperate his health. He had been drinking to excess for some time, and was suffering from the effects of it when he arrived. After staying a short time he strayed off to the mountains Northeast of this place and did not return. His brothers advertised for the lost man, offering $100 reward.
>
> On the 17th [of July] a farmer found the body some 4 or 5 miles from here, nearly nude, and in an advanced stage of decay. The gold watch and ring of the deceased were missing, and nearly all of his clothing. The ring was subsequently found in a small brook a short distance from the body, and the reasonable conjecture is that in his delirium he threw away his watch, ring and clothes, and found death in the wretched plight in which his body was discovered, and not by murder....

Mr. Seimers, I am informed, was a member of the Masonic fraternity, and, with the one weakness which led to his death, an excellent citizen.

The fourth of Harbin's springs might seem nearly as ominous as that ghastly account. It was, and is, an arsenic spring, but the water contains only trace levels of the mineral. It was a hot spring (115°), with a flow of about 15 gallons an hour. Today it is used only as a footbath, for the relief of athlete's foot and other fungal conditions. But in the 1880s, the arsenical waters were drunk by a small percentage of the guests, and in small dosages, to relieve the ubiquitous dyspepsia, along with scrofula and gout. They were especially touted as being serviceable in cases of female complaints, with "the proprietor assuring me that they are more valuable in such diseases than in any others."[18] Anderson claims that they were especially tonic, both for drinking and in topical applications, for skin diseases including eczema, psoriasis and acne, and also effective in cases of syphilis.

The claim that the water of any resort cured syphilis was very rarely heard after a while, and with good reason. Word of mouth about the services, accommodations and miraculous waters of a resort could make or break its reputation.

Witter Springs was a large resort located in the northern portion of Lake County in the late 1800s, also known for the efficacy of its healing waters. One gentleman who had been suffering from syphilis when he arrived at the springs, believed that, because of the waters, he had left the disease behind when he departed, and unfortunately was effusive in telling his friends about his cure. Its reputation for the curing of venereal diseases became so well known that the mere mention of the name "Witter" could produce ribald laughter among visitors on the springs circuit. A large hotel had been built on the

---

18 Female complaints ranged from menstrual problems and the after-effects of pregnancy to "that form of nervo-hysterical troubles frequently observed in the young ladies who are fond of late evening parties, theatres, balls, etc., and who spend most of the following day in bed or in the house reading exciting novels." Cold water poured down the back was thought to be the cure for that particular "affliction."

property, but, due to its dubious claim to fame, no one wanted to admit that they went to Witter Springs. The clientele dwindled, the resort declined, and the magnificent hotel never opened. When it was dismantled in the 1940s, some chandeliers, bathroom fixtures and other furnishings were found in the rooms, still in their original crates.

❖ ❖

NO SUCH CALAMITY BEFELL HARBIN SPRINGS. ITS POPULARITY continued to grow, in part because of all the Lake County resorts it was the closest to San Francisco, and in part because of the effusive testimonials that filled its advertisements and the newspapers of the day.

> One old gentleman from Sacramento who was paralyzed for seven years was cured here....His complete recovery was sudden, after the first favorable signs commenced. And when at last one morning he was able to throw his crutches away, half wild with delight and excitement, he set off on horseback for home in such haste that he rode the horse to death.

> A mechanic from the Mare Island navy yard, named Mother, is now here. He was paralyzed while at work on the United States ship *Resaca* two years ago. He lay helpless for three months afterward and was finally carried up here. He was completely cured in five weeks and is here again because he felt the old symptoms returning a few days ago.

Business improved with each passing summer. Although the resort was open year-round, "the season" was from June to September, after which only the hardiest tourists or most desperately infirm patients lingered. At the height of the season, more than 100 visitors could be accommodated in the hotel buildings and cottages, with additional guests able to camp in tents or wagons. Rates ranged from $2 a day to $12 or $15 a week, depending on the lodgings desired. An 1874 business directory notes that the facilities were so attractive that they would serve "to give our readers an idea of how cheap valuable property is sometimes disposed of when its real value is unknown; in 1866 this property was sold for $3000, but an offer of $100,000 today would be refused."

Richard Williams might have taken that somewhat inflated offer for his property, had anyone made it. Still, despite the exaggeration, in the first ten years that he owned the land, he *had* increased its value geometrically. By reinvesting most of each season's profits into buildings and improvements for the resort, he had taken it from an undeveloped piece of real estate to one of the premier watering places in Northern California.

The Napa *Daily Journal* interviewed Williams in June of 1875, at which time he had:

> ...expended upon the property, in grading, building, furniture, etc., between $70,000 and $80,000 and still engaged in making improvements. He is just finishing a new kitchen and adding an addition to the dining room. He proposes putting up one more new cottage this season and changing the bath-rooms, setting aside a certain number of rooms for the exclusive use of female patients.... There are about 60 guests here now, among that number about 15 ladies. By far the largest number of sick folks here are rheumatics. Paralytics, neuralgics and dyspepsics are also well represented.

The well-represented dyspepsics, along with their fellow invalids and a handful of pleasure seekers, came mainly from the Bay Area to visit the resort. The trip from San Francisco to Harbin Springs cost $5.70 and took a little over nine hours. Starting very early in the morning, city dwellers drove their buggies to the wharf at the foot of Market Street, where they could catch the 7:30 ferry to Oakland, and meet the train there for Vallejo Junction (now Crockett). At that point they again changed conveyances for the ferry ride across the waters of the Carquinez Strait to the city of Vallejo. A train on the Napa Branch Railroad line left Vallejo at noon, running up the Napa Valley through the vineyards to Calistoga.

The terminus of the railroad line was at the Calistoga Station, where passengers going to the resort areas farther north once again rearranged themselves and their luggage for the last leg of the journey. For those unwilling or unable to go any further that day, the Harbin Springs stagecoach also called at the Calistoga Hotel.

Williams (and a succession of partners) owned and operated a livery stable in Calistoga, and from it conducted a private stage line whose route was from Calistoga over the mountain to Harbin. The daily departure was scheduled to connect with the train from Vallejo, which carried passengers from Sacramento as well as San Francisco. Williams owned a team of a dozen horses and three coaches, ranging in size from an eight-passenger stage to one that could hold 17 travelers. A six-horse stage made the 21-mile trip over the mountain every afternoon (except Sundays), "over a route affording some of the most picturesque and magnificent landscape views in California."

For a few miles after it left Calistoga, the stage followed the route of what would one day become Highway 29, veering right toward the mountains after crossing a small creek, at a junction that is today marked by a sign that says "Lawley/Old Toll Road."[19] This road meandered up the mountainside in a series of sharp turns, but gradual grades. It was (and still is) extremely narrow, barely six feet wide, cut into the side of the mountain so deeply in places that the trees and rocks overhang the road. As the passengers on one side of the stage came close enough to the hillside to touch its mossy rocks, their fellow travelers on the other side of the coach were treated to the view of the craggy pinnacles across the valley, and to a sheer drop of hundreds of feet, only inches from the edges of the horses' hooves. It was a truly magnificent stretch of road, but those whose illnesses were nervous in origin were probably not soothed by their journey.

The stagecoach is a romantic vehicle, rivaled only by the wood-burning locomotive as the nostalgic hallmark of the American West. But its image far surpassed its reality. The journey from Oakland to Calistoga (approximately 70 miles)

---

19 When Highway 29 was constructed, it followed the course of the toll road from Calistoga to this junction, then continued straight to go up the mountain, on a steep grade that the horsepowers of automobile engines could handle, but the actual horsepower of the stagecoach could not. The two roads merge again about two miles before the summit.

Harbin Springs Livery Stable, Calistoga

took about five hours, and was relatively comfortable; trains featured such luxurious amenities as upholstered seats and windows. The stagecoach trip from Calistoga covered less than a third of that distance in nearly the same amount of time, all of which was spent bouncing up and down the rough dirt road.

In the winter, the trip was likely to take even longer, as the wheels of the coach sank into the mud; by the time they reached the springs, passengers were quite often soaked to the skin by the cold rains. They may have fared better than summer visitors. Temperatures on the journey during "the season" often topped 100°, despite advertising claims of a balmy climate.[20] Nevertheless, one author noted that "summer clothing will be found comfortable, but persons in delicate health, as most are who seek the springs, should never discard flannels."

---

20 Many brochures of the time claim that the temperature in the summer never rose above 90°. Either this claim, like many others, was also exaggerated to make a resort stay more appealing to potential customers, or the climate has changed somewhat in the last hundred years. In the 1980s, temperatures in Lake County occasionally reached 110°.

Ten or twelve people (or more), most of them sickly, dressed in what amounted to long underwear, sat cheek to jowl in the stagecoach, jostling against each other for several hours in the summer's heat. But the worst part of the journey in the summer was the dust. The stagecoach had no windows, only canvas flaps that could be rolled up or down. The heat in the summer months required the flaps to be rolled up in order to provide any ventilation at all; the dry dirt from the roadbed obscured any glimpse of the picturesque and magnificent landscape, and nearly suffocated many of the passengers.

It was a ride...under a blistering sun, through dust twelve inches deep which the heavy hooves of the horses and the wheels of the lumbering coach tossed ten feet in the air, half smothering the inside passengers and coating those on top within and without. Thorpe had secured the seat by the driver, thinking to forget the physical discomforts in the scenery.

But the prettiness of the valley was obliterated by the shifting wall of dust about the stage, and he resigned himself to misery. Even the driver would not talk, beyond observing that it was "the goldarndest hottest day he'd ever known, and that was saying a darned sight, *you* bet!" It was late in the afternoon when the stage pulled up at the hotel....

The Harbin Springs Stagecoach,
crossing St. Helena Creek just outside Middletown.

It is no wonder that most people stayed at the resort for weeks at a time; the return journey was no less harrowing. Upon their arrival at Harbin Springs, all but the most frail of the dust-caked passengers were immediately taken to the baths.

The Harbin Springs livery stable also furnished horses and carriages for parties who wanted to visit the resort, but did not want to take the stagecoach. The road was no less rough, and the ride was no less exhausting, but it could at least be made in private, in the company of a few select friends.

❖   ❖

BY THE END OF THE DECADE, RICHARD WILLIAMS HAD IMPROVED the area around the springs themselves so that a large number of people could bathe in a variety of therapeutic settings.

The bath rooms were in several white wooden buildings in about the same location as today's Hot, Warm and Cold Pools. The main building contained small, interconnected rooms, offering individuals privacy during their baths. The Harbin visitor could choose from any of 15 separate baths: one mud bath, nine individual tubs and five "plunges"—tubs or pools in which a person could be completely immersed.

The mud bath was small and extremely hot; one source describes it as a mud footbath, with a temperature of 101° on the surface and 121° in the mud and rocks below. At least one of the plunges was hot, and was about the size of the Hot Pool. The rest were cold, with one being cited as very spacious, large enough to be referred to as a "swimming tank."

The water was piped into the bath rooms from the various springs. The baths were arranged with a natural system of cooling, so that baths or douches of varying temperatures could be enjoyed; the closer the room or tub was to the spring, the hotter the water. One source notes that each bath also had a facility for the application of steam, although just how this worked was not explained.

Bathing in the 1800s was not just a matter of walking up to the bath rooms and soaking for a while. Unlike today, bathing was seen less as a pleasure than as a prescription, and there was a definite structure to the bathing ritual, complete with rules and customs that the patient was advised not to ignore.

Although some of the more robust men enjoyed a vigorous cold plunge upon arising, most invalids were counseled to bathe several hours after breakfast, at ten or eleven in the morning, once or twice a week. Dr. Anderson warned:

> CAUTION: Do not commence a course of treatment at the springs by bathing once or twice daily. The American fashion...of hastening and rushing through everything may be well enough for business, but where the life of an individual or the treatment of an obstinate disease is at issue, this plan is not only deleterious, *but may prove fatal to the life of the patient!*

The bi-weekly bath was the focus around which the rest of a person's schedule revolved while on vacation. It was not a casual dip, but an all day affair, incorporating not only the waters, but often a massage and several other ablutions as well. Anderson again:

> The bather undresses in a warm, comfortable room, wraps a blanket around himself, puts on slippers to protect his feet from the hot floor, and then enters the bath-rooms proper.[21] Here are plunges of hot and cold water, douches of hot and cold water, and hot steam. The bather soon breaks into a general perspiration. This lasts from 5-15 minutes.
>
> The next step is a plunge into the cold water...[after which] the bath attendant may stretch the bather on a table, pour warm water and salve over him and begin to press, squeeze and twist his whole body with wonderful dexterity...the whole body is then rubbed with soft soap and the bather plunges into the hot water.
>
> Here he remains a few minutes, then is taken out and rubbed dry...the hair and beard are trimmed and the bath proper is completed. The bath lasts about two hours and makes one feel as if he were born anew.

---

21 No mention is made about whether or not the bather undressed completely, or retained a bathing garment of some kind; nor whether nudity was acceptable for both men and women when bathing in private. In any communal bathing—as in the cold swimming plunge—men and women may have taken the water together, but all were nearly fully dressed in the heavy woolen swimsuits of the time.

After all that, the bather frequently napped for a few hours on a cot in a warm room next to the baths, set aside for that purpose. For the next few hours, he was advised to take a gentle walk, or remain quietly in his room. The rest of the day, it was suggested, the bather would feel a genial sensation of luxurious contentment, a relief from pain, and a feeling of enjoyment and physical well-being that he would wish could last forever.

On days that were not dedicated to bathing, patrons read, wrote letters, strolled the grounds and socialized with one another in order to pass the time. Harbin Springs was quite isolated from the rest of the world, and an abundance of relaxation sometimes proved too much of a good thing:

Harbin Springs, Lake Co., Sep. 7, 1879

My Dear Henry,

...If the affliction was only in the left instead of my right side, the time which now hangs upon my hands so heavily could be made pleasant to myself.... About election time the guests (some sixty in no.) cleaned out leaving a few grunters like myself, behind. There is only one with whom I can exchange a thought, and she is a splendid woman, one in whose company I could enjoy every moment spent, but she is too much of an invalid to endure even the sight of a face only for a few moments at a time. So you can imagine how a letter from anyone would break in upon the monotony of my forced stay here. A bundle of papers would be acceptable—weeklies I'd prefer as they contain the summary of what I've not seen.

The water has had a powerful effect upon Alice, showed the face irruption [sic] to be an impure condition of the blood which the continual use of mineral waters for a few weeks will cure, but I fear she will not remain long enough to have it benefit her much. I am doing very well, but it is difficult to tell which it is, freedom from harassing cares or the water. If I do gain strength sufficient shall write to Mrs. Pomeroy, so please send her address....

Your devoted Mother,

M.C. McPike

As the proprietor, Williams tried to relieve the tedium of his guests by providing every service he could. Besides the recreational activities offered, the principal newspapers from Napa and San Francisco were sent up on the stage, and there was daily mail delivery. A telegraph office was located in the main hotel building, there was a barber shop near the bath houses and "the servants are polite and accommodating. The visitor immediately feels he has found a first-class watering place, under the management of a man who thoroughly understands the wants of the traveling public....Harbin Springs is the Saratoga of the Pacific."

The facilities at Harbin Springs were not as elaborate as those of New York's Saratoga Springs, which boasted a casino, race track, ballrooms and a truly grand Grand Hotel.[22] But when they got off the stagecoach, Mr. Williams' arriving guests did find comfort, if not luxury.

❖   ❖

IN ORDER TO PROVIDE CONGENIAL LODGINGS FOR HIS GUESTS, Williams continually invested his season's profits into new construction. In mid-July of 1879, though, his plans for the future exceeded his capital. He acquired the needed funds by taking out a three-year, $14,000 mortgage on the property, placing the title to the land in trust with a wealthy real estate magnate from Vallejo named Thomas Mathews.

With cash in hand, Williams completed his grand layout, and by 1881, Harbin Springs was a small village of more than 25 buildings. Besides the bathing facilities, there was a main hotel building, a smaller hotel/rooming house, a dining room and kitchen, an office, a dance pavilion, eleven cottages, and various outbuildings.

Most resorts, Harbin included, provided a wide range of lodgings to accommodate the needs of their clientele. Those who wished to stay at the spa with a maximum of comfort and luxury booked rooms in the main hotel. Families with children, and those who preferred to do their own housekeeping, rented cottages; the robust (especially many younger, single gentlemen) preferred to rough it in tents, while still enjoying the society of others in the evenings.

---

22 It was also the place, in 1853, where the potato chip was invented.

The hotel itself was a large, two-story white wooden building with pillars, porches and balconies, facing the road and the main plaza area. A parlor, reading room and four bedrooms were located on the ground floor; eleven more bedrooms, with either single or double beds, were on the second floor.

The hotel rooms were, by the standards of the 1880s, pleasant but not opulent. The walls were hung with the typically florid wallpaper of the time, probably with brown or green designs on a beige or cream background. A matching border print with scrollwork in the same basic colors ran in a band around the top of the walls, and the ceiling paper was of yet another pattern, light and open, in the same color scheme. The windows were covered with pull-down shades, rather than curtains, and the wooden floors were concealed by dark carpets woven with either a floral or a scroll motif.

There was no electricity.[23] Lighting in the evenings was provided by candles, brass-based oil lamps and (probably) some gas lights in the hallways, whose illumination filtered into the room through the transoms above the doors. (There may have been gas fixtures on the walls or ceilings of the guest rooms as well. They were in common use at the time, but no sources specifically mention their use at Harbin.) The round globes of the oil lamps gave out a rich, warm light, softening the corners of the rooms and shadowing the floral walls. Outside the hotel, all was black except the flickering of lamplight in the windows and the stars above; the guests must have found their rooms very cozy.

In contrast to the ornate wall and floor coverings, the furniture in the rooms was fairly plain and simple. An iron bed or a wooden bed with a tall headboard was covered with a spring mattress and an excelsior mattress. On top of this relatively soft pad were cotton sheets, two wool or cotton blankets (depending on the season), two pillows and a fringed

---

23 Edison patented the incandescent bulb in 1879, but it was many years before it was in common use, especially in rural areas.

bedspread. When the bed was fully made up, a bolster, covered in the same material as the bedspread, lay decoratively atop the pillows.

Next to the bed was a wooden washstand with a mirrored back, a drawer, and a cupboard beneath. On top of the stand stood a porcelain washbowl and pitcher painted with delicate flowers; in the cupboard was a matching porcelain tureen with a lid and a handle on the side—the chamber pot. There were no bathrooms or toilets in the hotel. Guests washed and shaved with the pitcher and bowl, bathed at the springs, and used the chamber pot for other matters.

The only other piece of furniture in the room was a chair. Presumably the guests hung their long dresses, dark pants, white shirts and flannels in a closet and used their steamer trunks as bureaus.

Downstairs, patrons could spend the sultry afternoons in the comparative coolness of the reading room, which was furnished with about two dozen comfortable chairs and a few tables with bright lamps. The walls were decorated with framed pictures, mirrors and a clock; Williams stocked the room with current newspapers, a selection of the novels of the day, and the usual conglomeration of books that are left behind by guests at any summer resort.

The parlor next door was the place where non-readers gathered, and where the ladies met after dinner while the gentlemen played billiards. Several lounges, chairs and rocking chairs provided seating for guests who wanted quiet conversation; a piano offered both solitary and group entertainment.

A smaller version of the hotel building, to the right, contained the kitchen and dining room, which could seat up to one hundred people. Each of its twelve tables was covered with white linens and gleaming silverware, an elegant background for the bill of fare.

Nearly all of the food for the dining room was provided on the property. Harbin Springs was more than just a resort in the 1880s; it was also a working farm. Twenty-six horses pulled stagecoaches and wagons; a handful of mules helped harvest over four tons of hay and barley. The barn was shelter for the animals; storage for hay, harnesses, saddles; and housed a complete blacksmithing shop for shoeing and wagon repair.

The gardens yielded fresh produce seasonally; Williams and his gardening staff raised more than 35 different fruits and vegetables. An article about the Lake County Fair of 1880 claimed that "garden productions from Harbin Springs, by Dick Williams, would have taken the premium at the State Fair for variety, quality and excellence...and the great variety of garden seeds from Dick Williams' garden [are] all fine, plump and fresh." The judges at the fair awarded their blue ribbon to Williams and his gardeners, Louisa Ferare and Gracoon Gelarane, for their lavish harvest.

In addition to the garden, Harbin Springs also had its own dairy, under the direction of an Irishman named Patrick Connolly. His herd of nearly 50 cows (and one bull) provided more than 400 pounds of butter each season, and all of the cream, milk and buttermilk for the dining room table. Annie Williams, her daughter and step-daughter churned the cream themselves; the judges at the same 1880 fair awarded them a ribbon for their rolls of fine butter. The dairy products and eggs (from several varieties of chickens that Annie raised) were stored in a cool room cut into the hillside at the back of the kitchen, to protect them from the summer heat.

Harbin-raised livestock supplied meat for the guests' meals as well. The farm supported chickens and a few dozen hogs, in addition to the cows. Advertisements for the resort boasted that the fresh and smoked meats produced on the premises at Harbin Springs were beyond compare with any resort, world-wide.

Few components of a visitor's meal had to be purchased beyond the gates. Receipts indicate that Williams went to San Francisco several times a season to purchase such items as tea and coffee, pepper, salt and vanilla, as well as wines and spirits.

Although Harbin Springs called itself a "health and pleasure resort," when it came to dining, pleasure appeared to be more important. Many of the invalids who came to the springs were suffering from the effects of alcohol abuse, but healing and consumption seem to have been treated as separate issues. The hotel maintained a well-stocked and presumably profitable bar for the enjoyment of the discerning gentleman. An 1882 "shopping list" included five gallons each of gin and brandy, two gallons of hard cider and one of blackberry brandy (perhaps a tipple for the ladies), two kegs of beer, a gallon each of sherry and port, and three bottles of absinthe.

Some wine may have been served with dinner, as was the European fashion, but the atmosphere at Harbin was more homey than posh. It is likely that the majority of the spirits were consumed, as was the prevailing custom, when the gentlemen retired to the bar in the wine room after dinner for brandy, billiards and cigars. For the summer season of 1882, Williams stocked several thousand cigars, 500 cigarettes and 30 pounds of tobacco for his guests.

Guests who were not quite as well-to-do, or those who wanted more solitude than society, preferred to stay in the cottages or in the rooming house, rather than in the luxury of the main hotel. According to an 1881 description, "the cottages are genuine. There is no 'shake shanty' nor rustic log cabin about them, but they are enclosed with siding painted white, with nice doors and windows."

The rooms in the cottages were quite similar to those in the hotel proper; the walls were painted rather than papered, and the beds and the washstands were slightly more utilitarian. Maids cleaned the hotel rooms daily, making the beds and emptying the chamber pots; people in the cottages were usually families or very long-term guests, and did their own housekeeping chores.

The *Jenny Lind* cottage[24] had four single rooms completely furnished, as did *Rose*, which was also carpeted. *Hayward* had four rooms and could accommodate six people; the four rooms of *Mills* were designed to sleep seven; *Fern* had five single

---

24 Information about the names, sizes and accommodations of the individual cottages come from two sources: a listing in an 1881 Lake County history, and a probate inventory filed at the Lake County courthouse. They differ slightly: the inventory does not mention *4th of July, Yuba* or *What Cheer*; the historical account leaves out *Jenny Lind* (but *Pine* is called *Jenny* in at least one place). It is possible that the historian got a name wrong, or that the appraiser missed a cottage or two. Fortunately, the two sources agree about the majority of the facilities.

rooms, and three or four people could stay in *Pine*. Two other four-room cottages were called *4th of July* and *Yuba;* the tiny *What Cheer* cottage had only a single room.

Myrtle seems to have been an odd cottage. It had four rooms, which contained two beds, three bureaus, three washstands etc., eight chairs and two sofas. Perhaps one of the rooms was a parlor; it was the only cottage with bureaus, and with more "toilet" facilities than beds. Larger families or groups could share the cottages called *Bartlett* and *Tom Collins,* each containing two rooms with four single beds and two washstands, chairs, pitchers, bowls, etc. per room.

The cottages were on the opposite side of the road from the hotel building, set in a line among the trees going up the hill to the baths. Hayward was at the bottom of the hill, closest to the dining room, and Pine[25] closest to the baths. The building nearest the baths (on the site of today's Redwood) was a three-story hotel called *Capitol*. It had 20 small rooms, furnished very plainly with iron beds. Many of the rooms were private; in others guests slept dormitory-style in rooms containing several beds and a shared washstand. *Capitol* was referred to in some literature as a rooming-house rather than a hotel, and its rates were lower than those for the main hotel or for the cottages.

Tents were set up in front of this building, a fairly level piece of ground. Much more elaborate and sturdy than the camping tents of today, they were made of heavy canvas stretched over a framework of wooden posts and beams, anchored securely to a raised wooden platform. Visitors brought their cots (and sometimes chairs, tables and lamps) and set them up in the tent. At least one family, it is noted, brought a rug to spread over the wooden floor of the tent, creating a cozy, canvas-covered parlor.

❖   ❖

---

25 *Hayward* no longer exists; *Azalea* is now on that site. *Pine* is the yellow cottage known today as the "Shiatsu Building". It is at least 100 years old, and is by far the oldest building at Harbin, the only one still existent from the days of Richard William's resort.

BY THE SUMMER OF 1882, HARBIN SPRINGS HAD BECOME ONE OF the largest and best-patronized resorts in California. The range of its accommodations appealed to a wide variety of people, and visitors flocked to the springs from all over the state. It was a booming and prosperous site. Fifteen years after he first began excavating the rocky hillsides, Richard Williams' dream had become a reality.

But it was a reality he did not live to enjoy.

One Thursday in late June of 1882, at the height of the summer season, Richard Williams contracted typhoid pneumonia. On Saturday morning, July 1st, after two days in the delirium of a high fever, he died at the age of 48.

His obituary in the local paper called him:

> A man of great executive ability. Prompt, active and energetic, he succeeded in whatever he undertook, and having a high conception of the beautiful, he ornamented and improved his grounds in a manner both tasteful and artistic, making the place a public resort for health and pleasure second to none in the county....Liberal to all and generous to his friends, we cannot but view his early death as a loss to the public, as well as to his friends and family.

The Lakeport paper echoed its associate's sentiments, adding that:

> That elegant resort, Harbin Springs, one of the most famous in northern California, is almost wholly the offspring of his energy and enterprise, and we trust may always flourish as a monument of the good he has done. That it will suffer greatly from his loss there can be no doubt, but that the wheels of its enterprise may not be stopped is the wish of all.

The wheels didn't stop, but their revolution became more complex for a while. After a brief trip to San Francisco for the funeral and burial in the Odd Fellows Cemetery, Richard Williams' family returned to Harbin Springs and to the business of running it.

He had died without a will, and with a mortgage on the property. His heirs (his wife, Annie and their son, Richard, Jr., who was seven; his 21-year old son William; and his daughter,

Maggie, who was then 19) agreed to divide the property equally between them, pending closing of the probate of the estate. Thomas Mathews, as the legal owner of the property, agreed, and Annie and William became joint administrators of the estate, with the legal power to pay off old bills and to run the resort. They completed the season of 1882 with no loss of business.[26]

Just prior to her husband's death, Annie Williams had applied for, and received, a grant for 166 acres of land abutting the Guenoc land grant and immediately south of the Harbin Springs land. At about the same time, Richard Williams was posthumously granted an additional 40 acres of land, which became part of his estate. (See map, page 128.) In October of 1882, Annie sold her 166 acres, along with her quarter of the whole estate, to Thomas Mathews, for $15,000 in gold.[27] At that time, she and Richard Jr. moved to Vallejo, leaving Harbin Springs in the hands of Maggie, William and the staff.

For the next year, William (and Annie, more as a legal signature than as an active

Richard Williams, circa 1881

---

26 The business of running a resort in the 1880s covered a wide variety of concerns. One memorable invoice notes the purchase of 2 cans of axle grease, 100 pounds of corned beef, and a charge of $2 for the removal of a dead horse, all provided by the same firm.

27 She would later buy back the irregularly-shaped tract from Mathews, for the sum of $1, placing the land in trust for her son, Richard Jr., until he turned 21. When Annie died, in 1886, the guardianship of Richard Jr. and this piece of land went to her third husband, Patrick Murphy.

participant) continued to administer the estate while he and Maggie ran the resort. They covered such mundane matters as taxes, insurance and the mortgage payments from the previous summer's profits, and invested some additional money into repairs and new construction.[28]

William petitioned the Lake County courts to allow the as-yet-unsettled estate to continue operations for the season of 1883 at the resort:

> In order to prevent depreciation in the value of said estate by reason of loss of custom and the good will of the health- and pleasure-seeking public...and that conduct of such business by the administrator has resulted profitably to the estate.

The court granted his request. In September of 1883, after another successful summer season, the estate was finally settled. William, Maggie, Richard Jr. and Mathews were each given one-quarter of the property and resort.[29] The mortgage which Mathews held had been almost completely paid off, and Maggie bought out her brother William's share of the title for $20,000, paying the same to Mathews for his portion.[30]

Sometime in 1884, 21-year old Margaret Williams married James A. Hays, a tall, dark-haired man ten years her senior, who had worked for Richard Williams as a stagecoach driver. Jim Hays, his new wife, and her brother ran the resort jointly,

---

28 An October, 1882 invoice for cement, brick, lime, etc. has the words "Harbin Springs" in several different and elaborate typefaces, doodled on its back in pencil. Perhaps young William was considering a new image...

29 William bought back 1/2 of Maggie's share of the estate in December of 1884, for $30,000. At that point he owned 3/8 of Harbin, Jim and Maggie jointly owned 3/8 and little Richard Jr. owned 1/4. This extraordinarily confusing share-swapping continued in the family for some time: in 1888, Richard Jr.'s 1/4 was sold to Jim and Maggie for a little over $12,000. On the same date, William bought an 1/8 share from them for $5, giving William and Jim and Maggie (as a couple) an equal portion of the property—1/2 to each party.

30 Nowhere is there any mention of how Maggie came to have $40,000, nor whom, if anyone, she borrowed the sum from. The records merely show that she purchased land from the two men, and for that sum.

with Jim as the proprietor and genial host, and William behind the scenes as the business manager.

Jim Hays proved as able a hotelkeeper as his late father-in-law, continuing to build new facilities for the resort, and advertising it aggressively. In an 1885 listing in a business directory covering most of northern California, the services and personnel of Harbin Springs take up nearly a page.[31]

One of the people listed in Hays' employ was John Claudius Mottier, a vineyardist. Mottier was a short, florid Frenchman who had come to California in his early twenties during the Gold Rush, and eventually settled in a valley near Harbin Springs in the 1870s. He was one of the pioneers of California's wine industry, fascinated by the possibility of producing wine from native grapes, rather than from stock imported from Europe and transplanted. A solitary and scholarly man, Mottier spent his life experimenting with various grapes, in an attempt to determine which native strains were viable.

He planted the hillsides above what is now the Village with hundreds of grapevines, and produced some bottles of excellent wine. Arpad Haraszthy, one of the wine-fathers of the Sonoma Valley, proclaimed that Mottier's claret was so fine that his vines ought to be exported back to Bordeaux.

Mottier probably provided some of the wine for Harbin's hotel bar. At any rate, he and Jim Hays got along well enough that in February of 1888, Hays sold him four acres of land for $100. (Mottier's four acres would create a legal muddle for nearly forty years; each time any of the acreage around the springs was bought, sold, or traded, the four acres had to be excepted, and described. The description, which takes up nearly half a page, begins with "Commencing at the post in a mound of rocks at the southwest corner of the southeast quarter of the northwest quarter of section 20 from which a pine stump 5 feet high and 20 inches in diameter bears north 6.5 degrees..." and becomes even more confusing from there. The position of

---

31 More than 30 people were employed full-time at Harbin by the mid-1880s, a staff that included clerks, horsemen, stage drivers, cooks, bartenders, teamsters, bath tenders, maids, gardeners and various laborers.

FIGURE 4

Early Land Acquisitions
(1867-1888)

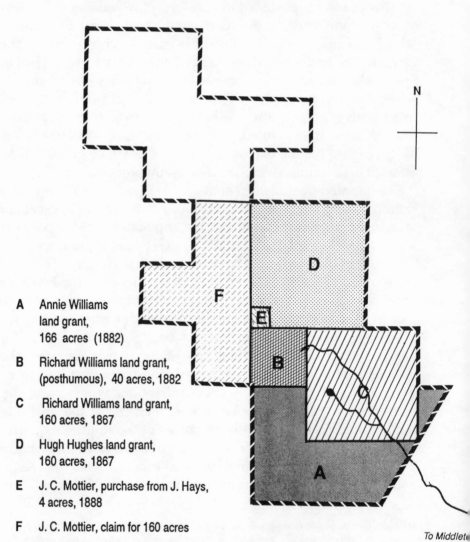

A   Annie Williams
    land grant,
    166 acres (1882)

B   Richard Williams land grant,
    (posthumous), 40 acres, 1882

C   Richard Williams land grant,
     160 acres, 1867

D   Hugh Hughes land grant,
    160 acres, 1867

E   J. C. Mottier, purchase from J. Hays,
    4 acres, 1888

F   J. C. Mottier, claim for 160 acres

▪▬▬▪ 1991 Harbin property line

Mottier's land on the map [page 128] is therefore slightly approximate.) Mottier had claimed 160 acres of public land for his vines and cabin (which was in approximately the location of the Mountain Lodge of today); it seems likely that he purchased the four acres from Hays in order to have access to, or to build, a road that would connect his land to the Harbin Springs road.

Land deals were rife that February. The mortgage had been paid off, and Williams and Hays, collectively, owned Harbin Springs again. Thomas Mathews and his wife, Margaret, offered them $37,000 for their acreage (minus Mottier's small plot), and they accepted, with the proviso that if they repaid the money within five years, the property would again belong to them. The Mathews agreed, and immediately leased the land back to the trio for the same five years, with an annual rent of about $3000, and their own proviso that Williams and Hays buy insurance on the property with a value of no less than $6000, naming Mathews as the beneficiary.

For the next five years, William Williams and Jim and Maggie Hays continued to run Harbin Springs. The resort thrived, the Hays family had four children, two boys and two girls, and Jim continued to expand and improve the premises.

In 1893, the lease and insurance were renewed for another five years, and the Southern Pacific Railroad Company published a pamphlet about Lake County, which boasted of Harbin Springs:[32]

> It would be difficult to find a more delightful and picturesque spot than this. It is one of the oldest and most popular resorts in the state, and justly merits the fame it has earned. The improvements are so elaborate and extensive that, when viewed

---

32 Literature of the 1880s spoke glowingly of Lake County, and even more glowingly of how prosperous it would be once a railroad was built, and it was more accessible. No less than five attempts to bring trains to the area were made—bonds were raised, corporations were formed, land was bought by the thousands of acres—all awaiting the railroad boom that was just around the corner. It never happened, and the Southern Pacific Company's monopoly, and its less-than-congenial attitude towards competitors, is frequently cited as the cause. But SP did print this brochure: "A Trip to the Geysers and Into Lake County, Famous as the Switzerland of America, Quickly and Easily Made, Delightful and Not Expensive."

from some one of the many surrounding eminences, there appears to be a neat little village nestled cozily down in the canyon.

Harbin Springs, late 1880s. The baths are at the upper right, the Main Hotel building at center, and the barn and stables at the lower left.

❖ ❖

AFTER "THE SEASON" OF 1894, ONLY A HANDFUL OF GUESTS remained at the springs with the owners and their family to enjoy the balmy September weather. On a Saturday evening, after the last billiard game had been completed and the ladies and gentlemen had finally left the porch and retired to their rooms for the evening, disaster struck.

Fire was discovered in one of the wooden buildings, perhaps from an overturned lamp or an unattended candle. The cabins were very close together, and summers are very dry in Lake County. Within minutes the fire had spread to the other buildings.

Some of the cold spring water had been diverted into a 30,000 gallon tank in case of just this sort of emergency, and Jim Hays and his men began to fight the fire with water from the tank and from the springs themselves, while someone telephoned to Middletown for help. Maggie and other members of the staff assisted their few guests in evacuating the rooms, and rescuing what belongings they could.

It is most likely that they went to the garden, below the main area, where there were few buildings, and there was less danger of injury. From the garden, this handful of men, women and children, clad perhaps only in their nightgowns, or in whatever hastily-donned costumes they had been able to gather, watched Harbin Springs burn.

The sky on the west side of the canyon was full of smoke, obscuring the stars and back-lit by the eerie orange glow and the sweeping brightness of the flames. The painted wooden walls of the cabins and the main hotel blistered and blackened, crackling as the fire reached them, and consumed them. Windows exploded with great booms and showers of glass. Furniture, bedding, clothing, and even the piano were dragged out of the main hotel building, but the heat was so intense that, even outside, they smoldered and burst into flame.

Additional men arrived from Middletown, to form a bucket brigade, but by that time the fire was completely out of control. As the night passed, all anyone could do was watch and listen as, one by one, the cabins and hotel of Harbin Springs fell in on themselves in a fiery roar and a massive shower of sparks that lit the night sky for miles around.

On the morning of Sunday, September 9th, 1894, much of the resort was gone. Although there has been no loss of life, and surprisingly few injuries, to either the owners, their guests or their livestock, nineteen buildings had been burned, most of them beyond repair.

The main hotel and the dining room were in smoldering ruins, as were almost all of the cabins. *Pine* cabin and the Capitol building had been spared any severe damage because of their proximity to the holding tank and the springs; bucket brigades were able to use the healing waters to dampen and save them. The buildings around the baths themselves were somewhat blackened by the smoke and a few other buildings were intact, some of them damaged only slightly by the smoke or singed by the heat of their neighbors' destruction; others were gutted, but still standing.

Although their lease had called for insurance of $6000, the losses from the catastrophic fire were closer to $80,000. The Lower Lake *Bulletin* noted that:

> Messrs. Hays and Williams have the sympathy of the entire neighborhood, though this must seem poor consolation to those who have lost the labor of half a lifetime. We have not learned of their plans for the future, but presume they will proceed at once to rebuild. The burning of the village of Harbin Springs is a great misfortune to the people of the vicinity, as well as to the proprietors.

By early October, some of the debris had been hauled away, building materials were being ordered and plans for new construction were beginning. But the Victorian spa that had once stood was gone forever, and the Harbin Springs that would rise from the ashes would be a very different resort.

CHAPTER FIVE

Pugilists in Paradise

JIM HAYS DIDN'T, AS FAR AS IS KNOWN, KEEP A DIARY, and the rebuilding of a resort isn't nearly as newsworthy as its destruction, so very little is known about the period immediately following the fire.

Early in November of 1894, about two months after the blaze, the *Clear Lake Press* reported that:

> J.H. Ford and his wife have moved to Harbin Springs. Mr. Ford has the contract for building the hotel at that place. Work will begin at once.

Two weeks later, the local paper noted that

> Large quantities of building materials is [sic] being hauled to Harbin Springs. William Spiers sent up three large wagons loaded with shingles on Tuesday. Work is being pushed forward as rapidly as possible.[1]

There were very few paying customers at Harbin Springs that winter. The Hays family, the Fords and other construction workers, the livestock handlers and a few members of the resort staff lived in the available buildings while they began the reconstruction of the hotel and other guest facilities. Any buildings which had escaped the wrath of the flames were repaired as quickly as possible—window glass and roofs were

---

1   Wm. Spiers was the owner of another stagecoach line and Spiers (now Ettawa) Springs.

replaced and enough maintenance was done to make them habitable through the cold rainy season.

Although the 1893 lease had three more years to run, the property involved had changed quite a bit, and in February of 1895, another lease agreement was made between Thomas Mathews and his wife and Jim and Maggie Hays.[2] The earlier lease had specified rent of approximately $3000 per year, with a five-year term. The new lease was for 10 years, with rent reduced to $1500 per year. Mathews agreed that for the first year, due to high construction costs and extremely low revenues from the resort trade, no cash rent would be paid, but that Hays would be responsible for all taxes. The lease also stipulated that Hays would continue to provide insurance on all existing buildings, which at that time had a total value of less than $10,000.

In 1897, the Mathews sold the furnishings and fixtures of the resort (except the new stove in the kitchen) to the Hays family for $1000. Later that year, Jim and Maggie sold "all the personal property belonging to or being on the premises of the Harbin Springs Health and Pleasure Resort" back to Margaret Mathews, for the sum of five dollars. The transaction gave Mrs. Mathews the goods as further security for the lease. As long as the lease terms were followed, the sale was in name only; if Jim and Maggie defaulted on the lease, Mathews could take over the furnishings as well as the land and the buildings.

In exchange for this guarantee, the Mathews used some of their capital to rebuild and protect their investment. When Thomas Mathews died in 1897, at the age of 77, he left over half a million dollars in real estate to his wife, Margaret. Without the income from these investments, which included property in Vallejo, Oakland and Berkeley, the rebuilding of Harbin Springs would have been unlikely, if not financially impossible. Jim Hays was a capable and innovative manager, but without the Mathews' backing, Harbin would have suffered the same fate

---

2   William Williams, possibly feeling that being the business manager of a ruined resort was a job with a tenuous future, was not a partner in the lease, although he appears to have continued to live at Harbin and help in the rebuilding.

as most other resorts in the county—a disastrous fire, a lack of labor and capital to rebuild, and a gradual decline into ruin and decay—until it would have been nothing but a name on a tax roster or in a history book.

Like his father-in-law 30 years before, Jim Hays opened his resort to the public as soon as he had beds and baths to offer them, and used the profits from each season to continue construction and expansion. But where Richard Williams had been starting from scratch in a veritable wilderness, Hays had the advantages of some financial backing, and of building from an existing resort and clientele. Lake County had changed a great deal between 1872 and 1897; there were good roads for the delivery of materials, telegraphs and telephones for ordering supplies and labor, and a thriving town within a half-hour's ride. All of these factors made the reconstruction of Harbin Springs a great deal easier than the original construction had been.

A year and a half after the fire, the bulk of the rebuilding had been completed, although additional building and remodeling continued for several years. The 1895 summer season had been very slow because of construction, but Hays made sure that the resort was ready for the 1896 season. In April he placed ads in all the major San Francisco papers, assuring potential guests that Harbin Springs was, indeed, open for business as usual, and that it now offered "a handsome new hotel, large and commodious rooms, a large new dining room, and everything newly furnished throughout the hotel and cottages."

Hays was an astute businessman. He realized that if he merely remodeled a Victorian spa, the facilities would soon be outgrown by a clientele that was changing as the century was ending. And so he did more than rebuild—he modernized. He equipped all of the hotels, cottages and other buildings with an acetylene gas system for lighting; gas fixtures were considerably cheaper and cleaner, not to mention safer, than kerosene lamps, oil lamps or candles. It was the most modern utility available in the county at the time; the widespread and economical use of electricity in the rural area was still some years away.

He expanded the bath areas, boasting that:

The baths are unsurpassed in the world. The tubs and plunges are of hot sulphur and iron water. A natural mineral or medicated mud bath has just been discovered, nothing like it known. Many improvements have been made at this popular resort, and it is more attractive than ever.

By 1900 business at the Springs had recovered sufficiently for Jim Hays to publish a new brochure about the resort, replacing the 1890 version which was quite out of date. On its cover he claimed that Harbin Hot Sulphur Springs was "The Best Summer and Winter Resort in the World."[3] For the first time this brochure included actual photographs of the resort, not just woodcuts or line drawings. Opening the tiny pamphlet gave the prospective visitor (and, later, the historian) a realistic view of the resort buildings and the land upon which they stood, as well as a glimpse of the type of visitor that frequented the spa.

Men in bowler hats and shirt sleeves and women in ankle length cotton dresses stood next to the stagecoach in front of the white-pillared Main Hotel Building. Some of the same people are also shown standing inside a hexagonal "park" surrounded by a white picket fence, in the location where a gazebo would soon be built. Still another picture depicted the three-story Capitol Hotel and the platform tents in front of it, on the hill just above the Pine cottage.

Rates for guest accommodations in 1900 were, surprisingly, a fraction cheaper than those published 10 years earlier: a one-day stay at the Springs ranged from $1.50 to $3, depending on the type of lodgings; a week cost $10 for a tent, up to $18 for

---

3   In 1899, only four resorts (Harbin, Highland, Bartlett and Adams) were declared "Class Number One" resorts by county officials. The distinction came with a price—these resorts were charged $150 per year for their liquor licenses, while all the other resorts paid a mere $50.

a room in the Main Hotel; monthly visits began at $40 and went up to $60 for the best the resort could offer. Baths were, naturally, included in the price, as was access to Long Distance Telephone service, U.S. Mail and the Wells Fargo Express wagon. Stagecoach time from the city was about the same as in 1890, but the fare had risen from $5 to $7.[4]

Letters from satisfied customers accompanied the photographs and descriptions, all praising the miracle cures afforded by Harbin water:

A MARVELOUS CURE OF DROPSY

Napa, Cal. Jan. 17, 1900
J.A. Hays, Esq.

Dear Sir:

Firmly believing that my life was saved at Harbin Springs by the use of the water and baths, it gives me great pleasure to recommend your Springs to suffering mankind. In November, 1896, I was taken down with dropsy and confined to my bed for five months, until the first days of April, 1897; during that time I was tapped four times.[5] During the month of April I gained little strength, and as my physician gave me but slight encouragement, I went to Harbin Springs the first week in May, and stayed until December 8th, drinking the water and taking the baths, and coming home feeling like a new man. Today I feel better than I have for five years past. The baths at Harbin are great, and I cannot say too much for them, as they are the best I have ever seen, and I have seen many of them.

Yours sincerely,
L. Christin, proprietor
Alta Napa Winery and Distillery

---

4   On August 3, 1901, a fire swept Calistoga, destroying most of the town's buildings, including the Harbin Springs stable. Because a change of horses and additional stages were kept in the other stables at the Springs itself, regular service was only interrupted for a short period of time.

5   Dropsy is an archaic term for edema, the abnormal swelling of tissues because of a severe accumulation of fluid; tapping was a painful procedure that, like tapping a barrel, drew off some of the liquid.

REMARKABLE CURE OF KIDNEY DISEASE

Stockton, February 10, 1900

Dear Sir: I cannot sufficiently express my appreciation of the benefits derived from the use of the water at your Springs.
I was thoroughly disheartened when I came to your place, thinking that my case of kidney disease was incurable. But now I am completely recovered, and feel like a new man.
I hope all who are affected similarly may know of your health-giving Springs, and I shall certainly do all I can to acquaint others of their virtues.

I am, yours very truly, A.H. Foster

FIVE YEARS AFTER THE FIRE, HARBIN SPRINGS HAD REGAINED ITS prominence as a Lake County resort, and could accommodate 200 people. It had two large hotels (the refurbished Capitol, near the baths, and the rebuilt Main Hotel in the central area); 15 cottages; 39 platform tents; a fully-equipped bath house, steam room and plunge; a barber shop; a bar; a dance hall; and a large building containing a dining room and a gymnasium.

Gymnasium and Bowling Alley Pavilion. Entrance gate is at far left.

A life-long sportsman, Jim Hays probably built the gym as much for his own pleasure as for that of his guests. It was his most successful innovation, and influenced the change in clientele that the resort would experience in the next few years.

A resort under construction was not as attractive to families or to those in very delicate health, who required a great deal of peace and quiet. Although he continued to publicize the healing nature of the waters, after the fire Hays began to put additional emphasis on the recreational pleasures that a stay at Harbin offered, especially to fellow sportsmen. Hunting and fishing had been mentioned in the earlier brochure as pleasant pastimes for the visitor who had come to take the waters, but at the turn of the century, Hays also presented the waters as a refreshing diversion for the serious sportsman.

> Mountain quail, dove, grouse, wild pidgeon [sic] and deer are plentiful during the season. A fine pack of deer hounds and horses are always on hand for hunters. The famous Harbin Creek, which flows through the Springs' property is stocked yearly with mountain trout, and fairly teems with the speckled beauties.

The appeal to sportsmen had several purposes. First, men coming up from the city to hunt and fish were content with much less luxurious accommodations; they were up there to "rough it," and were unconcerned if the new carpets hadn't been installed yet, or if the hotel dining room was less than elegant, as long as they were well-fed.

Another advantage was that Hays could extend "the season" well into the late fall for deer hunting, and even into the winter, when the trout-teeming streams were running deep and swift from the heavy rains. Like the Lake Miwok hundreds of years before, the men of Harbin in the first years of the twentieth century established seasonal camps.

A group of men could be housed together without any impropriety or slight of hospitality, and many cabins which had held two or three genteel ladies and gentlemen could be used in the off-season to sleep six or eight men with the addition of a few beds and the subtraction of a few dressing tables. By the time most of the major rebuilding was completed, Harbin

Springs had developed a reputation for being a resort that catered to the sportsman, as well as continuing to be a health spa.

Many of the visitors to Harbin at this time were businessmen from Vallejo, Oakland and San Francisco, who came up for a week or two of vacation in the woods. During the summer they were likely to bring their wives and children; fall and winter visitors were predominantly male. Some of the "businessmen" who came up were in a field that was quite new—the business of professional sports, primarily boxing.

❖   ❖

MEN RESORTED TO THEIR FISTS TO SETTLE ARGUMENTS LONG before anyone thought of staging fights to entertain others. Boxing is one of the oldest sports; in ancient Crete and in the early Olympic games in Greece, men boxed, not for money, but for honor. However, with the coming of Christianity, boxing, as a sport, disappeared, resurfacing in England in the early part of the 18th century.

Schools in London taught the techniques of pugilism, rules were established and, for the first time, men regularly fought for money. But prize-fighting was still regarded as not much better than street brawling, and not respected or followed by the "better" classes of people. By the time of the Civil War, boxing's popularity had spread to the United States, where some good fighters were adding a decidedly American flavor to the sport.

The first prize fights here were amateur contests, fought with very few rules by bare-fisted men who hoped to make a couple of dollars, mainly from the spectators' betting. Fights were few and far between, and fighters seldom made a living at the sport. The bouts were held in secrecy, since prize-fighting was illegal in every state; the location and time of a fight was passed by word of mouth days before. If the fight was discovered, the local sheriff could arrest and jail the participants, charging them with disturbing the peace. Most sheriffs were fighting men themselves and were usually content with breaking up the match, scattering the crowd and,

Early fights were often community affairs, with one town matching its best man against the neighboring town's premier fighter, and the two communities putting up the prize money. By the 1880s, boxing's popularity had increased so much that athletic clubs were formed in most major cities, with private bouts staged (in theory at least) for club members only. Outside the arm of the law, these private matches were well-attended, often with as many as several hundred spectators, and were consequently well-funded.

The staging of boxing matches between clubs began to take on the air of a business—events needed to be scheduled and publicized, crowds needed to be managed, and greater and greater sums of money were involved. Boxers who were particularly popular began to demand more concessions from their clubs, creating a need for managers, fight promoters, trainers and the like.

Prize-fighting was legalized in New Orleans in 1890, and became legitimate, if not completely respectable, in many other areas as well. It became, symbolically, the ultimate test of American masculinity, and journalists soon propelled interest in fighters and their matches from the local to the national level. The *National Police Gazette* was a shocking-pink weekly tabloid that sold for a dime. Distributed to barbershops, saloons, livery stables and private clubs, it was one of the first papers to have a sports section, and it popularized prize-fighting as it exploited an American thirst for the sensational.

Editor Richard Kyle Fox offered cash prizes and trophies to acclaimed fighters, including a belt for the "heavyweight champion of the world."[6] Going against public opinion because of his own personal prejudices, he awarded the title to Jake Kilrain. But Kilrain lost it in a 75-round fight in 1889, to the man that most of America *knew* was the champion—an immensely popular Irish boxer named John L. Sullivan.[7]

---

6   Not a sports purist by any means, Fox also offered prizes for competitive oyster-opening, steeple-climbing and one-legged dancing contests.

7   Most sources say Sullivan won the title in 1882, at the age of 24. He is listed as the first U. S. heavyweight champion, despite what Richard Kyle Fox might have thought.

Sullivan was more well-known than any athlete in previous history. He was the first truly national sports hero, something out of myth and legend, but real enough that the details of many of his fights were broadcast by telegraph, blow by blow, to saloons and billiard parlors across the nation.

In 1892, the Marquess of Queensberry rules were adopted for American prize-fighting, which, among other things, required the boxers to wear gloves rather than fighting bare-knuckled, and created three-minute rounds for the fights.[8] That year John L. Sullivan faced "Gentleman Jim" Corbett, a San Francisco native and one of the originators of the scientific and strategic school of fighting. In the 21st round of the fight, in New Orleans, Sullivan, the bare-knuckle champion, lost to the Olympic Club-sponsored Corbett, who had occasionally trained in Lake County, at Bartlett Springs.[9]

Many of the early champions were from California, and Lake County was very popular among Bay Area boxers as a location for their pre-fight training camps. For routine training, most boxers went to places that were out in the country but still very close to the city; there were camps in Larkspur, Alameda, San Rafael and San Leandro, among others. But for championship matches they trained for a concentrated period of time, and usually went away to a more remote area. The resorts of Lake County offered the fighters several advantages

---

8   These rules were established in England in 1867; previously, under London Rules, a round ended only when a man went down, and could last anywhere from a few seconds to fifteen minutes or more, making the match often more of an endurance contest than a test of skill. Before and after the change in rules, the fight ended when one man couldn't get up, or when his second "threw in the sponge" or towel, signifying surrender.

9   According to one source (not identified in Henry Mauldin's notes), in 1892, while Corbett was training across the county at Bartlett's, Sullivan was training at Harbin. The 1892 fight between Sullivan and Corbett was the first title fight to be fought with gloves and timed rounds, and as such is one of the most famous fights in the history of boxing. It would be nice for the mythos of Harbin if Sullivan had indeed trained here for that momentous fight. But the fight was held in New Orleans; neither fighter would have trained on the west coast. And, unfortunately, other than that one cryptic note, there is no evidence that Sullivan was ever at Harbin. Since there is no other mention of *any* fighters training at the Springs before the fire, much less John L. Sullivan himself, it was apparently just wishful thinking.

over training in urban areas, primarily isolation, heat, elevation and recreation.

The top boxers of the time were major celebrities. Only royalty or the very rich could draw more of a crowd than a sports hero. Training in the city for a major fight was filled with too many distractions for a serious contender. People flocked to gyms and clubs by the hundreds to watch their heroes work out, and followed them into the streets when they did their early morning roadwork. The fans and the congested traffic of the cities, filled with horse-drawn wagons and buggies, streetcars and even some of the new automobiles, made running on the streets difficult for the pugilists.

❖   ❖

HARBIN SPRINGS DISTANCED FIGHTERS FROM THIS TURMOIL. THE four-mile road to Middletown was level and smooth and usually free from any traffic, and the miles of paths up and down the hills offered an equally serene, but more strenuous, work-out. The isolation of the resort also offered the men some degree of freedom from admiring fans, although the better-known fighters had camp followers by the score, even in a remote location.

Most of the fighters who trained at Harbin were heavyweights—Jim Jeffries, Bob Fitzsimmons, Tommy Burns, Jess Willard. They were big men with big appetites during their off-seasons, and usually had to drop a lot of weight quickly before a title match. The summers in the Bay Area were too cool for rapid weight loss, but the high temperatures in Lake County during the summer months were perfect for that purpose.

Despite Jim Hays' claims to the general public that the climate at the Springs was as mild and desirable as any in the world, the boxers came because it *wasn't* mild; excess weight came off much more quickly when they were working out in 90 to 100 degree weather. (The fighters may have been guests at the Springs in the fall and winter for hunting and other recreation, but usually *trained* there in the late spring and summer; the winter climate was too cold and damp for good weight-loss or muscle flexibility.)

Harbin was also a beneficial spot for men getting into fighting condition because of its elevation. Ranging from about 1500 feet in the main area to more than 3000 feet at the crest of the ridge, Harbin's varied and mountainous terrain provided more strenuous exercise for the boxers' legs than the sloping meadows of the surrounding countryside. Trainers also touted the mountain air at Harbin; it was cleaner and healthier than the air in the city. They also believed that, because of the altitude, it was "thinner" and taxed the lungs of the fighter, strengthening them with every breath.

The fourth advantage that Harbin and other Lake County resorts had over more urban locations was the recreation they offered. The warm pools were used for relaxing stiff muscles (long before the locker room jacuzzi was invented), as was massage, and the swimming pools were used for both fun and exercise. The fighters often swam or soaked without suits during training, but were attired in a more socially acceptable manner for recreational swims.

Most of the men who trained at Harbin played as hard as they fought, and enjoyed the fact that diversions were as close at hand as their dumbbells and punching bags. Wading upstream against the current in pursuit of a wily trout, hiking the trails for hours at a time with a ten-pound gun, or carrying back the even heavier result of the hunt was more fun than running or lifting weights just for the sake of exercise.

The first major fighter to train at Harbin was James J. "Jim" Jeffries, affectionately called Jeff by an admiring public. Jeffries was born in Ohio in 1875, but his family moved to the Los Angeles area when he was very young. He grew up to be a boilermaker, a big man, over six feet tall and weighing about 225 pounds at his fighting weight. He boxed locally and in 1896 moved up north to San Francisco, where he fought most of his early bouts.

He came to the attention of Gentleman Jim Corbett, and served as Corbett's sparring partner while the champ trained in Carson City, Nevada for an 1897 title match against "Ruby Bob" Fitzsimmons. An incredibly strong, sturdy man, Jeffries was not particularly skilled in his early fights, relying on sheer power to win, but learned much of the "science" of boxing from watching and sparring with Corbett.

Jeffries used what he had learned from the former champ when he won his first heavyweight title at Coney Island in 1899, knocking out Fitzsimmons (who had defeated Corbett two years before) in the 11th round. According to many sources, Jim Jeffries was possibly the greatest boxer in the early days of the sport. He had height, speed, strength, strategy, science and equal hitting power in either hand, along with more endurance in the ring than any other man of his time. He could sprint 100 yards (in full roadwork clothes weighing more than 30 pounds) in 11 seconds flat, and high jump almost six feet, both close to the records for the day.

Jeffries came to Harbin in the first week of October, 1901, to train for a fight against Gus Ruhlin the next month in San Francisco. He brought along his sparring partners (his brother, Jack and their friend, Robert Armstrong) to train with him, as well as a few coaches and a small group of camp followers. Harbin's gym was well stocked with weights and other fitness equipment; Jeff brought his own training gear as well. Besides the time he spent in the gym itself, lifting weights, using the punching bag and sparring up to 16 rounds a day, he also did wind sprints on the road, swam laps in the pool and ran between eight and 14 miles a day.

Jim Jeffries in the gymnasium at Harbin Springs, circa 1902.

When he wasn't working out, he spent a great deal of time napping in a large hammock on the porch of his cottage, Hayward. Several times a week he went hiking in the hills, or went deer hunting with his buddies and Jim Hays.[10] He left Harbin in early November, storing all his training equipment in the gym and planning to return in the spring to train again. While Harbin's atmosphere can't take all the credit, Jeffries did win his San Francisco fight handily, knocking out Ruhlin in the fifth round.

❖ ❖

LEGAL MATTERS CONCERNING HARBIN SPRINGS WERE NOT AS decisive as Jeffries' punches, and things were not going smoothly in the off-season. That winter, Maggie Hays' younger brother, Richard Williams, Jr., died very suddenly in a San Francisco hospital. He had been a small child when their father died in 1882, but had inherited a portion of the estate, and of the resort. The bulk of the Springs property was sold and traded within the family, and finally sold to the Mathews in return for the lease. But Richard's mother, Annie, had secured a 166-acre piece of property in her own name, which she put in trust for the boy.

At the time of his death he was 27, and was married. In his will, written on his deathbed, he left all his personal property, including their home, to his wife, Dorothy. His sister Maggie received the rights to the 166 acres adjacent to the Harbin Springs property; the small parcel of land was valued at $300 by the court. The rest of his estate, 410 acres in Napa County, was valued at $8500. He left this land to his step-father, Patrick Murphy, who had raised him since he was 11, when his mother, Annie, died.

---

10 Jeff was such an avid hunter that some of the terrain was named after him. About halfway up the south side of Boggs Mountain is an area of loose dirt called "Jeffries Slide." Jeff often hunted with the McKinley brothers, and they would block the trails on either side, forcing the deer to run across the slide, so that Jeff could pick them off with his gun.

Richard's death seems to have been surrounded by confusion. He died in San Francisco, and was buried in Vallejo, where he and his wife and step-father all lived. Six months later, a permit was given to move the body to the Odd Fellows Cemetery in San Francisco, where he was again buried, next to his father. A year after his death, Maggie Hays sued to contest the will.

Neither his sister nor his wife were happy with Richard's last decision to give the bulk of what he owned to his step-father, and the 166 acres he had left to Maggie was in a legal muddle. In 1900, Richard had deeded the parcel over to Murphy "in consideration of the love and affection which he has shown, and for his better support and protection." A month after his step-son's death, Murphy in turn deeded half of the property to the young man's widow. Meanwhile, Richard had left the whole parcel (which he appears not to have owned anymore) to Maggie.

There was no love lost between Maggie Hays and Patrick Murphy. She claimed, in a long series of legal documents, that he had exerted undue influence over her brother while he was the boy's guardian, and had extended that influence to his final days. She claimed that Richard was not of sound mind or competent to make a will when he was in the hospital dying, and that Murphy had taken advantage of that, inducing Richard to leave the most valuable property to him. Richard, accustomed his entire life to obeying the man's every word, had complied.

Eight years after Richard's death, Murphy complicated the already tangled legal matters by giving the other half of the 166 acres to his niece, Clothilda Monreal. A month later, Dorothy (Williams) Blessing sold her half to Jim Hays. (What happened to Clothilda's portion is a mystery; there is no record of any sale, but Jim Hays ended up with it: a 1909 parcel map of the county shows the small parcel wholly owned by Hays, surrounded by lands belonging to Mathews.)

The question of Richard Williams Jr.'s will would drag on for almost 20 years. Finally, in 1920, a public administrator was ordered by the courts to close the estate; by that time Murphy had died, and neither Dorothy or Maggie could be located.

❖ ❖

BUT IN 1902, MAGGIE WAS STILL AT HARBIN WITH JIM AND THEIR four children: Nellie, age 15; Edna, age 11; and Richard Williams Hays, age 8. Their oldest boy, Eddie, was 13, and a sportsman like his father. That summer he was old enough to hang out with the fighters, and run errands around the training camp. He spent the spring eagerly awaiting Jim Jeffries' return.

Jeff came back to Harbin on May 27th, to prepare for a July rematch with Fitzsimmons, who was training a few miles north at Skaggs Springs. Once he was down to fighting weight, Jeffries preferred to work out in the early morning and in the evening, avoiding the intense summer heat, and leaving his days open for various other activities. He trained hard, and was a serious fighter, as evidenced by his string of titles, but Jeff was also a showman, a dedicated practical joker, and very fond of publicity—an idea of which Jim Hays heartily approved.

The details of sports training are, in themselves, not very interesting, even to athletes. Sports writers worked with boxers, promoters and managers to glamorize the non-sports aspects of athletes' lives, and so the local and regional papers are full of the 1902 exploits of Jim Jeffries, World Champion, at Harbin Springs.

Among other adventures during his two-month stay, the public was treated to the fact that he captured a pair of wildcat cubs while on a raccoon hunt, presenting them to Hays (who presumably let them go again). On another hunting trip, a skunk was shot so that the oil could be extracted from its scent glands and used on Jeff's sore arm—a little-known and perhaps little-desired folk remedy.

On at least one occasion, he and his friends took some of the other visitors at the resort out on a snipe hunt. The fighters had spent most of the day talking among themselves, loud enough to be overheard easily, about how plentiful snipe were that year, and how much they were looking forward to going out that evening for a fine hunt. Naturally, a few of the other men, whether impressed by the game or the hunters themselves, asked if they might come along. Jeff and his cohorts readily agreed, and told the fellows about the special equipment necessary to hunt snipe.

First, it seemed that snipe were plentiful, but rather stubborn, and needed to be scared out into the open; plenty of noise makers were required. Pots and pans, allowed the champ, could be banged on with spoons from the kitchen to make just the right sort of noise. Then, he went on to explain, while everyone else was flushing the snipe out of their hiding place, one man was needed for the most important part of the hunt.

The chosen man was to wait, quietly and patiently, beneath a bush or other protective covering, until the snipe, strutting along on the ground, was within reach. At that point, the crafty hunter should hold out a canvas bag in front of him and sweep the snipe into it with a small broom or a bunch of feathers.

Of course, Jeff offered to let the guest have this important role in the hunt and, of course, the man accepted. Jeff and his buddies told the unsuspecting guest to meet them around twilight for the hunt. The party went into the hills and reached a clearing. Jeff pointed the guest to a likely looking bush and told him to wait there until he caught the snipe, cautioning him that it might take a long time, but that he needed to be completely silent.

The man crawled under the bush and Jeff and his friends banged away at their pots and pans for several minutes. At the end of the cacophony, they tiptoed quietly back to Harbin, leaving the guest under the bush, holding the bag.

❖   ❖

JIM HAYS PUT UP WITH JEFF'S PRANKS (AND PROBABLY encouraged them), because Jeff was so enthusiastic about promoting Harbin, and invited many of his friends to come up and watch him train. Far from the invalid passengers of a decade earlier, during Jeff's visits the stagecoach carried some very large, robust travelers. It was not uncommon to see three or four prizefighters and/or half a dozen policemen from San Francisco's Mission District alight from the stage for a week's stay at Harbin. Although his brother was his favorite sparring partner, Jeff often held practice bouts with the men who had come up for a visit, and other resort guests were occasionally treated to a small, private match between two famous heavyweights.

Harbin Springs soon became known as a fine training camp, as well as a resort. According to many Lake County sources, the fighters, especially Jeffries, had such a large following that:

> The resort became a young city during the appearance of the trainers and the training camp staff. It was a well-known fact that many of the guests, rather than be denied accommodations, slept on the pool table and in the halls of the buildings, where small cots were placed during training camp periods. It was not uncommon for as many as 500 persons to demand accommodations, when there was actual facility for little more than 200.

Although this account may be somewhat exaggerated, there is little doubt that Harbin Springs was much rowdier during Jeff's visits than it had been as a spa with a clientele made up primarily of invalids.

With Jeff's deft, if flashy, hand directing it, the Fourth of July, 1902, must have been quite a spectacle. He had hired a band from Calistoga, which arrived on the stage the night before. On the morning of the Fourth, a huge parade was held at Harbin for a delighted audience of several hundred men, women and children, complete with a brass band and the Heavyweight Champion of the World, in a flamboyant costume, as the Grand Marshall. An enormous barbeque, with sack races and the like was held that afternoon for all the guests, young and old to enjoy. The day ended with a baseball game played by an odd assortment of resort guests and some of the biggest names in boxing.

The combination of Jeffries' Harbin training regime and extracurricular activities paid off—he returned to San Francisco on July 23rd and two days later faced Fitzsimmons once again, in a specially-built arena near Woodward's Gardens. Fitzsimmons' blows landed repeatedly, and Jeff took a lot of punishment, but at the end of the eighth round, Ruby Bob was on the mat being counted out, and Jeff maintained his title.

There had been heavy betting on whether the fight would go over eight rounds, because:

> The wife of one of Jeff's close friends, who was at Harbin Springs during the training period, told Jeff's fortune one day, and she said the cards predicted he would win the fight in eight rounds. A lot of the sports around there took it as a hunch, and bet their money that way.

Convinced by Jeff's public relations skills as well as by his fists, Fitzsimmons accompanied his ring crony to Harbin the next year, arriving on June 20, 1903, to help the champ train for another meeting with Jim Corbett.

Robert Fitzsimmons was 41 when he came to Harbin with Jeffries, and was described by many as "that bald kangaroo." He was almost six feet tall, weighed a trim 165 and was covered from head to toe with freckles; what little hair he had left was a fringe of gingery red over his ears. Born in England, he had worked in Australia as a blacksmith, which resulted in his peculiar physique—long, knock-kneed knobbly legs and a massive, solid upper body with long muscular arms.

His body structure influenced the way he fought, his long legs giving him a lot of speed and agility, and his arms providing him with an extraordinary reach that was also immensely powerful. He was famous for his "solar-plexus" punch, a paralyzing blow to the stomach, and infamous for an 1894 fight after which his opponent, Con Riordan, died. (Fitzsimmons was exonerated of any blame.)

Because of his weight, he boxed as both a middleweight and a heavyweight, winning his first title in the former category in 1891, and in the latter in 1896. He tried to recapture the heavyweight crown twice against Jeffries, each time unsuccessfully. After their last bout, Fitzsimmons and Jeffries teamed up to do exhibition matches, traveling throughout the West, boxing each other and taking on all comers.

In the summer of 1903, Ruby Bob and Jeff made quite a pair at Harbin, elaborating on Jeff's solo adventures of the year before. Jim Hays had acquired a pet bear, as an added attraction for visitors to the resort and, as the newspapers reported it:

Fitzsimmons had built a pen for the bear, and he and Jeffries tried to get the bear into the pen. The bear balked at the attempt, so Jeffries' fox terrier got into the act. The bear got the dog in its grip, and in their attempts to free it, both fighters received a number of bites from the bear. Fitzsimmons attempted to sew up Jeffries' wounds with a needle and thread, but his skin was so tough the needle failed to puncture it, and a hammer was used to drive the needle through.[11]

Jeffries developed a case of blood poisoning after the incident, either from the bear's claws or the first aid methods involved, but that didn't stop him from pulling a prank so outrageous it made the daily papers as far away as Los Angeles.

Prizefighters outside the Harbin gym. (l to r): Jim Jeffries, Joe Kennedy, Jack Jeffries, Ruby Bob Fitzsimmons. (Barn and entrance gate in background.)

---

11 Part of the job of a boxer's second, his back-up man, was to carry the necessary supplies for emergency first aid in training or in the ring—a sharp penknife, a bottle of tincture of iron, a small brush, a bottle of smelling salts, a roll of adhesive tape and a clean sponge. Most boxers had worked as seconds at some point in their careers, and were used to dealing with bruises, stopping the flow of blood and stitching up any cuts. Except for the rather grisly detail of the hammer, Fitzsimmons' nursing was not outside the regular line of duty.

❖   ❖

JEFF WAS SCHEDULED TO FIGHT JIM CORBETT ON AUGUST 14TH, IN San Francisco. On Saturday, July 12th, the referee for the fight, Eddie Graney, and Jim Coffroth, manager of the club that was conducting the match, came up to Harbin Springs to confer with Jeffries about the upcoming fight.

"Sunny Jim" Coffroth had become the first true fight promoter in California when he assumed control of the 10,000-seat Mechanics Pavilion in San Francisco, with seats at $1 to $3, and offered the boxers a percentage of the gate. According to boxing historians, Coffroth had revolutionized the management of public boxing exhibitions by sparing no expense to get the boxers he wanted, and by offering reserved seat tickets for the bouts. He was credited with making boxing in San Francisco a first-class sport, rather than a small private affair.

Graney was no less a pivotal figure in boxing. Known as "the honest blacksmith," the short stocky man was the first referee to appear in the ring in a tuxedo, making a tremendous sensation. He had been a featherweight contender, but turned to refereeing in 1899; due to his own experience in the ring, he was known as a referee who handled boxers well. Because he had their confidence, he officiated for years without ever having to lay a hand on one of the participants, which permitted him to dress as he did.

Coffroth and Graney had intended to spend the weekend at the Springs, but late Saturday afternoon a telegram came for Graney, informing him that his wife had suddenly taken ill. The daily stage from Harbin had already left, but Coffroth volunteered to drive him over the mountain in a private buggy, so he could catch the next train out from Calistoga.

Graney was completely unaware that Jeffries, Fitzsimmons, Coffroth and several other men had decided to take advantage of his sudden departure to stage an elaborate hoax, "in order to relieve the monotony of life at Harbin Springs."

Graney was carrying $5000 with him, the deposit for the fight from Jeffries and Corbett. The plan was for Jeff to play the highwayman, rob Graney of the money, and then return it via the first express wagon on Monday morning. Jeffries dressed the part with great care, donning high boots, a flannel shirt, a black mask and a big slouch hat.

Feigning an excuse to go into Middletown, Jeffries met a local policeman named Andy Gorman and, armed with Winchester rifles, they set out on horseback to a spot on the mountain road a few miles from town. They were accompanied, according to reports, by a crowd of visitors from Harbin. The guests were to be supporting players in the charade, hiding in the bushes at the site of the "ambush" and watching the fun, but not actively participating in the prank until after the money was taken.

All was going well. According to one San Francisco paper:

> As the vehicle drew into the shaded spot where the amateur brigands were concealed, Graney, who was handling the lines, was startled to hear the call of "hands up!" and to see two giant horsemen advance from the darkness.

Jeffries was a very large, fierce looking man, and he could make his voice quite savage. Graney fell for it and jumped out of the wagon, throwing the reins over the backs of the horses and putting his hands in the air as he faced the "bandits" and their rifles.

Unfortunately, Graney and the horses were the only living beings within miles who weren't in on the joke. Graney surrendered, but the horses bolted, running for their lives, leaving Coffroth (who had originated the idea for the caper) helpless in the runaway buggy.

Graney screamed, "Jim can't drive!" and to his utter amazement the erstwhile highwayman took off, sprinting down the road to capture the fleeing team. Coffroth jumped from the wagon after a few hundred feet and was stunned by the fall; Jeff ran right by him in the growing darkness.

The horses were very frightened and, fortunately, Jeff was in very good condition, because it was more than three miles up the mountain road before the champ was able to catch the team, gather in the reins, and drive the buggy back to the spot where the rest of the shaken pranksters waited.

Meanwhile, at the scene of the "crime," an embarrassed Andy Gorman identified himself as a policeman and took charge of the matter, finding Coffroth and determining that he was only winded from his fall. Someone rode back to Harbin to get Jim Hays, who brought another buggy and drove Graney to Calistoga in time to catch the last train, after the stocky referee had accepted an apology from the tired and somewhat shaken Jeffries.

The crowd from Harbin had been deprived of their part in the playacting. The plan had been for Jeffries to take the money and order both Graney and Coffroth to drive on, "under pain of instant death if either of you turn around or make an outcry." After a hundred yards or so, Coffroth was to turn and yell, "Thief! Robber! Murder!" at which point all the Harbin visitors would shoot their guns into the air, wait a moment, and then leap out of the bushes, laughing.

The horses, alas, had not learned *their* lines, and the crowd got to be witnesses to an entirely different drama.

Fitzsimmons went to San Francisco two weeks later and married an actress who had just closed in *When Johnny Comes Marching Home*. The newlyweds were met in Middletown by a crowd of 200 cheering people led, of course, by Jeffries, and escorted back to the springs amidst hurrahs.

The fighters' fun was not limited to pranks and parades that summer. Grateful for a place to come and train (and let off steam), Jeffries volunteered to stage an exhibition bout, sponsored by Harbin Springs, at the rodeo in Lower Lake, boxing with his brother, Jack. Being the heavyweight champion at the time, he drew a large crowd, and the rodeo benefitted greatly.

On an even more local level, they helped organize a benefit at Harbin on August 3rd for George Nutter, a man who had worked at the Springs for many years and who had broken his ankle. Former blacksmith Fitzsimmons went to Middletown and made a horseshoe, to be auctioned off. A gala show was put on in "the Music Hall" at Harbin (inside the gym building), where Mrs. Dan Hogan of Oakland won the shoe with a bid of $50, which went to Mr. Nutter.

The summer of 1903, full of fun and games and sprinting after terror-stricken horses, was again good for Jeffries. He left Harbin on the 12th of August and KO'd Jim Corbett in the 10th round of their San Francisco bout two days later. The fight took place at the Mechanics Pavilion, promoted by Coffroth, and set a new record for the gate: over $62,000.

❖   ❖

FIVE MONTHS LATER, BACK AT HARBIN, ON DECEMBER 9, 1903, tragedy again came to the resort with the sudden and unexpected death of William Williams at the age of 42. Although he was no longer the business manager, he had worked until his death rebuilding and helping his sister and brother-in-law run the hotel. It was a long and bleak winter.

❖   ❖

IN THE SUMMER OF 1904, JEFFRIES ARRIVED FOR WHAT WOULD BE his last stay at Harbin, in training for what would be his last consecutive title fight. This time his entourage included not only his brother and other fighters, but also a different member of his training team—his new wife.

Jeff's exploits were somewhat toned down by marriage.

> While resting in the shade one afternoon [he] told the gatherers, including his wife, that he was "going to drink a pail of blood to make him mean and eat a wildcat steak to make him wild." His wife did not appreciate Jeff's rough humor.

He needed nothing to make him strong. One day several of the men were trying to get a side of beef into a wagon, without success. Jeff impressed the onlookers by casually lifting the 510-pound carcass onto his shoulder and then into the wagon.

The biggest event of Jeffries' last summer at Harbin had very little to do with him or his penchant for practical jokes, as far as we know. On August 1, 1904, there was another fire. Fortunately this one was confined to a small area of the Main Hotel building, and little damage was done. Jeff and the men in his camp turned out instantly, using their strength and their endurance to contain the fire and keep it from spreading.

Jeff's last month at Harbin was as beneficial as his other stays. He returned to Oakland on August 20th, and a week later in San Francisco he knocked out Jack Munroe in the second round. Finishing his career with a triumph, Jim Jeffries announced his retirement from prize-fighting.

He was 29 years old.[12]

❖   ❖

THANKS IN PART TO JEFFRIES' PATRONAGE, HARBIN SPRINGS, TEN years after what could have been a cataclysmic fire, was fiscally on its feet again. In November of 1904, Margaret Mathews renegotiated the lease with Jim and Maggie Hays, the new contract to begin on February 1, 1905 with the expiration of the 10-year agreement signed in 1895.

The new lease, also for a 10-year term, raised the rent by only $50, to $1550 a year, and required that insurance of no less than $10,000 value be purchased against loss or damage by fire. It seems that a lot of new landscaping must have been done around the turn of the century, because in addition to financial matters, the new lease also specified that Hays agree to "protect the growing trees and shrubbery at all times during the terms of this lease, and do not permit any waste or damage to the same."

Margaret Mathews inspected the property before drafting the newest lease, and also required that Jim and Maggie "at once erect and build a new flume of cement in place of the wooden flume now in use,"[13] build a new four-room cottage,

---

12 Five years later, Jeff was urged to come out of retirement to fight Jack Johnson, who had become the first black fighter to win the heavyweight crown when he defeated Tommy Burns. At first Jeff refused, but was finally persuaded to try and win back what many sports figures saw as a white title. He had been out of competition for five years, and weighed more than 300 pounds when he began training. Jeff was dispirited by having to lose that much weight, along with the ugly racial overtones of the fight and the incessant demands on his time by the media and the sporting public. He never regained his previous form, and was solidly defeated by Johnson in the 15th round of the fight in Reno on July 4, 1910, and retired for good. He died in Burbank in 1953.

13 The flume in question was a narrow trough, an aqueduct, that carried the run-off from the pools down to the stream. Its probable location was from the pool area, beneath the current Massage Temple, and then down the slope to the stream. Remnants of the cement flume can still be seen in the area.

and restore the Capitol Hotel to good repair. Mrs. Mathews agreed to provide one carload of cement for the flume and all the necessary lumber for the hotel repairs.

Proud of the improvements he had made, in 1904 or 1905 Hays had a series of black and white photo-postcards printed, showing the scenes that a visitor to Harbin enjoyed. Guests at the resort sent these cards all over California, sharing their vacations with family and friends in a new way. The picture postcard was a fairly new phenomenon in the United States; postal regulations had changed in 1898 to allow cards with a message and address on one side and a picture on the other to be sent anywhere in the country for a penny.

Sales and use of postcards exploded, providing the public with a cheap and easy method of communicating; literally millions of postcards were sent each year. They also provided later historians with an invaluable record—no other source reflects as accurately what the resort looked like at any given time, or what real people actually said about it.

One card showed a wooded road and a buggy full of people, with the caption "On the Road to Harbin Springs." Sent in October of 1905, the message on the back read:

This is certainly the candy up here—a bunch of fun. Back, back to the high stool for me on Monday—I hate to think of it. I've had such a good time and feel fit—see!!—"Kop"[14]

Others pictured the stagecoach and the hotel (one card had the names Blanche, Alma, Evelyn, Edith, Bessie and Marguerite written in pencil along the side); a couple in a horse-drawn cart ("Out for a Drive at Harbin Springs"); and a man wearing a suit, including hat and vest, standing next to a cow ("Country Life at Harbin Springs").

---

14 Quotes are from individual postcards in the collection of the author (on permanent display at Harbin Hot Springs) or from those in the collection of Irl Rickabaugh of Ukiah.

❖ ❖

IN 1906, AN EARTHQUAKE AND FIRE DEVASTATED SAN FRANCISCO, and had repercussions in Lake County. Hot springs are dependent on water and steam escaping from fissures deep in the earth's crust, and any seismic activity can cause changes in their flow. Many resort owners found that some of their springs no longer flowed at all because the underlying chan- nels had been closed off by the quake; others found them- selves with new springs in unex- pected places.

No long-lasting changes were re- corded in the hot or cold springs at Harbin, but a fluc- tuation in the flow rate indicates that the 1906 tremblor did have some geo-

Jim Hays (inside cover of 1907 Harbin brochure)

logic impact on the baths, and an economic one as well. The season started a little earlier that year, as people fled north from the ruined city in April. Families who could afford it vacationed for that entire summer while their homes were being repaired, or new homes built. Many men stayed in the city to try and create order out of the chaos that was the aftermath of the quake; they sent their wives and children to the country until the city was once again habitable.

❖ ❖

SOMETIME AROUND 1907, A NEW HARBIN SPRINGS BROCHURE WAS printed, replacing the 1900 version. The new piece had a stiff red paper cover with a circle cut out of it, through which the smiling face of the genial innkeeper, Jim Hays, appeared. When the cover was opened, there was a picture of Hays, his thumbs in his vest, below type that claimed Harbin Springs was "the finest hot sulphur springs in the world."

The new brochure was mostly a reprint of the earlier pamphlet, with some different photographs and a few facts that were changed to reflect new prices. (The prices for one-day stays had risen to $2 to $5; weekly rates to an $11 to $21 range; and the most expensive monthly stay was now a princely $84.)

Recreation and healing appear to have been equally important at the resort itself, but the brochure again begins with boasts about the medicinal value of the waters, along with the usual testimonial letters supporting these claims. The two letters from the 1900 brochure are reprinted in the 1907 one; another letter (originally dated March 1, 1900), was changed to appear more current.

WITNESSED MANY STRIKING CURES

Stockton, March 1, 1907

My Dear Sir: It affords me pleasure to testify to the medicinal virtues of Harbin Hot Springs. During my sojourn there, I received great benefit from the use of the baths and the waters myself, and also witnessed many striking cures in others, especially those suffering from rheumatic troubles. Of a certainty, the waters of Harbin have great healing power.
Yours very truly, Geo. S. Harkness, M.D.

Except for a repetition of Dr. Anderson's 1888 water analysis, the rest of the brochure is dedicated to describing the bill of fare offered, and the recreation possibilities. Hunting and fishing still come highly recommended, and saddle horses and mules (for ladies and gentlemen) and ponies (for boys) are available for trail riding. Under the heading "Amusements," Hays offers Billiards, Quoits, Shuffle Board, Croquet and "lovely walks over easy and winding mountain trails."

The brochure repeats a detailed description of the gym, which had been in use for at least eight years; Hays didn't bother to update the opening sentence.

One of the finest Gymnasiums in the State has just been built. Hand Ball Court, Ten Pin Alley, Billiard Room, Exercising Room, Reception Room and Bath Room. All connecting and furnished with all kinds of apparatus to exercise with, which makes it very attractive.

The gym's facilities had been highly praised by Jeffries as well. Although he was in retirement, he continued to encourage other fighters to come and use Harbin as a training camp. The San Francisco fire destroyed many of the athletic clubs and their training facilities, causing a temporary slump in local boxing promotion, but also bringing business to out-of-town camps.

In February of 1906, a 25-year old Canadian named Noah Brusso, who fought under the name Tommy Burns, won the heavyweight crown. Jeffries had vacated the title by retiring in 1904, and the fight between Burns and Marvin Hart had been an elimination bout for the championship. Burns won the fight with a decision in the 20th round, and became the new heavyweight king.

Following in Jeff's tradition, Burns came up to Harbin on June 3, 1907, to train for a match with Australian Bill Squires. A stocky fighter, the 5'7", 175-pound Burns liked to hike and hunt, and used the same guides and the same burro that Jeffries had used three years before. Unlike the former champ, Burns stayed out of the hot baths, because he thought they would drain his strength. His bathing preference was for a natural swimming hole that he had found in the woods about five miles from the resort.

Tommy Burns wasn't as widely known when he won the heavyweight crown, so the press didn't give him the kind of publicity that the well-known and well-loved Jeffries had. The only anecdote available from Burns' three-week stay at Harbin is a cryptic note that he liked to "catch snakes and scare his dog with them."

The combination of fearsome snakes, no hot water bathing and the famed Harbin gym was as fortunate for Burns as the Springs had been for Jeffries: he knocked Squires out in the first round of his 4th of July San Francisco bout.

At about the same time, in a flurry of self-promotion, Hays had another series of postcards printed, this time in full color. Britton and Rey, a San Francisco postcard company, printed a set of 12 different Harbin Springs cards in 1907 or 1908, from photographs taken by Fowzer Photo. When viewed in order, the cards duplicated the succession of views that travelers encountered on their way to Harbin.

The photographs were black and white, and artists at the printing company hand-tinted them for color printing. Unlike modern color photographs, the color on these cards is rich, but slightly muted. They are quite beautiful, but have a drawback as a historical record; there is no way of knowing whether the yellow barn on a card is yellow because it actually *was* yellow, or because the artist thought it ought to be.

The first card in the series, "The Harbin Springs Stage Coach," showed at least twelve people in a stagecoach pulled by six horses, crossing what is supposed to be Putah Creek, just outside of Middletown.[15] Following was "The Lone Pine Tree on the Road to Harbin Springs"[16] which showed seven women in hats, shirtwaists and long coats, standing at the base of a 50-foot pine. The tree itself stood on a rocky promontory which was either well off the road or well above it; nothing was visible in the background but some very distant hills.

As the traveler's journey from Middletown came to an end, the stage passed through the tall, sign-topped gate of a white picket fence, proclaiming to the passengers that this was the "Entrance to Harbin Springs." On the right was a barn of at

15 Postcard companies had stock photos—beautiful sunsets, scenic views, etc.—which were used across the country, merely by personalizing the caption. ("Moonlight on Timber Lake, Boise, Idaho" and "Beautiful Night Scene, Buckeye Lake, Ohio" might be identical images.) Cards with this stagecoach scene have also been found with the caption "The Stage to Bartlett Springs." The exact location of the photo is unknown; it does look a great deal like Putah Creek, and may well be.

16 I have tried to find the location for this card, and either the tree fell years ago and the rock is overgrown, or it is a stock photo that was not, in fact, taken around Harbin. Or I looked in the wrong places. At any rate, it's not on any "Road to Harbin" that I'm aware of.

Entrance to Harbin. Barn is at right, gym at left.

least two and possibly three stories, built into the hillside so that the entrance was on the second floor. Across the road was the gym and a ring for horseback riding. Some buildings in the garden could be seen on the far right. The message on the back of one card (sent in August of 1908) said:

> *I will most likely remain here as it is all right, but I miss the lakes anyhow. Regards to all, Dave.*[17]

"The Gymnasium and Bowling Alley Pavilion" was a sprawling, multi-level wooden building just inside the entrance. It was (at least in the mind of the artist) painted yellow and topped with a red-shingled roof. The main entrance to the building was on the ground floor, through a small covered porch. The building itself, again built into the hillside (on the site where the main Harbin office is today) may have been three stories, or two with a very high-ceilinged second floor, suitable for a gym or a dance hall. A split-rail fence-lined road led up the hill behind the gym.

---

17 The cards were printed in 1907, but postmarks ranged from 1907 to as late as 1915, as visitors used up the stock of printed cards.

Jim Jeffries had divided his indoor time between the gym and his four-room cottage, *Hayward*, which he shared with 11 other men and his dog. The cottage, located where the front porch of the Azalea Building is today, was pictured on postcards as a yellow building with a green roof and slim white pillars. It was perpendicular to a light green cottage named *Del Monte*, which sat on the edge of the hillside, overlooking the canyon. A card showing a view of these two buildings was sent to Alameda in 1909, offering a counterpoint to Jim Hays' claims for his better accommodations:

> *Last night I slept in a tent and it was much nicer than the room I had the first night. Am anxiously awaiting a long letter from you. Dave.*

Up the hill from *Hayward*, behind a widespread line of tall trees, were three or four cabins, located where the Walnut Building is now. They are all depicted as bright yellow wooden buildings with white trim and green roofs. The last cabin, *Pine*, was flanked by tall flowering bushes, and its front door opened onto "The Croquet Ground at Harbin Springs." On the front of the card, five dark-suited men and two long-skirted women, one with a parasol, were pictured in the midst of a game on a

The Capitol Hotel, with tent platforms, as seen from Shady Lane.

164

circle of bare ground surrounded by a lush green lawn. Postcard messages have not changed much over the years, and the back of this card offered a bare-bones description of one gentleman's stay:

> Dear Mrs. Fenton. Well, here I am up here. There are not many up here. Am taking the baths. Yours truly, Walter.

On the other side of the croquet grounds were the platform tents, behind which stood the Capitol Hotel. A green and white building with red accents, it had eight rooms opening onto a porch on the ground floor. Another set of rooms opened onto a second-floor porch at the back of the building, level with the bath area. A third story provided rooms with access to a balcony overlooking the baths and stairs down to the pools.

The baths themselves were pictured on a card captioned "Bath House and Plunge," which offered a view of the dressing rooms from the back porch of the Capitol. At an angle to the dressing rooms was a two-story building with arches and stairways leading to the baths themselves.

Another card in the visitor's pictorial journey, "Drinking Sulphur Water at Harbin Springs" showed a very up-to-date lady dipping a ladle into a basin of healing mineral water. The photo appears to have been taken near where the cold plunge can be found today. On the back of this card, an unknown woman wrote a contemporary glimpse of Harbin healing to her friend:

> Dear Cora, Mr. and Mrs. S. came home from Harbin Springs Wednesday, fat as ever. I am fine, weighed today, weigh 143—how's that? Write soon, Love, May.

More than 80 people gathered for a photograph in front of the "Harbin Springs Hotel." It may have been the Fourth of July, as the porches were draped with red and white striped bunting. The men were uniformly clad in straw hats, white shirts (some with dark vests) and dark pants; many stood with their arms crossed or their hands on their hips, as if waiting for this foolishness to be done. The women were dressed in high-necked, long-sleeved white blouses and floor length skirts;

some were wearing hats, others were holding them, or their parasols or small children.

The stagecoach was full and stood to the right of the crowd, ready, it would seem, to leave at any moment. The picture showed quite a prosperous resort on a pleasant summer day, which was exactly what Jim Hays wanted. However, the message one guest wrote on the back of her card gave a very different, and possibly more realistic, picture:

> *Dear Sis and Bro: It's a shame I haven't written. I have had my hands full. The boys are just doing fine and Will is feeling fine. I am about settled, although we intend moving, as this place is so dirty and the water isn't good. It was the only vacant house when we got up here. My how we miss home, and this is such a small place. I'd write again, but there isn't any news. Love from, Dora.*

The message on this card may have expressed the dissatisfaction of an overly-fussy and complaining guest, or it may have been a glimpse into the realities of a stay at Harbin, a reality that contradicted the gloss of the brochure. The card was mailed in 1909, and by 1909 the resort was a much different place than it had been two years before.

❖   ❖

1907 HAD NOT BEEN A VERY GOOD YEAR FOR JIM HAYS. SOMETIME that year, he was returning from a trip into town when his horse spooked.[18] The buggy tipped over, and Hays was thrown several yards, critically injuring his neck in the crash. At the time of the accident he was 53, and due to his age and the nature of his injury, he never really recovered. He was no longer able to lead hunting trips or to travel any distance in a buggy or on the stage because of the pain that the bouncing caused him. He began to stay more and more on Harbin property and around the Main Hotel area, and became a

---

18 The exact date is not known; most of the copies of the Middletown newspaper (The *Independent*, published from 1888 to 1918) were destroyed when the town was ravaged by fire in 1918; accounts of local Middletown and Harbin events appear to be lost forever.

Bath house and plunge. Building at far left is at location of Fern dressing room; railing at right is Capitol Hotel porch.

Main Hotel, circa 1905. Small fenced area is now Gazebo .

Croquet grounds.

Cabin in center is now Shiatsu Building.

Other cabins, downhill to right, are where Walnut is today.

semi-invalid, using the waters he had praised for so long to try to heal and recuperate.

Maggie and Eddie continued to run the resort under Jim's guidance; the evidence shows that they were not altogether successful. Business began to decline slightly without Jim's drive behind it and, without his overseeing, some of the physical facilities of the resort deteriorated. Eddie attempted to take his father's place as the resort's chief sportsman and hunting guide, but the boy was only 18 and, though enthusiastic, just didn't have the experience or the panache that his father had developed after running a resort for 25 years.

The family tried valiantly to keep the resort going, hoping for Jim's eventual recovery. But he had been hurt too badly. After almost two years of pain and increasing immobility, he had a stroke, and died on July 31, 1909.

❖   ❖

AFTER THE FUNERAL, A DISTRAUGHT MAGGIE HAYS FOUND herself at the height of the summer season, with money coming in from guests, an annual rent that was due, and bills that needed to be paid. Jim hadn't left a will, so his estate was in probate; all the assets were frozen until an inventory could be taken and a value for the estate determined. No one, including Maggie, could legally pay any of the bills until the court appointed an administrator.

On August 9, 1909, Maggie petitioned the court to appoint her as special administratrix of her husband's estate, so that she could continue to conduct the business of the resort. She especially urged the court to act quickly in the matter because the annual rent of $1550 was due on August 20th.

If she failed to pay the rent on time, Margaret Mathews could terminate the lease and take over the property. Mrs. Mathews was in her 80s and was interested in Harbin Springs primarily for its value as an investment; Maggie Hays was 46 and had lived at Harbin since she was two years old. For her, the question of paying the rent was a matter of losing the only home she had ever known.

The court agreed to her petition, and appointed her special administratrix. Mrs. Mathews, knowing what it was like to be a widow and deal with financial matters, gave her a grace period on the rent. Maggie paid $550 of the outstanding rent, most of the past-due bills and, at the end of September, reported to the court that the estate had taken in over $6300 in August and September and paid out $2900, leaving a positive cash-flow of $3700 as a cushion for the slow winter months.

The revenue was almost all from the resort and livery stable business, with about $400 more coming in from the profits of the saloon. The saloon was a separate business, run jointly by Jim Hays and H.T. Quigley, providing beer, liquor and cigars to patrons of the Springs.

Expenses noted for the court give an intriguing look at the complexities of running Harbin Springs in 1909. In a little over one month, Maggie spent $35 on eggs, $150 on groceries, $225 on meat, $42 on beer, $85 on cigars and $75 for ice. Operating expenses included money spent for such diverse things as hay, wood, stamps, attorney's fees, paint, freight hauling, advertising, "drugs for the springs"[19] and tuning the piano. On top of all that was the cost of labor. The payroll for the month of August was over $1300 (nearly equal to one *year's* rent), $700 of which went to the hotel cook, Fong Don.[20]

At the end of September, Maggie Hays was appointed the permanent administratrix of Jim's estate, and appraisers were selected to determine a value for the property involved. She also petitioned the court for a $150 per month family allowance for the support of herself and her two minor children, Edna and Richard; the court agreed that she could take the money from the balance left from the summer.

A preliminary inventory of the resort just after Jim's death showed that the value of the estate was about $12,000. This figure included $5000 for furniture and fixtures in the hotels and cottages; 30 horses and various saddles at $1150; $1200 worth of buggies, wagons and other vehicles; $500 for 25 head

---

19 I assume that this item was for chemicals of some sort to treat the water, fight algae, etc.

20 This is an awful lot of money, even for a great cook. It seems likely that the $700 entry on the accounting sheet was the cook's wages for the entire season.

of cattle and $400 for 130 hogs; $700 in stock of groceries, liquor and cigars and $500 in cash.

In addition, the appraisers found real estate valued at $2000—139 acres of unimproved Lake County timber land and a few unimproved lots in town—and interests in several quicksilver mines in the southern portion of the county. The inventory also notes "13 and one-half acres of land adjoining Harbin Springs, improved with a Club House Building," valued at $1200. The small acreage was a part of the 166 acres that passed from Annie Williams to her son Richard and then into confusion; the Club House was located on the eastern side of the canyon, away from the main hotel area.

The official court-ordered appraisal of the estate was made late in November, detailing the furniture, fixtures, livestock and equipment. From the number of blankets, sheets and other bedding, it seems that there were 105 beds available for guests at the resort, although all publicity material mentioned accommodations for 200.

The property itself, land and buildings, belonged to Mrs. Mathews, with the exception of the gas plant pipes and fixtures and the gymnasium. The gym building and all the equipment are listed as part of Jim Hays' estate, so he must have owned it outright. Other than the Club House, it was the only structure that belonged to him at the time of his death; it had not existed at the time of the 1895 lease, and so was not included.

Maggie and Jim Hays had run Harbin Springs together from 1882 to 1909. In those 27 years, in addition to raising a family, Maggie had served as the hostess for the hotel and dining room, and was in charge of overseeing the maids, the kitchen staff and the garden. The rest of the business was the province of Jim and her brother, William. With both of them dead, Maggie attempted to manage the resort herself, but it appears that, like most women in 1910, she knew little about the nuts and bolts of business or finance.

The summer season of 1909 had made enough of a profit that Maggie was able to live on that money for several months. But in the winter of 1910, more and more bills began to come in as claims against the estate, offset by income of less than $800 a month. By March the claims against the estate totaled over

$12,000, and Maggie was down to her last $700. In Jim Hays' probate file, one document alone lists 31 creditors who were demanding payment on their bills, for the newspaper subscription, for the crockery for the hotel dining room, for the lumberyard and the hardware store. Margaret Mathews was demanding the $1000 balance of the unpaid rent, and a non-productive mining partnership had been judged to be a $1500 liability, not an asset.

Maggie petitioned the court to give her a few months to meet these debts, arguing that Harbin was a summer resort; it made a profit during the summer months and operated at a loss during the off-season. She informed the court that during the slow winter months she had been preparing the premises so that business could continue, and that:

> ...now everything is in satisfactory condition and ready for the entertainment of guests....[I] have already received many enquiries from intending guests at Harbin Springs for the coming season, and am of the opinion that the business can be carried on successfully and profitably during the season of 1910.

The court agreed, and Harbin was open for business as usual during that summer.[21] It was a profitable season; the revenues for April to October of 1910 totaled just over $14,000.[22] Unfortunately, that was almost exactly what it had cost, in labor and supplies, to run the resort for the summer.

On October 1, 1910, Maggie Hays discontinued operation and closed the gates of Harbin Springs.

❖   ❖

IN A LETTER TO THE COURT SHE EXPLAINED THAT ALTHOUGH SHE had made every effort to run the business profitably, it had proved impossible, and that "it would be inadvisable and

---

21 They planned for a prosperous season. The local papers noted, in June of 1910, that "Eddie Hays met a consignment of trout at the toll house Wednesday and bought over 45,000 of the speckled beauties for Harbin Springs Creek."

22 It is interesting to see the seasonal fluctuation in the figures from her financial report: April brought in $450; May $840; June $1700; July $5100; August $2800; September $520, with an additional $1200 from three guests who stayed for the entire summer.

unprofitable for the estate to further carry on the business at Harbin Springs." She asked the court's approval to close the resort completely, except for one hired man who, for an expense of about $30 a month, would care for the cattle and caretake the land and buildings against further deterioration.

The court sent a referee out to examine the books, talk to Maggie, and determine what ought to be done. He spent a week at Harbin going over the business in minute detail, and his conclusions were not promising. He reported that all of the claims against the estate appeared to be valid, and that "the manner in which the books have been kept shows a lack of knowledge of bookkeeping...and many accounts do not balance." On October 28, the family allowance of $150 a month was discountinued because the estate was insolvent.

The rent for 1909 had not been paid in full, and the rent for 1910 was owing completely. On December 15, Margaret Mathews agreed to drop any claims for back rent in return for the surrender of the lease that had been signed in 1905. It must have been an agonizing Christmas; on January 1, 1911, Maggie Hays surrendered Harbin Springs to Mrs. Mathews. The elderly landlord allowed the Hays family to continue to live on the property until the whole legal matter was settled and new tenants could be found to run the resort.

Two weeks later, Mrs. Mathews leased the property to the firm of Booth, Carr and Booth—Newton S. Booth of Crockett, his brother Dr. E.F. Booth of Vallejo and their brother-in-law, A.W. Carr—the family who would run the resort for the next 50 years.

The terms of the lease were similar to the Hays lease: a ten-year agreement with rent of $1550 per year, increasing to $2000 per year after four years. The lease covered all the hotel buildings, cottages and other fixed improvements on the premises, and once again called for the new tenants to build a four-room cottage and take care of the shrubbery.

According to the 1897 sale, all the property on the premises was forfeit if the lease was delinquent; Margaret Mathews appears to have declined this option. Perhaps she was feeling charitable and allowed Maggie to keep the property, or (more likely), taking over the assets of the estate might have left her legally open to being responsible for its enormous debts as well.

Early in 1911, creditors petitioned the court to force Maggie to sell off all real property and real estate at auction because "the Harbin Springs property is deteriorating in value to the detriment of the creditors of the estate."

Faced with $12,000 in debts, Maggie began to sell off the property piecemeal in the early months of 1911. A man named Frank Snow bought some hogs and cattle for $900 in January. In February, Dr. Booth, the new tenant, bought a few tables and some lamps. In March and April, bit by bit, friends, neighbors and even the employees of the Springs came and bought things from Maggie Hays: a cow, a mule, a saddle, the cash register, four chairs, a quilt, a stage coach, a bedroom set—all left Harbin one-by-one in a season-long garage sale.

In May Dr. Booth bought a large number of items, including the bar, the ice boxes, the bowling alley and the oven, presumably leaving them in place until he took over the premises.[23] More horses and wagons were sold, along with some of the tents, the piano and various pieces of furniture. On June 7th, it is noted, a Mrs. Harris bought "six towels, one dozen spoons and one dozen large spoons."

All told, between January and June, people came to Harbin and spent a little over $2500 on miscellaneous bits and pieces of what had been the resort.

In order to satisfy the creditors, Maggie posted a notice in the newspaper that all of the remaining hotel furnishings and equipment, wagons, animals and bar fixtures would be sold at auction. The sale was held in Middletown from July 21 to July 26, 1911.

The objects that collectively had once been the Harbin Springs Health and Pleasure Resort were spread all over the county. A young man named Max Hoberg bought the billiard table and almost all of the beds, linens and dishes, to furnish his

---

23 Why Booth, Carr and Booth (having leased the premises for ten years) didn't buy *all* the furnishings for their own resort business is something of a mystery.

family's resort up on Cobb Mountain. Booth, Carr and Booth bought more small items, including 54 soap dishes at a nickel apiece. The total proceeds from the five-day sale amounted to $1552.25.

At the end of the auction, everything was gone. Harbin Springs was a few hundred acres with a lot of pretty, empty buildings.[24]

---

24 Maggie Hays was discharged as administratrix in 1912. In 1916, when probate finally
closed, the estate had over $7000 in debts, none of them deemed collectible. When her
brother Richard's 20-year old probate file was finally closed, in 1920, the courts were
unable to locate her. She died in Vallejo on August 26, 1936, at the age of 72.

CHAPTER SIX

A Family Resort

HARBIN SPRINGS HAD CLOSED ITS DOORS TO THE PUBLIC after the summer of 1910, and remained closed for nearly two years. After the 1911 auction was completed, 35-year old Newton S. Booth and his wife Lela (along with his brother and brother-in-law as general business partners) began the task of refurbishing and re-opening the resort.

In the four years since Jim Hays' accident, while Maggie and Eddie had struggled to make ends meet, the resort had become somewhat dilapidated and rundown. It took the Booths more than a year just to complete the repairs necessary to open Harbin to guests once again.

Most of the furnishings of the resort had been sold at auction, leaving only the buildings, some major pieces of equipment and a few head of livestock for the new managers. One guest remembered the animals from her childhood visits to Harbin in the early days of the Booths' management:

> My earliest recollection of Harbin is the pigs! The pigs were the first to greet one at Harbin. After the pig pens, one drove up through the gate and stopped at the office, where the Booths were usually standing on the steps to greet the newcomers when the stage arrived. Even at an early age, I could never understand why the pigs came first!

The pigs didn't come first for very long. Like Jim Hays after the fire of 1894, the Booths decided to modernize the resort rather than merely restoring it to its former condition. One of the first improvements that they made was to build a large cold-water swimming tank, replacing the smaller "plunge" that

Hays had built. They did an excellent job of construction; present-day visitors to Harbin swim in the same pool.[1]

Swimming pool, about 1915. Visible through the trees to the left of the pool are the second and third floor balconies of the Capitol Hotel.

The Booths also planned a dancing pavilion on the hill below the Main Hotel and built a gazebo (which still stands) in the center of the "Social Plaza" at Harbin. An octagonal kiosk with shaded benches around its perimeter and a fountain in its center, the Gazebo was directly in front of the lobby door of the Main Hotel, and soon became the favorite gathering spot for guests relaxing between meals and baths. Booth also repainted the exteriors of all the buildings on the property to give them a unified look—green wooden sidings with white pillars and trim. The only exception seems to have been the Main Hotel, which was entirely white.

The local papers were enthusiastic about the new, improved resort, and predicted that "under the capable management of

---

1   If you look carefully, you can see the date "1912" and the initials "RW" drawn in the cement at the shallow end of the pool.

Mr. Booth, Harbin Springs bids fair to regain all her old time popularity."

Dear K: Arrived Harbin 5 o'clock. Had a breakdown on top of mountain. Had supper at 5:30, went for a little walk. Gee, but this is a lonesome old burg—all of the alt hands. I don't know how I'm ever going to kill time, but the waters and the baths here are excellent. I think they are going to do me good.—Oscar.[2]

Water therapy was not nearly as well-regarded as a cure-all by this time, but many of Harbin's visitors did come because of some medical condition that would benefit from taking the waters. As Harbin grew (and "modern" medicine evolved), the invalid class of guests decreased, and there was a need to appeal to other visitors. Jim Hays had begun the transition from an invalid-oriented spa to a resort, and in the late 'teens the Booths decided to "modernize" the clientele they attracted to Harbin as they had modernized the facilities. They began to change their advertising so that it appealed to a "family class of people" as well as invalids, sportsmen and hunters.

Although he focused primarily on families and amateur sportsmen, Booth certainly didn't discourage professional athletes from vacationing at Harbin; throughout the decade a few boxers continued to use the gym facilities,[3] and Harbin was also a favored training camp for some early baseball players in the off-season.[4]

---

2 All quotes in italics are from postcards in the collection of the author or Irl Rickabaugh of Ukiah.

3 One notable guest was Jess Willard, the 6'6" "Pottawatomie Giant." Willard trained at Harbin in April of 1913 for a fight with Gunboat Smith. Although he lost that match, he did go on to defeat Jim Jeffries' erstwhile opponent Jack Johnson in Havana in 1915, and retained the heavyweight crown until 1919, when he lost it to Jack Dempsey.

4 The 1925 and 1927 Pittsburgh Pirates baseball teams were the National League champions, winning their first World Series from the Washington Senators, and losing the second to Babe Ruth and the New York Yankees. Their primary training camp was in Southern California, at Paso Robles, but for two or three weeks each season, before spring training formally began, the team came to Harbin Springs to take the hot baths and begin limbering up. During their stay at Harbin, the Pirates team took time to coach the Middletown high school boys in the fine points of baseball.

Many of the Booths' other guests in the 'teens and '20s were San Francisco firemen and policemen. Beginning in Jim Jeffries' days, law enforcement men from the predominantly Irish Mission District came up to Harbin to hunt and fish and relax, sometimes as a group, sometimes with their wives. An officer who came and enjoyed his stay would tell his buddies, until a sizeable clientele was built up by word of mouth.

In the early years of Booth's management, Harbin still had a lot of the rugged aspects that had characterized the prizefighter years. In 1916, a small article appeared in the local papers, noting the demise of an old Harbin resident:

> The bear which for years was an attraction at Harbin Springs broke out of its cage Saturday. When men attempted to recapture it, it became vicious and had to be shot.

This may have been the same bear that wrestled with Jim Jeffries' dog some years before, or perhaps it was one of a succession of tame bears at the resort. At any rate, the death of the bear seemed to signal the end of a somewhat rough and tumble era, and Booth began downplaying these aspects in his brochures and newspaper ads. That same year a guidebook to California resorts noted that:

> The present management have lived down the "sporty" reputation that the place once had, and it now has a deservedly select patronage.

Harbin was already well-known for its mineral waters, and under the Booth's management it became popular throughout the county for its hotel facilities and fine food. The select patrons of the resort were treated to simple home-grown and home-cooked meals in the dining room. Roasts and stews were complemented by fresh produce from the garden during the summer months, except on Fridays when a fish entreé was provided. Lela Booth ran her dining room with a firm hand, making sure that meals were delicious, but not extravagant. The Friday staple, oyster stew, was prepared by placing three oysters in each soup bowl, then ladling a cream soup over them.

Lunchtime in the Main Hotel Dining Room in the 1920s.

On hot summer days, and especially on holiday weekends, the screen door between the white-painted dining room and the steamy kitchen banged continuously. Three times a day the ten apron-clad high school and college girls who worked as waitresses hurried from stove to table with trays of food and Harbin's renowned iced tea.[5]

The kitchen itself was the province of the cooks, and no one, not even Lela herself, dared to enter without their permission. For more than 30 years the cooks at the resort were all Chinese, and lived in a cabin next to the bar, hidden from view by a thicket of bamboo. They had a unique status at Harbin. Inside the kitchen, the word of the head cook was law, and he and his assistants had their own dining room, and their own hour to use the pools (which they entered in order: head cook, second cook, third cook and dishwasher). But outside the kitchen, they were second-class citizens. They left their cabin, walked across "the yard" to the Hotel, and then back again at night. Other

---

5   Waitresses (circa 1925) were paid $35 per month, plus room, board and tips.

than for their daily bath, they were not permitted on any other parts of the property.

The home-cooked meals were accompanied by iced tea and the carafes of Harbin spring water which sat at each table. Those who wanted stronger fare went to the bar, or club-house, patronized primarily by the male guests, and a few scandalously "modern" women.

❖   ❖

THE YEAR HARBIN REOPENED, 1912, WAS ALSO THE YEAR THAT Lake County voted itself dry, with a complex and confusing set of liquor laws.

No beer could be shipped into the county, but locally-brewed beer could be legally delivered directly to the customer. County residents could have liquor shipped in from other areas, but only for their own personal consumption, in their own homes. Non-residents—strangers, travelers and hotel guests—were forbidden to consume alcohol within the county. Selling liquor by the drink was forbidden, which outlawed saloons and taverns and hurt the larger resorts, but created a number of unofficial establishments.[6]

According to an article in a local paper colorfully titled "Blind Pigs on the Run," in mid-July of 1914, the Lake County Sheriff and his deputy raided a number of speakeasies and resorts.[7] Included in the raid was Harbin Springs, where they found "a quantity of liquor." The article noted that the resort was run by Booth, Carr and Booth, and that warrants had been issued. No further legal action was reported in the paper, so the management most likely received a fine, or perhaps just a warning.

---

6 Nearby Napa County was not dry. Out Butts Canyon Road, on Oat Hill Road, just over the county line, was a flat with an enormously popular saloon, which drew its business primarily from the men and boys of Middletown.

7 The term "blind pig" was journalistic slang for a speakeasy or illegal saloon. According to one dictionary, the term came from the practice of many establishments purporting to be museums of "natural curiosities" as a front for their back room liquor business.

The county came alive in 1914 with a motion on the fall ballot to repeal the liquor laws, with the "drys" campaigning for moral decency and the "wets" arguing that prohibition was hurting Lake County's greatest industry—its hotels and resorts. The Lake County Hotel and Summer Resort Association, of which Newt Booth was an active member, campaigned to have "table licenses" permitted, with the provision that liquor could only be served at resorts and restaurants during lunch or dinner hours, and then only with a meal that cost more than fifty cents.

In November of that year the State of California voted to be "wet" by a three to one margin, but Lake County voted to stay dry. The county prohibition remained in effect until the 18th Amendment banned all alcoholic beverages nationwide in 1919. Alcohol was not officially served again at Harbin for almost twenty years, until Prohibition was repealed in December of 1933; presumably Newt Booth, who has been described as "quite a drinking man," continued to have a private supply for himself and his regular customers.

❖   ❖

WHATEVER HE DID PRIVATELY IS A MATTER OF SPECULATION, BUT he was quite public about the changes he was making in the resort facilities themselves, and the local press frequently gave him a few lines of publicity, mentioning that:

> Newt Booth is busy putting the Harbin Springs road back in shape after summer travel.

or that:

> Mrs. Booth of Harbin Springs, having a few early guests, has engaged Millie Harp to help her cook for a short time.

or even:

> Mr. and Mrs. N. S. Booth of Harbin Springs resort motored to Santa Rosa on Thursday.

Perhaps the most significant changes at Harbin in the early days of Booth's management had less to do with new construction or whether many of the guests were athletes, than with how the guests arrived at the springs. The bouncing stagecoaches and private livery that were kept at the stable were being replaced by a new form of transportation—the horseless carriage.

Automobiles were manufactured in the 1890s, but were the toys of rich men, and could be driven in very few places. They were not particularly reliable machines, and did not travel well on anything but smooth, hard roads without breaking down and getting stuck. At the beginning of the 20th century, they were becoming a familiar sight in most cities, but it wasn't until 1908 (when Henry Ford introduced the Model T) that the automobile gained real popularity.

In 1900 there were 8,000 automobiles in the United States; by 1920 over eight million. America evolved into a nation on wheels, and it changed the way people lived, the way they traveled, and the way they vacationed. Trains and stagecoaches had been faster than traveling on horseback or on foot, but the passengers had traded the freedom to roam about the countryside for the speed and convenience of the rails. No longer dependent on train, ferry or stage schedules, or limited to the areas served by those lines, motorists were more mobile and more spontaneous in their recreational plans.

An automobile could travel on the same roads as a horse and buggy, but much faster, and for greater distances. The motorist could go where he wanted to go, *when* he wanted to go, limited only by the condition of the roads (and the availability of gasoline). For the first time in history, it was possible to travel more than 100 miles in a single day, with the power to stop at leisure, or change travel plans on a whim. But this new-found freedom did have its disadvantages. The trains, stages and ferries of Northern California had coordinated their schedules so that travelers on one line could make connections on another. The modern motorist, with his own individual timetable, could easily find himself stranded.

> We had to leave Harbin's right after breakfast, because it was necessary to leave Calistoga early in order to reach Benicia before nightfall. The ferries that crossed the Carquinez Straits from Benicia didn't run at night. Stranded travelers had to stay in Benicia where the hotel rates were exorbitant—if you could find a room.

The automobile promised more than just transportation; it was also a symbol of up-to-date affluence. Driving became the great American entertainment, as thousands and then millions of motorists took to the roadways to watch new sights and scenery continually unfold through the screens of their windshields.

Harbin and other Lake County resorts had long been summer homes for many Northern California travelers, who bundled up their trunks and came to stay "for the season." But as the use of automobiles grew, guests who formerly thought of Harbin as a remote vacation spot began to go even farther afield for their extended holidays. Harbin's trade turned more to vacationers, weekenders, and even some overnight guests. A new class of people was born—the tourists.

> Lake County was now thought of more as a weekend and mountain resort center within easy reach for a few days' relaxation....A new generation grew up untutored in the joys of spending a few weeks bathing, drinking mineral water, hiking, dancing, playing croquet and reading in the seclusion of a mineral spring retreat. Instead of rest, quiet and rural recreation, the modern resorts featured city comforts and pleasures in the fresh air of the mountains.

An association of northern California resort owners, including Newt Booth, held a meeting at the Vichy Springs in Mendocino County, to promote a resort-oriented advertising campaign aimed at motorists. Large ads in every major northern California newspaper in June of 1916 urged tourists to "Loop the Loop"—a motoring tour that began in San Francisco and went through Sonoma and Mendocino Counties, over into Lake County, and down again through Napa, Solano and Contra Costa. Maps of the route were printed, and drivers were urged to take the beautiful, scenic drive as soon, and as often, as they could, and to encourage their friends to travel the route.

> Have not heard from you for a long, long time. Did you get the map I sent you? We arrived here yesterday for a two weeks visit. The trip up is wonderful. You would enjoy it. You could come in your machine....Kindest regards, M.E. Skaggs.

Newton Booth saw that the future of Harbin lay not with the playful roughhousing of boxers or the sedate gentility of the Victorian invalid, but with the new and prosperous Californian, who was on the move. The watchword of the day was *modern*, as an ad in the San Francisco *Chronicle* boasted that Harbin was:

> The best equipped resort in Lake County, the only resort having modern baths, modern steam room and modern indoor hot plunge. Only 5 hours from San Francisco by auto. Make this your next week end run.[8]

❖ ❖

IN 1916, BOOTH BOUGHT OUT THE INTEREST HIS TWO PARTNERS had in the lease and became the sole manager of the property. On July 2, 1917, Margaret Mathews, who was well over 90 years old, died in Vallejo. The probate files on her very considerable estate (more than half a million dollars) are over a foot thick, and it took several years to untangle her assets. In the meantime, Booth continued to lease Harbin from the executors and to make improvements to the property so that business could go on as usual.

BOOTHS SPENDING $22,000 AT HARBIN HOT SPRINGS

> There is being erected a new brick building which will contain several steam bath rooms and a hot plunge. There is also under way a large open-air dance hall and a new laundry room with all the modern equipments. The dining room has been refitted and is one of the best in the county....next season an electric plant will be installed.

After World War I ended, the trickle of tourists became a deluge. In 1918 Booth published a new brochure that prominently featured the advantages that a post-war resort had to offer. Although only about 10 years lies between the brochures of Jim Hays and Newton Booth, the world had

184

changed dramatically between 1908 and 1918, and the changes at Harbin reflected that.

There is no mention in the Booths' brochure of the gymnasium that Jim Hays was so proud of, nor of the horses and stables. But, according to this pamphlet, the new Harbin did provide the *motoring* guest's every need.

> Supplies such as gasoline, greases, oils, batteries, spark plugs, etc. are kept on hand. There is a garage, wash rack, pit and facilities for ordinary repairs which are free to guests.

Mineral water was still a bigger draw than any modern amenities, and between 1916 and 1918, Booth completely remodeled the bath area, replacing some of the buildings that Richard Williams had built nearly half a century before, and extensively renovating some others.

The building that had held the dressing rooms was partially razed; Booth remodeled the right hand side and continued to use it for changing rooms. On the site where the other section had been, he built an entirely new building for the hot springs, claiming that it was one of the country's finest enclosed baths.

The baths area. From left to right: the building housing the nurse's office, massage rooms and barber shop (now Fern dressing room); the Warm and Hot Pool building; the changing rooms.

A small set of steps led up to the windowed front of the ivy-covered stucco and brick building. Inside, a large room was filled with a Warm Pool surrounded by wrought iron railings with a distinctive circle motif.[9] A walkway along the right side of this warm plunge led guests to the smaller hot bath at the back. A doorway on the left wall of the hot bath room led outside and to a new cold plunge and footbath[10] that had been built on the hillside in back of the building.[11]

Because it was enclosed, the back room served as a steam room as well as a hot plunge. Half of the hot bath room was filled by the four-foot deep Hot Pool itself; the hot springs on the hillside flowed from a pipe directly into the pool. Often the splashing of the water was the only sound in the dimly-lit stone room with its high, timbered ceiling. To the right of the pool was a windowed chamber lined with benches where those who wanted to take the steam, but not the waters, could sit or lie down. A doorway led from this steam area back out into the Warm Pool room.

The waters in the '20s were praised as much for their relaxing effects as for their curative powers. Therapeutic bathing is only mentioned briefly in the brochure, which seems to stress the modernity of the facilities slightly more than the medicinal virtues of the water itself.

---

9   This is the same building in which the Hot Pool is now located. The Warm Pool, which is now an outdoor pool, was enclosed in this building until 1975, when most of the structure collapsed. It has never been rebuilt.

10 The footbath (which no longer exists) was also known as "the corn springs" because of its therapeutic effect on calluses, bunions and corns. A small, shallow bath, it was filled with less than a foot of water and a few inches of fine, mineral-laden silt. Two people could sit together and soak their feet in the callus-softening ooze. It was also known among the Harbin staff as a good place to go neck at night.

11 The baths were more and more modern and civilized, but the countryside surrounding them was still virtual wilderness. One local man tells of a time in the early '20s when he and a high school buddy came up to use the tubs. They were sitting and talking at one end of the cold plunge and looked up to see a mountain lion and her two cubs casually getting a drink from the other end of the pool.

The new Plunge and Steam Room is the only modern natural steam and plunge in the State. The Hot Sulphur water runs through this plunge at the rate of 2000 gallons per hour. The vapor bath, with steam from Nature's furnace, in conjunction with the drinking of the waters, are very beneficial in cases of liver, kidney, stomach and other complaints, and are a wonderful cure for rheumatism.[12]

Resort guests who came to use the baths in the early 1920s were less leisurely about their leisure than their counterparts had been even a decade before. Although some of the guests were invalids or long-term visitors to the springs, others just came to the resort for a weekend getaway, a brief break from the hectic pace of the modern world. The changes in what the guests wanted from the resort are apparent from the highlights mentioned in the brochure. In a section about amusements, Booth points out that:

There are quiet and shady nooks where the tired city worker can sit or lie in peace after his bath or meals, and simply do nothing.

The Harbin guest could do nothing, but it seems that he was to do it rather quickly.

The location of Harbin permits one to make this their regular weekend run. Only 6 hours (easy) from San Francisco. Try it. Harbin is the favorite stopping place for Auto parties in Lake County.

❖ ❖

HARBIN WAS NOT ONLY ONE OF THE MOST POPULAR PLACES IN the county, it was also open for the season of 1918, while many other Middletown area businesses were not. On Sunday, March 3, 1918, a tank house in the back of Spiers Auto Stage garage caught fire, and the flames were swept across the town by heavy winds. Within two hours the business section of Middletown—the newspaper office of the Middletown

---

12 An ad in a Lake County guidebook from the same era (1918) notes in boldface type that "the waters are of no benefit to consumptives, so none are taken."

Independent, Snow's butcher shop, Spiers' garage, the Herrick Hotel, Read's drugstore, Piner's store, Barker's candy shop, Koopman's billiard hall and fourteen other buildings—had been completely destroyed. Newton Booth opened his hotel and dining room to his unfortunate neighbors, as Middletown began the slow task of rebuilding.

❖   ❖

IN 1919, MARGARET MATHEW'S ESTATE WAS SETTLED, AND ITS executors, Noah Hathaway and Joseph Raines, became the new owners of Harbin Springs. On July 2, 1920, on behalf of the estate, they sold the property to a man named James J. Griffin.

It is not clear whether the Booths' improvements had been, at least in part, financed by Mrs. Mathews, and therefore belonged to her estate, or if they had been made by the Booths with an eye toward eventual ownership of the upgraded property. In any event, Griffin "neglected and refused to comply with the terms of the sale," and on October 4, 1920, Newton S. Booth purchased Harbin Hot Springs for $40,000—one half down and the other half to be paid in four yearly installments of $5000 each, plus interest.

Shaded tents at HARBIN SPRINGS

Tent camping in front of the Capitol Hotel.
At far left are steps leading up to the tents on Shady Lane.

During the next seven years, the Booths paid back the note on the purchase of the property, and used the land as collateral to borrow an additional $30,000 to continue remodeling and upgrading the resort. In 1920 Harbin's capacity was 200 guests, but five years later the owners decided that a hotel, a rooming house, a dozen platform tents and 10 individual cabins were not sufficient accommodations for the number of visitors that they hoped to attract to the springs.

The summer of 1925 was the last season for the tents in front of the Capitol Hotel and up on Shady Lane—the Victorian ideal of luxuriously roughing it was going out of style; those who wished to camp out could easily drive to more remote wilderness locations. The modern traveler wanted a comfortable room for a night or two.

With an automobile, city dwellers could get out into the country for brief periods of time, and were not limited to stopping and staying in places where there was a hotel in close proximity to the train or stage stop. As they explored previously un-hoteled territory, many travelers took their own tents with them, stopping and camping for the night in a convenient field. Almost overnight, it seemed, private tourist camps sprang up, competing with established resorts for the motorists' business. The auto camper was provided with water, showers, and a level spot to pitch a tent for the night, all for a dollar or less. Some camps even offered a few amenities, like a grocery store run by the camp owner.

In the mid to late '20s, as the novelty of automobile travel began to wear off, and people grew weary of sleeping in tents or of missing the last ferry and having no camping gear along, enterprising tourist camp operators built rows of small cabins alongside their campgrounds, and found that these more permanent facilities attracted more business. All-season, all-weather mini-resorts, called auto courts, appeared on the sides of highways across the country, many offering services that used to be the province of fine hotels—a laundry, a bakery, a barber shop—for the private use of their guests.

By the early '30s there were more than 30,000 auto courts in the United States. Most of them were merely clusters of cabins, painted and furnished as cozily, but inexpensively, as possible, providing the illusion of a home away from home. But as the number of tourists and the market for overnight lodgings increased, so did the ingenuity of the auto court proprietors. Newt Booth found himself competing for business not only with other spas and resorts, but with tourist camps that offered cabins shaped like teepees, missions, English cottages or log cabins, all trying to lure the traveler looking for someplace new and different to stay.

❖   ❖

IN ORDER TO COMPETE WITH THE FLOOD OF THEME RESORTS AND roadside attractions, Booth continued to make improvements in the *quality* of his accommodations, counting on the natural attraction of the hot springs and the quiet peace of the woods to bring guests to Harbin. In the off-season, the winter of 1925-26, he finished the remodeling of the Main Hotel—which he had begun in 1918 with the addition of "sanitary plumbing" (a flush toilet in or next to every room)—by repainting the structure and renovating the lobby.

There are no photographs of the interior of the Main Hotel after Jim Hays rebuilt it in 1895, so it is not clear what Newt Booth was starting from when he remodeled it 30 years later. But a photograph of the lobby, taken in the late 20s, shows a large, windowed room with a fieldstone fireplace at one end. The furniture, a couch and several scattered chairs, is wicker with cushions in a large leaf and flower motif.

Windowed double doors open onto the large porch that faced the Gazebo. Across the room is the counter and registration area for the hotel—a wooden and glass booth with shelves of candy, gum and cigars beneath it. Above the booth and the doors opposite it are mounted deer heads, souvenirs of Harbin hunting trips. Flanking the counter are several one-armed bandits—slot machines—for the private amusement of the guests.

No doubt guests were told, with great solemnity and a knowing wink, that the machines were for decoration only, since gambling had been made illegal in Lake County in 1910. But until the late 1940s, almost every resort in the county had slot machines; although the slots were not set to pay off to the

Lobby, Main Hotel, 1925.

guest's advantage, people played them "pretty heavy" and for many resorts a large percentage of the rent was paid by the dimes and nickels that were fed into the machines.[13]

During that same, rainy winter of 1925 most of the smaller cottages were razed, *Hayward* among them, and in their place two large hotel buildings were constructed.

In the past, travelers had stayed at resorts or hotels for two reasons: in order to have a place to sleep, and in order to socialize and meet people. Twentieth century motorists often just wanted a room and preferred to have a choice about being social after a long day on the road. Individual cabins allowed

---

13 When the state attorney general cracked down on the slot machines in 1948 and ordered them out of the county, a rather indignant article in the Lake County *Bee* defended the devices, claiming that "Lake County [is] one of the few and possibly the only county in the state free of vice and gambling rackets....these machines are operated without 'payoff' or 'protection money,' and served as amusement devices for the thousands of vacationers coming to Lake County. They were operated out in the open, and not behind closed doors."

the tourist a degree of privacy not possible in a hotel, and offered the illusion that they were in their own, albeit tiny, home; there was no lobby to cross, and no other guests to run into.

But cabins also required individual plumbing and heating, which made construction more costly. In order to alleviate some of the expense, and to allow the guest a sense of privacy as well, new resort buildings were designed as a series of connected rooms. These long, low structures were like a string of small cabins, all opening onto a common front porch.[14]

Harbin's two new buildings, Walnut and Azalea, were built along these lines, with individual private rooms, but no common areas. They were built on the northern hillside, perpendicular to the Main Hotel; the three hotels encircled the Social Plaza with the Gazebo in the center—the main area of activity at the resort. Guests who wanted to socialize merely had to walk across the lawn to the lobby, the dining room and

Walnut (center) and Azalea (behind trees at right), and parking lot, around 1936. The two small wooden structures on the hillside were sunbathing decks.

14 This style of architecture would become very popular in the '20s and beyond as "motels" sprang up along America's highways. Originally "motor hotel," the term was coined in 1925, and usually indicated an establishment less luxurious than a hotel, and one which also furnished lodgings for the tourist's automobile.

the bar or walk up the hill a short way to the baths. Each of the new structures contained 16 guest rooms on two floors; they opened out onto railed balconies that overlooked the main area. The space in front of the buildings (now a lawn) was used for a solving a problem that Jim Hays never had to think about —parking.

Accommodating families or people who wanted to come up and stay as a group was a problem with single hotel rooms, so Booth remodeled the few remaining cabins to meet modern plumbing standards. On the small rise across from the Capitol Hotel (the area known as Shady Lane) he replaced the line of tent platforms with five or six brand new cabins. He also built a modern home for his family (his wife, Lela, their 15-year old daughter, Helen, and their 21-year old son, Newt Jr.) next to the *Del Monte* cabin. What was once the Booths' home is now the (vastly remodeled) Stonefront Building.[15]

Until he had their home built, Newt Booth and his family had lived in part of the Main Hotel building. The building had no guest rooms, but housed many of the staff members, along with the lobby, dining room, office etc. In the summer months, the waitresses lived on a long, screened sleeping porch above the dining room, with the hotel porter and bookkeeper in larger rooms across the hall.

Harbin guests—mostly upper middle class city dwellers, newlyweds, some families with children and some college-age singles hoping for a summer romance—were accommodated in the cabins and other hotel buildings. A few of the facilities were only opened for holidays and busy weekends, or on those

---

15 In the 1950s, when Newton Booth Jr. had a family of his own, he and his wife and children lived downstairs, and Newton Sr. and Lela lived upstairs. It's not clear where the Hays or Williams families had lived. In the early years and after the fire they probably lived in one of the cottages. It is likely that their permanent quarters were a separate suite of rooms in the Main Hotel, perhaps connecting with (or near) the office and reception desk.

occasions when a company rented the resort for an employee outing.

To welcome guests to the new and improved Harbin, Booth replaced the painted wooden entranceway to the resort, building in its place a huge stone arch with "Harbin Hot Springs" emblazoned in foot-high brass letters.[16]

The improvements in the resort facilities naturally brought an increase in the price of a stay at Harbin. In 1918, tent camping was $15 per week and rooms were three or four dollars a day; a room with a bath and lavatory commanded $21 a week. By the mid '20s the tents were gone, and a room with a private bath was $30 a week. As always, room rates allowed a guest full use of the baths, pools and steam rooms, and also included meals and a few other amenities.

> This famous resort is open all year. The hotel rooms and cottages are all equipped with running water and toilets connecting with room, thus assuring clean and sanitary accommodations. We have accommodations with hot air furnace where winter guests have all the comforts of a modern city hotel. A large free garage is provided for your car.

❖ ❖

HARBIN CHANGED TO PROVIDE FOR THE NEEDS OF THE NEW motoring public, and so did the rest of Lake County, as along with the automobile came a need for road improvement. Buggies and stagecoaches could travel on dirt roads, even in the mud, relying on the brute strength of the horses to pull them out when they got stuck. But early automobiles were not as powerful, or as easily controlled, so in the 1920s, America experienced a massive highway building program.

Like many rural areas, Lake County in the '20s had many roads, but very few that were suited to automobiles. Most were plain dirt, and some still bore the stumps of trees that had been

---

16 The word "Sulphur" was dropped from the name of the resort at this time, as "Harbin Hot Sulphur Springs" sounded too medicinal for the new, recreation-minded type of guest. See back cover for a photograph of this archway.

cleared when the road was cut through the hills. An anonymous writer described his trip to one of the resorts as he traveled over:

> ...narrow roads where dust disguised ruts, and sharp turns and pitches so occupied a driver's attention [that] many of the magnificent views were missed....Lake County roads are no places for a man to linger if his heart is weak.

The condition of the roads was decidedly not an advantage to the local tourist industry, and local businessmen (as evidenced by newspaper headlines and fervent letters to the editor) did their best to lobby for some immediate and comprehensive measures. The "Loop the Loop" campaign of 1916 had included an exhortation to travelers to write to their Congressmen and demand nationwide road improvement.

In 1916 and again in 1921, the federal government had passed two Road Acts to provide funds for building new routes, and for widening older roads, turning them into hard-surfaced, two-lane highways. In 1919, the State of California, using this federal money, had begun construction of the Ukiah-Tahoe Highway, the major east-west link for the northern part of the state, and approved funding for a highway to run from Vallejo through Calistoga and Middletown, to join the Ukiah Highway at Upper Lake.[16]

The state could take over the funding and maintenance of county roads, but could not legally allocate money to improve the privately-owned Lawley Toll Road that crossed Mt. St. Helena between Calistoga and Middletown. So in 1922, Napa and Lake Counties jointly bought the Toll Road for $30,000, and continued to collect the toll. By 1924, toll revenues had paid for the purchase of the road, the tolls were dropped, and the state began to fund the maintenance of the road, rebuilding it and regrading it. A large portion of the route of the Lawley Toll Road was abandoned; a new grade was built to wind around

---

16 Consistent highway numbering was uncommon in the late '20s. Many roads changed their routes, and their numbers, in the years following. The Ukiah-Tahoe Highway officially became State Route 20 in 1964; the Vallejo to Upper Lake road is now Highway 29. For convenience, I will refer to these roads by the numbering system being used in 1990.

the mountain, foregoing the old, more direct route, which it joined just below the summit.[17]

Highway 29 remained a hard-packed dirt road for many years, but in 1927, a local contractor, Charles Kuppinger, received the bid to gravel and oil the road from Middletown to the county line.[18] The men worked for several months, at $5 for a 12-hour day (plus a bonus of five cents for every cubic yard of gravel spread). All the work was done by hand-operated dump trucks—the trucks not only had to be started with a hand-crank, but had to be cranked manually to dump each load. The section of road from Middletown to Lower Lake was similarly improved in 1929; construction of Highway 29 would finally be completed in 1948.

At about the same time that the road improvement projects were in full swing, standard electrical service also came to the area. Many resorts and sizable businesses, including Harbin, had provided their own electricity by means of small power plants and private generators for some years, and Middletown had become the first location in the county to have a public electrical utility when the generator at George McKinley's mill began to operate on January 1, 1906.

The mill, located northeast of Middletown on Highway 175, was a flour mill, powered by a large water wheel.[19] The wheel powered the mill during the daytime, and was operated by the Callayomi and Middletown Power and Light Company from 7:00 to 10:00 each night, supplying electricity to a small portion of the town through its three miles of electric wire. (There was

---

17 The 10-mile road lay in both counties—8-1/4 miles in Napa and 1-3/4 miles in Lake, and so the cost was prorated accordingly. Lake County's share of the $30,000 purchase was $5250.

18 Previously, outside of some major cities, most roads were merely packed dirt, which became mud in the winter. The highway building programs in the 20s widened the roads to accommodate two opposing lanes of traffic, and surfaced the roads with macadam. Macadamized roads were graded and then spread with road oil—a thick, tarry emulsion—over which layers of finely crushed gravel were spread. The gravel sank into the warm goo, which solidified as it cooled, and together they formed a hard, permanent, all-weather surface.

19 It had originally been built in the 1870s as a saw mill—by Mat Harbin.

not enough power to run the mill *and* generate electricity at the same time and there were times in the driest part of the summers when there wasn't even enough water flow to power the generator. At those times, McKinley would supply the town's electrical system by hitching the generator up to his tractor; on a few occasions there was simply no electricity at all.)

In June of 1927 the McKinleys sold the power plant to the California Telephone and Light Company for $9000. The company was part of a network of northern California utilities which was in the process of becoming Pacific Gas and Electric. Construction of the network of power lines was completed in September of 1928, at which point Middletown received publicly-supplied electricity 24 hours a day. The utility began furnishing Harbin Springs with electricity almost a year later, in August of 1929.

Reliable electricity and the new and improved roads created an era of prosperity for many of the resorts in Lake County. But it was a death-knell for many other resorts, as the new roads bypassed them, leaving them isolated in the hills, not easily accessible by electric wires or automobiles.[20] Because it was so near to Highway 29, and was the closest resort for the motorist coming up from the Bay Area, Harbin prospered from the road improvement program.

❖   ❖

BUSINESS WAS GOOD AT HARBIN IN THE '20S, AND BOTH THE resort and its owners thrived. The Booths and their resort were frequently mentioned in the "Middletown" column of the Lake County papers, and readers were informed that: "Harbin Springs has an unusually good opening season, with guests

---

20 Bartlett Springs, the largest, most elaborate resort in the county at the turn of the century, lobbied vigorously, but unsuccessfully, to have the Ukiah-Tahoe Highway (Highway 20) turn east into the mountains near the springs on its way into Colusa County. But the road was built following the eastern shore of Clear Lake, more than 15 miles away. Because of this bypass, Bartlett lost business steadily (and finally closed), as the resorts and towns along Clear Lake grew and prospered.

arriving almost daily," that Newton Booth had bought himself a new Studebaker sedan and his son, Newt Jr. a Studebaker coupe, and that Mr. Booth and his daughter, Miss Helen, enjoyed a month-long motor trip to Southern California at the end of one season. Newton Booth, like Jim Hays and Richard Williams before him, had transformed the resort to meet the changing needs of the vacationing public, keeping pace with the times, and profiting nicely from the changes.

Harbin began to develop a fine reputation throughout Northern California for its accommodations and services, and was picked as the site for numerous local and regional festivities. In 1922, the members of a San Francisco Yacht club celebrated the holidays at Harbin. In 1926 and '27, the Callayomi Masonic Lodge held its annual ball in May, filling Harbin's new dance pavilion, with its view of the gardens.

Summer fun for some of the female guests—a beauty contest in front of the Capitol Hotel, 1926.

> Music was furnished by the splendid jazz orchestra of the S.S. Manchuria, the musicians having recently completed a cruise around the world. Newt Booth is a very affable host and his resort is extremely popular. The new hotel under the shady pines is quite an asset.

The Dance Pavilion was, second only to the baths, Harbin's premier attraction at the time. Until the Depression, the Booths hired an orchestra of young men for the June to September season. They all lived together in a large tent, and their job was to play for the dances which were held each evening after dinner. On weeknights the music ended at 10:00 p.m. sharp; on Saturdays the boys played until midnight.

After the dances, weenie and marshmallow roasts were held around a campfire, with young hotel guests mingling with the waitresses and orchestra boys (who were considered to be the elite of the resort staff). On weekends, they too went dancing, at some of the "after hours" resorts near Clear Lake.

Harbin's orchestra had such a good reputation that dances were attended not only by Harbin guests, but also by local couples and people vacationing at other nearby resorts. Business was so good that, even with the new Walnut and Azalea buildings, Booth needed more rooms for guests, and a headline in the paper proclaimed:

HARBIN SPRINGS TO HAVE NEW HOTEL

A new hotel of 35 rooms, steam-heated and with bath is to be built at Harbin Springs by Newt Booth. To make room for the structure, several old buildings will be torn down.

The three-story Capitol Hotel was the largest of the old buildings to be demolished. Richard Williams had built it as a rooming house in the 1870s, and it had survived the fire of 1894. But by the late 1920s, it was in drastic need of repairs, including major plumbing renovation, and Booth decided that it was more economical to replace the antiquated structure than to remodel it. He razed it and a small cabin next to it, and built a new three-story hotel, complete with modern toilets in every room. The new "Main Annex" building (also referred to as "Capitol") was nearly identical to Walnut and Azalea, creating a unified line of hotels on the hillside.

Guests on the second and third floor of the building could choose rooms that faced down the hill toward the Gazebo, or that faced the pools. Second floor rooms opened directly onto the swimming pool; the rooms above opened onto a balcony overlooking the pool area, with an outside staircase leading down to the plunge.

Harbin Springs continued to attract new guests, many of whom came up with their families or in groups and wanted more space and more privacy than a single hotel room could provide. To accommodate them, Booth decided to expand the resort as a whole, rather than building any more cottages in the Main Area. In 1930 he took out a loan for $20,000 and

"Main Annex," 1936. (On site of Capitol Hotel; now Redwood)

purchased almost 500 acres of land just north of Harbin. The property included the pools, cottages and other buildings of the recently-closed Stuparich Resort.[21]

❖   ❖

THE LAND THAT BOOTH WOULD RENAME THE HARBIN ANNEX came to him as a parcel with a 50-year old history of its own, a history that involved much of the economics, politics and resources of Lake County.

In 1891, Henry C. Boggs, founder of the Farmer's Savings Bank of Lakeport and one of the men who had financed the first toll road into the county after the Civil War, bought 80 acres of land on the wooded slopes of what would later be called Boggs Mountain.

Boggs was the son of the Governor of Missouri, and had traveled to California as a young man, adding to his fortune by investing in lumber, beginning with his acquisition of a large mill on Cobb Mountain, near Kelseyville. He owned that mill

---

21   An area today known as "The Village."

until 1881, when he moved his facilities to "a location about three miles north of the Harbin springs, in a well-timbered section." The new mill was on a 160-acre parcel owned by his business partner, Henry Long. After Long's death, Boggs purchased the land from Mrs. Long in 1891.[22]

In 1893, an aging Boggs sold the land to a man named Pierre G. Somps for $650 "in lawful money of the United States." Two years later Somps received a government grant for an adjoining 160 acres, later selling all 320 acres to Emma Fenton of San Francisco, who paid $10 in gold for the property in 1901. (See map, page 204.)

Mrs. Fenton kept the land for almost two years before reselling it in 1903 to Lillian M. Hickmott, also of San Francisco.[23] The Hickmotts are sometimes credited with starting a small resort on the property, but there is no evidence that they ever began, much less completed, any building. The only structural remains on that section of land are a large stone foundation and chimney, located near where the "Gulch House" is today.[24]

---

22 The mountain was named after Boggs, an extremely prominent man in the county, and his mill. His prominence was enough to supercede the notoriety that had led to the mountain's previous name—Digger Jones Mountain.

    William "Digger" Jones is an interesting character in early Lake County lore. He was a white man who had taken a native wife —a Digger Indian in the epithet of the day. He lived on a ridge of the mountain about one and a half miles northwest of Harbin, near Gifford Springs. He had a plot of land with fresh water and a garden, and made his precarious living hunting, fishing, and cutting wood with his partner and son-in-law, Henry Long, (no relation to Boggs' partner) who lived with his wife two miles north of Harbin in a small cabin.

    Both men were heavy drinkers. One night in 1882, Jones was told that Long had "sold off some wood and drank up the profits." Drunk and enraged, Jones went up to Long's cabin, argued with him, then shot and killed him as he lay in his bed. Jones was arrested and found guilty by the jury. In June of 1883, he was hanged by Sheriff L. H. Boggs (Henry Boggs' brother) at the jail in Lakeport—the only white man ever legally hanged in Lake County

23 Lillian was the wife of Robert Hickmott, whose claim to fame, it is noted in many histories, was that he was the first man to can asparagus in the Sacramento Delta.

24 These ruins have been (erroneously) thought to be the remains of "The Old Stagecoach Inn." In fact, they are all that is left of the Brookins Saw Mill, which operated from about 1905 until it was abandoned (or possibly destroyed) in 1918; a logging road on the side of Boggs Mountain connected the mill with Harbin and other springs.

The Hickmotts took out a Deed of Trust on their parcel in 1908, and used it as collateral to borrow money. In 1919, legal wrangling over the property ended with the Hickmotts defaulting on the deed and their note for the $2000 they had borrowed; to satisfy the debt the property was sold at auction for more than $4000 to Henry C. Wulf. Why the property appreciated from $10 to $4000 in 15 years is something of a mystery, even considering the increase in value that might have been expected along with the new road construction.

An even bigger mystery is why, in November of 1924, Wulf resold the land for $10 again, to a woman named Georgia Clark. Mrs. Clark didn't hold on to it long; three days later the real estate (and the $10) changed hands again when she sold it to Paul and Emily Stuparich, of San Francisco.

The 320-acre transaction brought the Stuparich's land holdings up to 484 acres of land. (See map, page 204.) Paul J. Stuparich was an Austrian native who had emigrated to the United States in 1888, and had settled in San Francisco. He formed the Stuparich Manufacturing Company, which made photographic cards and cardboard, in partnership with his brothers, Nicholas and Stephen. After the 1906 earthquake, when the building that housed the firm was severely damaged, Paul went into business for himself as a vendor of photographic supplies.

By 1911, he had become a building contractor, and had again gone into business with his brother Stephen as a partner, in order to build a health resort in Lake County. They purchased a 164-acre parcel of land known as "The Old Frenchman's Place" from a young entrepreneur who called himself E. W. Hays.

Eddie Hays had bought the property from the estate of Claudius Mottier, the vineyardist (also known as "the old Frenchman") who had lived on the land for more than 30 years before his death in June of 1909. Mottier had purchased a tiny, 4-acre plot from Jim and Maggie Hays in 1888, and was awarded the other 160 acres posthumously in a government land grant. He had applied for the grant some time before; federal paperwork gave him actual title to the land four months after his death.

In 1911, as Maggie Hays was embroiled in her final struggle to save Harbin from bankruptcy, her 22-year old son Eddie purchased Mottier's acreage from the estate for $500. Perhaps he was hoping to help keep Harbin alive, either by relocating the business or by selling off his new real estate at a profit. At any rate, he and his bride, Ruby (formerly a secretary in the Harbin office) held on to the land for a little more than six months before selling it to Paul Stuparich for $10 (and, presumably, "other considerations").[25]

The Stuparich family began building on their property in 1913. Paul lived with his wife Emily and their daughters Helen and Rena in a house in the North Beach section of San Francisco, using his Lake County land as a summer home; Stephen lived year-round in a house in Middletown. Once a private residence was built, the Stupariches began construction of the hotel and guest buildings, excavated much of the wooded hillside, and drilled a well to provide more water for the resort.

For three or four years, as construction slowly progressed, Paul continued to live in the city, commuting up to the country occasionally to supervise the building; the bulk of the construction was overseen by his brother Steve. (Local residents remember both brothers as being "kind of odd characters.") Paul spent time each summer in Lake County, with his wife and younger daughter joining him for several weeks during the season. In 1918, the family began spending the entire summer on their "ranch."

Paul was 57 when the doors of the Stuparich Resort finally opened to the public in 1922. Billing itself as "a modern place in a wondrous locality," the resort had the seal of approval as an "official hotel" of the California State Automobile Association, and was affiliated with American Express, Thomas Cook and

---

25 Eddie Hays moved out of the area soon after the sale. In 1927, an article in the Lake County paper (referring to a lawsuit he had filed against the San Francisco Board of Supervisors over an accident involving a captive bear in Golden Gate Park) had him living in Stockton with his stepson, Richard Harvey Polinghorne, aka Percy Hays. Eddie died in St. Helena in 1960, at the age of 71.

FIGURE 5

Later Land Acquisitions (1893-1924)

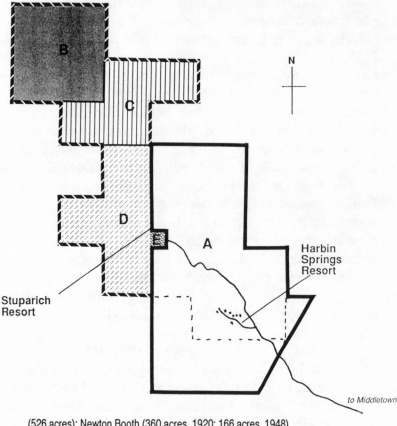

A	(526 acres): Newton Booth (360 acres, 1920; 166 acres, 1948)
B	(160 acres): Pierre Somps grant from U.S. (1895)
C	(160 acres): Henry Boggs to Somps (1893)
B & C	(320 acres): Somps to Fenton (1901); to Hickmott (1903); to Wulf (1919); to Clark (1924); to Stuparich (1924)
D	(160 acres): J.C. Mottier, posthumous grant from U.S. (1909)
E	(4 acres): J.C. Mottier from J. Hays, 1888
D & E	(164 acres): Mottier estate to E.W. Hays (1911); to Stuparich (1911)
———	Harbin property line (1924)
▬▬▬	Stuparich property line (1924)

other major travel agencies, who booked vacations for city dwellers.

Stuparich had designed the buildings himself, along fairly modern lines. Most of the resorts in the southern part of the county that were still operating in the late '20s were remodels of Victorian spas; Stuparich's Resort was brand new from cabin to plunge, and was considered very "artistic" by local critics. It was a posh place, in many ways more elegant and elaborate than Harbin.

Harbin guests and staff enjoyed walking around the mountain to Stuparich on warm summer evenings, although one waitress remembers that it didn't have the same feeling of freedom that Harbin did. At the time it was considered more of a "dress for dinner kind of place."

> Accommodations to please the most fastidious guest. We supply "city comforts in the mountains," (rooms with baths, etc.). The cottage idea is used to perfection at the Stuparich Resort, where the comforts and conveniences of a first class hotel are provided, but with the added advantages of separate "bungalettes" or summer cottages.
>
> Meals are served in the large central Dining Room. All buildings as well as the grounds are lighted by electricity. Comfort and cleanliness are ever kept in mind. The furnishings at this first class resort are finished in ivory enamel and the beds are the most comfortable money can buy. Everything is new and inviting.

The Stuparich Resort was about a mile north of Harbin, on a continuation of the Harbin Springs Road, which paralleled the creek. The entrance to Stuparich's was marked with two elaborate fountains, past which was a narrow lane with a row of a dozen one and two room cabins. On the right side of the lane, overlooking the small creek which ran the length of the resort, was a large building housing the dance pavilion, surrounded by the elaborate decks, trellises and porticos that enclosed the cold swimming plunge.

Above the cold plunge, at the far end of the lane, was the dining room, social hall and main hotel building, which faced the Main Plaza of the resort. Surrounded by cabins, the hotel, and the Turkish baths, it was a flat area of hard-packed dirt where guests could park their square, black Fords, Reos and Hupmobiles.

On the left side of the Plaza were some of the "bungalettes"—green, lattice-fronted cabins of natural wood, nestled into the hillside, and reached by short, zig-zag flights of steps. On the right were cottages with railed wooden decks; facing the entrance to the Plaza was a large, single-masted wooden ship (bedecked with nautical flags) which housed the resort's ice cream parlor. It served a complete line of soda fountain items and soft drinks, very much in keeping with the novelty architecture of roadside refreshment stands in the 20s.

The heart of the Plaza area was the main hotel building, a long, low natural wood building that had a lattice-covered porch with wicker chairs and rockers facing a flower garden with a fountain at its center.[26] Across the Plaza in front of the garden and next to the Ship was the building that housed the baths.

Although any functioning hot springs at the site are minimal today, in the early 20s the resort did offer hot baths in a charming building. A long flight of steps led up to the entrance of the pseudo-Moorish structure, which stopped just short of minarets and instead had columns topped with the crescent and star of the Turkish flag.

> Turkish baths in charge of competent attendants. Hot plunge, steam room, electric and massage rooms add to the completeness of this important department.[27]

Guests could walk down a flight of stairs from the hotel garden to the large white concrete swimming plunge (still used occasionally by current Harbin residents), which was fed by cold spring water and situated in an open area that offered the

---

26 The fountain is still there, in a tangle of blackberry bushes and the remains of some stone foundations, just off the road at the end of the Village.

27 For a period in the '20s there was a health fad involving the use of small amounts of electrical current, thought to cure many problems, especially those involving the nerves. "Turkish baths" usually indicated a series of steam rooms of increasing temperature, followed by a rubdown, a massage and a cold shower.

Swimming
pool, Stuparich
Resort. (Now
the "Village
Pool.")

Main Hotel
building and
garden,
Stuparich
Resort.

Fountain in center
is still visible
at the end of the
Village.

"On the Plaza"
at Stuparich.
One of the
bungalettes is
at the left. Far
left, just visible,
are the flags of
the ship ice
cream parlor.

swimmer plenty of sunshine. The Stuparich Resort was open only during the summer season, and its advertising definitely appealed to the Bay Area traveler.

> Climate is dry and delightful—no fog at Stuparich's! A complete change is offered to those residing in the coast climate.

The season of 1923 opened on May 19th and closed October 1st. A price list from that summer shows that the hotel rooms and "bungalettes" could accommodate a guest population of 85; rooms were all offered on the American Plan. Rates included the room, all meals, use of the baths, use of the garage, dancing, games and other amusements.

Rates for the 1923 season ranged from $4.50 a day or $25.00 a week (for a room with hot and cold running water and an adjoining toilet) to $5.75 a day or $38.00 a week for a private cottage with running water, a toilet and a shower. In between the cheapest and most deluxe accommodations, guests could select from a room with private toilet ($28 per week), a one or two room suite with a

Turkish Bath building at Stuparich

screened sleeping porch ($33 per week), a two-room cottage with a bathtub ($35 per week) or a one-room bungalow with a shower ($35 a week).

Plumbing was an important selling point in the Stuparich literature. All the rooms had cold running spring water; many had hot water as well. The more expensive rooms came with a tub or shower and, while many of the rooms had a toilet adjoining, the suites and deluxe cottages had that sanitary feature that distinguished the hotels of the 20th century from their predecessors—the private toilet. Curiously, the brochure that Stuparich published goes on to boast that "no expense has been spared to make the plumbing at the Stuparich Resort a distinctly different feature."

This fascination with plumbing extended to the dining room:

> The only dining room in the world with running ice water piped to every table. This unique feature is a complete success and is the invention of Mr. Paul J. Stuparich, the designer, builder and owner of this picturesque property.

Old-timers who visited the resort more than 60 years ago fondly remember the little spigots at each table from which they could have all the ice water they wanted in the heat of the summer, without ever summoning the waiter.

Ice water was not the only attraction of the dining room at Stuparich's. It was widely known for its wonderful meals, prepared by a European-trained chef, who had worked for Stuparich at his Miramar Café in San Francisco.

> Meals are the most important feature at our hostelry. The table is our chief concern, and the favorable reports which guests have spread during the past seasons have placed us foremost on the list of Desirable Resorts.

Interior of the Dining Room, Stuparich Resort

The Stupariches had spent nearly ten years developing their resort and, although it was never one of the most prominent places in the county, it was popular, and was acclaimed for its modern facilities. But it appears that the revenues generated four and a half months out of the year were not enough to offset the cost of constructing the picturesque buildings, and the resort wasn't open for very long.

On June 2, 1926, after only three full seasons of operation, Paul and Emily Stuparich sold their Lake County land to a man named Victor Klinker. The local papers reported that the sale was made to Herbert Fleishhacker, the San Francisco millionaire, but the deed recorded with the county is in Klinker's name. In fact, Klinker was the senior vice president of the Anglo and London Paris National Bank, a financial institution run by Fleishhacker. The Fleishhacker interests bought the resort from Stuparich for $10 and held the title to the property for a year and a half before selling the land to Joseph and Helen Greenbach, for the same $10. (According to the deed, the sale mentioned below as Stuparich to Greenbach was actually between Klinker and Greenbach; the bank had held the title to the property for Stuparich as a business go-between.)

STUPARICH'S SOLD TO J. GREENBACH

One of the most important realty deals consummated in the Middletown district for some time was the sale of Stuparich's Resort by Paul Stuparich to Joseph Greenbach of San Francisco, prominent builder and owner of much valuable property in the metropolis.

The Stuparich Resort is one of the show places of the Southern section of the county, with its new and modern hotel, 20 well-furnished cottages, bath house, artistic dance hall, gardens, etc.

In this deal, P.J. Stuparich acquires title to the new cooperative apartments building on Broadway between Fillmore and Webster, and the building at Hays and Octavia, which has 16 apartments on the upper floor and the French-American bank occupying the lower floor.

The results of this transaction? Paul Stuparich traded his Lake County holdings for some prime Pacific Heights real estate, the Fleishhacker interests acquired the bank building and Joseph Greenbach bought himself a ready-made resort.[28]

Greenbach apparently intended to continue running the resort as a commercial venture, planning to reopen it for the summer season of 1928. But in February of that year, the following story appeared as a small item on the inner pages of the Lakeport newspaper:

NEGRO SOCIAL CLUB PURCHASES RESORT

The Eureka Club, a Negro social organization, is reported having made arrangements for the purchase of the Stuparich Resort, one of the most attractive summer resorts in the county. According to reports, the club contemplates making extensive improvements. The club undoubtedly intends using the resort as a vacation place for its members.

There is no record of any such sale, nor is it likely that Greenbach would have made this sort of agreement. It appears that someone was trying to set Joseph Greenbach up. Lake County's population was very predominantly white and the Ku Klux Klan, a white supremist organization that began in the South just after the Civil War, was flourishing in California in the late 20s.

Open air meetings of the Klan were occasionally held on Mt. St. Helena, just west of Middletown. According to the local papers, "Whether or not anyone from Lake County joined the organization, no one knows. The Klan don't tell very much," but it is assumed that at least a few local men had an interest in keeping the county white and Christian. They would know that a rumor about Stuparich's Resort being sold to a black group would have serious repercussions for the property owner, who happened to be Jewish. (The Booths accepted no "coloreds" as guests at Harbin as a matter of policy.)

---

28 Paul and Emily Stuparich moved back to San Francisco. Emily died there in 1936, at the age of 63; a few years later, in very poor health, Paul moved in with Stephen, who cared for him until he succumbed to his long illness, in a San Francisco hospital on July 14, 1945, at the age of 80. Steve Stuparich stayed in Middletown until his death in 1959, at the age of 90.

The rumor spread like wildfire through the Middletown area, and was widely believed. Two weeks later, the front page of the same paper blazed with the headline:

NEGRO INVASION AT MIDDLETOWN SAID FALSE RUMOR
New Owner of Stuparich Resort Will Conduct Place As In Past, Claims
All fears of any Negro invasion of the Middletown vicinity have been set at rest through the announcement of Jos. Greenbach....that the South Lake County resort will be run on the same plans that have governed its operation in the past.

For the past several weeks, rumors have been running rather wildly through the county that the resort originally built by Paul Stuparich had been sold to a Negro organization, and that the plans of the purchasers called for making the resort into a country club for its Negro members.

Greenbach, the new owner, states positively that the resort will be open for business again the coming summer on the same lines it has been operated in the past.

On an inside page of the same issue of the paper, a small item noted quietly that on March 8th a large barn at the Stuparich Resort had been destroyed by "a fire of unknown origins."[29]

Greenbach's troubles did not end with the burning of his barn. A month later, Newton Booth sued him for $5000 for illegally diverting water from Harbin Creek for use at the Stuparich Resort. (Two years earlier, Booth had been granted a permit by the State Public Works Department to take 90,000 gallons a day from the creek to irrigate his 11 acres of gardens and to water his livestock.)

In May of 1928, just before the season began, Greenbach and his wife created the Paso Robles Hotel Corporation, and deeded

---

29 The rumor about the sale of the resort had been quite effective—more than 60 years later, local sources still claim it as fact. One man, who was a high school student at the time of the incidents, told me that "They sold it to a bunch of Negroes. Negroes were very unpopular then. One night the KKK, they said it was, burned these fiery crosses all over the hill and the barn burned down. So they didn't get the message, and about a month or so later [*In fact, six months.*] the whole resort went up one night. They claimed some of the other resort people burned it down, but whether they did or not, I don't know."

the land and the resort to it. Greenbach became the president of the corporation that owned the resort, but not, as an individual, the legal owner. He doesn't seem to have ever changed the name of the resort from Stuparich to Paso Robles Hotel, and there is no evidence that he opened the resort to the public that summer.

On October 7, 1928, the Stuparich Resort burned to the ground.

STUPARICH RESORT DESTROYED BY FIRE

Stuparich's summer resort was visited by fire of unknown origin at 5:00 Sunday morning, totally destroying the hotel, private residence and nearby cottages. The dance hall and several distant cottages were saved. Volunteer fire fighters rushed to the scene from Harbin Springs and Middletown, but the blaze had gained such headway that efforts to save the property were futile. The fire is believed to have originated in the power house....The property is reported to be covered by $40,000 insurance.

The true cause of the disastrous fire will probably never be known. It is possible that it was just an accident, one of dozens of Lake County resorts to burn at the end of long, dry summers. Or it may have been deliberately set, whether because of racial tensions, as alleged the previous spring, or because of a disagreement between Greenbach and parties unknown.

Joseph Greenbach was prepared to use the insurance money to rebuild, and hired former owner Paul Stuparich as the architect and planner for the new construction. In the summer of 1929, both PG&E and the telephone company were granted rights of way through the property to extend public utility lines to the resort. That summer Greenbach also won the suit with Booth, and acquired the right to divert Harbin Creek water.

But despite these events in Greenbach's favor, the resort never reopened. Perhaps the stock market failure in October of 1929, which sent the country into the Depression, affected his financial situation. Four months after the crash, in February of 1930, he sold all his land (along with the water rights) and what was left of the Stuparich Resort to Newt Booth. The purchase brought Booth's total real estate to over 1000 acres. He planned to use the Stuparich property as accommodations for families and long-term visitors.

❖   ❖

THE DEPRESSION DOESN'T SEEM TO HAVE HAD A PARTICULARLY dramatic effect on the operation of Harbin Hot Springs. Newton Booth was in a more fortunate position than many other businessmen; he owned the resort and the land free and clear, and almost all of his investments had been in real property rather than on paper. He continued to keep the resort open year-round throughout the '30s and, while business was steady, there wasn't the surge of growth that there had been during the boom time of the '20s.

He did very little building in the main area of the resort, other than routine repairs and maintenance, with the exception of adding "the finest doubles tennis court in Lake County" (located   just below the entrance, where the lower visitors' parking lot is today) sometime in the early '30s. His only major construction project during the decade came in 1935, when he took out a $10,000 loan in order to renovate the old Stuparich resort, which he renamed the "Harbin Annex."

Although Newton S. Booth arranged the financing for the Annex remodeling, it was his son, Newton G. Booth—Newt Jr.—who supervised the job and managed the Annex once it was completed. Newt Jr. began to take over more and more of the day-to-day operations from his father, who was then in his sixties; Lela Booth continued to manage the dining room and guest facilities.

The main hotel at the Annex was never rebuilt, nor were the fabulous Turkish baths, the Ship ice cream parlor, or many of the other amenities that had made Stuparich a unique resort. But the younger Booth cleared out the debris, leveled and replanted most of the grounds, and repaired and remodeled those cabins which had escaped the flames. The large dance pavilion had been relatively untouched by the fire, and throughout the next two decades it would be used for large dances, parties, and holiday celebrations, gaily lit by colored paper lanterns.

Annex cottages were a 10-minute walk by trail from the Harbin baths, or a ¾ mile drive by car from the Main Hotel. They were designed for small groups who wanted to come up and stay for a few weeks, doing their own housekeeping. For a fraction of the rate for a single room in the Main Hotel, a person could stay with family or friends in a large, screened cottage with a private bath and shower. The standard cottage ($7 per person, per week) offered bedding, cooking utensils, an ice chest and an electric hot plate. The deluxe cottages ($10 per person, per week) featured a small refrigerator and a gas range. The management furnished everything the guests needed for a home away from home, except silverware and towels. Clean bed linens were provided once a week and although meals were not included in the weekly rate (as they were with rooms in the Main Hotel), grocery service with free delivery to the cabins was promised at "a reasonable price."

Guests in the Annex could use the cold, spring-fed pool there, or hike over to the main resort area to enjoy the hot baths, cocktails, dinner in the dining room, etc. The row of cottages provided a cozy retreat for families on vacation, and guests were on their own as much as they chose, rising and eating on their own schedules. This was especially a draw for the families who vacationed at Harbin with young children and for others who didn't want to interrupt their swimming or relaxing by the pool in order to get dressed and go to the hotel for dinner. Most guests cooked their own suppers, going "out" to dinner at the Main Hotel once or twice during their stay. For a week or two they had their own small home in the woods, as one guest wrote home on a postcard of a shady path.

Dear Mom: It's swell here. Peg and I have a great big cabin all to ourselves, and this is the trail we walk over when we go to the Hotel proper. Cabin 7 is our home, we're across the hill in the Annex. Even have a swimming pool at the front of our cabin. This is a big improvement over the Lake.—Helen.

It was not the artistic and modern resort that it had been before the Stuparich fire, but it was quiet and picturesque and away from the city. The Harbin brochure wisely counseled guests that "reservations must be made in advance due to the popularity of these cottages," some of which were booked as much as a year ahead of time. Many people returned season after season, got to know the other guests in the row of cabins, and often planned their vacations so that they could all be together for the same weeks the next summer.

Cottage rentals supplied a steady income each summer, but were not as popular in the off-season, while some hotel rooms were booked year-round. Harbin also continued to offer its services as a convention and conference center, and was one of the more popular sites for local organizations to hold their meetings.

Both Newt Booth and his son were great boosters of Middletown and Lake County, and each belonged to several local fraternal and civic groups, including the Shriners, the Masons, and the Chamber of Commerce. Their special area of interest was recreational sports—hunting and fishing—and they were both very active in sportmen's organizations on the county and the state levels.

Their involvement was for both business and pleasure. The county's primary attraction for visitors was its scenery and recreation, and the resort owners had a vested interest in keeping up with what was going on in the state, as well as lobbying to make sure that any Fish and Game laws that were passed or changed were to their benefit. Owners of many of the larger resorts, including Harbin, also profited from their memberships by hosting the associations' monthly or annual meetings.

The Lake County Associated Sportsmen held many of their annual dinner meetings at Harbin Springs, attended by fishermen and hunters from surrounding towns and members of the State Fish and Game Commission.[30] Their annual meeting in the spring of 1935 featured a surprise guest, Jimmy

---

30 Newton G. Booth was at one time president of the Middletown Rod and Gun Club, and was appointed to the California State Fish and Game Commission late in 1938 by then-governor Frank Merriam. He served a little over a year, and was replaced (along with most of the other commissioners) when a Democratic governor, Culbert Olsen, took over the office from the Republican Merriam in 1940.

Durante, an avid sportsman who was visiting his wife's relatives in Clearlake.

In the fall of that same year, the Associated Sportsmen of California met at Harbin Springs for a two-day meeting attended by over 300 delegates. At an elaborate banquet held on the first evening of the convention, Newt Jr. was elected treasurer of the Association, and Harbin got a lot of favorable local publicity.

In selecting Harbin Springs as the convention headquarters, mem- bers of the Associated Sportsmen and Newton Booth, Jr., in particular, who led the fight for the convention to be held in Lake County, are to be commended for the manner in which the delegates and their friends were taken care of, and the excellent service rendered by the management.

Newton G. Booth, 1940s, in front of Walnut.

Throughout the '30s Harbin Springs was often able to beat out the competition from San Francisco, Santa Cruz and Monterey for Northern California convention business. Harbin was host several times to the Associated Sportsmen, both county and state, and the Northern California Chamber of Commerce; its hotel, guest facilities and dining room developed a state-wide reputation for excellence.

❖ ❖

BOOTH DID EVERYTHING HE COULD TO PUBLICIZE HARBIN AND increase that reputation. When he first reopened the resort in 1912, he had a brochure and some postcards printed to show the improvements that had been made. He continued this practice, taking new photographs and having new materials printed as he completed each major phase of building. One set of black and white photo postcards—showing views of the entrance gate, the Main Hotel, its lobby, the baths and plunge, the renovated croquet grounds, and a successful deer-hunting expedition—was published in 1926, when he finished the remodeling of the Main Hotel.

A second set of postcards was published in 1937. Scenes of Walnut, Azalea, the Harbin Annex, the Dining Room, the Gazebo and the Snack Bar were available in racks in the lobby of the Main Hotel. Then as now, people sent vacation pictures home to friends and family. No brochure's claims could ever be as convincing as a few lines from a friend.

> *Dear Ed and Margaret: Here we are, up at Harbin's and having one grand rest. It is surely lovely. Wish you could take a run up sometime while we are here. If you will let us know, we will have a nice chicken dinner for you. Lovingly—Ma and Pa.*

Many of his guests came up to Harbin because of favorable reviews from their friends and relatives, but Newton Booth benefitted from other forms of publicity as well. In 1939, as part of the tremendous preliminary publicity for the Golden Gate International Exposition—the California World's Fair on Treasure Island—25 "Information Girls" representing the Redwood Empire[31] toured its member counties by Greyhound bus on a "fact finding expedition." Their Lake County destination was Harbin Springs, where they "enjoyed the warm plunge and some of them braved the chilly [February] atmosphere in the out-of-doors plunge."

The Information Girls' job was to visit prominent spots in each county and then to "sell" its attractions to World's Fair visitors. Each of the nine counties had its own booth in the Redwood Empire Building; Lake County's exhibit was an illuminated diorama. A miniature Mt. Konocti rose above a tiny Clear Lake with a scale-model hot springs resort

---

31 The Redwood Empire Association was formed in 1920 to promote tourism along the new Redwood Highway (now Highways 1 and 101) and the scenic, cultural, recreational and business attractions of its nine member counties—San Francisco, Marin, Sonoma, Napa, Lake, Mendocino, Humboldt and Del Norte in California, and Josephine County, Oregon.

(incorporating features of Harbin, Adams, Siegler and other springs) in the foreground. The background lighting of the diorama changed the scene from day to night every three minutes.

The Fair opened in San Francisco Bay in February of 1939, and "Lake County Day" was celebrated there on April 23rd. That morning, at 8:00 am, a caravan of hundreds of Lake County citizens, including the Booths and several members of the Harbin Springs staff, left Middletown to travel to the Fair as honored guests.

The county's booth at the Fair stimulated a lot of interest in Lake County and its resorts for the next few summers, and records show that business was very good at Harbin in the first years of the '40s.

The summer of 1942 was busy, but very different. With the bombing of Pearl Harbor in December of 1941, America entered World War Two and everything changed on the "domestic front." Almost every eligible man enlisted or was drafted into the armed forces, including 37-year old Newton G. Booth, who joined the Navy. The war effort depleted much of the local labor force; some jobs were filled by women and older men, and others were left vacant "for the duration."

Rationing became a fact of life and changed the way Lake County resorts operated. Butter, meat and many other foods were available only with coupons issued by the government. Harbin had been almost self-sufficient at one time, but by the 40s only a few domestic animals and livestock were raised on the property. There was an extensive garden, so the resort was able to provide at least some of the food for its own dining room, but like all other resorts in the county, the menu had to be modified to accommodate what was available. Building was also sharply curtailed, as all materials were allotted to the war effort as a first priority and anything left was on an individual need basis, mostly distributed by government agencies.

The most dramatic change for the tourist industry in the county came from the rationing of tires and gasoline—essential elements in traveling to a fairly remote area not served by a railroad. Strict tire quotas were established for each county; one month Lake County was allotted 8 new tires and 14 retreads, to be distributed among over 8,000 residents. In 1942, the production of automobiles was suspended and nationwide gas rationing went into effect, sharply curtailing the free and easy, spur-of-the-moment traveling that had become the habit of Americans in the preceding decades.

People did not stop vacationing altogether, but the number of overnight and weekend guests dropped sharply. Instead a lot of people, especially women who had husbands in the service, began to use what gas they could get to come to Harbin for several weeks or for "the season" as they had 50 years earlier.

Many industries contributed directly to the war effort, and profited from it, by manufacturing vehicles, weapons, clothing, etc. to be used by the military. The tourist industry could not directly contribute to the war, but was still a vital part of the American economy, and the government encouraged people to get out of the cities and patronize recreation areas, which proved a boon to Lake County's resorts.

Eleanor Roosevelt, in her weekly newspaper column, told Americans that "we have not only a right, but an obligation to take vacations," and people responded, filling Harbin and other resorts in the spring and summer of 1942. A large advertisement in newspapers that spring declared that:

TRAVEL IS POTENT STIMULANT
FOR WAR PRODUCTION, MORALE

It is not only "patriotic to go vacationing" but it is highly essential to the success of the war effort and ultimate victory since relaxation, sports and change of scenery contribute to the health, morale and confidence vitally essential to the winning of any war.

A plea to patriotism during the war years was more effective than any other form of advertising. The summer of 1943 was the most successful season Harbin had ever had; every cabin and room was booked to capacity. Business was booming, but it was also quite a strain on the Booths. Newt Jr., who had been managing most of the business, was off at war, and his parents were nearly 70. They had difficulty in hiring people for the summer; there were few men available and although over the years the majority of their seasonal employees had been housewives, college students and retirees, many of them had found more patriotic (and more lucrative) work in defense plants.

Harbin had always prided itself on being one of the few resorts to stay open year-round, but because of their age and poor health, and the difficulty in hiring staff, the Booths made the decision to close at the end of the summer season. On September 12, 1943, for the first time since Maggie Hays had gone bankrupt in 1910, Harbin Springs closed its doors, with plans to reopen in April or May of 1944.

Four days later, the plans were changed, abruptly and dramatically.

❖   ❖

AT TEN O'CLOCK ON THURSDAY NIGHT, SEPTEMBER 16, NEWT Booth looked out of his living room window and saw flames coming out of the west end of the Main Hotel. Within an hour the building, containing the office, lounge, dining room, kitchen, and service quarters, had burned to the ground. The Middletown Volunteer Fire Department and the State Fire Suppression Crew responded to Booth's call for help almost immediately; while they could do nothing to save the hotel, they were able to stop the fire from spreading to other buildings.

A small cabin used for linen storage was destroyed, along with over $2000 worth of blankets,[32] sheets and towels, but the guest cottages and other buildings were spared. The building housing the bar and cocktail room caught fire several times, but each time the flames were extinguished and it suffered only external damage. The baths and the other hotel buildings were not affected by the blaze.

---

32 Harbin blankets were wool in the winter and cotton in the summer. Each was white with a green stripe and "Harbin Springs" embroidered in green script along one edge.

Fortunately, because the resort had closed the weekend before, no guests were in residence and there were no injuries. But the Main Hotel and all its contents were gone, and damage was estimated at over $75,000; insurance covered only a portion of the loss.

If tourism was Lake County's greatest asset, fire was its major liability. Bartlett Springs burned in 1934, and was never reopened as a resort. A fire at Laurel Dell resort closed it in 1942. Adams Springs, one of the largest and most prominent resorts in the county was partially destroyed by a blaze in July of 1943, and burned again in July of 1954. Highland Springs burned to the ground in 1945. Several other smaller resorts were ruined by fire over the years. None of them is open as a resort today.[33]

Harbin was not completely destroyed; if more buildings had been burned it seems likely that its story would end with "closed in 1943." But as Jim Hays had done 50 years before, Newton Booth decided to try to rebuild and reopen.

In January of 1944, he announced that he would attempt to open for business that summer. He planned to remodel the bar into a temporary dining room and kitchen, and house the few remaining staff members in the other hotel buildings until a new Main Hotel could be built. But there was a war on, materials were scarce, and labor scarcer.

> Priorities to rebuild the destroyed structure have been obtained by Booth from the government, but so far he has been unable to secure the needed labor for the construction work. The remodeling plan will not require the amount of labor a new structure would, and Booth is hopeful of obtaining the labor.

Booth may have been hopeful, but the labor was simply not available that year.

It's not clear just how long Harbin remained closed. It was closed for the summer of 1944, and opened for part of the season of 1945 on a limited basis. Booth made what

---

33 Bartlett's is now a bottling works; Adams is a golf course and housing development; many others have been developed or bulldozed over and are gone.

improvements he could during the war; a brief notice in the Middletown newspaper in July of 1945 stated that the largest reach-in refrigerator in Lake County had been installed at the "newly opened" Harbin Springs.

After the war ended, although the new hotel wasn't completed, Harbin was again the site for many local business meetings. February of 1946 was an especially busy month—the Lake County Peace Officers Association (with guest FBI agents), the county Chamber of Commerce and the Northern California Game Wardens all met in "newly erected buildings." In its publicity, the Lake County Chamber of Commerce urged its members to support the recovering resort.

Newt Jr. had returned home from the war with an injured back, but once again joined his parents in managing and rebuilding the resort, and Harbin Springs was up and running for the summer of 1946. That fall Newt Sr. took out $55,000 in loans and they proceeded to finish replacing the Main Hotel.

For the third time, the rectangular plot on the west side of Harbin's canyon was the construction site for a large, white hotel building. This third hotel was remarkably similar to its immediate predecessor. Each was a long, narrow, two-story building with a wide first floor porch and a railed second floor balcony overlooking the Gazebo. The major changes in the hotel built in the late '40s were four windowed gables on the roof, a deeper porch area, and a small flight of stone steps leading up to the lobby door.

Except for these few details, it is easy to mistake the two buildings in photographs (the vintages of the cars parked in front of each hotel are the most striking clues that the year has changed) and without knowledge of the

Booth family and friends in the ruins of the Main Hotel, 1943.

1943 fire, it would be easy to conclude that the old hotel had just undergone some exterior remodeling.

It appears that Newt Booth took advantage of the materials, labor and money available that winter and leveled a portion of the western hillside to build the 14-room Fern Building. Designed to provide lodging for people who wanted rooms close to the baths, but not directly overlooking them, the building was constructed on the same general plan as Walnut and Azalea. Its lower floor was level with (and perpendicular to) the second floor of the Capitol/Main Annex building; a flight of stairs at its northern end led directly to the changing rooms and the baths.

Some of the former guest cabins were saved and used as housing for the people who worked at the Springs. Most of the maids were college-aged girls working on their summer vacations, and they lived in the old *Del Monte* cabin, just below Azalea. Many of the staff lived in Middletown and simply went home each night.

❖   ❖

THE NEW HOTEL AND DINING ROOM WERE COMPLETED IN THE spring of 1947, and Harbin business returned to its pre-war prosperity. That year, Booth had another opportunity to increase his real estate holdings, with the purchase of a small parcel of land adjacent to the resort.

When Jim Hays died in 1909, the only Harbin land that he had not already sold to Margaret Mathews was the irregularly-shaped 166-acre parcel that Maggie inherited from her step-mother, Annie Williams.[34] After Jim's death, Maggie

---

34 Herbert V. Keeling, Maggie's attorney, bought the acreage at auction in 1912. A dispute with Dorothy Williams Blessing (Richard Williams Jr.'s widow) over the property was finally settled in 1920, at which point Keeling sold it to W.S. George and Robert Harkinson for the standard $10 in gold. Harkinson died in 1925 and left his half of the parcel to his daughter, Maude Roberts. W.S. George died in 1927, leaving his half to his daughter, Alice Marie, who promptly sold her share to Maude for $10. Maude Roberts held on to the land for 20 years, finally selling it to Newt Booth in 1947 "for value received."

sold the section of land, along with some mining property that Jim had owned, in order to help pay off his creditors.

This piece of land passed from hand to hand over the years, finally coming to Booth in 1947 and bringing the total area of the resort to almost 1200 acres. At the time of Jim Hays' death the parcel had been listed in the probate files as "improved with the addition of a Club House," but it's not clear whether the structure was still standing (or usable) when Booth bought the land.

❖   ❖

HARBIN QUICKLY REGAINED ITS POPULARITY AS A FAVORITE vacation spot, and its parking lot was full of cars sporting bumper stickers that proclaimed "Harbin Springs: It's the Water." A few of the cars belonged to celebrities who knew the Booths—Robert Stack was a Navy buddy of Newt Jr., and entertainers Aldo Ray and Sophie Tucker were also visitors in the late '40s.

Year after year, people returned to this familiar spot. Several people, (now in their late fifties) have shared their childhood memories of coming up to Harbin with their families. For those staying in one of the hotels or in a cottage on Mainside, the day began with breakfast in the hotel dining room. One man described the menu as "everything you could think of—from ham and eggs to fruit and waffles."

Everyone gathered at breakfast to discuss their plans for the day: men mapped out hunting or fishing expeditions; kids headed for the swimming pool or to the stables[35] for horseback riding, with promises to be back in time for lunch, and begged for a few nickels to play the slot machines or the punchboards at the snack bar;[36] the women may have chosen to read by the pool in the morning and then, after a hot luncheon of chicken or

---

35 Horses hadn't been used for transportation for 40 years, but the big three-story barn just above the tennis courts (the lower visitors' parking lot) housed about 20 horses used on trail rides around the property.

36 The slot machines were removed around 1948, when large-scale gambling raids occurred at the resorts on Clear Lake.

veal cutlets, to rest in their rooms or play a few rubbers of bridge or a game of canasta at the circle of tables in the shade of the Gazebo.

And, of course, there were the baths. People mostly bathed for relaxation and because it was "good for you" rather than for any specific medical problems. (Postwar "miracle drugs" had replaced mineral water as a cure-all.) One guest sent home a postcard of the bath house in August of 1948 and commented:

Dear Hainsey: The baths are so hot they parboil one! What a heat. Very nice place but very hot.—Ethel.

Although parboiling was unlikely, a nurse was on staff during the summer months for cases of poison oak, sunburn, splinters and other vacation-related maladies, as well as for the benefit of any invalid and elderly guests. Her office was in a white two-story building next to the baths, along with a few amenities like a barber shop and a room where therapeutic massages were administered.[37] In 1950, a beauty shop was opened, serving the ladies of Middletown as well as their vacationing counterparts. A few years later the Pine (Shiatsu) Building was fitted out with some exercise bicycles and served as an exercise room.

The "back to nature" folks staying at the resort could go up to one of two green wooden structures on the hill behind Azalea and sunbathe in the nude, if they chose (*see photo, page 192*). The buildings, one for men, one for women, were designed to provide a maximum of privacy, for both the sunbathers and the other guests. The wall at the back of the structure, where the door opened onto the trail, was about ten feet high. There was no roof inside and the wall sloped down to about six feet in the front, where it was screened to provide a view of the main area.

The end of a day in the sun, in the water, or on the trails came at about five in the afternoon, when a woman named Sadie and "an old guy named Willie," would go up to the pools

---

37 This building has been remodeled and today houses dressing rooms, bathrooms and showers downstairs and a large community kitchen upstairs.

and lead the guests down to the main area, around the Gazebo and into the bar in what has been described as a Conga line orchestrated by accordion and banjo. The bar (and snack bar) was in the front of the building next to the Booth's home; the back was an open deck where dances and dance contests were held.

Supper was usually in the Hotel Dining Room, but on some nights barbecues and picnic suppers were held on a flat rise just before the main gate (today the upper visitors' parking lot). The area had a large stone barbecue and picnic tables, and in the evenings was lit by a string of colored lights and paper lanterns.

After supper many people sat on the porch of the hotel until twilight, played shuffleboard in the cooler evening air, or went to the mahogany-paneled Game Room next to the Dining Room for gin or canasta. Others retired to their rooms or danced on the deck overlooking the moonlit gardens, to the music of Wendy, the organ player.

Sometimes as many as 60 people gathered around the Gazebo for sing-alongs with Willie and Sadie, reminiscing with pre-war songs like "Bell Bottom Trousers" as their voices and

Club house, containing the bar and cocktail lounge, dance floor and snack bar, 1930s. (Note gas pump, just behind truck—it's still standing, near the entrance to Harbin's Theatre.)

the accompaniment of Sadie's accordion floated out over the resort.

Several nights a week Bingo games or other special events were held in the Game Room. Once in a while, on a very hot night, someone would hose "the yard," to keep the dust down, and bring out all the chairs from the Game Room. They were lined up next to the Gazebo, facing the porch of the hotel, where a large movie screen was set up. The projector sat on a table in the midst of the chairs and, as the whirring of the reels drowned out the sound of the night breezes and the crickets, guests were treated to the Harbin Drive-in (or sit-in) Theatre.

It was a very pleasant place for a vacation, and very low-key. Unfortunately, this calm, relaxing atmosphere led to a gradual decline in business as America moved into the '50s. Post-war culture was bright and energetic and, as in the '20s, everything had to be *modern*.

❖   ❖

MOTELS AND RESORTS IN GENERAL HAD SUFFERED FROM automobile-related rationing, and after the war they boomed; the number of such businesses doubled in the decade following the war. The majority of pre-war resorts had been "mom and pop" businesses, and most of them lacked the financial reserves or management skills needed to compete with corporate chains like Best Western and Holiday Inn, who offered "more than the comforts of home" near every major recreational area in the country.

Americans wanted to relax on their vacations, but most of them also wanted to *do* something. Resorts dealt primarily in amusement, and places that offered miniature golf or boardwalks alongside their swimming pools and modern hotel rooms were increasingly more of a draw to families than a quiet hot springs with quaint wooden buildings.

Between 1949 and 1954 Newt Booth had to take out more than $38,000 in loans, some of it for maintenance and repair, and some of it just to keep the resort open. Harbin was still a popular *local* resort, but the number of guests declined, as improved air travel opened Europe and Hawaii to the casual

The Gazebo and the front porch of the Main Hotel
on a busy summer afternoon in the late 1930s.

tourist, and places like Disneyland, which opened in 1955, catered to families.

New business was minimal, and even the regular clientele had dwindled. A lot of the young people who had "motored" to Harbin in the early 1920s had continued to patronize the resort, but had aged along with it. Some had become too elderly to travel; others moved on because their children and grandchildren wanted to go someplace more exciting. The pace at Harbin was a bit slow.

> On the broad verandas of the white frame buildings at Harbin Springs, dozens of middle-aged and elderly folks sit in rocking chairs in the evenings and talk contentedly of how the sulphur baths have eased their aches and pains, and do you remember the long twilight back in Peoria?...

Just as the Victorian spa cure had fallen out of vogue half a century before, vacationing at a hot springs lost popularity with any but senior citizens. Those who did come to Harbin again came as much for the benefits of the water as for the resort activities. A 1952 pamphlet, published by the League for the Development of California's Mineral Springs, noted that:

The one type of vacation that is most beneficial for those who have reached middle age and beyond is that offered by our curative mineral springs....The climate, altitude and wholesome routine in equal proportions give needed rest and relaxation that can only be found at this type of resort.

But it appeared that, even among the senior population, more people wanted their vacations with diversions than without them.

Newton Booth was 80 in 1956. As his health failed, Lela had taken over the management of their finances as well as the kitchen and the hotel. Newt Jr. was 52 and had five children to support. The family had invested their whole lives and most of their assets into Harbin Springs, but it seemed that the time of the old-style resorts was coming to an end. Many Lake County resorts which survived the Depression, the fires, and the war succumbed to changing times in the late '50s. One source said he'd stopped at a gas station in Nice, on Clear Lake, and asked the operator:

"What happened to all the health resorts in Lake County?"
"All the health resorts closed down," was the reply. "Everybody who went to them got old and died. Now people want fun resorts."

Harbin Springs didn't close down, but the Booth family finally made the painful decision that they could no longer afford the money and the energy it was taking to keep the resort open themselves.

On May 15, 1957, after 45 years of management,

Lela and Newton S. Booth at their fiftieth wedding anniversary party, mid-1950s.

Newton and Lela Booth sold Harbin Hot Springs to Robert J. Ramsey, an Oakland hotel owner, for $176,000. A gala farewell party was held at the Springs.

BOOTHS WERE HONORED ON MONDAY NIGHT

Starting with a caravan from town, residents of Middletown went to Harbin Springs on Monday evening to honor Mr. and Mrs. Newton S. Booth and Mr. and Mrs. Newton G. Booth with a farewell party....Potluck refreshments being provided by many local residents and a buffet arrangement at the resort.

Later in the evening, Assessor Jim Tichin acted as Master of Ceremonies and called upon many of the old-time residents who have been close friends and associates of the Booths for 45 years. All of the resorts in the area were represented and extended good wishes. In all about 150 were present to extend good wishes for their retirement from the resort business and every happiness in their new plans.

Because of their poor health, the senior Booths opted to live in St. Helena, to be near doctors and the hospital. In August of 1957 they moved to that Napa Valley town and settled in their "first real home in nearly 50 years."

For them, and for Harbin, it was the end of an era.

CHAPTER SEVEN

Failed Dreams

IN THE SUMMER OF 1957, THE HARBIN SPRINGS THAT PEOPLE had visited for 100 years slowly began to disappear. When the ownership passed from Richard Williams to Jim Hays and from Maggie Hays to Newt Booth, there had been a sense of continuity. The resort evolved and changed, but each successive manager had built on the efforts of his predecessor.

Robert J. Ramsey was a real estate investor, not the genial host-in-residence that Hays and Booth had been. For him Harbin Springs was an investment, another in a series of properties he had spent his life buying and selling.

He was born in Napa in 1898 and earned his living as a peach farmer after graduating from college. In the '30s he moved to Oakland and got his real estate license, opening an office downtown at 14th and Broadway. Within a few years he expanded his business to include a collection agency, and began investing in property with various partners. In the '40s he was the president or treasurer of several different companies;[1] his very diversified holdings included part ownership in the Oakland City Club and a punch press factory in Richmond.

In 1946 he entered the lodging business when he purchased the Coit Hotel for over half a million dollars—one of the largest real estate deals in Oakland that year. He renamed it the Coit-Ramsey Hotel. Three years later he and his wife Catherine

---

1   The Ramsey Corporation, The East Bay Credit Service, Ramsey-Fairchild Realty (Coit Hotel), RAN Corporation (punch press factory), Western Broadcasting Co. (radio station KWG in Stockton), and Developers Corporation ("engaged in developing a 320-home subdivision at Walnut Creek").

bought the Highlands Inn south of Carmel, a "famed honeymoon hideout." The Oakland *Tribune* article announcing the sale also lists him as the owner of the Hotel Berry in Sacramento, the Hotel Oxford in San Pedro, and part owner of the Palm Springs Pueblo. Ramsey later joked that he began buying hotels "when smart people were selling them."

New Main Hotel, about 1959.

His first foray into Lake County real estate was in 1946 when he and W. Kelly Day, a local entrepreneur, bought out the interest in the Mirabel Quicksilver Mine Co. The mine had closed in 1945 due to a lack of any new mineral discoveries and a big drop in the value of mercury. The papers noted at the time that "quicksilver future [is] not too bright."

It may have been a better tax shelter than a mine, but it got Ramsey a foot in the door of Lake County and an acquaintance with local people and local land potential. He was aware that the health of the senior Booths was failing in the 50s, visited Harbin a number of times, and finally made an offer on the property that they somewhat reluctantly accepted.

Ramsey took out a 15-year mortgage with the Booths for $176,000, buying Harbin Springs lock, stock and barrel. His purchase included over 1000 acres of land; the hotel buildings and all the furnishings in 110 guest rooms, the lobby, bar and dining room; two pick-up trucks; and miscellaneous tools and equipment. For an additional $10,000, he also took over the liquor license. On May 14th, 1957, Harbin was open for business under the Booth's ownership; on May 15th, under Ramsey's.

Robert Ramsey never lived at Harbin. He hired a manager, Douglas Ross, to handle the day-to-day running of the resort, replaced him almost immediately with another manager, and returned to his home in the exclusive suburb of Piedmont. Business at Harbin went on more or less as usual.

> Lake County's Foremost Fun and Pleasure Resort, Same Ownership as Fabulous Highlands Inn, Carmel, and Slender Springs Beauty Lodge.[2] Cocktail Lounge. Live Music. Special Family Rates include three excellent meals by Chef Tierney. Four Swimming Pools. Natural Hot Mineral Plunges. Fishing. Horses. Tennis. Deer Hunting. Call Harbin Springs #1[3]

Obviously health was no longer considered the primary reason to visit Harbin; the baths were well down on the list of attractions. Ramsey tried for a while to operate Harbin as a private membership club with a more vacation-oriented clientele, because that was where the money was in the resort business. No details of this phase are available, but in a 1958 interview, the latest in a string of managers, Jim Johnson, said:

> All is changed at the resort and [I] extend a cordial invitation to all local people to drop in any time and enjoy the facilities of the resort. The club plan is still being operated, but there is always room for guests who are not members.

---

2   The Slender Springs Beauty Lodge appears to have been a separate weight-reduction clinic, managed by a Dr. Lawrence Wing, with facilities located in Harbin's Main Hotel building.

3   Dial telephones came to Middletown on Saturday November 2, 1957, changing the operator-assisted Harbin Springs #1 call to YUkon 7-3193. The local papers noted that "this will bring Middletown within a nationwide numbering plan that eventually will make it possible for people here to dial their own long distance calls...but it will be some time yet before people in Middletown will be able to dial long distance calls to people in other places." People were requested to refrain from placing calls "just to see how it works."

The resort attracted some new guests, but lost many others who had found it a cozy getaway spot under the Booth's management. According to a few sources, when Ramsey took over some of the heart went out of the place, and it was never quite the same.

❖   ❖

HARBIN SPRINGS AND ITS GUESTS WERE THE LEAST OF RAMSEY'S problems in the late 50s. In 1958 the IRS imposed a lien of $19,000 for unpaid employment taxes and social security contributions. The California State Employment Department filed a smaller lien for delinquent payments, and additional judgments were levied against him by other state agencies and private firms. In order to back up his shaky finances and generate some cash, Ramsey took out a series of loans, raising almost $135,000, putting his Harbin Springs property up as collateral each time.

Very little money was going back into the resort—enough to keep it open and make minor repairs, but not enough to make any improvements. Harbin began to deteriorate, bit by bit: the landscaping wasn't done quite as carefully; the hotel service was a little less efficient; a few buildings had paint peeling here and there.

On Thursday, September 17th, 1959, Newton S. Booth died at his daughter Helen Wiggin's home in Orinda. He was 83, and was survived by his wife and daughter, son Newt, and seven grandchildren. He had been the holder of the notes from Ramsey's original Harbin mortgage, which passed on to the family.[4]

Ramsey had owned the property for nearly two and a half years, and had made few payments on the principal, interest or

---

4 Newton S. Booth's estate was settled in December of 1960. Lela received their household goods and family car, along with 1/2 interest in Ramsey's promissory notes, which then totalled $141,000. Newt Jr. and his sister Helen each received 1/4 of the estate, including 1/4 interest in the notes on Harbin.

taxes, but the Booths took no action until after Newt's death. In December of 1959, acting as executrix of Newt's estate, Lela Booth filed for default. Ramsey was ordered to pay off the entire mortgage, or to sell the property in order to satisfy his obligations. He appears to have gotten himself into quite a financial hole.

Ramsey defaulted on three separate notes for over $200,000 and had judgments filed against him for another $15,000,[5] all in the first months of 1960. In September of that year, in order to satisfy his creditors, he was served with a notice to foreclose on Harbin.

Following on the heels of the foreclosure came what appeared to be the final blow—on October 4, 1960, the Lake County Sheriff's Department was ordered to attach all the property at Harbin Springs, and begin the process of closing it.

In an unlikely "coincidence," six days later the Main Hotel was completely destroyed by fire.

MAIN HOTEL GOES DOWN IN FLAMES

By 3:00 a.m. Monday morning on October 10, 1960, the top floor of the Harbin Springs Hotel was one mass of flames! Ten fire trucks on the scene could not prevent the building from burning to the ground.

Fortunately there were only two guests in the hotel, and they were led to safety by hotel receptionist Wanda LaVelle....The fire had downed the phone lines, so Miss LaVelle, without waiting to save any of her belongings, drove the hotel's station wagon to Middletown for help....

In rapid succession five Forestry rigs, four [Middletown Volunteer Fire Department] trucks and one truck from Clearlake Highlands moved in on the fire. No additional help was called because no more trucks could get into the narrow confines of the burning hotel and the buildings opposite.

---

5 Including nearly $5000 filed by the State Labor Department for violations in non-payment of his employees at Harbin Hot Springs.

The firefighters struggled to contain the blaze, but gusting winds blew the flames from the west end of the building to the kitchen and dining room on the east end, and onto another building beyond that housed the bowling alley and gymnasium.[6] They saw that it would be impossible to prevent the destruction of the hotel, and concentrated their efforts on saving the other structures, extinguishing many smaller fires and leaving a few buildings with minor roof damage.

> Fire hoses were pouring water from the pool, Harbin water system and the tanker, which was refilled time and again at Middletown....The maintenance man and his wife, Joe and Mary Coleman, had that afternoon moved into the east end of the hotel. For 20 minutes while the fire tore great holes in the roof and top floor of the building, the Colemans both slept soundly. Only the boom of an exploding oil tank woke them....they made their escape through the window and through burning brush to the safety of the cocktail lounge.

Amazingly, the only people that sustained any injuries during the blaze were two rangers who suffered superficial facial burns.

> Owner Robert Ramsey hastened from his Coit-Ramsey Hotel in Oakland to the fire scene. He expressed his sincere thanks and admiration for the fire fighters confining the fire as they did. He also stated that he fully intends to rebuild and create an even more beautiful resort hotel in that ideally located spot: good news to the thousands who have loved the seclusion and the peaceful charm of Harbin Springs.

❖ ❖

SIXTY-SIX YEARS AFTER ITS FIRST FIRE, THE HARBIN SPRINGS HOTEL once again lay in ashes. But this time there would be no phoenix. The hotel has never been rebuilt. Today the site is a wide lawn where volleyball games are played. The only

---

6 Yes, this was Jim Hays' gym building. The Booths had used the bowling alley, but the top floor had been primarily for storage. Ramsey's managers restored the gym to its original function, probably for the use of Slender Springs Lodge patrons.

evidence that hotel buildings had stood there for nearly a century are remnants of a concrete foundation in the hillside and five wide cement steps that once led to a front porch where men in straw hats and ladies in summer dresses sat in a row of wicker rocking chairs.

There is no evidence that the fire was deliberately set; none of the newspaper accounts mention any cause at all. There is also no indication that anyone at the time was aware of Ramsey's financial situation, or of the attachment order on the property. It was, perhaps, just a very convenient fire for Mr. Ramsey. Damages were estimated at over $150,000, and he collected an unspecified amount of insurance, which enabled him to keep the damaged resort open.

Faced with several thousand dollars in additional judgments against him and his companies in 1961 (primarily by the Labor Department and state tax agencies), Ramsey began to restructure his empire, trading the Coit-Ramsey Hotel for a block of apartment buildings in Stockton valued at $650,000. In a more mundane fund-raiser he (and yet another new manager) had a fire sale.

HARBIN SPRINGS SELLIN' THINGS

Harbin Springs Resort's big rebuilding program gets underway this weekend with an open yard sale of salvage from the hotel fire. All types of pipes, fittings, etc. will go fast and cheap. On display will be the plans for the big, beautiful building to be erected. Plumbing, brick, soil pipe—if you need building materials, here's the chance to get them cheap.

His nickel and dime event may have raised a little capital, but not enough to finance what he seems to have been planning.

A few months after the fire, Ramsey had a professional appraiser come in and evaluate both the damage to the property and its potential.

The resort's inventory in 1961 included: four large structures with hotel rooms, all in good condition, although not modernized (Fern, Capitol, Walnut and Azalea); an office building containing the resort office, lobby, manager's quarters and dining room (Stonefront) and a Western-character tavern with a good view of the valley. Fifteen cottages on Mainside and in the Annex, along with the pool buildings and bath-house were listed as having "little or no value."

The appraiser called for a new tennis court, a fountain and a miniature golf course as costly but necessary improvements if the property was to continue as a resort. He recommended that the "highest and best use" of the land would be to build a 9-hole golf course, and have the baths serve as a recreation center for the 500 to 800 single-family homes to be constructed on Mainside, in the Meadow and in the hills.[7]

With a large housing development in mind, the resort buildings and land were appraised at $1.2 million in November of 1961. Whatever future plans for the development or potential sale of Harbin land Ramsey had, he was keeping them to himself. Publicly, he claimed that he was going to rebuild the old hotel, and restore the resort to its pre-fire charm. He had plans drawn up and prominently displayed at Harbin, and made sure that the public was reminded periodically of the pathos of the fire and the hope of beginning anew.

> At the east end of the Main Hotel Building lay a little garden plot between the hotel and the shed....to the rear of the plot was a shrine of St. Francis of Assisi. The shed burned, the hotel burned and the statue was intact but smoky, while the redwood shrine was charred an inch deep....It will be placed in the Garden Court of the new hotel, to be built soon.

In May of 1961 Ramsey announced the opening of a new kitchen and "view dining room," under the supervision of yet another new manager, Art Broughton. The new restaurant was in the lower level of Stonefront (next door to the cocktail lounge building), and overlooked the garden. It was also air-conditioned, a first for Harbin and the only modernization Ramsey seems to have completed. (A newspaper ad in August of that year also noted that a "Pitch and Putt" golf course was

---

7   Obviously, such a development was never completed on the Harbin site, but Ramsey's appraiser's recommendation is quite similar to a development that *was* built outside of Middletown in 1968, on the site of the old Hartmann Ranch—Hidden Valley.

nearing completion, but it was never finished and where it was to have been remains unknown.) The ad also emphasized the joys of *outdoor* dining: barbecues, picnics and breakfast rides—the new facilities weren't as spacious as the old hotel dining room.

Ramsey advertised extensively in 1961, with ads in the major Bay Area papers as well as the local press. A new brochure would have been welcome, but expensive; in its place he sent out press releases—single sheet typewritten pages and price lists—extolling the merits of Harbin.

By this time, Harbin Hot Springs was an older resort, a little run-down, with a charred patch of ground where its Main Hotel had been. Ramsey creatively publicized what was left:

> Harbin Springs is reminiscent of Early California both in its primitive appeal and hospitality. An unforgettable vacation land, rich in history, and famous for its natural beauty—the majestic mountains and inspiring hill formations that roll gently down to the valley that embraces this popular resort.

*Swimming pool, with changing rooms at far end, Main Annex
(now Redwood deck) to left, early 1960s.*

Such romantic hyperbole sounds more like Richard Williams at the end of the Civil War than most advertising in the first years of the Space Age. But the prices were decidedly modern. Hotel rooms on the American Plan, which included all meals, were $25 per night or $152.50 per week (double occupancy); cottages were $25 a night or $160.50 a week. People who wanted to stay in the Housekeeping Cottages in the charmingly named "Western Town" (formerly the Annex) paid only $50 a week, but had to provide their own linens, bedding, kitchenware and food.

In 1959 it was "Lake County's Foremost Fun and Pleasure Resort;" in 1961 it became a resort for "Health, Relaxation and Pleasure." In the hopes that people whose main concern was health would not notice the lack of luxury, Ramsey's ads lauded the mineral baths, which were again "world-renowned, and whose Curative Powers have been recognized for over a century." To hedge his bets, he also noted that Harbin was only 20 minutes from the nearest golf course, and would soon have one of its own.

Charming advertising, quaint names and a mythical golf course were not enough. Despite his efforts, business at the resort was way down, and the rest of Ramsey's investments don't appear to have been in much better shape. Additional liens and judgments were filed against him almost monthly. He needed to sell Harbin, hopefully to a developer that would pay for the land's potential value, rather than for what it was worth as an old-fashioned resort.

So he discovered gold. Or at least filed a claim. In June and July of 1961 he filed notices of "Location of Quartz Carrying Copper, Silver and Gold,"[8] duly notarized by Oakland attorney Patricia Smith (who was also Ramsey's new wife).

It seems highly unlikely that there was any gold; Ramsey wanted to increase the appraised value of the land, with an eye to selling it as soon as possible. A month after he filed the

---

8   The exact locations of Ramsey's "discoveries" are listed in the Lake County courthouse, on pages 219-224 of Book 353.

mining claim, Lela Booth again filed a notice of default on his notes, and he was sued by the State of California, the local lumber company and the laundry that handled the hotel's sheets and table linens—all for non-payment of debts.

In May of 1962, the property was put up for public auction. The Booth family was the highest bidder, and regained ownership for $75,000. Robert Ramsey and his wife moved to their Highlands Inn; the Inn was quite successful and Ramsey was a prominent figure in Carmel's humanitarian and charitable organizations until his death in 1978.

❖   ❖

A SMALL NOTICE IN THE *TIMES-STAR* REMARKED THAT LELA Booth and her daughter Helen spent several weeks at Harbin in June of 1962, presumably cleaning the place up and checking out what needed to be done.[9] Harbin seems to have been open that summer; the article goes on to say that "there are still many, many buildings with plenty of room for vacationers—and you just can't beat those wonderful mineral baths!"

The Booth family couldn't keep the resort open year-round. It was too big a job, especially with the fire damage and general deterioration. The family held onto the property for about nine months after the auction, and then in March of 1963 sold it to an East Bay developer named Maurice Abend, for $163,000.

Very little is known about Maurice Abend. He, too was a real estate agent, and an acquaintance of Ramsey's, which is probably where he heard about Harbin. He borrowed $153,000 from Sandy Estates Company, a group of San Francisco real estate investors, and $40,000 from Ramsey's former partner, W. Kelly Day, in order to make the purchase.

---

9   Newton Jr., his wife Jane and their four daughters—Pam, Linda, and the twins Penny and Patty—had moved to Napa some time after the senior Booths moved to St. Helena. Newton G. Booth didn't return to the management of Harbin. He worked as a nursing assistant in the Veteran's Home in Yountville, retiring in 1973. For some years he lived at Smith's Trout Farm, on Western Mine Road, outside of Middletown. He died in 1981, at the age of 77.

Harbin was not open during the summer of 1963. Abend had plans for completely revamping the resort including, for the first time in Harbin's history, changing the name. He christened it "The Golden Spa."

He filed a preliminary development plan with the county that was quite similar to Ramsey's "highest and best use" appraisal: more than six hundred A-frame summer cabins in the Meadow and on the gentler slopes of the hills northwest of the main area; a nine-hole golf course on 28 acres along Harbin Creek; and a five-acre lake for recreation and water storage. In the main area he planned to build a new gymnasium, a sauna, game room and a large pavilion.

He may have vacillated on the name change somewhat (although "Harbin Hot Springs" doesn't seem to have been in the running)—an article in the *Times Star* in May of 1964 stated:

> Complete with six sauna baths, what used to be Harbin Hot Springs is now in the process of becoming "Clear Lake Spa," though it is just outside of Middletown a few miles off Big Canyon Road. Lots of signs to show where 500 homesites on a 1,000 acre development is programmed by the Clear Lake Spa firm.

Maybe the preliminary plan didn't make it through final county approval, or maybe Abend couldn't get enough working capital to get the development off the ground. At any rate, in July of 1964, he took on a business partner, San Francisco marketing and public relations executive Art Blum, to concentrate on turning Harbin into a luxury resort.[10]

The Harbin plan for 1964 was to create a spa—The Golden Spa—modeled after the posh and profitable Golden Door in Southern California.

The Golden Door, formerly an Escondido motel, was one of America's most exclusive, and expensive, spas. Its clients were wealthy women who paid $500 to $800 for a week of exercise,

---

10 Nearly 30 years later, Blum has no recollection of any plans for a housing development or a golf course; Abend may have shelved that idea before bringing Blum in.

massage, yoga, herbal wraps and a very rigorous diet (a typical breakfast was black coffee and half a grapefruit).

In the early sixties "health" and "weight loss" became synonymous for most Americans, especially women. Most of the women who came to the Golden Door came to reduce ("at the Golden Door you come to grips with what ails you, and what ails most of us happens to be fat.") but others came simply because they could afford the luxury. Three dozen guests were attended by nearly 90 staff members; the women were pampered into what passed for health.

The
GOLDEN
SPA

Lake County's Newest (and oldest)
Vacation Resort and Diet Centre

Area Code 707   Phone: 987-3193   Middletown

Recreation — Rest — Rejuvenation in the true tradition of the European Spa. Marvelous mineral springs; luxurious hot baths and pools; massages; medically supervised Slenderizing Centre. A forest playground with swimming, hiking, riding. Continental dining; smartly furnished accommodations; nitely dancing in our lounge — on the lanai. American plan.

Reservations — call Lee Puthuff, Mgr.
The Golden Spa — Middletown

Blum and Abend intended to follow the Golden Spa's goal of "offering for money what one thinks cannot be bought—health and fitness and improved looks." In order to achieve the level of luxury needed to attract wealthy guests, they planned to remodel every aspect of Harbin, modernizing each building and constructing new facilities for massages, whirlpool baths and the like.

> In addition to a chef who sings opera, Virgil Straus, lots of shade-cool rooms, a regular pool and a hot pool, and an outdoor barbecue lanai, you have this Western Hideaway which partner Art Blum prefers to call Golden Spa Slender Center.

The Golden Spa was not to be strictly a weight-reduction clinic. A Bay Area physician supervised the "Slender Center" portion, which planned to offer exercise classes (under the direction of a physical therapist), serve special dietetic food, and return the resort to its previous health-oriented focus. But the resort also catered to "today's vacationer and those locally who wish to dine in the finest dining room anywhere."

Local residents appear to have been somewhat skeptical of this new plan to transform and upgrade Harbin. One source commented that Abend came to Lake County with delusions of grandeur, and the *Times Star* published this tongue-in-cheek account of the goings-on at the resort:

NEW SPORT: THE CLIMB TO THE TOP OF HARBIN PEAK

...The race originated on the cool, comfortable greens of what used to be Harbin Springs Resort, but is now known as the Golden Spa, or Gordon's Pa, or Grandma's Bra...something to that effect. Anyway, Maurice Abend and his new partner, Art Blum, might have a fine new gimmick going for them in that timed climb to Harbin Peak...at the top [you] have to climb a flagpole and fly a banner....

Business in the summer of 1964 came primarily from local residents, as Blum worked to promote the new spa, promising such innovations as an outdoor teahouse overlooking the swimming pool area with a hot sulphur footbath for "soaking your tootsies while sipping tea and eating crumpets." But none of their dreams made it to reality. Like Ramsey, Abend was having major financial difficulties, and had a large number of judgments filed against him by private firms and collection agencies as his unpaid bills continued to increase. The resort was running only on its cash flow, which wasn't very much; there were no reserves or working capital to build from.

Abend has been characterized by several sources as a charlatan who misled his partners and investors in order to fund his projects. He promoted Harbin Springs as a ready-made resort, ripe for transformation into an elegant and lucrative spa. In fact, by 1964, the buildings were in need of major repairs and foundation work, the plumbing was antiquated, and the septic system was almost non-functional.

Blum recounts that, besides a lack of funds to make the place presentable, (much less build a teahouse) there was simply not enough money to hire a good staff, or to do sufficient marketing and advertising to build up a clientele for the new spa. Neither Abend or Blum had ever run a resort before; that and the lack of money soon led to The Golden Spa being abandoned.

Dozens of creditors were suing Abend, Abend and Blum, or the Golden Spa Corporation, which had stopped paying most of its bills. Finally Blum himself sued Abend and extricated himself from the not-so-golden mess that the development had become.

❖   ❖

HARBIN'S FINANCES WERE A MESS, AND THE RESORT ITSELF WAS gradually deteriorating, but the natural beauty of the land and the soothing power of the waters continued to attract visitors. In August of 1965, Abend deeded the Harbin property to CKB Corporation, a Los Angeles firm, for $65,562.20. The proceeds from the transaction enabled Abend to pay off his creditors by the end of 1965. CKB Corp. was headed by a man named Bob Schneider, who had yet another plan to turn a profit from the old resort.

HARBIN SPRINGS SOLD TO BECOME PRIVATE CLUB

Bob Schneider of Los Angeles announced to the *Times Star* on Saturday that the deal had been closed with Maurice Abend the day before—on Friday the 13th. Schneider has Rodal Realty in Los Angeles, and states that 90% ownership will be his. Plans are to close the resort to the public after Labor Day weekend and begin remodeling. Harbin Springs will remain closed to the general public and become a private club, states Schneider.

One of Schneider's stockholders, Bob Kies, moved his wife and his family up to live at Harbin while he managed the resort. The other investors used Harbin as a private retreat; in return for their money they got free and unlimited use of the property.

In September of 1965, 33 charter members of the Harbin Springs Hunting and Health Club flew up from Los Angeles in a DC-3, landing at the Hoberg airport. Most of the members were from Southern California, and were impressed by the Northern California countryside; the local papers predicted a new boom for Harbin.

Many of the "old timers" who have been coming up for as far back as 40 years from the Bay Area are now spending their weekends at the old Harbin place....[Bob Kies] works from sun-up to sundown supervising the new face-lifting and general clean-up of the place....The place will be closed in a couple of weeks and reopened as a private club, but in the meantime, everyone is invited to come up and get acquainted and look over the place. The hot pools and mud baths are always open and the restaurant and cocktail lounge will be open in a matter of days.

Schneider and Kies planned to dam Harbin Creek at the foot of the Meadow, creating a stream-fed 30-acre lake for the boating and fishing pleasure of their members. The lake would be surrounded by camping sites and a large RV area with hook-ups for water and electricity. Revenue from the camping and RVs, combined with investors' capital, would be used to finance building, remodeling and restoration. All the old hotel buildings (except the Capitol) needed extensive repairs; once the existing buildings were in good shape, the owners hoped to rebuild the Main Hotel.

Bob and Marilyn Kies became great Middletown boosters, and promoted Harbin as a site for many local events in early 1966. The Lion's Club and other organizations hosted up to 100 people at some outdoor barbecues and a couple of sit-down dinners in the air-conditioned dining room. In January, the Middletown Luncheon Club had a "night out" at Harbin:

....The Smorgasbord dinner will cost $2.50, and it'll be an interesting evening. There's a possibility that Bob Brennen will sing *The Last Time I Saw Lodi*; Norm Evans might recite *Dan McGrew*, or find somebody who can; and we'll try and coax Ken Reinertson and Earle Wreiden to do the twist to Henry Egnor's harmonica rendition of *The Penny Opera*....The resort, under the friendly methods used by this community-minded young couple, is regaining the popularity it once knew.

Community support was solidly behind the latest "new" Harbin Springs. Unfortunately, financial support was not. Kies urged Schneider to go slow, concentrate on local business and shut down most of the resort to save operating expenses until they could raise the working capital to make improvements. The dining room did a fairly steady business, but the hotel trade was slow and most rooms were vacant.

Kies noted, more than 25 years later, that if Schneider had actually gotten all the investors he expected, the project would have had over $75,000 in capital to keep the resort in good running order. But the money just wasn't there.

Operating costs were staggering. Newt Booth had owned Harbin free and clear, and had no mortgage payments. He provided some of his own food for the dining room, and had a very small overhead. What he made in the summer months financed the operation of the resort in the off-season. But Schneider and Kies were in an entirely different situation. Mortgage payments were $1700 a month, and utilities ran about the same. Phone bills, food, etc. added another thousand or two. With over $5000 a month in expenses, and insufficient income from local trade alone, there was not only no working capital, but the resort was operating continually in the red.

In June of 1966, Kies left Harbin. He couldn't support his wife and daughters on a resort that had no profits, and so by mutual agreement he turned the management of the property over to Schneider.

A month later the property was again up for auction, as Schneider defaulted on his deed with Abend. Abend continued to be the owner-of-record of Harbin Springs, but it doesn't appear that the resort was open on a regular basis between the summer of 1966 and the spring of 1968. There is no record of any activity at the resort, no mention of it in the local papers, and no sale or lease on the books at the county courthouse. Bob Kies no longer lived at the site, but worked part-time for Sandy Estates, doing enough routine maintenance to keep the buildings and the springs from deteriorating completely.

The only people living at Harbin in that year and a half were part of a school that leased the Annex area briefly late in 1966. The school was a sort of half-way house for several dozen boys aged 12-17. Apparently there was little control or supervision, and one day, after a few months of occupancy everyone left, leaving behind a lot of unpaid bills and broken windows.

❖   ❖

IN 1968, ABEND WAS ONCE AGAIN IN FINANCIAL HOT WATER, AS thousands of dollars in judgments were filed against him. In the spring of 1968, he negotiated with a San Francisco homophile organization that wanted to buy the property and use it as a "gay country club." There is no record of any sale completed, and there is no mention in the local papers of a change in ownership—a change that would have been more than a little controversial.

Several local sources remember "two queer boys" running the resort for a few months in the spring and early summer, while negotiations were continuing with Abend. A May, 1968 article in *Vector*, an early homophile publication, gives a detailed account of the proposed club.

> A new relationship concept between the management of business and the gay community has been initiated at Harbin Springs Club.
>
> This resort is being set up as a private club for the homophile community, as have many other businesses. The difference lies in structuring a Board of Directors which represents all aspects of the homophile community, that makes policy....
>
> The Board has set up a legal defense fund for members and the club that will be used in cases involving enforcement of laws pertaining to homosexuality...plans are under discussion for regular deposits to this fund from membership fees, profits, charges and special events that will insure regular fund growth in relation to the size of the club.
>
> The initial membership response has been surprisingly good. Membership does require sponsorship, manager review and review by a three-person committee selected by the Board. The purpose is to insure a future, secure country development for the use of the responsible gay community.
>
> The remodeling and refurbishing has already begun with the owners investing several thousand dollars in the development.
>
> This looks like a big step forward.

According to the *Vector* article, several homophile clubs had scheduled events for weekends in April and May, and the men who were organizing the venture had invited many other clubs from the Bay Area to come up and tour the property. Most agreed that Harbin had a lot of potential, but few were interested enough to invest any money in a venture that was so far away from the city.

The homophile resort quickly went the way of the Golden Spa and the other plans for Harbin, and for the same reasons: there weren't enough people coming up to run the resort at a profit; and there wasn't enough financial backing to make the improvements necessary to attract more guests. It may have been just as well that the money to open the club didn't materialize; especially in the pre-Stonewall days before gay culture was visible outside large urban areas, tolerance was low for a group seen by most as an affront to public morals.

❖ ❖

THE GROUP THAT EVENTUALLY DID OCCUPY HARBIN SPRINGS IN the summer of 1968 would turn out to be an even bigger affront to the public morals and would, within eight months, ruin Harbin's reputation in Lake County. Easily the most colorful and outrageous people to occupy the property, the Frontiers of Science Fellowship took over the resort in August of 1968.[11]

The Frontiers of Science had begun in San Rafael in January of that year, the brainchild of Donald James Hamrick, a six-foot two, 250-pound, balding nuclear physicist and mystic. Hamrick had worked for Syndyne Corporation in Vancouver, and moved to the Bay Area to work for an Oakland research firm. He also operated a private company, Novatron Labs, in Berkeley, where he did research in electrohydrodynamics, holding 16 patents in that field.

Hamrick was a man of very complex interests. He had also been a Church of Christ minister and was excommunicated from that body because of his radical, mystical views. He claimed to have been taken up by a flying saucer one night, and given a mission to enlighten the world. According to some, Hamrick believed that he was Jesus, returned to complete the salvation of the world. To others, he was one of the brightest and most progressive scientists in the country.

Lecturing at weeknight gatherings at Grace Memorial Church and the College of Marin, he preached a humanistic religion based on scientific principles. He formed the Frontiers

---

11 Again the Middletown paper reported that Abend *sold* the property to the FOS, and the Marin *Independent-Journal* said that the group planned to purchase the secluded resort for $210,000, but there is no paper trail to indicate that such a sale was ever completed. Abend certainly may have attempted to sell the land in 1968—he was in default on the deed—but the exact nature of FOS's tenancy is a mystery; they probably had some kind of informal leasing agreement with Abend.

of Science "to establish order and unity on Earth and to connect the physical and metaphysical aspects of science."

In May of 1968, Hamrick and two other men—Donn F. Pennell of Berkeley and Thomas G. Stone of Pebble Beach—formed a religious and educational non-profit corporation, Frontiers of Science Fellowship, whose primary purposes were to:

> Extend the frontiers of knowledge through research and to disseminate knowledge and guidance in the preparation of humanity for a distinguished civilization....

and

> To promote the synthesis of the physical, life and social sciences...[and to] establish medical and psychological health centers...to actively influence the personal, social and economic development of the World Community.

Their secondary purpose was to finance these visions with tax-deductible gifts, donations and bequests of money, stocks and real estate.

Their first headquarters was in Marin County, but petitions were circulated by their San Rafael neighbors, protesting the group's presence, and in the summer of 1968 they rented "a huge run-down country club a few hundred miles north of San Francisco, and began to put together one of the most outlandish communes on the coast."

In hindsight, the first mention of the Frontiers of Science's arrival at Harbin is foreboding. A small article in the *Times-Star* reports that a burning candle was left on a table unattended, and fell over, causing one of the Annex cabins to go up in flames. A photo of two men surveying the damage identifies them as a Forestry investigator and a research technician for Harbinger Research.

Hamrick told reporters that Harbin would serve as the headquarters for the over 11,000 people allegedly involved in the FOS, with 100 people actually living on the premises, and serving as the nucleus for the organization. Frontiers of Science presented itself as a scientific research foundation with a religious inclination, and an interview with Hamrick in the

Times-Star one week after the candle incident, described it to the people of Middletown:

> The group intends to make a permanent residence there as a self-sustaining community, where each member contributes his special talents for the overall group benefit. Numbered among them are scientists, engineers, mechanics, teachers, writers, craftsmen, photographers, musicians, artists, lawyers, actors, film-makers, farmers and many others with specialized training and abilities.
>
> ...Dr. Hamrick stated that in addition to the scientific and economic aspects of the foundation, there are also religious ones. He uses both religious and scientific philosophy to illustrate principles of human relations...The name Harbin will be changed to "Harbinger," meaning "the Herald," suggesting the work of the Fellowship in exposing the inner nature of man and preparing him for a new and better ordered future.

This introduction goes on to mention that there had been a lot of activity at the site since the group first moved in, supposedly because the condition of the facilities required monumental repairs to bring the buildings up to liveable conditions, in compliance with county health and building codes. Hamrick requested that Middletown residents not visit the springs, to give the FOS a chance to finish moving in and make the repairs.

A private institution—Harbinger University—was set up at the site. Hamrick, at one time a fairly wealthy man, had given up all his other enterprises to found the Frontiers of Science and turned over all his resources to the Fellowship, getting additional financing for the Harbinger venture from his fellow directors, Stone and Pennell. The assets of Harbinger University included over $350,000 in laboratory equipment and a private plane, which Hamrick used to travel from Harbinger to give lectures and seminars all over the state.

"We really mean the Frontiers of Science," he said in an interview with the Marin *Independent-Journal*. "We're right out on the edge." His classes and seminars included such esoteric subjects as "Codification of Consciousness," "Physiology of Higher Bodies," "The Skills of the New Man," and "Far Field

Contributions to Consciousness." When he lectured in Marin, hundreds of people crowded into rooms at churches and recreation centers to hear him:

> ...Disclose the nature of the forces at work on this planet as we enter a new sector of the galaxy and a New Age of Man...We can see that at the extremity of science we must acknowledge God and at the extremity of our perception of spiritual values we must perceive science. There's a bridge to be travelled there....

Obviously, Harbinger University was unlike any other enterprise that had been at Harbin, unlike anything the people of Lake County had encountered before. The Booths had been part of the local community, and the various people who came after them continued to be part of the business and social structure of Middletown. All of them had the same basic purpose in mind for the Harbin property—to run a resort. And that wasn't what Harbinger University was about at all.

The people involved with Harbinger, followers of Hamrick's philosophy of the unity of science and religion, came across to the people of Middletown as sincere, if a little strange. The *Times-Star*'s editor ran a column about Hamrick and his venture that indicates Middletown citizens were skeptical, but willing to give Harbinger the benefit of the doubt:

> Hamrick, the executive director of the "brain factory" was in the office the other day to give a brief rundown on the operation. We guess that the average IQ of Middletown area people will shoot up about 50 points....In talking to them we were impressed by what we gathered, but most of the time the stuff was way over our heads...if we had paid more attention to our chemistry teacher while in school, we might have been able to get a better understanding.

Hamrick said the reason the group had chosen Lake County was its non-contaminated air, a low level of fallout and a minimum of electrical interference, so the Fellowship's electronic brain research devices could operate unimpeded. Another reason he cited was privacy, and he again expressed his desire for local residents to stay away from Harbinger unless invited, so the participants in the "think factory" wouldn't be disturbed in their research projects.

What Hamrick didn't mention was that they had not gotten along well with their previous neighbors and a run down, isolated old resort was ideal for them. In addition, after their initial investments, the group's resources were limited, and they don't appear to have made any large payments for the property. The Frontiers of Science survived entirely on donations and funding from people who came to Harbinger.

Seekers turned over everything they owned—money, property, cars, etc. In return they were given a room, fed, and became one of the "family." "There are no membership rules or dues in Frontiers—persons become a part of it by functioning with us. They must care about the same things we care about," Hamrick said.

In September of 1968, the editor of the Times-Star, the manager of the Lake County Chamber of Commerce and the local bank manager were invited up to the "campus" for a very guided tour. They were shown the research facilities and the lab (in what used to be the cocktail lounge), and even given a sample "treatment" with an electronic device supposed to raise one's IQ level.[12]

The tour went well and seemed to dispel most of the fears about these new strangers. But the editor did ask two questions that indicate he suspected something else was going on:

> We did inquire about the hippie (should that be capitalized?) situation...we were told that one of the functions will be to analyze hippies and "see what makes them tick." Many volunteer. As we understand it, non-hippies are analyzed also.
>
> We asked Hamrick about a rumor we heard around town concerning the use of narcotics or any dope. He assured us there

---

12 The electronic device they sampled was probably the same machine that Stephen Gaskin describes as "a bar of non-conducting material about 3/4 of an inch around and about six feet long, with copper coil wrapped around it, and you were supposed to come and aim this thing at you somewhere and plug it in and throw the switch. It was called the Zendyne Zapper. Folks said you could really get a high off the Zendyne Zapper. And the vibes around it were very paranoid and Frankensteiny."

was no basis for the rumor. We found the attitude of the people we talked to very friendly and very cooperative, and are looking forward to [them] becoming part of our community.

Hamrick's public statements about the Fellowship repeatedly emphasized that its research was investigating the mind and expanded consciousness without the use of drugs. Hamrick himself is said not to have used drugs, but with 100 people at Harbin experimenting with mind research in 1969, it seems highly unlikely that no psychedelics were being used.

In a bizarre part of their first interview, Hamrick and the *Times-Star* editor Joseph Aniello were chatting about the long, winding road up Mt. St. Helena, and Hamrick replied that the trip wasn't a problem for Fellowship members because "there is a way to poke a 'hole' through the mountain without blasting. We can't give you the correct technology," said Aniello, "but as we understand it, these people have found some 'chemical' that would 'disintegrate' rock."

A chemical called LSD.

❖   ❖

LYSERGIC ACID DIETHYLAMIDE-25 MAY NOT HAVE BEEN ABLE TO actually dissolve rock, but it was certainly able to change someone's perception of the mountain, and had a profound effect on the character of American society in the '60s.

It was the hippie sacrament, a mind detergent capable of washing away years of social programming...a consciousness expander, a tool that would push us up the evolutionary ladder. Some even claimed LSD was a gift from God, given to mankind to save the planet from a nuclear finale.

A Swiss research chemist named Albert Hofmann first synthesized LSD in 1943; experimenters with Sandoz Laboratories called it a powerful psychotomimetic—a drug that temporarily induced symptoms of psychosis in ordinary individuals. Subjects experienced vivid, fantastic and kaleidoscopic hallucinations, and an astonishing change in perception that swept away all objective reality. The drug reached America in 1949, and psychologists here conducted a number of empirical tests in their laboratories. But there was a major problem with the testing procedure and with the results:

> If I were to give you an IQ test and during the administration one of the walls of the room opened up, giving you a vision of the blazing glories of the central galactic suns, and at the same time your childhood began to unreel before your inner eye like a three-dimension color movie, you would not do well on the intelligence test.

As more and more doctors experimented with LSD, a distinct pattern began to emerge. Almost all subjects reported that the drug had taken them on a journey, a trip, to a world that lay beyond the realms of ordinary consciousness. Scientists were disturbed by the fact that descriptions of this Other World by various subjects were very similar, as if they'd all gone to the same world: a world in which Love was the primary and fundamental fact of the universe. Subjects repeatedly described the journey in terms that were more mystical or religious than scientific. As Jay Stevens comments, "to discover, in the recesses of the mind, something that felt a lot like God, was not a situation that organized science...wished to contemplate."

By the mid-50s, LSD research was being conducted all over the world, and the researchers themselves were splitting into two camps. The "lab boys" saw LSD as an empirically valuable tool for studying brain chemistry under measurable conditions; others thought that it might be the key to the next step in human evolution—not physical change, but mental change, from self-consciousness to the cosmic consciousness attributed to such advanced beings as Christ and Buddha.

Many experimenters began to move away from sterile lab settings and questionnaires to their own living rooms where the music, lighting etc. that created the set and setting could be prepared and manipulated to create different "trips." Trips were taken with a guide, someone who had taken the drug before and was familiar with the otherwise unknowable "landscape" of the Other World. Use of the drug grew from a tiny number of brain researchers out to a larger, but still very select group of their colleagues and friends. Psychiatrists in Los Angeles and New York began to offer LSD therapy, and found their client lists growing as word got around about the "creativity pill."

Controlled, almost ritualistic LSD use was widespread by 1960, but only in a very elite circle of academics, writers, artists and the like; it was not well known to the general public. The man who would change that forever was Timothy Leary. Leary was a Harvard psychology professor who had been introduced to psilocybin—another hallucinogen, synthesized from the sacred mushrooms of Mexican shamans—and formed a research group to study its effects. It began as very academic research, but soon his graduate students too were talking about Love and God and ecstasy, not graphs and results, and Leary's house filled up every weekend with Harvard students eager to explore their own inner reaches.

After Leary tried LSD, he abandoned most of his psilocybin project and introduced the drug to the intellectual and artistic communities of Cambridge and the East Coast. More conservative researchers were afraid that Leary's enthusiasm would ruin what they had worked to build, and that he would destroy the credibility of psychiatric studies on LSD with his mystical talk.

One half of Leary's desk was piled with psychology monographs and studies of the drug; the other with books on psychedelic trips like Huxley's *Doors of Perception*, along with Hindu scripture, Buddhist texts and the *Tibetan Book of the Dead*. There was no model in the Western scientific world for describing the LSD experience, but Eastern religion provided descriptions of mystic journeys and altered states of consciousness that fit exactly. Leary, the arcane scientist, became a very public figure and took LSD out of the relatively small, respectable medical sphere, and brought it to the attention of the media.

Harvard was not pleased with the attention. Drugs and mysticism were not consistent with its image, and so it fired Leary and his colleague Richard Alpert in 1962; the press branded them as irresponsible scientists when they spoke of "expanded consciousness." They moved to an estate in Millbrook, New York to continue their experiments and their publicity.

On the West Coast, novelist Ken Kesey had been given LSD while he was participating in a medical research project, and he too decided that this new reality-bender must be shared. LSD was still fairly easy to buy from Sandoz and other drug companies, as long as a legitimate-sounding research project was proposed; Kesey got a large supply. He and his friends, calling themselves the Merry Pranksters, dressed in day-glo super-hero costumes and travelled across the country taking and distributing "acid" in a psychedelically-painted bus, and gathering a lot of attention wherever they went. The Pranksters and their crowd, which included the Hell's Angels, sponsored large, public parties they called Acid Tests—total sensory experiences with light shows, rock music and a lot of LSD.

Leary's camp advocated the benefits of controlled LSD use for consciousness expansion, and the Pranksters' only rule was that there were no rules, but both were very public about their own visions for an LSD future. The media responded with alarm, and soon the papers were full of stories about the LSD epidemic. After a few months of almost entirely unsubstantiated horror stories about the new menace, most psychiatric research projects and legitimate supplies of the drug were curtailed, and LSD was made illegal in 1966. Those who had studied LSD were forbidden to use it; supply and demand were in the hands of the "hippies."[13]

Obeying Leary's exhortation to "turn on, tune in and drop out," many collegiate LSD users withdrew from conventional values and conventional society as they experienced "higher consciousness." These young acid-heads, dissatisfied with the corporate-suburban lifestyles of their parents, formed their own "families" and societies. Some viewed this with alarm, as a force that could destroy America, but others saw it as optimistic evidence that the evolution away from a materially-oriented society towards a spiritually-oriented one, had begun.

---

13 "Hippie" was a term coined by San Francisco *Examiner* reporter Michael Fallon. It was seen as a derogatory put-down by hippies themselves, who preferred "freaks" or "heads." It is used here as the most common term.

The largest of these new societies, or countercultures, formed in the Haight-Ashbury section of San Francisco, where by 1966 over 15,000 hippies had gathered. In the next year, almost a hundred thousand more joined them. As the Haight grew, it too became a focus for the nation's media, and soon tourists were coming by the busload to take snapshots of the "natives," and disillusioned teenagers poured into the Aquarian Mecca. It's estimated that over 100,000 doses of LSD were sold each week; some stayed in the Haight, some went back to Ann Arbor or Boulder or even Cleveland.[14] Seekers came, but with them came the usual percentage of criminals and hustlers.

Crime hit the Haight, along with malnutrition, overcrowding and an influx of drugs like heroin and speed. Police raided houses and business on a daily basis, sweeping the streets and making arrests for possession, or picking up runaways. Leary, Kesey and some other movement leaders were arrested on a variety of drug charges, and faced stiff prison sentences.

> The psychedelic movement ground to a close. The drugs were still available, more so than ever, but it was a rare person who took them to push the envelope [of consciousness]. For the kids, a trip to the Other World was like a trip to Disneyland: lots of scary rides and laughs, but no wisdom.

What had begun as a quest to open the doors of perception, to expand the boundaries of the human mind, had gone awry. Scientists found it difficult to embrace the mystical aspects of the frontiers of the mind, and LSD had moved from the controllable realm of science out into the chaotic hands of the masses. In any culture where achieving a higher form of consciousness is a goal, the journey is reserved for a very small

---

14 Rumors abounded in the '60s that any high school student could manufacture LSD. In fact, after 1966, the key ingredients—lysergic monohydrate and ergotomine tartrate—were virtually unobtainable in the United States, and acquiring the chemicals and equipment required to synthesize the drug could cost as much as $100,000. A very small number of chemists, the most famous of which was Augustus Owsley Stanley III, set up illegal, "underground," labs, even portable labs in the backs of semis, and turned out millions of doses.

number, who respect its power and are trained to use it; only the shamans and the priests have access to the sacred mushrooms, because "the shaman is the connection to the God residing in the sacred plant." To the hippies, everyone was a shaman, but most lacked the respect for the power of the drug.

As the utopian days of the Haight ended, people began to reconsider their search. For many, LSD had been an entry point, drawing them into the world of transformation. But as philosopher Alan Watts said, "Psychedelics are like a boat one uses to cross a river; once on the other side, the journey continues on foot." Leary, Alpert and many others turned to Eastern religion and meditation, to find enlightenment and altered states of consciousness that didn't always require drugs.

❖   ❖

DON HAMRICK APPEARED ON THE SCENE NEARLY TWO YEARS after the height of the Haight, a johnny-come-lately guru espousing the same sort of ideas about consciousness as the later Leary and Alpert (now Ram Dass), and expanding the concept of the connection between religion and science that had arisen in LSD research. Like them, he claimed to be searching for new answers to ancient questions, continuing the quest for advanced consciousness. Most Western scientists saw powerful psychoactive substances in terms of biochemistry, rather than as supernatural. Hamrick's view of consciousness embraced both science and metaphysics; he claimed not to use drugs to unlock the doors to the Other World. But it appears that most of the people who came to Harbinger University did.

According to Mario Vassi, a chronicler of the Aquarian Age of the 60s:

> The scene at Harbinger rapidly became one of dope and spirituality. The notion was that if a group of people could get it together and raise huge positive vibes, they would form a center from which salvation would flow....They also had some of the most beautiful hot springs baths in the area, and on any given afternoon there would be a small group of people sitting in the healing waters, gently stoned and smiling at each other.

The atmosphere at Harbinger was so bucolic that it began to attract a number of people who sought similar adventures into altered states, and who were looking for a place that offered them the privacy and freedom to explore their inner landscapes.

> They started to interest IBM executives and mathematicians and scientists from all parts of the country....Now at Harbinger they could move in a company of peers, for there were gathered some of the finest acid heads of the day....At Frontiers there were people who had a high degree of native intelligence and who had mastered the vicissitudes of acid. In addition there was the countryside, hundreds of luscious and often nude women, healthy babies and pulse-pounding music.

The Frontiers of Science and Harbinger University almost seem to have been two separate entities, or at least two distinct factions among Hamrick's followers—one appears to be spiritual, rural and into alternative living and the other seems to be involved with esoteric religions and psychedelic drugs.

In October of 1968, the Frontiers of Science, in conjunction with the Six-Day School in Glen Ellen and the Zen Center, published a magazine called *The Changes*. The 32-page publication was devoted to astrology and tips on gentle, rural living (herbs, geodesic domes, composting) for new communal back-to-nature seekers. Hamrick wrote a very long piece, taken from his lectures, in which he described his philosophy of science and mind, human consciousness and caring.

In the first few months of its existence, Harbinger University was considered by some to be "the psychedelic country club of the nation's hip intelligencia." At about the same time *The Changes* was published, some Harbinger University people put out a 24-page publication, *Harbinger*, modeled on the San Francisco *Oracle*, to take their message out to the world; it cost a quarter an issue, or 35 cents for those outside the Bay Area.[15] Contradicting Hamrick's claims that FOS did not advocate drug

---

15 How often *Harbinger* was published, how many copies were printed, how many issues it ran are all unknown. Some sources said that there were several different issues, but research in archival collections has turned up only several copies of the same one.

use, the main theme of *Harbinger* was psychedelic—poetry, art, personal accounts of acid trips and reprints of articles by some of the leading lights of the LSD movement (Alan Watts's "Psychedelics and Religious Experience" and Timothy Leary's "Government Violations and Non-Violent Hippies"). Readers were invited to share their own:

> Projections along the perennial trip—art expressions, ideas, feelings, communications from similar energies. Send efforts to Harbinger, Box 504, Middletown CA 95461.[16]

The *Harbinger* production staff was decidedly creative in their use of colors and layout. One page had a dark purple background with (mostly illegible) white text; another was printed in triplets—the first lines in yellow, second lines in red and third lines in purple, repeated endlessly down the page; mandalas and collages in greens and oranges seemed to vibrate off the paper.

Harbinger advocated psychedelics, one-ness with the universe, love, consciousness, creativity and complete freedom of expression. Ironically, it was this promise of freedom, and the idyllic setting of the old resort, that led to Harbinger University's downfall. More and more people were drawn to Harbinger, wanting to experiment with the new Aquarian mixture of drugs, Eastern religion and rock and roll; they brought their friends, and their friends' friends, and within a few months the word had spread that there was a huge commune up in Lake County.

The lawns in front of the Pine Cabin (known as the Magician's cabin, where resident and visiting magicians and wizards stayed) were filled with the beautiful people—in faded blue jeans and tie-dyed shirts, headbands, day-glo tights, serapes, desert robes, Indian beads and Errol Flynn dueling

---

16 *Harbinger* was not a unique name for a publication. The first *Harbinger* was published by the utopian Brook Farm community between 1845 and 1849 and was "devoted to social and political progress." Other *Harbingers* have been published in Toronto (1968-1971), South Carolina ("A Carolina Grassroots Journal," 1981-83), Sebastopol, California (1969), and New York ("The Journal of Social Ecology," 1983). The current resident newspaper at Harbin Hot Springs (1987 on) is also called *The Harbinger*.

shirts—sitting beneath the sycamore trees talking and giving massages. Women in long soft dresses nursed babies and painted mandalas; gentle men with flowing hair and beards wove God's eyes and played guitars. The smells of fresh baked bread and huge pots of vegetable soup wafted out of the kitchen as naked children laughed and ran across the grass.

Front cover of the Harbinger, 1968

It was "a community of intelligent, open, out-front people, all sharing an incredible adventure in living." Visitors to Harbinger remember it as full of smiling people, most of them very young, most of them from middle class families, living in their new tribe like benign gypsies. Free from the restrictions of American society's requirements about clothes or jobs, they announced that they would live on their own terms, experimenting with alternative ways of working, thinking and living.

Following the Summer of Love in 1967, the counterculture population of the Haight-Ashbury had fragmented into a lot of different sects and cults, and many people left the city for communes or farms in Marin and outlying areas. Dozens of communes started in the late '60s, but few of them began with the resources of Harbin.

> They had a hot bath, medium hot pool, swimming pool, hundred room hotel, machine shop, wood shop, auto shop, chemistry lab, a library with all the back issues of scientific magazines back to 1900 in several different fields—tons and tons of *things*.

It was a ready-made playground with a vast amount of space. When the Booths owned it, the resort could accommodate over 200 guests in hotel rooms and cottages. Harbinger often housed three or four times that number, in sleeping bags and on mattresses on the floor of every room.

The playground rapidly took over the laboratory.[17] By the end of 1968, Harbinger was *the* weekend party place for San Francisco hippies, and a temporary home for an uncounted number of people, many of whom had heard that it was a free and easy place to crash. Hundreds and hundreds of people came up on weekends and "partied their brains out." And when the party got to be more or less continuous, many of the original seekers went somewhere else—back to the city, down to Esalen, off to land of their own—anywhere there was some semblance of order and a little peace and quiet.

Conditions deteriorated very rapidly. The scientists and mystics whose dream it had been to found Harbinger University as a learning center were relatively few, and they were hard-pressed to hold that dream together in the face of the hordes of people who came and did as they pleased. No one really had any idea who was there, or who was coming or going. The population expanded and contracted daily— expanding into the hundreds for parties and happenings, and shrinking down to a handful when it came to paying the bills or providing enough food.

Harbinger's income relied on the people who lived there donating their money and belongings to the common fund. Unfortunately, the numbers of people grew and grew, but the percentage of donations was small in relation to the expenses. It's estimated that hundreds of thousands of dollars, most of it the original investors', were cycled in and out of Harbinger in a little over six months.

Hamrick was a visionary and a charismatic speaker, but he was often away from the property lecturing, and the dream he

---

17 The lab itself was in the old cocktail lounge. Obviously, the bar trade at Harbinger was non-existent, so in the fall of 1968, Abend boosted his failing finances by selling Harbin's liquor license to the new Hidden Valley Country Club for $17,000.

had for Harbinger was changing too rapidly for him to remain in control—of the vision or the reality.

> I saw H. lecture up there one time. The place sprouted out with pictures of him three feet high, full face posters of this great bald-headed baby face, looking like a nude or something. And then the next time the place sprung out in big signs with pink hearts on them, saying stuff like "We love our Director!" And the next visit, you came up to the place and you find those signs smashed to flinders up against a concrete wall somewhere.

According to sources who were at Harbinger, there was a continual stream of "hotshots" from the Haight who came up to try and take control of the operation, and run the commune according to their own visions. On any given day, the person with the loudest voice or the strongest energy ran the place. A new regimen, a new organization with a new set of rules, was posted on the bulletin board every two weeks or so. But none of the rules could be enforced, because by that time no one was really in control.

> We came charging up the hill and got about halfway up toward the place, and there were two big thrones by the road. There was a pair of nice young hippies, a guy and a girl, and they had these big thrones, eight feet high up the back of them, with big arms and decorated up like thrones. The couple was wearing crowns and they were all done up like royalty. They had told them they were the King and Queen. Talk about being sent up in a box kite. They didn't have no juice, no authority, no say-so. They just had those thrones and those crowns, and all the speed-freaks who came by would just take a bite....We felt somewhat sorry for them that this funny organizational system had put them in an untenable situation.

Hamrick's dream of a small research community, a nucleus of dedicated seekers, had exploded into a chaotic picnic. Harbinger has been described as a *hummingator* commune, a thing with the mouth of an alligator and the body of a hummingbird. Hundreds of people expected to be fed and housed and taken care of, without giving much of anything in return, or taking responsibility to see that anything got done.

Once a person became a part of "the family"—which involved learning a subtle set of mannerisms that indicated he was one of "us," not one of "them"—it was possible to live at Harbinger for months without any money. Few of its residents had any money or any plans, and even fewer cared who was there, if the place was maintained, how the bills were paid or what happened next.

People lived in the former hotel buildings, playing guitars, smoking marijuana, painting, dropping acid, and acting almost entirely on their impulses. If it was too hot, they broke a window to get air. If it was too cold, they used the furniture for firewood. If the room seemed too small, someone would get a sledgehammer and knock down walls until the space seemed right. Parts of Azalea and Walnut became open spaces—four or five rooms long with the connecting walls knocked out—where musicians set up their amplifiers and loud, weird music echoed out over the valley at any time of the day or night.

Drug use was more or less continuous, and came with membership in the family. One man remembers that there was a drug tray circulated each afternoon to people sitting on the lawn and on the porches of the buildings. Two bowls of marijuana joints and hashish were surrounded by smaller bowls containing hits of LSD, and capsules and tablets of every type of psychedelic, upper or downer available—all provided free by "the management."

The baths were used for every conceivable purpose. There were frequent all-night parties, with what Harbinger people called "free love" and Middletown people called "orgies." Musicians played their instruments in the Hot Pool because of the acoustics. People took baths in the Hot Pool with soap and shampoo so that the water in both hot and warm pools was murky. The drains clogged with soap scum and hair and stopped working; the therapeutic baths became stagnant cement ponds.

What had begun as cordial relations with the Middletown community turned sour very quickly. The local people were willing to be tolerant as long as their way of life wasn't threatened, as long as Harbinger didn't impinge on Middletown. Of course, it did. A group of long-haired scientists was one thing, but within a few months, hundreds of hippies descended on the town on their way to Harbinger, behaving unconventionally (at the very least) and invading the rural area with what citizens saw as frightening displays of weirdness.

> The young people had no sense of propriety. As far as they were concerned, the Earth was theirs, totally, and they would allow others to live on it as long as they didn't interfere with their own sprawling, chaotic ways. They insisted on wearing the wildest of hippie-type costumes and driving through the streets in psychedelically painted trucks. They flaunted their beards and bra-less chicks and smoked dope outrageously.

The town responded. The local sheriff made a few trips up to Harbinger, officially looking for underage runaways, and the Sheriff's Department and Narcotic Division began to keep a very close eye on the "colony," which Frontiers of Science members called harassment.

❖   ❖

MAURICE ABEND WAS EITHER UNAWARE OF WHAT WAS happening to his property, or simply didn't care. He had been in default on his loan on several occasions, and finally in December of 1968 the land reverted back to Sandy Estates Company, the group of San Francisco investors who had originally loaned Abend the money for the purchase, and who held the deed.[18]

Within three weeks of acquiring the property, Sandy Estates and the Lake County Health Department were in communication. Late in January of 1969, Richard Nixon became the President of the United States and inspectors from the Health and Building Departments took a tour of Harbinger.

The building inspector cited numerous violations of the county code, such as new electrical work done with open and

---

18 After 1968, I can find no trace of Maurice Abend. No one who had any dealings with him in the 60s has any idea of what happened to him, and few of them seemed to care. There is no record of his death in the State of California.

exposed wires and bundles of live electrical wires hanging loose next to combustible materials; drainage and sewage lines obstructed and with holes punched in them; and waste from toilets flowing directly onto the lawns and into the streams. He recommended that all buildings be vacated immediately, and deemed unsafe for human occupancy.

The Health Department imposed a 50-day quarantine on the property because of a number of cases of infectious hepatitis. Road blocks were set up on the road to Harbinger, and no one was allowed to enter or leave the property. The next day the county conducted a mass immunization, giving shots to 94 Harbinger residents, including 20 children. Food was sent in from a federal food program distribution center in Lakeport; a photo on the front page of the *Times-Star* captioned "Food for the Hippies" shows a group of long-haired, bearded men on a rainy country road, loading boxes into a Volkswagen van.

The quarantine was lifted after six days, and many of the people at Harbinger decided it might be a good time to move on. By mid-February, less than 50 people remained. In addition to the building and health departments' inspections, the *Times-Star* (in a story under the banner headline "Hepatitis Hits Harbinger"), also reported that:

> Numerous violations, including others that have nothing to do with the Health Code, are being investigated, and action is expected shortly. The District Attorney would not spell out the "other violations" but rumors around town persist that narcotics are being used freely on the site.[19]

Early in February the local Parent-Teachers Club held a meeting to discuss the area's growing drug problem, which was not limited to Harbinger and its residents. The Sheriff brought samples of various drugs, pipes and other paraphernalia, and told the group that LSD could be purchased almost anywhere in the county. Eight Harbinger residents attended the meeting,

---

19 It seems unlikely that drug use could still be considered just a rumor after the publication of *Harbinger*, a blatantly pro-psychedelic newspaper; perhaps the publication wasn't widely read in Middletown.

and argued that since alcohol and marijuana have similar effects, marijuana should be legalized. Their viewpoint was not shared by other members of the audience.

The Health Department issued an eight-page notice with more than 30 violations of the Health and Safety Code, including: raw sewage flowing above ground; open drainage ditches; broken and unsafe appliances and unsanitary walls and floors in the kitchen; insects and vermin in the kitchen and restaurant; contaminated water used for cooking and washing; pool waters unsafe for bathing, and cracks and broken cement in pools, with no pool maintenance in evidence; buildings with an "accumulation of debris, filth, rubbish, garbage, vermin and other offensive matter"; lack of adequate heat; buildings unfit for human occupancy because of general deterioration; and female food handlers not wearing hairnets.[20]

Harbinger was given three days to correct the sewage problem. The pools were ordered closed and could not be used at all until they were drained, cleaned and repaired. Most of the other violations were ordered to be corrected within a 14 or 30 day period. Hairnets were required immediately.

Nothing much was done. A week after the inspections, editorials and letters from Middletown people began appearing in the *Times-Star*, pleading with county officials for an end to the "hippie menace." More people left Harbinger because "the trip was getting heavy." The Health Department served the commune's inhabitants with an order to clean and repair their quarters or vacate, and Sandy Estates told the District Attorney that they planned to begin eviction proceedings.

A few weeks later the Lake County Narcotics Division made its first real raid on Harbinger, late on Saturday night, February 22, 1969. According to one of the officers present during the weekend raid, the department went up with four officers and a paddy wagon, expecting to find 30 or 40 residents. Instead they

---

20 Obviously, long hair at Harbinger wasn't limited to women, but the county code had no provisions for citing long-haired men.

walked into the largest and wildest party ever held at Harbinger.

❖   ❖

THE PARTY WAS THE CULMINATION OF A FIVE-DAY CONFERENCE sponsored by the Frontiers of Science, which included a concert, a meeting of the Congress of Concerned Educators at the College of Marin, and a two-day gathering at Harbinger.

Invitations in medieval Irish script were sent out for the first event of the conference—The Frontiers of Science Celestial Synapse, produced by Bill Graham at the Fillmore West in San Francisco, on Wednesday, February 19th. 1500 people in music and a broad range of psychedelic tribes—from Rancho Oompali[21] and other communes, to the Hell's Angels—were invited; more than 3000 people showed up. *Rolling Stone* said:

> [The Celestial Synapse had] to do with the crystal in the center of the living Earth, which is affected by human vibrations and which may either change shape (a creative change) or change size (a destructive change, since it would cause earthquakes). The idea [was] to send down good vibrations to change the shape of the crystal, and the Celestial Synapse may very well have done just that.

The good vibrations of the evening opened with an oboe and bagpipe introduction by The Golden Toad, a local band whose members included Bob Thomas, John Paul and Don Brown. Don Hamrick addressed the crowd:

> Goodly company, it is our hope that this evening there will be an opening and a free interchange, so that something new may emerge. Let the barriers fall. Let there be a merging.

The Grateful Dead facilitated the merging with a flowing, improvisational four-hour set, which Rolling Stone called "some of the best music the Fillmore had seen in some time." During

---

21 Rancho Oompali was a communal ranch just off Highway 101 in Novato, frequented by the Grateful Dead and many other acid-rock groups formerly headquartered in the Haight.

the set the crowd, most of whom were tripping on LSD and other substances, danced, danced on stage, took off their clothes and danced, greeted strangers, hugged, and passed out joints and flowers. There were 3000-person OMs, sending vibrations throughout the hall and into the Earth. According to Stephen Gaskin's account, Bill Graham stopped security guards from hauling the naked dancers off the stage, and "Tim Leary was there, behind the amps, staying out of trouble. Women and kids and Tim Leary behind the amps." The concert went on until the wee hours of the morning.

Many of the thousands of concert participants went up to Harbinger to continue the celebration after the concert finally ended. It was a huge party, with 500, 600 maybe even 800 people dropping acid, playing music and dancing in the baths, around the Gazebo, in the "hotel" buildings, and then in the big dining room down in Stonefront when it started to rain.

It was to be the last of the great Harbinger parties. Some say that the word had gotten out on the street that the scene at Harbinger was turning into a bummer, and there was going to be one last-gasp party before it was over, and as many hippies and counterculture celebrities who could get up to Lake County were there. The Golden Toad supplied the music; Stewart Brand, originator of the *Whole Earth Catalog* was there; and Tarthang Tulku, leader of the Nyingma Buddhist Center in Berkeley held court, sitting on a throne of pillows, smiling and engaging people in discussions of Eastern metaphysics. One source says Ken Kesey was also at the party, but no one else remembers him being there, although there was certainly a Pranksterish acid-test feel about it.[22]

The acid flowed freely; thousands of hits had been donated by underground chemists from the Bay Area. Most of the people at the party had taken some combination of

---

22 A few people were not so ecstatic. Hamrick's wife Jonna was pregnant with their fifth child, and she and her six-year old son drank LSD-laced apple juice at the party. She was taken to the hospital minutes before the sheriff arrived. The boy was sick for three or four days; the baby died in the womb later that night. According to the newspaper, Mrs. Hamrick claimed she was unaware that there had been any drugs in the juice.

hallucinogens, and a few hundred of them were dancing, ecstatic and naked, when the Sheriff arrived.

No one was particularly impressed or bothered by the arrival of the law. A lot of the discipline of the raid fell apart when the deputies discovered that they were dealing with people who didn't really care about sheriffs or badges or arrests. The people at the party weren't experiencing the same reality as the officials, and to them the deputies were just men in beige suits with stars on them. Only one man really resisted arrest; the others just didn't accept the concept of arrest, and kept dancing.

> Stalwarts from the local constabulary...pulled a surprise raid. Except it was they who suffered the greater surprise. They found six or seven hundred naked freaks, dancing and swilling acid punch, setting up a soaring cry which set the leaves on the trees to spinning. They rushed into the dining hall where the bulk of the party was going on, and froze to the spot. To a man, they blushed. They stated their official business...and quickly left.

They did make a few arrests for possession of narcotics and/or dangerous drugs, but even that had its surprises. One source who was at the party relates that the sheriff pulled some people over and barked, "Okay, we're going to have to search everyone, now!" Several dozen men and women smiled at him and simply took off their clothes.

According to the San Francisco *Chronicle*, the officers left Harbinger having arrested 12 of the 500 or so people present.[23] After they were gone the party continued, although a lot of people left because the "good vibes and party energy" had been destroyed by the presence of the authorities. Many of the

---

23 There's another story, told to me by a dozen different sources, with variations on the details. It may be an embellishment of something that actually happened; it may also be completely apocryphal. It seems that during the raid, one of the officers was offered a glass of juice by a young woman. The fireplace was blazing away, the room was hot and stuffy, and he accepted it gratefully. The juice was spiked with acid, and within an hour, as the story goes, the cop was sitting on the stairs with his hat in his lap, scared, freaked out and tripping. Half a dozen naked hippies surrounded him and tried to guide him through the trip, saying "Just relax. Let go. Go with it. It's okay. We love you." The other deputies eventually found him and took him home.

people who stayed went up to the baths for the rest of the night, where they drummed and blew conch shells, which reverberated off the walls of the Hot Pool. Dozens of others sat in the soft darkness of the Warm Pool room, chanting and OM-ing until dawn.

Local response to the event was accompanied by a photo taken near Harbin Springs of a Middletown man pointing to a sign that said "Hippy Heaven":

> We noted that most of the people arrested during the weekend raid at Harbinger University were picked up for possessing something other than marijuana...this sort of proves to us that marijuana leads to other narcotics...the idea came up that possibly the "students" at Harbinger University are manufacturing the "stuff." If so, and if any of our tax dollars are being spent aiding the place, maybe the citizens of Middletown ought to check into it. We certainly don't want our tax dollars used to aid in the manufacture and propagation of narcotics.[24]

❖　❖

THE JIG WAS RAPIDLY BECOMING UP.　MORE AND MORE Harbinger residents left each week, although a few new people from the Bay Area continued to arrive.

The front page of the next issue of the *Times-Star* contained a plea from the Middletown community: "D.A. Asked to Move on Harbin Hippies Now!" District Supervisor Earle Wreiden demanded action from the District Attorney's office to evacuate Harbinger immediately, citing the fact that over 40 days had passed since the Health Department's inspection, and no attempts had been made to correct any of the violations.

The District Attorney's office had contacted the property owners, Sandy Estates, and told them that the hippies would be given a March third deadline to vacate. The investment group

---

24　There is no evidence to support this idea. Although the use of LSD was extremely widespread at Harbinger, it is highly unlikely that the drug was actually being manufactured on the site. See footnote, page 259.

asked the D.A.'s office to refrain, and again assured them that evictions would take place soon.

But Wreiden warned the County Board of Supervisors that unless they took immediate action:

> Other alternatives may be taken such as the residents marching on the Courthouse demanding action or contacting the State Attorney General's Office or the local residents taking matters into their own hands. [Wreiden] also emphasized that it was a county problem and they should not wait for the owners of the property to rectify it.

The article ended with the mention of an unconfirmed rumor that Sandy Estates had sold the property to Otis Electric Company, which planned to develop the site into apartments and condominiums.

Public opinion in Middletown was running very strongly against the continuing presence of Harbinger University and the Frontiers of Science Fellowship in Lake County. The Health Department was preparing to close "the campus," David Luce, the District Attorney, was readying a case against the Fellowship, and private citizens were writing indignant letters to the paper.

> We moved here because we were tired of fear, violence and hippies. When we heard about what was happening to Harbin Springs, we were amazed and very displeased. Truthfully, I can't understand the hippie philosophy of life, but maybe it's because our children are normal, average citizens....In Middletown there are fine boys and girls. Won't we be letting them down to let Harbinger exist as it is? —A Proud Citizen.

On March 13, 1969, Harbinger was served with a three-day notice to quit the premises because of failure to comply with the Health Code, and the Lake County Board of Supervisors passed a resolution. It directed the D.A. "to abate the nuisances of Harbin Springs and other hippie colonies by whatever means necessary."

Five days later, on March 18, 1969, the Lake County Sheriff's office, assisted by two State Narcotics agents and two Federal agents, made a pre-dawn raid on Harbinger. Chastened by their somewhat abortive first raid, they came prepared with dogs, several paddy wagons and search warrants. They confiscated "marijuana, drugs and paraphernalia used for smoking and injecting narcotics." They met with little resistance.

The property was evacuated completely. Sixteen people, all in their early to mid 20s, were arrested in the raid; two were released immediately for lack of evidence. Two Mill Valley girls, aged 11 and 16 were picked up as well; the Sheriff noted that although they were juveniles, they were not runaways.

After the raid Luce denied that the arrests had anything to do with the Supervisors' order, and called the raid "an independent action of the Sheriff's office." He issued this statement:

> A temporary restraining order was served on the occupants of Harbin Springs on Tuesday, March 18, 1969. This order enjoins all persons from occupying the premises until all building and sanitary conditions have been corrected and approved.
>
> No one occupied the premises the night of March 18, and the moving out process has commenced. It is expected that within two days the Frontiers of Science, Harbinger University and all individual occupants will have moved from the premises all machinery, equipment and personal belongings....The occupants have cooperated with the authorities in complying with the court order.

After eight tumultuous and powerful months, the great Harbinger experiment was over.

❖   ❖

THE FRONTIERS OF SCIENCE FELLOWSHIP AND HARBINGER University relocated; small groups of Harbinger alumni moved into houses in Mill Valley, Oakland and Berkeley, and were looking for a house to rent in Novato. Ten to 15 members moved to a laboratory in Richmond to "conduct an experiment in lifestyle, one of our main concerns," FOS public relations man Stuart Papell told reporters. He went on to reiterate that "the policy of the Fellowship doesn't allow drug use, and those arrested were those who weren't aware of the policy."

Sixteen people from Harbinger appeared in the Lake County Justice Court on Thursday, April 3, 1969. All entered pleas of "not guilty" on charges of possession of drugs.

Immediately after the second raid, Don Hamrick went to Mill Valley, where he stayed at the home of FOS members. By the end of March, Papell said the Frontiers founder was in New York, and had been given office space by the National Council of Churches, to continue his work.

The Frontiers of Science continued for a while in its diaspora. Members produced a radio show once a month (at the beginning of each zodiacal sign) on Berkeley's KPFA, and Harbinger University Press, located in Oakland, published the third and last issue of *Changes* in April of 1969.

Changes final issue was much more professional than either its first two attempts or *Harbinger* had been; it was a standard sized magazine and although its artwork was still fairly psychedelic and colorful, it didn't interfere with the text.[25] Metaphysical bookstores, herb shops, natural foods stores and other counterculture businesses had advertisements in *Changes*, presumably financing its printing and distribution, since the FOS wasn't in the best financial standing.

Articles again reflected a less drug-oriented, more ecological and holistic viewpoint than *Harbinger*. "Introduction to Herbal Medicine," "Natural Areas in the Urban Environment," and the "Smokey the Bear Sutra," were offered, along with an editorial by Stephen Levine and a history of the Haight by Allen Cohen, former editor of the San Francisco *Oracle*.

A long, philosophic piece entitled "Cycles, Seasons and Codes" was written by the Frontiers founder as the lead piece for that issue. It said, in part:

---

25 The issue is also memorable because its inside back cover was an illustration by underground comic master R. Crumb—the first appearance of Mr. Natural on a tractor, "Twas Ever Thus."

Do you know how many people stand without and try to understand what goes on within?....We are all simply what we are seasonably, giving what we can at the right time....Various ones of us have appeared and taken roles we have had through the ages to make preparation for this day, this season, this era.

The article marked the end of his era; it's the last known appearance of Don Hamrick. An ad in the revived, second generation San Francisco *Oracle* in October of 1969 offered the complete series of his lectures on reel-to-reel tape; his work was available from Harbinger Recordings in Fairfax, but there is no further mention of the man himself.

One source said he left the country in the early '70s and moved to New Zealand with his family. Another remembers reading about a connection between Hamrick and John Lennon, involving UFO research in New York in the early '70s. What really happened to him remains unknown.

❖ ❖

TWO WEEKS AFTER THE HARBINGER RAID, A COUNTY CREW CAME out to change the road sign on the outskirts of Middletown. They painted out the "ger" and lettered "Springs" back in. The sign may have said "Harbin Springs" again, but the resort that had gone by that name for so long no longer existed.

The buildings were empty, and the D.A. decided that no one would be allowed to occupy the premises in the future until all building work was completed and the property was brought into compliance with the county Health Code, neither of which looked at all likely.

One man who had been at Harbinger said he went back a few months after the raid and walked around.

I could see it as I saw it then—spiderwebs covered with jewels and glowing tapestries. Then suddenly none of that was there and it was just a decrepit resort.

No one lived there. The abandoned area became a forbidden late-night hangout for Middletown youths to go drinking, or do some target shooting at what was left of the old hotels. Rusted beer cans littered the ground. The pools were stagnant and filthy, the springs barely trickling in; the windows had been broken or shot out of all the buildings. Harbin was not only deserted, it was destroyed.

And at the entrance, just below the spot where Newt Booth had once built a stone archway with gleaming brass letters that said "Harbin Hot Sulphur Springs," there was a rusted car body, riddled with bullet holes and dripping red paint that said "Welcome."

CHAPTER EIGHT

Renaissance and Community

T HE SIXTIES HAD BEEN A VOLATILE DECADE FOR HARBIN, one in which everything that had come before was changed and ultimately abandoned. As the '70s began, the former resort was a shambles—the buildings and grounds had been thoroughly trashed, first by the Harbinger University "students" and later, after they had been evicted, by vandals and (some say) by vigilante groups who wanted to make sure no more hippies would ever live there again.

After over 100 years of being the pride of the Middletown area, "Harbin Springs" had become a bad word.[1] The property was officially closed, but occasional squatters lived in what was left of the buildings, and in the relatively unscathed Annex. The Sheriff patrolled the area to keep people from trespassing, but security was lax, and the baths continued to be popular as a local after-hours party site.

Sandy Estates had originally invested in Harbin Springs in 1963 not as a resort, or even as a potential housing development, but primarily because of its geothermal and mineral resources. In the early '70s, the property was not on the market, but the real estate group was exploring the possibility of selling the land to an oil company or the federal government for development.

The State of California also had its eye on the property. In October of 1971, a meeting was held to discuss turning the historic resort site into a state park. The State Parks and

---

1   As late as 1988, at least one Lake County guidebook continued to erase all memory of the Frontiers of Science with the terse entry: "Harbin Springs—closed 1960."

Recreation Department made a survey and inspection and recommended that further surveys be done and that Harbin Springs be placed on a priority list for incorporation into the state system.

> When money is available, possibly in 1972, the purchase of the land may be made, and the conversion of the property into a state park can begin. This will be an attraction to campers and tourists from all over the nation.

Sandy Estates apparently decided not to wait for state money to materialize, and put Harbin up for sale in the spring of 1972. A few months later it was purchased by a 39-year old Gestalt philosopher and erstwhile Miami real estate investor named Robert Hartley.

❖ ❖

BOB HARTLEY WAS BORN IN WASHINGTON D.C. TO A WEALTHY family, and attended private schools until he matriculated at Harvard. After a two year hiatus with an Army rifle company in Germany, he got his degree and went on to do graduate work at Columbia, specializing in the economics of underdeveloped countries. He took his failure to secure a job in banking in New York as a sign that he should go into business for himself and went to Mexico. Because of strict regulations governing business by foreigners, his Mexican venture was unsuccessful; while he was there he embarked on a life-long course of self-education, concentrating on philosophy, psychology and comparative religion.

He returned to New York, got married and moved to Miami, where he put some money he had inherited into both real estate and the stock market; within nine months, his investment has increased five-fold. He used the money to manifest some of the ideals he had been reading about, and financed two Summerhill-type schools in New York and Florida. After his divorce, he lived at one of the schools for a few months, then traveled around the world for six months of study.

In Taiwan he met and married his second wife, Teresa, the daughter of a member of the exiled Chiang Kai-shek government. After they returned to the U.S., Hartley managed his real estate holdings and continued to increase his assets in the stock market.

In 1966 he was 33 years old, successful, and bored with the business world. The developments in alternative living that were happening in Haight Ashbury and elsewhere fascinated him, and he began to devote more and more time to study and less to business. The couple moved to Hawaii for about a year; Bob began to think about finding a spot to fulfill a life long dream—establishing a community where he could live and study.[2]

> I had a dream of community. The most ideal living situation I'd ever had was in college. Each [350-person] House had its own dining room, and I used to spend four or five hours a day there, hanging out with people and discussing things. It was a very creative, very enjoyable period for me. I wanted to have that kind of environment.

More and more radical changes were developing in California, and in 1967 the Hartleys moved to Berkeley, living a few blocks from Sproul Plaza and the anti-war protests for eight months before buying a home in nearby Kensington. Bob had read all of Fritz Perls' work on Gestalt therapy years before and, after two years of training, was accepted at the Gestalt Therapy Institute of San Francisco for continued training and study.

Gestalt work excited him more than anything else he had studied and he totally immersed himself in the program, doing therapy in groups as a participant and a leader, and doing therapy with himself, using a tape recorder alternately as patient and therapist. One thing he didn't like about the work was the unequal interaction of the therapist and the patient. He didn't particularly want to be an authority figure; he wanted to

---

2   He explored the possibility of buying a South Pacific island, but soon discovered that most of the islands were owned by European governments who were no more hospitable to American entrepreneurs than Mexico had been. He also realized that, on an island, there was really no defense against pirates coming in and taking everything that had been created, and abandoned the idea.

use Gestalt techniques in an atmosphere of equality and honest communication.

Hartley visited a Gestalt Kibbutz which Perls had founded in Canada and rekindled his own vision of living in community. Two of his teachers at the Institute, Richard Miller and Larry Bloomberg, had also been exploring this idea, and the three men set out to find a piece of property suitable for a small, Gestalt-oriented center.

The two teachers were to be the leaders of the community; Bob didn't feel capable of starting or organizing it, but he was in a better position to finance the purchase. "I was sort of a third person, tagging along, with money to contribute and a lot of zeal," he said. He developed a "wish list" of ten attributes the ideal property would have—reasonably priced; not too far or too close to a town; good road access, but no through traffic; no close neighbors, so that nudity would not be a problem; phone, electric and water lines; within a two hour drive of the Bay Area; existing housing and—definitely an ideal but not a necessity—a hot springs.

The Santa Cruz Mountain area was appealing, but none of the properties that were available met more than six or seven of the criteria. The group made a few offers in Sonoma County, but nothing panned out. They finally made an offer on Bartlett Springs, on the far eastern edge of Lake County; another group made an identical offer and the sale went to them. The real estate broker handling the sale said that the owner of Bartlett's was "an extreme conservative and suspicious of psychologists and psychiatrists," which had probably been the deciding factor. Years later, Hartley would call it "divine intervention."

❖   ❖

WHILE MILLER AND BLOOMBERG WERE ON A TRIP TO MOROCCO, another Lake County property came on the market—Harbin Hot Springs. The two teachers had liked the property when they visited it a year or so before, and said that it was beautiful, but horribly neglected, and had a very bad reputation. Hartley had never seen it, so when the broker called to say it was available, he took a drive up the mountain to take a look.

His first view of the property was the bullet-riddled car and, as he made his way up the road, while he saw the abandoned buildings, the roads rutted by run-off from heavy rains, and the obscenities painted on the sides of the buildings, he also saw what he'd been looking for. The place was a wreck, but it met every one of the ten criteria on his wish list.

Sandy Estates had originally been asking half a million dollars for the property, but by the time Bob looked at it, the price was down to $250,000 for over 1000 acres and what was left of the resort. In order to stall for time, he made the broker a low offer, which he fully expected to have rejected. By the time he and the broker began to negotiate, he thought, his partners would be back from Morocco, and they could get down to dealing.

To his surprise, the Sandy Estates accepted his offer of $180,000.

A contract was drawn up, including a 50/50 split of the mineral and geothermal rights (which Sandy Estates had wanted to keep outright), and Hartley gave the broker a $5000 deposit. When Miller and Bloomberg returned, they were quite happy with the property, but during the process of negotiating the down payment and mortgage arrangements, the three men came to some disagreements and their partnership dissolved.

Faced with the choice of losing the deposit or going through with the deal alone, Hartley drove up to look at the dilapidated former resort site again. It was April, and the air was warm, the trees were in bloom and the hillsides were a deep rich green. He walked around for several hours, again struck by the beauty and power of the land. The deal was closed in May of 1972.

Bob Hartley held the deed to Harbin Hot Springs, but he had no plans for it. Instead of being an apprentice watching his teachers form and lead a community, he was the sole owner. He had a wife and two children and almost all of his money was tied up in real estate, but he "just couldn't believe I had ended up with such a beautiful piece of land."

He readily admits that he was very naive about what would come next. There were grumblings and heated rumors locally that another bunch of hippies was going to take over Harbin, and the county's health and building departments quickly made it clear that no one could move in and no repairs or new construction could be done in the Main Area until the sewage and water systems were brought up to code. The building department further recommended that most of the existing structures (except the Fern building) should be torn down because they were unsafe and were beyond repair. The top floor of the old cocktail lounge was dismantled, and the barn was torn down in stages. One resident remembers that the lumber from the demolished buildings was used for bonfires that lasted for days.

Two couples who had been loosely connected with the Gestalt community in the Bay Area—Louis Figone and Al Svanoe and their wives—moved into the first two cabins in the Annex (renaming it "the Village"), which had suffered the least destruction and deterioration, and began to fix it up. A man named Jimmy[3] moved into the Pine (now Shiatsu) cabin, and served as the caretaker for the main area while arrangements were made with the county.

Since the buildings were deemed unsafe for occupancy, but no repairs could be made to them until the sewage and water systems were completed, Hartley applied to the county for permission to consider Harbin as a construction site, with a maximum of 32 people living on it and working on the repairs. The county agreed to the proposal for one year. Hartley hired local contractor Larry Nardi to install two septic tanks and begin repairs to the water system, while he continued to try to sell his house in Kensington.

The Hartley family moved up to Harbin in June of 1973, nearly 14 months after the sale had been completed. They purchased a double-wide mobile home, which they placed by the entrance to the property. The structure served a dual purpose—it provided a home for the Hartleys and was also situated so that the occupants could monitor and have some control over who came onto the land. Once he was living on

---

3   In the very early days of the Harbin community, a lot of people came and went, and few records were kept. Nearly twenty years later, first names are all that are remembered in some cases; full names are used when available.

property and could keep an eye on what was going on, Bob put ads in the *Berkeley Barb* and other Bay Area underground papers, soliciting community members.

> Hot Springs in the country. Very rustic and unfinished. $30 per month rent, or work exchange, 1 to 1½ hours per day.

He had expected to be inundated with people who wanted to live in community, but made do with the scant handful of people who answered the ads, and did much of the physical labor himself in the first months that he lived there. The first residents were faced with the monumental task of cleaning foot-deep piles of trash, broken glass and paper out of their rooms before they could even put a mattress down. The next person found a clean, but bare room, with plastic over the open windows. There was no functional kitchen; people cooked on hot plates and washed their dishes behind the pools, in a bathtub filled with hot spring water.

The first project after the completion of the septic system was making Fern livable. A couple named David and Louellen were responsible for installing most of the windows in the building; Bob remembers making trips to the Bay Area and returning with the back seat of his car full of window glass. Work was progressing, but everything was very slow. There was very little cash available, and not enough people to do the enormous amount of work that needed to be done.

A 1973 mimeographed letter, sent to those who had answered the advertisements, described the ideal behind the work:

> The philosophy of the place is to have a community that builds itself, centered on a magnificent property rather than an ideology, with a minimum of controls to avoid the pitfalls of so many other communities...freeloaders and crashers or...an ideology that is more important than the individual. These do not exist at Harbin, as members are free to spend most of their time on their own needs and creativity. Most of us are interested in growing.
> I certainly am.—*Bob.*

❖　　❖

THE IDEALS WERE IN PLACE, BUT THERE WAS VERY LITTLE community feeling, just a handful of workers, many of whom were only looking for a cheap and rural place to live and kick back. A few organized groups from the Bay Area inquired about coming up and sharing the land, making improvements as they worked on their own, autonomous projects. Bob was enthusiastic about the idea of Harbin being a center for a variety of different "New Age" groups; the Health Department was not. Each time an application was made for a specific project, the officials countered with a list of repairs that must be completed first. The lists seemed to be endless.

Frustrated and discouraged by the battle between dream and bureaucracy, Bob decided to take a trip through Nevada, Arizona and New Mexico, to see if those wide open spaces also had wide open regulations. He traveled through the region looking for a site where a community could develop organically, at its own pace and with its own ethic. While he was in New Mexico he learned that Green Valley (the school he had financed in Florida) was in trouble and went there to try and straighten things out.

Green Valley had begun as an alternative school, and had gradually become a center for disturbed children and juvenile delinquents, with 60 staff members and 120 students. It had been successful as a treatment center, but a series of unfortunate incidents had put it into a bad financial position. Bob stayed in Florida as Executive Director of the school for five months, hoping to bring it around again financially, and perhaps merge his own community-oriented energies with its existing structures. But he and the staff of the school had very different goals, and his wife hated being there,[4] so he left it for the staff to run alone. It closed three months later.

Bob Hartley returned to Lake County in May of 1974 chastened by his experiences and determined to put all his energy into making a community at Harbin work. Things had

---

4   He and his wife had been gradually growing apart, mostly over differences in lifestyle. It was an amicable parting; she returned to San Francisco, and they were divorced soon after.

not gone well in his absence. The workers had the attitude that while the owner was on property they would work, but could relax while he was away, so very little had been done in five months. And there had been a fire.

The three-story Capitol Hotel overlooking the baths had been built by Richard Williams in the 1870s; in the 1930s Newt Booth had replaced it with what he called the "Main Annex." By the 1970s it was one of the few structures on property that was in decent shape, and its 40 rooms had housed a lot of the people living at Harbin. In March of 1974, a fire began in one of the rooms and quickly spread throughout the building. By the time the blaze was extinguished, over two-thirds of the Capitol was in ruins. The rubble was gradually cleared away, and a new roof was put on the now one-story building, renamed "Redwood." Decking was put on top of the roof, providing a sunbathing area next to the pools.

The Harbin Springs "community" was limping along, but Hartley was disappointed in the level of interaction and commitment among people who lived there. In the Bay Area, he had enjoyed a wide circle of friends—people inter- ested in Gestalt therapy, and in the "New Age." The situation at Harbin attracted a lot of loners, drop-outs and people who had rejected society and wanted to get away from it. Along with some sincere counter- culture seekers, there were a lot of people with "anti" energy, and much of it focused on him as the landlord and owner of the property.

Bob Hartley (Ishvara), late 1970s

When he returned from Florida, he attempted to eliminate some of that energy by getting together with the people who were serious about making a life at Harbin, to form a group that would join him in making decisions about the community and its direction.

He later commented:

> I didn't want to organize Harbin myself. I didn't want to do it as my personal thing, and I didn't want to have to be the person running around and making all the decisions.

In the fall of 1974 he sat down with a handful of other people—among them his new girlfriend, Elohym Heart, and builder Rod Johnson—and said, in essence:

> I'm tired of being the owner. I think it's time we decided what we want to do. Who are we? What do we believe? What's going to be the foundation of what we're going to do?

The group agreed that they were aligned with the growing New Age movement, and that they wanted to base the community's philosophical and social structure around its principles. They then struggled with the difficult task of defining what they meant by "New Age."

❖   ❖

THE NEW AGE MOVEMENT IS A DESCENDENT OF BOTH THE '60S counterculture and a long tradition of metaphysical thought in America. These very separate and widely divergent movements came together in the early 1970s to create a force that had never existed before, one based equally in science and spirituality.

Early protestant settlers in North America had battled fiercely to rid their society of any supernatural or occult beliefs, replacing spirits with a stern, patriarchal God. In the early 19th century, God was joined (and frequently opposed) by another strong force—science—which attempted to replace superstitions with observable phenomena and facts. But by mid-century, several separate movements arose to examine the nature of those things which were beyond science and forbidden (or whitewashed) by western religion.

Emanuel Swedenborg and his followers championed the primacy of an invisible, spiritual realm; Franz Mesmer introduced a method for inducing trances and altered frames of mind that many used to access "the other world." Henry Thoreau and Ralph Waldo Emerson, enthused by an early English translation of the Hindu scripture, *Bhagavad Gita,* advocated its religious precepts (combined with American values of individualism and personal responsibility) to form what they called Transcendentalism.

Many of the more radical thinkers of the 19th century were drawn to these ideas, out of which evolved such strong metaphysical movements as Spiritualism (which synthesized these earlier schools of thought with the added fillip of communicating with the dead while in trance) and Madame Blavatsky's Theosophical Society. The latter was responsible for a renewed interest in astrology, and was instrumental in introducing both Hindu and Buddhist texts and precepts to America.

Theosophy, Spiritualism and their innumerable offshoots were extremely popular in the early 20th century; a number of experimental communities were founded based on their principles, some with hundreds of members. But they were definitely "on the fringe," and looked at with distaste by both organized religion and science. The development of the science of psychology with its interest in mapping the "inner territories" of the mind, provided a great deal of intellectual support for the studying of the unseen; the goals of study and the terms used were, of course, quite different.

Psychology, especially the disciplines of psychic research and parapsychology, began to legitimize metaphysical thought by divesting it of its mysterious, supernatural and occult trappings. The Third Force or humanistic psychology of Fritz Perls, Abraham Maslow and others and the transpersonal psychology of the followers of Carl Jung provided a positive, scientific approach to what had previously been considered only matters of faith. They separated many "spiritual" practices such as yoga and meditation from their purely religious contexts, and lent scientific respectability to discussions of consciousness, creativity and the changes that often accompanied such practices.

The second "parent" of the New Age was the counterculture movement, which had its roots in the LSD research of the '50s and '60s, with its curious juxtaposition of God and chemicals. Hundreds of thousands of young people dropped out of mainstream society, searching for new answers and a new way to live. For many of them, including Harbinger University participants, the way to enlightenment was communal living and drugs. Drugs may have opened the doors to the exploration of consciousness, but people quickly discovered that they were not a long term solution, and they too turned to Eastern religion, meditation, yoga, hypnosis and other methods of exploration.

Scientists, seers and hippies were asking very different questions, but the answers were coming up the same; the common ground among them was what would come to be called the New Age.

❖   ❖

THE SMALL GROUP THAT MET IN THE FALL OF 1974 TO DETERMINE the future of Harbin examined their own experiences and conceptions of the New Age. They agreed that areas such as astrology might be *part* of the New Age, but were peripheral and did not define it. They found that they agreed that there were three basic elements which had never existed in their present forms: Universal Spirituality, the Human Potential movement, and the holistic, natural movement.

For them, Universal Spirituality meant recognizing the fundamental truths inherent in all religions, whether Christian, Hindu, Buddhist or Native American. They accepted the idea that there is a unity of spirit, within which all people are one with each other, the environment and life itself. Spiritual practices, no matter what their origin, would be accepted at Harbin Springs as a part of daily life, and each individual's conception of their own spiritual path would be welcome, as long as it didn't interfere with anyone else's.

They also embraced the principles of humanistic psychology and the Human Potential movement, which included: open, honest communication; individual growth; spontaneous and loving expressions of emotions and an emphasis on genuine relationships. Their dream for Harbin Springs was to create an atmosphere of love and trust for all who lived there.

Holistic, natural living was the third element of the New Age, a unification of body, mind and spirit in an atmosphere of health and healing. Harbin had always been a place for healing, and was a simple, rural setting; part of getting back to nature for most of its residents involved a healthy, primarily vegetarian diet and an emphasis on sound ecology, from organic gardening to recycling. They believed in respecting the health of the individual, of the land, and of the planet.

A common thread ran through each of these three elements of the New Age—growth, health, love, respect—that the group resolved would be the basis of their community and their religion—Heart Consciousness.

> We identify ourselves so completely with this new point of view that we call it a religion, and ourselves a Church. For what is religion but one's deepest identification and its conscious outward manifestation?...Heart Consciousness religion probably speaks in different words to different people; it is best to be gentle in defining it.

After months of discussion, they established Heart Consciousness Church (HCC), and incorporated it in February of 1975 as a non-profit religious organization. The Articles of Incorporation filed with the State of California stated that:

> The purpose of Heart Consciousness Church is to teach spiritual life and how it can be realized by individuals, manifested to others and made learnable by example, without this process requiring group conformity or adherence to a single teacher, method or creed.

Robert Hartley then sold Harbin Hot Springs to the new Church for ten dollars, and relinquished his role as its owner.

Heart Consciousness Church's first Board of Directors included Elohym Heart, Mick Zippert and Jo Ellen Burch; Bob was not included. At the time of the sale, he also donated two buildings to it, worth close to half a million dollars. The sale of the property and the donation was a potential conflict of interest if he, as a board member, had to do business with himself as the owner, and he chose not to be an official of the Church in its beginning stages.

The formation of HCC provided a conceptual framework and a focus for the energy of the fledgling community. One of the first projects to happen at Harbin under its auspices was the Village School, which offered a semester program of classes on ecology, psychology and religion for college age students. Peter Clark and his friend Judy had established their own non-profit corporation, and were instrumental in setting up the school program. As a school, it was a failure; no students signed up. But it brought the group together, trying to create something new, and that helped coalesce the feeling of community.

Peter and Judy also began offering workshops to people outside Harbin, holding the groups in the Stonefront building (the only usable structure) and charging $4 per person for the weekend. Harbin began to advertise itself as a workshop center for alternative seminars, which provided a small source of income for the new Church. In the summer of 1975, the Holistic Health Retreat was held at Harbin, with some leading names in Bay Area alternative culture, including the Berkeley Women's Health Collective. The event attracted over 500 people.

❖   ❖

HARBIN WAS A PRIVATE CENTER, BUT A FEW PEOPLE CONTINUED to come up to use the baths, many of them knowing about the place from the Harbinger University era. In the days when the community's identity was still being created, visitors were not particularly encouraged in Harbin's literature.

> Sunday is our regular visiting day...it is our community work day as well, and we find people get to know each other quickest and best by working together. We do not have a red carpet out for visitors as we are just too busy and too many people want to visit. You should write or phone before coming so we will know to expect you; with such an attractive place and Hot Baths, we have to be distant with strangers or we would have them all over us, and if you are not expected, you are a stranger.

Visitors who had made arrangements to come up were expected to work and contribute what they could. No admission was charged, but there was a donations box up by the door of the Warm Pool building. The average donation turned out to be about fifteen cents. When the Church was established, the Board of Directors decided to have a regular one dollar admission fee for each visitor using the baths, good for a day visit or for overnight camping.

Collecting the fee was hit or miss. Visitors were directed to a box at the front of the trailer near the entrance, where they were supposed to pay their dollar and sign their name on a list. Sometime in the afternoon, Bob would take the list up to the pools and ask people their names, checking them off as he found them. Naturally a lot of people had just sneaked in, and many of them complained (loudly) that the water was God's miracle, that the Earth belonged to no one, and refused to pay.

One of the Board members, Dennis Trager, decided it would be more efficient (and less disruptive) to collect the fee in the parking lot, and tell people that the fee was three dollars,

The Warm Pool, late 1970s

reasoning that if there was going to be that much hassle, it might as well be three dollars as one. To everyone's surprise, most visitors gladly paid the extra money; the complaint level stayed about the same.

The building which housed the Warm and Hot Pools, built by Newt Booth and company some 60 years earlier, was not particularly stable. The planning department had recommended that it be demolished, but nature saved the community the trouble. Early in 1975, an unusually heavy snowfall caused the roof of the structure to collapse, sending concrete and timbers into the water and denting the railing on the right side of the Warm Pool. A construction crew cleared the rubble out of the water and eventually cut the remains of the walls away cleanly.

The walls of the building and the pool itself had been covered with small tiles, many of which fell off during the collapse. The remaining back wall was, for a few years, a colorful, random outdoor mosaic. Replacing the roof and walls was discussed, but after a few weeks of bathing in warm water under the stars, open to the wind and the scent of the pines, everyone agreed that they really liked it better without a roof. It remains an open-air Warm Pool to this day.

❖   ❖

AFTER THE FORMATION OF HCC, THE REQUIREMENT FOR BEING A resident member of the Harbin community and its church was established as a donation of 15 hours of work per week; a few individuals were allowed to donate $75 per month in lieu of working. A notable exception was Michael Colton, who was a licensed contractor and was paid five dollars an hour for his skilled work in construction and remodeling. Under his direction the Stonefront kitchen was remodeled and brought up to code, and bathrooms were installed in that building and in the lower level of the building adjacent to Fern and the baths.

Conditions slowly improved at Harbin Springs, and more people came to join the Church and its community, many of them hearing about the center from workshop participants and word-of-mouth. Terry Reedy, his friend Chandra, Mort Reiber,

Mary Rivera and a man named Larry all arrived in 1976, and all would have a strong impact on the new Church and its future.

HCC was (and is) a non-dogmatic church; its members all shared a belief in some facet of its three-part vision of the New Age, and beyond that were free to pursue their own spiritual paths and goals. In the first three years of Bob's ownership, before the formation of HCC, there was almost no structure or organization at Harbin; about 25 people lived there, but little was accomplished as a group. HCC had created a kind of common identity, but it also gave a few residents something concrete to rebel against.

When the Church was formed, the decision-making role had passed from Bob as the individual owner to the Board of Directors of the Church. As a corporation, the Church had General Members, who belonged to the Church but had no legal say in its administration, and Voting Members, who had the power to elect or replace the Board.

A small group of residents who arrived in 1976 complained that the structure of the Church was elitist; they decided that all residents of Harbin should be Voting Members, and that the Church and the community should be run as a democracy. They declared that, as members of the Church, they were entitled to vote for their own Board of Directors, and with that voted themselves into power. Under the Church's corporate structure, their act had no legal validity, but this seemed irrelevant to them.

The legitimate Board of Directors (which included Bob by this time) had a long-range plan for Harbin to become a true spiritual center, dedicated to bringing the New Age into being by providing a space for teaching its precepts to anyone who shared in that vision. The "new board" was not interested in future visions; they wanted Harbin Springs to continue just the way it was—a small community making repairs to their buildings, growing vegetables, and raising their families away from the strictures of "society." They were quite content with their lifestyle, and saw no need to change it.

A schism developed between the leaders of the Church and the dissidents. Innumerable meetings were held to discuss the issues, some held in a spirit of harmony and compromise, others in an atmosphere of shouting and blame. Finally, in September of 1976, Mark Simms, Mort, Mary and Larry declared that they would no longer support the Church and its administration, and refused to contribute the $50 per month that was the residency requirement at that time.

After a few months of attempting negotiations, the HCC Board authorized Bob to begin eviction proceedings against the rent-strikers in early 1977. It took over five months for the matter to come to trial in the Middletown Justice Court; in the meantime, life at Harbin amounted to a civil war. About a quarter of the 30-person community sided with the rent-strikers, and an equal number with the HCC Board. The rest of the community was unwilling to jeopardize friendships with people who had taken one side or the other, and remained uncommitted, though most of them hoped the rent strike would succeed.

As eviction proceedings dragged on, active attacks against the Church accelerated. Job sites were vandalized, and rent-strikers began disrupting weekend workshops, telling the participants to pay the four dollar fee to them, not to Bob. One weekend group came up to find that the Warm Pool had been drained, and would not be filled unless payment was made to the strikers. The Holistic Health Retreat held another event at Harbin, but a lot of their participants withdrew when disruptions made it impossible to continue. Bob called the local sheriff from time to time when it appeared the situation was out of control, but the officers informed him and the strikers (who claimed it was Bob who was in the wrong) that it was a civil matter and outside their jurisdiction.

New people coming into the community were quickly approached by the rent strikers and told that if they joined the cause, they could live at Harbin virtually for free; Bob had to put locks on the doors of unoccupied rooms to prevent squatters from taking them over. At one point he met with the leaders of the strike to try and make some sort of compromise, and offered to expand the Voting Members of HCC to include two of them. Believing he had an ulterior motive, they turned him down.

Bob Hartley, understandably, felt lonely and betrayed during the rent strike. He had donated or loaned a large portion of his assets to the Church, but at almost every meeting he was shouted at and insulted. Encounters with many of his fellow community members were hostile and unpleasant, and he again looked outside Harbin for people who shared his dream of community living.

He made contact with a group called the Utopians, who had their own community in San Francisco called Kerista Village. Bob was impressed by what they had done—they had a small, but very well-organized community—and encouraged because they seemed to share his vision. He was continually looking for other groups to come and share Harbin as a teaching center (especially since the community at Harbin was floundering), and the Utopians were equally open to alliances with like-minded groups and were impressed by Bob's goals and the beauty of Harbin's land.

Beginning in early 1977, the Utopians held monthly workshops at Harbin, attracting people from the Bay Area. They also got involved in facilitating Harbin community

Front cover of Kerista Village's **Utopian Eyes**, *Spring 1977, showing Harbin's Warm Pool, and its mosaic walls.*

meetings, using their interpersonal processes to try and foster communication between the rent strikers and those aligned with the HCC board. Several members of HCC joined the Utopian organization, and about 20 Keristans became members of HCC, including two who moved up to Harbin as full-time residents.

The alliance bolstered both organizations—the Utopians had a place outside the city to hold their workshops, and in return contributed to Harbin's economy and produced its first brochure. But many people in the community were less than pleased with the Utopians' attitude toward Harbin; they felt the group was trying to take over Harbin and turn it into a rural Kerista Village.

The idea was not so far-fetched. The Spring 1977 issue of their newsletter—*Utopian Eyes*—featured a drawing of Harbin's Warm Pool on the cover, with the headline: "New School of Utopian Psychology at Harbin Hot Springs." It was terrific publicity for Harbin as a New Age center, except for the fact that the Utopians' text repeatedly referred to Harbin as "our first permanent rural base."

Harbin community members felt the Utopians were convinced that theirs was the one true message and were too dogmatic. Those allied with the rent strikers felt that Bob was selling them out to his new allies. They began disrupting the Utopians' workshops and making them unwelcome. The workshops were discontinued and, although there continued to be an HCC-Utopian alliance for some years, the dream of a jointly-sponsored center at Harbin gradually faded away.

Beginning in 1976, Bob had felt moved to find a more disciplined spiritual practice; he found Gestalt therapy less satisfying, possibly because of his separation from other practitioners. He and Elohym became involved with a teacher called Baba Hari Dass, but the practices they learned seemed too mild to Bob. His next spiritual encounter was with his housemates, Chandra and Terry.

Terry Reedy was a disciple of a man named Charles Berner, a yogi who had been given the spiritual name Yogeshwar Muni; Terry had taught a few Enlightenment Intensives at Harbin based on Yogeshwar's teaching. The form of meditation

Yogeshwar taught was almost exactly what Bob had discovered as part of his Gestalt Therapy work. It was taught as "surrender meditation," and was the basis of Kundalini Yoga, something Bob had always wanted to explore. Introduced by Terry, Bob met Yogeshwar and was soon initiated into Kundalini Yoga. It was a practice that would (almost literally) consume him for the next ten years.

As Bob drew deeper and deeper into his Yoga, sometimes meditating as much as twelve hours a day, he seemed withdrawn from the community. His attraction to the meditation, combined with the difficulties of the rent strike fight, contributed to his isolation—an isolation that he says gave him the strength to continue the struggle.

Some residents were afraid that since Bob was so involved in his Yoga, he might turn Harbin into an ashram and give it to Yogeshwar. Again, there was some basis for their fears, but they misunderstood Bob's motive and his vision of what Harbin could be.

> I fight hard to maintain structure, not because of a personal desire for power, but because if any one group came to control Harbin Springs or the Church, then the way would be closed to other groups that want to make use of what we have to offer. This is my one lifetime creative project. Whatever else I do, I will not sabotage it.

While he had no intention of turning Harbin into an ashram, in July of 1977, he did renounce his old identity. From that time on he was known by the spiritual name that Yogeshwar Muni had given him—Ishvara.

❖ ❖

TWO MONTHS LATER THE COURT DECIDED IN FAVOR OF THE original HCC Board of Directors, and (a year after the strike had begun) the four rent strikers were evicted.

❖ ❖

CALIFORNIA HAS HAD MORE EXPERIMENTAL COMMUNITIES FORM within its borders than any other state in the union, beginning as far back as the 1870s and continuing into the present. They have all been basically one of two types, religious or secular, and their successes and failures due largely to their philosophical structure.

Religious communities are based on a commonly-held belief system and generally have a single, charismatic leader. They usually operate in an atmosphere of unquestioning obedience, with little individual expression or personal freedom. They are, more often than not, run efficiently and successfully, gradually disintegrating at the death (or defection) of the leader.

Secular communities, on the other hand, base themselves on social ideals such as brotherhood or socialism, and most hold at their center the belief that all members have equal freedom to act and speak as they please. A majority of secular communities have been short-lived because of this unbridled freedom. As was the case at Harbinger University, those with the loudest voices are able to take control, and dissent and confusion reign until the community dissolves in the chaos brought on by a lack of organization.

Harbin Hot Springs had a unique amalgam of the two types of government—although it was religiously-based, there was no one religion or one leader to pay allegiance to, and individual endeavors were allowed to thrive. But the freedom of expression that caused the downfall of so many secular communities was tempered by the existence of the Church. Ishvara had carefully structured HCC to prevent the loudest voices from taking over, allowing for individuality, but not rebellion or chaos. He had created, in many ways, the best of both worlds. Because of its unique mix, the community was able to weather its first real crisis and not only survive, but move forward.

> Most communities were too coercive. I didn't want to live in an "everybody" community—everybody cooks one day, everybody sweeps one day, everybody does this, everybody does that. I think division of labor is important. Some people *like* to cook, others like to build. I think people live most fruitfully in an atmosphere of responsibility and freedom.

Ishvara had assumed that once the leaders of the rent strike were gone, most of the dissension would also disappear, which proved to be the case. There was more harmony in the community, but still very little sense of direction. The majority of people who came to live at Harbin still weren't as concerned about the long range goal of building a community and a spiritual center as they were in just enjoying a rural lifestyle. They were willing to work for a while, to help fix the place up and contribute their fair share to the community, but had no real commitment to Harbin or to the Church. Ishvara recounts:

> People would come in with tremendous energy to do some cottage industry, and they would have the energy to remodel, but not the energy to follow through on successfully getting the business started. They would leave a couple of months later and we would be left with the mess. There wasn't much consistency, in the work or in the population.

After six years of struggling to make Harbin the community he had dreamed of, Ishvara was finally joined by someone equally dedicated to the ideal of communal living. When Roger Windsor walked through the gate in 1978, fresh from training in Boston, his own dream was to live in a community that practiced macrobiotics.[5] He saw that his practice and Ishvara's vision were compatible, and set his considerable skills and energies towards making Harbin a place where both could prosper.

Ishvara had been doing all the administrative, legal and financial work, along with any other tasks that no one else would handle. When Roger came, he took over some of those duties—collecting fees, monitoring the entrance, answering the phones, and coordinating workshops. In a very short period of time he became Harbin's first General Manager, and was a strong force behind organizing the community.

To his relief, Ishvara finally had someone he could depend on enough to relinquish his unwanted role as the primary authority figure, leaving him free to concentrate more

---

5 Macrobiotics is a dietary philosophy that originated in Japan. Some of its tenets include a balanced intake of yin and yang food energies, a reliance on seasonal foods, and a grain-centered, vegetarian diet.

completely on his spiritual practice. Because of the rigors of his Yoga, his energy for functioning in the community was greatly reduced; he had moved out of the trailer into a circular hut on the hillside above, and spent most of his time in meditation.

Under Roger's leadership, Harbin's inner structure began to function more smoothly; its outer structures were still in need of great repair. The Fern and Stonefront buildings had been remodeled to meet the county's standards for use, but the renovation of Redwood had never been completed after the fire, and Walnut and Azalea were in just slightly better condition than the people of Harbinger University had left them.

A few months after Roger arrived, a contractor and merchant seaman named Ray Testman moved to Harbin, and started a five-year program of construction that would transform the former resort into a prominent New Age retreat center. He quickly gathered a construction crew—Alton, Bernie, Sage and others—and created a bathroom in the Meadow area to make it legal for use as a campground.

His first big project was remodeling Walnut and parts of Azalea so they were fit for occupancy. He and his team repaired walls, roofs and floors, rewired the electrical system, tore out most of the unusable original plumbing, put glass in the windows, and brought the buildings up to code. Once that was done, some residents moved into the remodeled Walnut building and, for the first time since Abend and Blum's ownership, rooms in Fern were available for guests. When he finished Walnut, Ray began the remodeling of Redwood for use as additional guest rooms.

Ishvara had initially thought that Harbin Springs would be supported through resident contributions, augmented by income from workshops such as massage, folk dance, weekend encounters and Stan Dale's pioneering "Loving Relationships." Rates for workshops were $10 per person for the weekend, or $20 if meals were included; meals for workshops were vegetarian and "without coffee."

With the availability of Fern, he and Roger began to examine the possibility of guest income as a contribution to the Church. Rates for day visits to the baths stayed at three dollars, with overnight camping at five dollars or a two-hour work donation. The new guest rooms were made available at a higher rate, and visitors paid a small amount of annual dues to become members of the Church. Although overnight guests were now welcome, Harbin Springs was definitely not on its way to becoming a public resort again; it was opening its spiritual center to non-resident members of HCC, who were expected to agree with its basic philosophy. A 1978 brochure noted:

> Visitors should respect the holiness of the land and natural waters by being quiet, not smoking or leaving trash, not drinking near the baths, leaving dogs at home and so forth.

Amenities for visitors were virtually non-existent; hotel rooms had no beds, just foam mattresses on the floor, and guests were expected to provide their own food, towels and bedding. While campers could logically be expected to bring their own sleeping bags, recently-arrived resident Chris Wippert felt that those who paid the extra money for a room should at least be entitled to a bottom sheet on their mattress. She took the initiative to go out and buy some linens for the beds in Fern and organized its cleaning and upkeep, creating a position for herself as the first manager of Housekeeping.

As accommodations and overall quality improved, Harbin Springs started to prosper. Before 1978, any construction or

Harbin residents in front of Azalea, during remodeling, late 1970s.

repair, the mortgage, and most of the operating expenses, had been financed by over a million dollars in donations and loans from Ishvara to HCC. Resident contributions and workshop income offset these expenses, but came nowhere near covering them. In 1976, the annual income from workshops and visitors was about $9000; the annual total for 1978 had risen to over $66,000.

By mid-1978, living accommodations for residents had also been improved by Ray and Roger's diligent work, and the residency requirement was established as 30 hours of work per month plus a donation of $60 to the Church in return for living space. People who were curious about becoming residents were sent a letter detailing what was expected:

> Only highly dedicated persons willing to become deeply involved in our Church program are now accepted as residents. Our work effort is: improving workshop and visitors' facilities, general beautification and maintenance, construction, teaching, spiritual leadership and administration...There is much sharing in decision-making, with final power in the Board of Directors of the Church corporation owning the land.

The community remained at about 30 people, but a greater percentage of the population was now willing to take on some of the responsibilities of management. The HCC board (Ishvara, Elohym, Rod Johnson and Roger) established a sub-committee for the "involvement of non-officers and non-directors in the active running of Harbin Hot Springs operations." For a while the committee—called The Servants of the Dream—replaced such early attempts at community government as The Committee of Five, the Committee of Eight and The Vision Committee. Harbin began to operate under the philosophy "government for all, by the responsible."

❖   ❖

WHILE THE SERVANTS OF THE DREAM HANDLED DECISIONS ON most of the day-to-day matters—housing, work reports, meetings, workshops, cottage industries, maintenance—the HCC Board was looking ahead to the future of Harbin as a locus for other centers to be developed. Ishvara had been in contact with Ken Keyes, author of *Handbook to Higher Consciousness*, whose organization had a 150-acre site in Kentucky called "Cornucopia." Keyes was planning to develop a West Coast center, and negotiations were underway for a 32-acre parcel of Harbin land to be leased to his group as a training center.

The "Living Love Center" was to be a model ecological complex of circular huts—dormitories, meeting rooms, storage buildings and a large dining hall—clustered on the hillside across the creek from the Main Area at Harbin. Keyes' center would be both residential and a short-term training site for those interested in the principles he had developed in his book.

The project was big enough to warrant write-ups in the Lake County and Santa Rosa papers, and Keyes addressed a meeting of a Middletown boosters association, explaining his plans for an open, loving environment just outside their town. Unfortunately, there was a lot of resistance from people in the county; letters were written to the papers and to county government protesting the development of any such center in the Middletown area.

Some of the objections had nothing to do with Keyes or his center, but with ironically bad timing. The planning commission hearings on his proposal for a Living Love Center came just one month after the massacre at Jim Jones' People's Temple in Guyana. Several local families had lost relatives at Jonestown, and were unwilling to have anything to do with what sounded like another cult.

Reluctance to approve a development at Harbin Springs may also have had a little to do with recent, very local events. After the rent strike had been ended in the fall of 1977, a handful of residents led by Al Svanoe left the Village area and moved up the mountain to the farthest corner of HCC-owned land, about two miles from the Main Area. They built three houses in that remote location and formed their own mini-community with eight or nine members. (Al built the *Gulch House*, Jim Strider built the tiny Doll House, and Swann Hover built a hut that would eventually be remodeled into *Arnell's*, later called *Aerie*.) They gradually severed any ties between the "upper property" and HCC's community on the

"lower property," other than paying rent to the Church.[6]
Unbeknownst to anyone in the administration, they had also
resumed an old cottage industry—growing marijuana and
psychedelic mushrooms.[7]

Marijuana use was still common at Harbin, and there had
been rumors of a major pot garden in the hills, but Ishvara
knew nothing definite until one Saturday morning in October of
1978. A member of the Sheriff's department came on property
and asked Ishvara for permission to search for illegal plants;
permission was quickly granted, as the Church wanted to make
it clear it had nothing to hide.

To Ishvara's surprise, a friend of Al's, who was living in the
Magic Inn just below Stonefront, saw the authorities and fired
three shots into the air to warn his buddies. Fifteen patrol cars
took off up the rutted dirt road that led to the outlying land.
Most of the people who lived on the upper property got away
before the sheriff arrived, but two women were found hiding
behind bushes and arrested.

GRASS GREW TALL AT HOT SPRINGS

A search of approximately 1100 acres of the Harbin Springs
area outside of Middletown by Lake County Sheriff's officers
resulted in seizure of 413 marijuana plants with heights of 2 to 14
feet. The 1300 pounds of "grass" was taken on October 7 at 9:00
am from the property of the Heart Consciousness Church.

The Board of Directors immediately wrote a letter to the
Lake County *Bee*, informing them that none of the growers in
the isolated area were members of the Church, which did not
advocate drug use or support illegal activity of any kind. Two

---

6   The building of the hut slowed renovations in the Main Area somewhat; Swann had
    stripped the windows and a lot of other materials out of Walnut and Azalea,
    disregarding any longer-range plans for those buildings.

7   One of the societal strictures that early Harbin residents were happiest to be isolated
    from was the illegality of marijuana smoking, which was as widespread at Harbin as it
    was in the rest of the counterculture in the mid-70s. It's estimated that in the early
    years, perhaps as much as 90% of the population of Harbin smoked marijuana
    recreationally, and there had been a few pot gardens cultivated in the Village area
    from time to time.

weeks later the paper printed a retraction ("Marijuana Growers Not Church Members") but the publicity had its effect on local opinions about Harbin, which were already somewhat negative.

(When Ishvara first bought Harbin, and especially after it was sold to the Church, relationships with Middletown residents were strained. The debacle of Harbinger University was still quite fresh in their minds, and they saw little difference between Heart Consciousness Church and the Frontiers of Science. A few local ministers even warned their congregations against associating with any of the people "out there" in the early years. As time went on, relations between the two communities went from guarded to civil to friendly. Harbin residents patronized local restaurants and stores, and gradually people in town realized that this new group was, on the whole, responsible and sincere, and quite different from the Harbinger University hippies.)

Ken Keyes became frustrated and discouraged by the county's response to his proposed center, and decided against the Harbin site. Relations between the two organizations continued to be friendly, and Keyes held several month-long training workshops in Stonefront before eventually establishing his own center in Oregon.

❖   ❖

THE CREATION OF COMMITTEES LIKE THE SERVANTS OF THE dream and the reorganization of day-to-day government gave Ishvara more time to study Hindu scripture, and to work on some creative projects of his own, including work on a manuscript that would put his dream into words. He called it Living the Future.

Living the Future not only described HCC and its underlying philosophy, but expanded the vision to include what the Church and Harbin could eventually become. Ishvara examined the current society's ways of dealing with problems such as the environment, housing, unemployment, education and care of the elderly, and contrasted them with what could be accomplished in the same areas using New Age principles. Positing the idea of the Harbin community as the first stage in the development of a network, he outlined plans for a second stage of offspring communities and educational institutions that would be geographically separate from Harbin, but still within the organization of HCC.

The third stage in his long range plan was the creation of a New Age University and alternative economic cycle in which businesses would provide money for facilities where teachers could offer courses to students who would, in turn, provide labor for the businesses. As part of this cycle, New Age teaching centers and experimental communities could be funded to allow for the expansion and evolution of workshops and programs offered at Harbin and other centers.

> A tremendous potential exists at Harbin Springs to develop innovative ideas which will help solve some of the problems of society....We are presently at work building the physical facilities in which to try some of the experiments mentioned, and others still to be conceived.

Innovation and experimentation were not always well-received. Perhaps the most misunderstood aspect of life at Harbin was that its retreat center and community had been "clothing optional" from the beginning. In the bath area and most other places on property (except the county-owned road), guests and residents could choose to be naked if they wanted.

Bob Hartley's original "wish list" had included no close neighbors so that nudity wouldn't be a problem. He believed that being naked was an important part of a free and open community because it created an atmosphere of honesty and openness, and fostered spiritual growth as ingrained cultural values were transcended. Many people in the county (erroneously) began referring to Harbin as "that nudist colony," and often equated nakedness with sex.[8]

---

8 Clothing optional areas are often confused with nudist camps or naturist gatherings. Nudists tend to band together, in private camps or resorts, for the express purpose of being naked (which is usually required). Naturists are those who fight for the right to be nude in public recreation areas (beaches, etc.), and who make a political statement of nudity.

Within the framework of the holistic movement, nudity is seen as a natural state, as healthy as vegetarian dinners and 100% cotton clothing; it is felt that the openness and honesty that comes from being naked encourages much more respect and communication than it does titillation.

Because Harbin was designed to be clothing optional, not nudist, those who chose to wear bathing suits in the pools were as free to do so as those who chose to bathe naked. Extending the principles of Heart Consciousness, it was a matter of personal responsibility and freedom—neither clothing nor nudity was required.

> Allowing people to do what they want where it does not disturb others is what we believe in. "Clothing optional" fits this belief while requiring clothes does not. There is no pressure one way or the other. We simply do what we do.

This laissez-faire attitude attracted a wide variety of people, many of them skilled workers who wanted to try a change in lifestyle. The last of the people living on the "upper property" had left by the fall of 1979, and Ray Testman and his wife moved up the mountain to the hut that Swann had built, which was little more than an extended shack with a great view of the valley. Ray remodeled the structure completely, creating a serene and private place for his family to live as he began a series of huge construction projects.

Ray and his crew spent 1979 and 1980 in the broad meadow north of the Main Area. Within a stone's throw of the place where the Lake Miwok had their fall encampment, the crew built a workshop center that was private and away from the center of activity. The Meadow Building was a light, airy, natural wood structure with a private bedroom for the workshop leader, a large kitchen and dining area and a main room, all surrounding a central atrium.[9] The space was perfect for almost any type of interactive workshop—from encounter groups to folk dance to massage intensives. Except for a few

---

9 The main room and the atrium were later merged into one large space with skylights.

huts and garden sheds, it was the first completely new structure that had been built at Harbin since the 1940s.

When renovation was concentrated on Mainside, it had made sense to have a tool and supply room close by, and two rooms on the bottom floor of Azalea (now Azalea Kitchen) had been allocated for that use. The area served as a tool room, wood shop and mechanics shop; construction equipment and pick-up trucks were parked on the lawn in front of the building. As construction moved to outlying parts of the property, the location of the tool room became less convenient. Guests walking from the office up to the baths or to Fern also found that the equipment and supplies detracted from the otherwise serene atmosphere of Mainside.

In 1981 the Pole Barn was built on a site just across the creek from the Village. It provided dry and secure storage for tools and equipment and ample space for lumber and construction vehicles. Part of the Pole Barn was set aside as an Auto Shop for the repair and maintenance of Church vehicles. In an interview some years later, Ray Testman described the construction:

> We decided we were going to build this barn, so we went around and gathered up all the materials that were lying around and we ordered this and that and we got a permit from the county...and we sat down and expressed a plan in the dirt and measured the lumber and basically built it so we could use up all the lumber that was around. We gathered that up and just started building, and that's what we had.

❖　❖

IN THE EARLY '80S THERE WEREN'T AS MANY MOMENTOUS EVENTS as there had been in the first days of the community, but rather a continual flow of people arriving and a gradual increase in the quality of both residents and their work.

> Most attempts to change society begin with people. This experiment starts with structure. There is no one here who was here the first five years, but the structure is evolving. The people from those days are gone, and yet there is no basic change in the structure; there has been evolution and development.

One of the problems in the evolution of Harbin as a viable community and center was continuity; the population was always in flux. Although it had increased from an average of 30 people to about 45, the turnover in population some years was nearly 70%—new people arrived each month as a few residents moved on to other parts of their lives. By 1980, only a handful of current residents had been living at Harbin during the rent strike; unaware of the political or social events that had preceded their arrival, each group of new residents tried, metaphorically, to reinvent the wheel.

In order to give new people some guidance and a sense of continuity in their first months as Harbin residents, a system of sponsoring was initiated. The members of the first Sponsors' Committee—Rod, Ray, Elohym, Alton, Sage, Claude and Ishvara—were all experienced community members willing to serve as mentors for newcomers. Six weeks of trial membership in the community was required before obtaining sponsors, which had to be accomplished in the following two weeks, or the person was asked to leave the community.

A person's Sponsors answered any questions about Harbin and how it was organized, mediated for the new resident in case of disputes with other residents or the administration and served as advocates in decision-making processes. Many of the Sponsors also served on the Board of Directors or one of its committees, and obtaining sponsorship gave new people the chance to voice their opinions on community policies in a direct way. Sponsors were also able to insure that residents were aware of existing policies and, if necessary, to see that they were enforced.

Harbin's "government" had been evolving since the formation of HCC. Changes in residency donations, housing policies and work requirements occurred quite frequently; under this trial and error method, some policies were abandoned quickly because they simply weren't efficient or effective, while others were adopted and used until they became obsolete. As facilities and management improved, community structures stabilized. By 1981 a Resident Handbook explaining all aspects of community life at Harbin was drafted and given to newcomers on their arrival, thus avoiding a great deal of confusion.

In the midst of his administrative duties, Roger Windsor found the time to invite a macrobiotic chef to Harbin and establish a community dining room in the lower part of Stonefront. Residents had the option of exchanging work hours for meals (at a rate of 7 meals for 5 hours of work), or cooking for themselves. The cabins in the Village each had private kitchens, and small communal kitchens were built in Fern, Walnut and Azalea. Shared kitchen space was strictly vegetarian, in deference to some people's strong feelings about eating meat; private kitchens had no restrictions.[10]

Many communities share common meals; Harbin was an exception. Although community dinners were held in Stonefront on a regular basis, eating in a group, like most other activities in the community, was a matter of individual choice. When he began the community at Harbin, one of Ishvara's core beliefs was in the freedom of individuals to maintain their own spiritual practices which, he felt, extended to eating.

> In most communities, everyone eats together. But *what* should we eat? Macrobiotics? Raw foods? Vegetarian? Meat? Kosher? The best way for people of different beliefs to live together in harmony is for people to have the freedom to do their own cooking.

Besides offering macrobiotic cuisine in the dining hall, Roger also gave workshops on the principles and techniques of the diet, and by 1981 had achieved his dream of a macrobiotic center. A number of students had been attracted to Harbin, and with their help he had built a house on the hillside about half a mile above the Village (on the site where, a hundred years earlier, Claudius Mottier had built his cabin and vineyards). Roger lived and taught at the house (now the Mountain Lodge), which he called the East-West Macrobiotic Center.

---

10 Azalea kitchen would later become a private, shared, non-vegetarian kitchen, with membership decided by consensus. Walnut kitchen (which eventually permitted the preparation of fish and chicken) was remodeled into guest rooms in the fall of 1990.

It was the first independent center to exist under the umbrella of HCC, but it was not the last; plans were underway for a number of New Age centers on Harbin land. Beginning in 1980, plans were made for a Spiritual Emergency Network facility called Aurora House to be built in connection with the Esalen Institute.

❖   ❖

ESALEN HAD BEEN FOUNDED IN 1961 BY MICHAEL MURPHY AND Richard Price, and gained an international reputation as a seminar and workshop center and as the birthplace of the Human Potential movement. Programs given by such seminal figures as Fritz Perls, Alan Watts, Abraham Maslow and Ida Rolf attracted thousands of people—and a lot of media attention—to the former hot springs resort on the Big Sur coast. In the late 60s, Dick Price had gotten involved with the work that Stanislav Grof and others were doing with schizophrenic patients. They were investigating the idea of "divine madness," using as a model the idea that what had been thought of as mental break-downs were actually spiritual break-throughs, processes that the human mind went through in order to access other states of consciousness—a process they called "spiritual emergence."

Dick Price wanted to establish a center where schizophrenic patients could be led through their own processes with love and support, rather than being suppressed with drugs. For a variety of reasons, it wasn't feasible to build such a center at Esalen itself, and he was looking for other locations close to the Bay Area where a pilot program could be set up. Harbin fit the bill nicely.

An anonymous donor gave Price $10,000 to help establish Aurora House at Harbin, and a double-wide trailer was purchased to house the staff, initially a psychiatrist and a director for the program. Two structures were built—one 12 by 12 feet, the other 16 by 16 feet—to serve as therapy rooms. The buildings were leased from HCC, and Esalen began publicizing the project internationally. Jane Hawes, a co-founder of the Spiritual Emergency Network in San Francisco, moved up to Harbin as the project's director, working with David

Purseglove, a resident who had been instrumental in organizing the project.

Initial construction costs were paid by Harbin; income to cover rent and other operating costs was to come from the fees paid by patients who were to be referred to the center by area hospitals, psychiatrists and the Spiritual Emergency Network itself. But no referrals were ever made. Part of the problem was that hospitals required the facility to be licensed before they would send patients, and the licensing process was time-consuming and costly. Jane Hawes and Ishvara brainstormed for several months and communicated with Dick Price to see what could be done about the situation from Esalen's end, but nothing happened. Aurora House was furnished and ready to operate, but there were no clients.

It became obvious that there wasn't enough money to keep the project going long enough to get licensing and develop a sufficient number of referrals. In April of 1982, the project was abandoned.

❖   ❖

AURORA HAD BEEN BUILT ON PART OF THE 32-ACRE PARCEL THAT Ken Keyes considered leasing back in 1978. As part of the groundwork for the Living Love Center, county approval had been obtained for the development of that area. When Keyes' plans fell through, HCC decided to use the county's approval to its advantage. The Board made its own plans for the development of an additional conference facility and a 20-room hotel on the site, which would be adjacent to (and possibly used in conjunction with) Aurora House.

Harbin's resident population had grown to nearly 60, and housing facilities on Mainside were near capacity. The Board had considered using Aurora's buildings as additional workshop space, but decided that they were more valuable as resident housing. The never-used therapy buildings were turned into residential and dormitory spaces and the trailer, with its kitchen and dining areas, became the nucleus for the housing cluster.

Workshops had become a vital part of the church economy, and both the Meadow Building and Stonefront were in use more weekends than not. A number of larger groups who had inquired about holding their trainings and seminars at Harbin had to be turned down because of the lack of adequate workshop space.[11]

Ray Testman spent two or three months of each year at sea, working as a ship's engineer. When he returned in April of 1982, he and a large construction crew set about building the largest structure Harbin had seen in decades. Connected to Mainside by a footbridge, by the time it was finished the Conference Center had a 40 by 65-foot meeting room, large enough to hold a group of 400 people on folding chairs (although most groups preferred pillows on the carpeted floor). The finished building contained a spacious bathroom, shower and dressing room, a catering kitchen, and a wide deck and terraced patio that extended the workshop environment into the wooded creek area. A few years later, two small hot pools would be added, creating an entirely self-contained and private space for larger workshops; an ambitious undertaking and an unprecedented achievement for such a small community.

During the planning stage of the Conference Center project a lot of new equipment and materials were purchased, which led to an expansion of the Pole Barn. The space above the Auto Shop was developed into a carpentry department—the Cabinet Shop—by Ron Berger. Berger was an experienced woodworker, and convinced the Board that it would be more economical to manufacture the interior trim for the Conference Center than to buy it, as they had done with the Meadow Building. He assembled a group of men—Peter Cumminsky, David "the Savage" Richardson, Robert Clark, Taliq Adams—and taught them to be quality woodworkers. They made all the trim for the interior of the Conference Center and designed and manufactured most of the windows and doors.

---

11 A few groups were discouraged for other reasons. When the Hell's Angels approached Roger about holding a convention at Harbin, he gave them the pertinent information, but stressed the Church's no-alcohol policy for workshops; the group decided against Harbin as a site.

The Cabinet Shop came together as a working unit in a way few other departments at Harbin had done. They functioned as a cooperative, sharing decisions on design, guidelines for work in the shop, and who came to work on the team. They got an order for three beds for Fern, to replace the mattresses on the floor, and eventually designed and built all the beds in Fern and Redwood (and later most in Walnut and Azalea), along with dressers, wardrobes and tables. Their skills and camaraderie grew with each project, and the men of the Cabinet Shop developed a reputation for professionalism—a rare quality at Harbin, with its basically temporary and amateur workforce. Taliq recalled:

> You could order something and get it done well and get it done on time, and we were very proud of that. We could deliver on time, we had a reputation to uphold, we loved wood, we loved our work and loved each other, and it was a good, good thing to be doing.

The dining area in Stonefront was being remodeled and expanded around the same time. Standard aluminum-frame windows had been planned for the room, but Ron and David Savage decided that would detract from the rest of the woodwork, and designed larger, natural wood windows that opened up the restaurant area to the view of the garden and the surrounding hills. They went on to make all the tables as well, transforming the community dining room into the Café Spontaneé.

The Café opened on Memorial Day of 1982, serving three primarily vegetarian meals a day (with occasional fish or chicken), under the capable and creative management of Robert Sousa and Lynley Lawrence—collectively known as "R 'n' L" ("Arnell").[12] The couple had arrived late in 1980 and spent their first Harbin winter with a simmering pot of soup on the stove and a steady stream of visitors. They expanded their culinary

---

12 R 'n' L were a colorful couple. Lindley was a ballerina and Robert had worked as a director on *The Dick Van Dyke Show* and later on *The Lucy Show*. As the story goes, he had been fired by Lucille Ball because he was drunk; actually, he had taken LSD.

efforts into making brownies and cookies for the Office Store, catering some workshops, and selling cookies and juices by the swimming pool in the summer of 1981. When Ray moved back into the Village, they moved up the mountain to his former house, which was there after known as Arnell's.

Their restaurant effort was open to both residents and guests; its pleasant setting and ever-changing menu soon made it a central focus for social life on Mainside and perhaps the most highly visible and successful "cottage industry" in the community.[13]

❖ ❖

THE FACILITIES AND THE RESIDENT POPULATION WERE IN A KIND of parallel evolutionary cycle—as more skilled and dependable people came to Harbin they improved its physical facilities and its management, attracting residents with higher standards of living, who then continued to improve the center and its community. Roger Windsor commented on the evolution of his neighbors:

> When I first got here, many of the people who were here were, frankly, crazy. Really crazy people. I'm talking about people with guns, people who would eat worms. I wouldn't apply the word crazy to people who are here now [1984], but they're definitely unusual and tend to be different from the people "outside."

Harbin was (and is) a community of individualists, some talented, some dedicated and responsible, some just different, but all people who wanted to live something beyond the ordinary American lifestyle. As the caliber of new residents rose, the arrival of one talented individual had less of a dramatic impact on the community as a whole than it would have had in the early years, but still almost everything that

---

13 They ran the restaurant until 1986, at which point the Church took over the management. It was managed by a number of different people in the community until 1989, when it became an independent operation.

happened at Harbin happened because one individual took the initiative to try something that hadn't been done before.

The basic structure of the community allowed for individual freedom of choice in work situations, and encouraged independent enterprises, which created an opportunity that didn't exist in many places: if your idea fit in with what the community needed at that moment, the money was made available to go ahead and do it.

The quality and diversity of the resident community was further reflected in changes in the guest population. Ishvara had long been hoping that Harbin would become an important New Age center, but for the first decade its facilities had been too limited—and much too rustic—to support the kind of growth that entailed. In the mid-80s, with the new conference buildings, a restaurant and increasingly more attractive guest rooms, Harbin's popularity as a retreat and workshop center grew dramatically. In five years income from non-residents jumped from $66,000 (in 1978) to almost $400,000 by 1983.

Guests, workshop leaders and students came from all over the United States and Europe, and participated in a wide assortment of programs. Unlike most spiritual centers, Harbin represented no one school of thought, and offered its visitors an eclectic sampling from traditional and innovative spiritual and psychological disciplines.

> The idea is that any given individual or group has a particular slant or interest, and their approach to the New Age is colored by that slant. Harbin Springs is like a university that represents a whole array of activities and fields of knowledge, not just the department of biology. It is a large, porous entity for dynamic small units to fit themselves into.

One of the dynamic units that fit itself into Harbin was the Niyama School of Massage, founded by bodyworker Phil Lutrell. The school offered classes in a variety of bodywork techniques, including Swedish and Esalen style massage and Japanese Shiatsu. Massage practitioners from all over northern California trained at the school, and many resident students found opportunities to practice what they had learned; massage services were increasingly in demand by Harbin guests.

Harbin's reputation as a health resort had declined in the '50s and '60s as the emphasis shifted from the "health" to the "resort." As the New Age movement spread, it brought a renewed emphasis on holistic, natural living, and health was once again a prominent factor in Harbin's popularity. The baths had always been its strongest single draw, but over the years claims for their medicinal and curative powers had given way to highlighting their recreational use. Visitors in the 1980s didn't come to "take the waters" in the same sense that their 1880 counterparts had, but they were much more conscious of the benefits of the natural mineral baths than the generations in between had been.

Health wasn't a separate activity, it was an integral part of life at Harbin, which advertised itself as "a center for growth and healing." Along with the waters, contemporary visitors were attracted by the natural environment, the lack of stress, the vegetarian diet and overall atmosphere of healthy living that Harbin offered.

> We provide a serene and beautiful place for New Age teachers to share their vision. We also open our environment to visitors to get away from the pressures of the modern world in our healing country setting. And finally, we are creating a living center in which our family, our resident membership, can live with the beauty of nature, work together to serve our dream, grow closer to each other and otherwise reap the benefits the community has to offer.

The free Health Treatment program was one of the more tangible benefits of residency. By 1983 there were 13 people in the community (out of a total population of about 60) who practiced some form of healing work, primarily massage. Each resident who fulfilled the work requirement (at that time, 24 hours per week) was eligible to receive two sessions per month free of charge. For this service to their fellow community members, the healers were given three-hour work credits for each session given. Guest rates for sessions from those healers who chose to offer them to the public were $25 and up for a one-hour massage.

The popularity of massage, along with an ever-increasing number of visitors who had heard of Harbin and came to enjoy its facilities, made it necessary to enlarge and remodel the inadequate dressing rooms next to Fern. Current guests who have been visiting Harbin since the early '80s describe the old building as "funky"—small curtained-off showers and toilets in a dark and run-down building. The structure had been built by Newt Booth in the early 1920s, and once housed the nurse's office and barber shop; it was gutted and completely redone in the winter of 1984-85.

New bathrooms with both indoor and outdoor showers were installed in the lower portion, along with storage cubicles and other amenities for bathers. The upstairs had been renovated into a large, skylit kitchen with communal cooking and food storage, and a dining area whose huge windows overlooked the whole pool complex.[14] Fern Kitchen was available for guests who chose to provide their own meals rather than eat in one of the restaurants[15] and for residents who didn't have other kitchen space. It quickly became a hang-out for late night discussions and impromptu potlucks and fostered a friendly, relaxed atmosphere where people could meet, and residents and guests could mingle.

The mix of residents and guests was another factor in Harbin's popularity; people who visited but who didn't choose to live and work in the community still felt like they were part of an extended family, with an open invitation to come back anytime.

❖   ❖

UNFORTUNATELY, HARBIN'S FACILITIES ALSO ATTRACTED uninvited guests; trespassers had been a problem since Ishvara bought the property. Under most of the previous owners, local

---

14 Current construction manager Neil Murphy describes the remodeling as "A neat piece of construction legerdemain. The kitchen was done first, resting on concrete piers, and was finished in the summer of 1984; the dressing rooms below were done the following winter."

15 The tiny Magic Inn had opened on weekend nights, offering macrobiotic dinners.

residents had visited the springs at no charge, coming up for dinner, cocktails or a bath, and sometimes just to visit. When the Church took over the property, business from a local clientele dropped off almost completely. Middletown residents were welcome, but required to pay the standard fee; most chose not to visit.

A handful of others felt they were entitled to use the baths for free if they wanted, frequently coming to that decision about 2:00 am when the bar in town closed. Every once in a while a pick-up truck full of young men, throwing beer cans and shouting, would circle the Gazebo, or someone would report that there was drinking and rowdy behavior going on in the pools in the middle of the night.

An all-night Security patrol had been formed by Stacey Moore in 1983, and he was able to deter most intruders (calling the sheriff on the rare occasions when the situation got out of hand), but their visits still shattered Harbin's peaceful atmosphere, at least for a while.

The community put up with these infrequent intrusions for over ten years; there were people in the community itself that were occasionally drunk and disorderly. But as Harbin became more civilized, the people who became residents no longer exhibited or tolerated that kind of behavior. Many community meetings were held to discuss the idea of putting a gatehouse at the entrance to the property, where the roads to Mainside and to the Village forked.

While almost everyone agreed that the trespassing had to be controlled, many were against the idea of putting a "guard" at the entrance. Security finally prevailed, and the Reception Center was built by Pete Fairclough, both to keep out unwanted visitors and to welcome guests to Harbin at any time of the day or night.

The Gate took a lot of pressure off the people in the Office, which had also grown more complex, handling guest reservations, resident work reports, health treatment forms and other paperwork. Roger was tired of managing the Office after five years, and moved on to other projects. He was replaced by NorVal Bhendra, a former legal secretary, who quickly established new, streamlined office procedures, including a personnel department (to handle the details of resident arrivals and departures from the community) and accounts payable department. She ran the office with a firm, no-nonsense approach.

A few people who had enjoyed the funky, laid-back atmosphere of Harbin complained that it was getting too bureaucratic, but with a resident population of close to 100, more than 150 workshops a year booked into three different facilities and thousands of guest visiting annually, it had become a rather complex organization.

Decisions about small projects and routine maintenance tasks (What furniture do we need for Fern 13? Which rooms need to be cleaned? Who's working the midnight gate shift?) were made by the people actually doing the work, supervised by working managers. By 1984, "Harbin" consisted of more than 15 departments, overseen by seven managers, handling every aspect of the resident community and the operation of the retreat center: administration, office, reception, housekeeping, landscaping, garden, maintenance, construction, auto shop, security, pools, cabinet shop, community food store, restaurant, workshops and healing staff.

Questions of policy and community-wide issues were decided by the Sponsors Committee and the Board of Directors at their regular meetings. It was a well-organized structure, but far from an ordinary bureaucracy. The members of the Board meditated together in a spiritual circle that met each week, in addition to their regular business meetings. This rapport made it possible for the group to make all decisions by consensus. Ishvara had stepped away from the day-to-day operations of the center, concentrating his efforts on long-term financial and legal matters.

One of those matters came about because of the efficiency and productivity of the Cabinet Shop. A lot of the major remodeling had been completed by 1984, and the men in the shop, who were by that time proficient woodworkers, were turning out beautiful pieces of furniture, and wanted to expand their enterprise to include customers outside Harbin. The problem was that HCC, as a non-profit corporation, couldn't legally engage in business.

A separate membership organization—the Religious Order of Heart Consciousness (ROHC)—was established in order to provide a structure for the Cabinet Shop and other large-scale cottage industries to operate within. Residents could join the ROHC partnership or not, as they chose. Benefits such as free health treatments and guest pass privileges were transferred to the ROHC membership, offsetting the minor liability that the individual's share in the partnership was taxable income.

The market for hand-crafted furniture turned out to be disappointingly small, but ROHC eventually took over many other functions at Harbin, including resident's pay, becoming the labor contractor providing the workforce for the HCC-owned retreat center.

❖   ❖

ALTHOUGH HARBIN'S WORKSHOP FACILITIES WERE BOOKED nearly every weekend, workshop publicity was somewhat haphazard. Individual workshop leaders advertised their own programs, but there was no central listing, no catalog of offerings. Roger Windsor had completed the building of North Star, a dormitory for his macrobiotic students, and decided to devote his efforts to improving public relations about the workshops, concerts and seminars being offered at Harbin.

He had assisted Bob Capell with a bi-monthly newsletter, *The Harbin Hot Springs News* (which kept residents informed of opportunities for classes or bodywork), but he wanted to reach the guest population too.[16] Late in 1984, he started a 16-page magazine, the *Harbin Hot Springs Experience*, which was primarily a workshop catalog, updated quarterly, with some articles about teachers and healers whose classes or services were available, and ads urging other workshop leaders to consider Harbin's facilities.

---

16 The *News* ran for twelve issues in 1984 and 1985. In October of 1987, another resident "newspaper"—*The Harbinger*—was begun as a weekly forum for news, events, notices, ads and other items of interest to the community. Edited by the author, it is still in circulation as of January, 1991.

An early issue of *The Experience* featured an interview with Peter Caddy, founder of the Findhorn Community in Scotland, who had visited Harbin that winter. Findhorn was internationally known, and was perhaps the premier community in the New Age movement (with Esalen being the top teaching center), and Caddy's favorable comments about Harbin's own community were a definite boost for the Northern California center.

The next issue profiled Charlie Thom, a Karuk medicine man and elder who traveled around the country leading sweat lodges and purification rituals. Although almost every spiritual discipline was represented at Harbin (Buddhists, Hindus, Christians, Rajneesh followers), Native American religion—the Red Path—had an especially large number of adherents, who brought some of the old traditions back.[17]

The first people who lived at "Harbin" regarded the land as sacred, especially the hot springs themselves. With the European colonization of Indian territories, most of that respect for the sanctity of the land had disappeared. But the New Age movement, with its emphasis on both spirituality and ecology, fostered a new respect for the earth and its creatures, and a new awareness of the existence of powerful spiritual places.

The "power spots" at Harbin were places on the land where many perceived spiritual energy to be strong.[18] Some of the places that were regarded as sacred by the members of HCC had also been revered by the shamans of the Lake Miwok—Indian Rock, the Grandmother's Circle and, of course, the baths themselves. But other spots had come to be held

---

17 Although the land was originally in Lake Miwok territory, what is referred to here is not the religion of any one tribe, but the values of the "universal spirituality" of the Native American world. Medicine men and women from many tribes—Cherokee, Lakota Sioux, Karuk and others—have come to Harbin to share the rituals of their own people with others who have come to visit Harbin's sacred land.

18 The seven primary power spots are: the hot springs; the top of Mt. Harbin; the South Ridge (especially the Medicine Wheel of rocks naturally found there); Indian Rock; the Great Rock Mountaintop in Boggs Mountain State Forest (just beyond the Harbin property line); the Great East Rock nearest to Middletown; and the cold water spring source and the cliff behind it.

sacred not for their "ancestral" energy but for the spiritual power that Harbin residents had found was present. They were places for dreaming, for meditating, for reaching "between the worlds." According to Ishvara and others, a network of seven primary power spots formed a protective ring around the property, with the Fire Circle in the Meadow at its center.

In order to assure protection for the spiritual aspects of the land, a non-profit corporation—The Holy Lands Preservation Trust—was formed. Many of the 16 trustees were Native American teachers who supported the efforts of the community at Harbin to preserve and honor the land. Not since the Lake Miwok had fished the creek and gathered acorns in the meadow had a group occupied the land *and* revered it. After more than a century and a half of secularity, Harbin and its healing waters were once again treated as sacred land.

The Church had operated Harbin since 1975, with the intention of creating a space for individuals and groups who identified with its founding philosophy to pursue their own spiritual practices. But Heart Consciousness Church itself had no formal rituals or ceremonies. In 1985, Suzanne McMillan LaRosa and her husband Sunny came to Harbin and began leading ceremonies honoring the full moon and the changes of the seasons. Full Moon ceremonies with chanting and musical instruments often took place at the Fire Circle in the Meadow or in the Warm Pool; two weddings also took place in the candlelit pool, with hundreds of people, decked with flowers, dancing in the warm water. Suzanne also held spiritual gatherings on Sunday mornings, eclectic mixes of rituals from all cultures, circles in which participants shared their own beliefs and feelings.[19] (In 1987 a Cherokee elder called Grandpa Roberts would move to Harbin and serve as the charismatic leader of

---

19 In October of 1990, Charlie Thom (Red Hawk) moved to Harbin to lead gatherings and sweats, and serve in the same capacity as Grandpa Roberts. In his newsletter, *Medicine Song*, he said: "I have been spiritually chosen to be at Harbin Hot Springs...a place where Indian people used to do many things. I find it's through communication with the Spirit here that it is very comfortable, where many people can come to visit such a sacred place and many sacred sites. It's a special retreat place."

these gatherings, and as the medicine-man-in-residence, until his death in August of 1988.)

Until Grandpa Roberts began holding them on the lawn, the gatherings were held in the recently-constructed Theatre. A room on the bottom floor of Azalea had been used as a community TV room, but as the resident population grew it became too small. Rooms in the lower level of the old cocktail lounge building had been used as storage spaces for electrical supplies and the odds and ends used by the maintenance crew in repair work. The supplies were relocated to a small tool room in the basement of the building, with the surplus going to the Pole Barn (and, when it was completed in 1986, to the Warehouse next door to the barn).

The former storage spaces were remodeled into one large, multi-level room; carpeted tiers covered with pillows were used for seating, with a large TV (later replaced with a VCR, projection unit and 10-foot screen) at the bottom of the room. The Theatre was open each evening until midnight for the viewing entertainment of guests and residents. A dubbing studio with a reel-to-reel tape recorder, a cassette deck, turntables and other audio equipment was built at the same time, and an audio library was created for residents' use.

The comfort and efficiency of Harbin's rural environment was discreetly enhanced with modern technology in other areas around the same time. Two small home computers had been purchased for bookkeeping use and, under the direction of Libby Hillman, the automation of routine office tasks was expanded to a complete computer system, which would ultimately be used to handle hotel reservations as well.

Libby had worked with Roger Windsor on *The Experience* as a production assistant, typing most of its third issue and providing her editing and graphics skills for the next. When Roger left Harbin in 1985, Libby took over the management of workshops and public relations. She redesigned the magazine, got rid of the typewriter it had been produced on and renamed it the *Harbin Hot Springs Quarterly*.

The first issues of the *Quarterly* were written on a word processor in the office. The files were taken to the typesetter in Santa Rosa (about an hour away); the galleys were taken back to

Harbin (with another round trip for any mistakes or changes) and pasted up under the art direction of Nita Miescke. This process was not only tedious, but costly, so Libby developed a proposal to the Board, recommending that the Church invest in a desktop publishing system of its own. The new system gave all of Harbin's literature a much more professional look, and its capabilities were extended to book production.

Becoming a book publisher, it was felt, was the next step in firmly establishing Harbin as a prominent New Age center, and enabling the Church to reach out to a much greater audience than those who were able to visit the property in person. The first volumes produced were for outside clients, but in 1986 Harold Dull (who had purchased the Massage School from Phil Lutrell) finished the manuscript of his book on bodywork, and asked the new enterprise to produce it. Harold had studied Shiatsu techniques in Japan, and had developed them into a new form of bodywork—water shiatsu or "Watsu"—which was given in the Warm Pool. It was a unique system, and one that was integrally related to Harbin and its facilities.

Bodywork Tantra was Harbin Springs Publishing's first title; distribution was almost entirely mail order, with the bulk of the publicity done by Harold himself, in his classes and through the *Quarterly*. In the next four years, the publishing arm of Harbin would expand into its own separate office in Middletown, with a growing list of titles, including the New Age Community Guidebook and Harbin Hot Springs: Healing Waters, Sacred Land. Harbin's books are distributed in bookstores nationwide, and are considered to be one of its most important resources for the future.

The hot springs have always been its most important natural resource, its most popular "attraction," and have given it a unique identity. The springs themselves had changed little over the centuries, but in the mid-80s the pool area looked very different than it had in Newt Booth's day.

The swimming pool had been refinished and repainted, the deck over Redwood had been built, and extensive landscaping had been done. In the years between 1985 and 1987, more modern additions to the pool area were made. Care of the pools had been a top priority in the community since its inception, and maintenance duties—regular scrubbing and frequent draining—were shared by many residents over the years. With large numbers of people using the pools 24 hours a day, seven days a week, cleanliness was of prime importance. Most public pools used chlorine to purify their water and control algae and bacteria growth, but Harbin was unwilling to tamper with the natural mineral content of the hot spring water by introducing any chemicals. Exhaustive research was done to find a healthier and non-toxic way of keeping the water pure; it was found that

The Hot Pool, late 1980s

a system using ultra-violet lights and hydrogen peroxide controlled organic matter without causing any smell or irritation to the bathers' eyes or skin.[20]

A soundproof pumphouse was built into the hillside and the filtration system for the Warm Pool was installed. The results were so good—crystal clear water with a reduction in maintenance—that the system was later expanded to filter the cold swimming pool.

Two new pools were also developed—one constructed and one discovered. Behind the Hot Pool building there had been, in times gone by, a small plunge filled with cold spring water.

---

20 The water passes through the U-V chamber, where the ultra-violet light neutralizes any organisms and turns the peroxide into its component water and oxygen. The particles are oxidized by this reaction, and all organic and non-organic matter is strained through a series of filters. The purified water is recirculated, a cycle that is completed six times a day.

The pool had been filled in with dirt and boarded over. In 1984, Hank Snavely removed the board and excavated the three-foot deep concrete pool; cold spring water was again piped into the pool to create an icy plunge.

The Warm Pool was (and is) a meditative spot where conversation, if any, is conducted in a whisper. Children find it difficult to whisper in a swimming pool, even a warm one, and both residents and guests who came into the pool to relax in its serene atmosphere had found the presence of a lot of children to be distracting. So, in the summer of 1987, a new children's pool was constructed next to the L-shaped plunge.[21] The new pool was built in the shape of a heart, and was slightly warmer and much shallower than the Warm Pool.

❖   ❖

AFTER WALNUT AND AZALEA WERE RENOVATED, BEGINNING IN 1978, they became home to Harbin residents who lived in the former hotel rooms. Each small room was decorated and furnished to suit its occupant's personality and needs—some were austere, almost monastic; some had cozy couches and chairs; some had massage tables; some had TVs and stereos. The atmosphere in the buildings was not unlike a college dormitory, with residents just walking down the porch to go visit each other, any time, day or night, or hanging out on the porch, talking and laughing as the sun disappeared behind the hills.

The number of visitors to Harbin grew each year, and rooms in Fern and Redwood were booked almost continuously. Beginning in the mid-80s, when a resident moved out of Walnut, the vacated room was remodeled—recarpeted, painted and furnished—and rented as a guest room. Incoming residents were offered spaces in other living areas, and gradually, over a period of years, both Walnut and later Azalea

---

21   The L-shaped plunge had at one time been inside a white wooden building that also contained tiny individual dressing rooms. The "shacky remains" of the structure were torn down in 1973. For a while the plunge had been fed by overflow from the Warm Pool, and was favored by couples "preoccupied by romance," but is now a cold plunge.

became hotel buildings again. The renovation, remodeling and refurnishing of guest rooms continues, as the quality of the accommodations rises to meet the needs of the guests of the 90s.

By the late 80s, Mainside was devoted almost exclusively to adult guests. Resident families with children were housed in cabins in the Village, and there were frequently more guest reservations than there were rooms available. The resident population had grown to 120, and housing was becoming tight. After Roger left, his house had been remodeled into a small, private workshop building—the Mountain Lodge—and the North Star dormitory became resident housing. Two structures on the hill above the meadow had been built—one as Ray's family house (Hill House) and one as Ron Berger's home (the Pyramid House)—and eventually they too were used for residents.

Because of a number of factors, including county regulations and Ray's semi-retirement (and later departure), it wasn't feasible to build immediate additional housing on Harbin property, so the Church began buying houses in Middletown for residents to live in, as Walnut and Azalea were phased into use for guests.

Between 1983 and 1987, the Church acquired the Key House (a portion of which later served as the offices for Harbin Springs Publishing), a house on Jackson Street and one on Douglas Street. A four-acre parcel a few miles outside of Middletown was purchased from the Nethercott family in 1986; it included a house and a barn that was, briefly, the site of a Harbin artists' cooperative managed by attractive potter Julie Adams.

❖   ❖

EXPERIMENTAL COMMUNITIES ARE OFTEN BELEAGUERED BY government bureaucracies whose guidelines cover only what exists, not what is possible. Harbin was no exception. In June of 1987, HCC was informed by the U.S. Department of Labor that the work hours for rent exchange that had been the basis for Harbin's resident economy was not in compliance with labor laws. Ishvara contended that, under the first amendment, the separation of church and state, the Labor Department had no jurisdiction over any exchange agreement between a religious body and its members; the government, of course, insisted that it did.

The Labor Department's information—that Harbin's workers were being oppressed and forced to work at an inadequate wage—had come from a disgruntled ex-resident. The reality of life at Harbin was quite different. The resident population had risen from about 30 in the mid-70s to more than 120 by the end of the 80s, but the "political" mix had remained about the same. Fifteen to twenty percent of the people in the community were "in charge," and an equal number complained that conditions were unfair, and demanded immediate change. The vast majority of the population lived fairly contentedly, working at their chosen tasks to serve the guests and the Church.

Most of the residents had joined the community to experience a non-urban, non-competitive lifestyle, one that was not based on material wealth, but on spiritual values. They found that the benefits of living in community and with nature far outweighed what was, for some, a decrease in take-home pay—adequate, but by no means affluent.

The Labor Department was finally satisfied, and did not file a lawsuit, and the state equivalent—the California Bureau of Labor Standards Enforcement—had written a letter in July of 1986, stating that HCC was not subject to state labor laws. Less than two years later, the state changed its mind, filing a lawsuit against the Church in 1988 for violation of minimum wage statutes. The bulk of their case was based on the Church using what the state claimed was the wrong method of accounting to track worker hours and pay. After months of legal paperwork and meetings between the state's attorneys and HCC's legal representatives, the case was finally settled out of court.

Because of government interference, Harbin policies regarding payment for residents' work were completely restructured in 1987; the freedom of the community to govern its own internal economics was severely diminished, but since then payments have been made in strict compliance with existing laws.

The government was unwilling to grant the community the opportunity to experiment with the possibilities of an alternative economic cycle, but other ideas put forth in *Living the Future* began to manifest late in the 80s. When he committed his dreams to paper in 1978, Ishvara's vision of the future of HCC was one in which the original community would eventually evolve into many separate centers, forming a New Age university. Some centers would be religious retreats, some would focus on alternative education, some would be self-contained businesses, and some would be family-oriented communities.

The idea was based on the premise that, after a few years' experience in the Harbin community, there would be those who would want to move on, and use their knowledge and skills to start their own communities, with the help of HCC. What he hadn't counted on was that most of the people with leadership skills who moved to Harbin loved it, and didn't want to move anywhere else.

This evolution remained only an ideal until 1988, when negotiations between Ishvara and rebirthing pioneer Leonard Orr were completed for the lease of most of Campbell Hot Springs. The Church signed a 99-year lease on the mountain property, two miles outside of Sierraville, California,[22] acquiring possession of about a third of the property (including a 100-year old hotel in the town) immediately, with an agreement to occupy its main

Ishvara, 1990

22 Completing an historic circle, Sierraville is about an hour's drive down Highway 49 from Camptonville, the town where Richard Williams ran a hotel before he bought Harbin Hot Springs.

lodge and cabins in 1992. The Church's share of the land was renamed Sierra Hot Springs and in January of 1989, Harbin Operations Manager Carol O'Shea became the first community leader to move on to her own center (leaving Harbin in the capable hands of Julie Adams and Constance McIntosh).[23]

❖   ❖

HARBIN HOT SPRINGS CONTINUES TO THRIVE. IN 1990 ITS Resident population neared 150—some living and working on the land, some living in Middletown, others working at jobs in local businesses but living in the New Age community. Its conference facilities are booked for more than two hundred workshops a year, and over 10,000 people visit annually. For the first time in its history, revenues in a single year approached two million dollars. But more importantly, the vision set out when Heart Consciousness Church was formed—providing a place for spiritual growth without conformity—has flourished.

Harbin Springs exists today because of the hopes of Richard, Williams; the tenacity of Jim and Maggie Hays, rebuilding when their life's work was destroyed; the constancy and business acumen of Newt and Lela Booth; and, in a way, because of the misfortune of Don Hamrick to have a dream that became too popular.

It has weathered many setbacks—from fire and bankruptcy to abandonment and rebellion—but it is still thriving. It was the first resort in this county, and is the only one, of all the old resorts, that still welcomes guests.

Countless people have come to bathe in its waters for hundreds, perhaps thousands of years. It has watched as history itself unfolded through its gates: Indians, pioneers, Victorian ladies, boxers, hunters, hippies and Heart Consciousness.

---

23 Sierra Hot Springs, as this is published in 1991, is home to a tiny community of people who are working to renovate the old hotel to provide living space for residents (and eventually, for guests) and to develop the hot springs property itself into small campsites and secluded pools.

It has been almost twenty years since Bob Hartley found himself the owner of a dilapidated former resort. In that time, Harbin Hot Springs has evolved from a place whose only future seemed to be certain demolition to a successful and prosperous community and retreat center.

In this last incarnation, it has been home to more than a thousand people, and a temporary haven for perhaps fifty times that number. It has succeeded where other churches, other communities, other living experiments have failed.

Why? Because of the vision of one man and his determination to hold to it, and because of the love and skill and dedication of the hundreds of others who shared parts of their lives in order to build their own dreams within his.

This book contains the story of Harbin Hot Springs' past. What about its future? It seems fitting to let Ishvara have the last word:

> I don't have any belief how things *should* be, because I believe that the evolving process is much more intelligent than my ideas are. And I believe that people will be guided to do the right thing at the right moment.

A Brief English - Lake Miwok Dictionary

Note: The following words are taken from Catherine A. Callaghan's *Lake Miwok Dictionary*, compiled from several years of fieldwork and interviews with native speakers of the language in the late 1950s. As a language, Lake Miwok is almost extinct; there is, in 1990, only one native speaker still alive. This was never a written language; many of its sounds are imperfectly represented by the English alphabet. Unlike English, there are no silent letters—all letters are pronounced, as follows:

	(used before words which begin with a vowel): a catch in the throat; a glottal stop.
á	as in *father*
áa	as in *father*, dragged out (*fa-a-ther*)
b	as in *boy*
c	ts as in *fats* (cc pronounced tss) (Hard C sound is written as K; a soft C as S.)
d	as in *day*
é	as in *they*
ée	as in *they*, dragged out (not ee as in feet)
h	as in *hard*
í	as in *machine*
íi	as in *machine*, dragged out
k	as in *skin*
kʰ	as in *kin* (said with more force than k)
k'	as in *kin*, followed by catch in throat
l	as in *let*
ł	a "hissed" l (no Eng. equivalent; also written hl)
m	as in *met*
n	as in *now*
ó	as in *poke*
óo	as in *poke*, dragged out (not oo as in shoot)
p	as in *spin*
pʰ	as in *pin* (more force)
s	as in *see*
ṣ	(back s), between Eng. S and Sh; an S with the tongue curled back, a whistling, sibilant S.
t	as in *tea* (but formed by pressing against the upper teeth with the tongue, not putting the teeth together)
ṭ	(back t) formed by curling tongue back
ú	as in *flute*
úu	as in *flute*, dragged out
w	as in *wet*
y	as in *young*

Double consonants (ww, nn, tt) are pronounced the same as a single consonant, but dragged out:
t = *mighty*   tt = *might tea*

Words marked with an asterisk (*) are cited in the text of Chapter Two.

A

*acorn	wáya
air	héna (also "breath," "life," "wind," "feelings")
arm	táwlik (also "wing" and "dime"— probably because of the winged figure on early 20th century dimes)
*arrow	kíwwa
ashes	wíilok
*atomic bomb	'ú'kaṣan háttuk
awl	hútik
ax	háaci (*haatsi*)

B

baby	púttu (also "child")
basket	'olúut (generic)
*beads	húuya
beak	húk (also "bill" or "nose")
*bear	kúle (grizzly)
belly	púluk
bird	méle
blood	kíccaw (*kitssaw*)
bone	kúlum
*bow	kóono (also, later, "gun")
boy	héena
bread	cíppa (*tsippa*)

C

*Camel cigarette	pʰúm'ele lúumakayaw
charcoal	kúṣṣa
chicken hawk	ṣúyyu
*chief	hóypu
*chief	málle (assistant)
*chief's wife	máayen (also "female leader," "queen")
child	élay (also "son," or "daughter")
*clam	káay
cloud	mólpa
coyote	'óle
cradle	túnuk (basket cradle)

D

dance	lákih
*dance house	lakíhniweyi
*dance caretaker	mállele
*dance dreamer	húuni

*dance timekeeper	heláama
day	híi (also "sun")
death	yóok
*deer	ṣúkki (also "meat")
digging stick	héllam
dirt	yówa (also "earth")
*doctor	húuni yómta ("singing doctor," shaman)
*doctor	lúubak yómta ("sucking doctor," shaman)
dog	háyu
door	káa
drum	tílle

E

eagle	ṣúul
ear	'álok
egg	pʰákpʰak
elbow	ṣíplik (also "nickel"; [half an arm]. See "arm")
eye	sút

F

*fall	wayáawali ("acorn season")
father	'áppi
feather	pákah (also "flower")
female gender	pócciwali (*potssiwali*)
finger[1]	k'úpum
fire	wíki (later, also "electricity")
fish (*n.*)	káac
fish (*v.*)	'ómah
food	yolúmni
friend	'óyyu
frog	kolóolo

G

*gambling	múlli (women's dice game)
*gambling	kóṣi (men's grass game)
girl	kóola
*God	líilewali kooca (*liilewali kootsa*) ("sky person")
growl	'oláakute (of bear)
growl	k'owóolodosi (of stomach)

---

1   As in English, each finger has its own name:
   index—kicínni (*kitsinni*) ("one that points")
   middle—kówuhk'upum ("middle finger")
   ring --láaktekhelak ("without a name")
   little—k'etélway (no translation given)
   thumb—nawáak'upum ("old finger")

H

hair	ṣáapa (of head only)
hand	'úkku
*Harbin Springs	'éetawyomi ("hot place")
*Harbin Creek	'éetawwuwe ("hot creek")
*hawk	wékwek ("bullet hawk")
head	cánna (*tsanna*)
health	hínah
heart	cíddidik (*tsiddidik*)
*heaven	líilewali ("high world," also "sky")
herb	wéne
*hell	wéyaawali ("bottom world")
hill	páwih
home	yómi (also "place," "nest," "people of a place")
horn	kílli
*hot water	'éetawkik
*house	wéyi
husband	míiw

I

*Indian[2]	kóoca (*kootsa*)
*Indian baking powder	'awáayowa ("red earth")
insect	cálay (*tsalay*)

K

kill (*v.*)	kátt

L

lake	pólpol
Lake Miwok language	kócca átaw (*kotsa ataw*) ("Indian language")
Lake Miwok speakers	'oléeyomi
large	'áde
laughter	yómu
leg	lóolo
lightning	kélip
*lizard	petéeli

---

2   The Lake Miwok used this word to mean "person," and later to indicate native person, rather than white person.

M

magic	'úṭel
male gender	táyhwali
man	táyh
*meadowlark	huyúuma
*money	'awáahuya (magnesite cylinders, "red beads")
*money	lúppu (clamshell disks)
*money	lúppuhuya (clamshell cylinders)
moon	káwul híi ("night sun")
*mortar	támih (large, permanent)
*mortar	tukúlli (portable)
mother	'únu
music	kóyanni (also "musical instrument")

N

naked	howóytu
necklace	poyénni (also, later, "necktie")
net	cáwah (*tsawah*)
no	hélla
no!	háccih! (*hatssih!*)
nuts	sának

O

*obsidian	cícca (*tsitssa*) (also "quartz," "flint," or "arrowhead")
*obsidian	tákse lúppu ("glittering rock")
ocean	'udíi pólpol ("huge lake")
old	náwa
*Old Man Coyote	'oléenawa

P

pain	húna (also "sharp," "disease")
pelvis	cúukin téepil (*tsuukin teepil*) ("fork of the hips")
*people	kóocako (*kootsako*) (also "family," "living things")
pipe	ṣúmkitumay ("smoking stick")
*poisoner	'amáayomi (also "enemy")
*poisoner	wállipo (renegade)
pregnant	púule
pretty	yomúnnaka

Q

quail	cokóoko (*tsokooko*)

R

*rabbit	nómeh (cottontail)
rain	'úupa
rattlesnake	holóomay
run (*v.*)	híccuw (*hitssuw*)

run (v.)	ṣóta (of nose)
run (v.)	cobooboṣi (tsoboobosi) (of water)

S

salt	kóyyo
*seaweed	haskúula
*shaman	yómta
sing (v.)	kóya
skin	ṣúluk
*skunk	káluk
small	k'úcci (kutssi)
smoke	ṣúmki (from tobacco)
smoke	káal (from fire)
song, magic	'uṭél kóyniwili ("magic happy song")
spider	pókkon
spring	'óla (water)
Spring	walintáke ("season emerging")
stick	túmay (also "wood")
sugar	kawáatsu (also "honey", "sweet," "sugar pine sap")
*sweat lodge	lámma

T

thunder	táalawa
thunder	tʰónonononono (sound of)
tooth	kút
*toyon berries	píila
*track	kólo (also "foot")
tree	'álwa
*trout	húul
tule	kóol (round)
tule	pʰátpʰat (flat)
turtle	meléeya

U

ugly	huwúmnaka
universe	walíiwali ("world world")
uterus	'elay ṣukúhni ("child resting place")

V

vegetables	ṣiwíiṣiwi yólumni ("green food")
*village	'oléeyomi ("coyote place")
*village	túuleyomi ("deep place")
*village	Kupétcu (located somewhere at Harbin)

W

water	kíik
weasel	cáti

whiskey	káykaykik ("hot water," post-contact word)
why?	'ée?
wife	kúlle
willow	káye
woman	pócci (*potssi*)
wood	túmay (also "stick")
woodpecker	panáak
*woodrat	yúllu
*wood tail	túmay kóok
world	wáli (also "year")

Animal noises:

sound of large animal falling	tʰóololololololo
sound of chicken hawk flying	psssss
sound of frog	watáak
sound of coyote running	tʰónonononono
sound of coyote coming	tʰánananana
noise made by coyote while running	kóol kól kól kól
Coyote exclamation	'ém 'ém 'ém 'ém ('ép 'ép hép hép)
noise made by bear	kúule
noise made by crane	wáak wáak

Counting:

one	kénne
two	'ótta
three	deléeka
four	'otótta ("two twos")
five	kedékku ("one hand")
six	páccadak (*patssadak*)
seven	semláawi
eight	'óttʰaya
nine	kénnenhelak ("one lacking")
ten	'ukúukoci ("hand" plus dual suffix *kotsi*)
eleven	kénne wállik ("one outside")
nineteen	kénnenhelak wállik ("nine outside")
twenty	'óttatumay ("two sticks")
ninety	kénnenhelaktumay ("nine sticks")

Exclamations:

for chasing animals away	fyúuuuuuuu
for calling forth game	hów hów
of applause	haháa
of surprise	háah!

Lake Miwok Creation Myths[1]

THE DESTRUCTION OF THE WORLD

1. The World is Set Afire

It ALL HAPPENED BECAUSE WEASEL GOT MAD. WEASEL GOT MAD because Hawk Chief stole his beads. They were all living at Tuleyome then, Coyote Old Man and his wife, Old Lady Frog. There were their two grandsons the Hawks, Hawk Chief and Grapevine Hawk. Lady Pelican was the wife of Hawk Chief. There was Bluejay. There was Turtle. There was Hummingbird. A lot of them were living at Tuleyome in one big house.

Hawk Chief used to hunt ducks for them. His grandfather Coyote had warned him: "If you see Weasel's house while you are out hunting, don't go there! Be sure not to go there! He is a mean one!" Hawk found Weasel's house. He went there. Weasel was away. Hawk was hungry. He looked for something to eat. He found some squirrel meat, and he ate it with acorn bread. Then he found the beads, strings of them, even well-polished flat disks of clamshell, a whole fortune of them. Hawk Chief stole out of Weasel's house and hid them in the creek.

Weasel came home. Right away he noticed the empty sacks where he had kept his beads. He kicked them. He cried. He cried for four days. Then he went out and built a fire. He built a fire. He was singing: "Somebody must be wanting to see me, somebody who is not afraid of me, somebody with plenty of power...!" Then, when the fire was hot, he stuck his spear in it. Then he pointed in all directions, looking for the thief. Then he cried: "Now the world is going to be destroyed!" Then the world caught fire. The whole world caught fire.

Then Hawk Chief got scared when he heard the fire getting near their house at Tuleyome. He cried: "Give him back his beads! I don't want them! They are in the creek!"

"Slowly, slowly, grandchild. What's the matter?" said Coyote Old Man. Then Coyote Old Man offered Weasel his beads. "I don't want them! It's too late now. You are all going to be burnt. It can't be helped now."

---

1 · As told by Maggie Johnson and confirmed by Salvador Chapo, both Lake Miwoks, to Jaime de Angulo and L.S. Freeland, circa 1928.

2. Coyote Old Man Puts Out the Fire With a Flood

THEN COYOTE OLD MAN DIDN'T SAY ANY MORE. HE SAT DOWN AND took up an elk horn and commenced boring a hole in it. He bored and bored a hole. Then he laid it away in his corner under the rafters, and he looked for his little buckskin sack, the sack where he kept the rain. He fumbled for it and found it. Then he went out. The whole world was burning. Coyote Old Man looked for his tree and found it. Then he struck the sack against the tree. Pretty soon the fog came in, foggy rain, foggy rain.

It rained for ten days and ten nights. There was too much rain. The water began to rise everywhere. Coyote went into his little hole he had bored in the elk horn. The water kept rising and came pouring in through the smoke-hole. Then Hawk Chief flew out of the house.

He could see nothing but water everywhere. He flew around the world four times, crying: we-e-ek, we-e-ek. He was pretty tired. Then he saw a twig of manzanita bush sticking out of the water. It was the highest top of Big Mountain [Mt. Konocti] and the water was just over the top. Hawk Chief alighted on that. But the twig kept ducking him up and down, in and out of the water. Hawk Chief called to his grandfather Coyote: "Grandfather, grandfather come and help me!" But Coyote was singing inside his elk horn and didn't hear him. Coyote was singing:

Nenneo-nennaya, nenneo-nennaya,
Mother, give me some acorn-mush,
Nenneo-nennaya, nenneo-nennaya,
Mother, give me some acorn-mush,
With a roast of rabbit-ham.

Then Hawk saw two ducks swimming about, two Duck Old Men swimming about on top of Big Mountain. "Grandfathers, grandfathers, save me! I am going to die!" "All right, boy, jump on my back...but be careful of the sore place." (Note: He refers to the chronic sore that old men developed from lying too near the fire in the sweat lodge, of which they were quite vain.)

Then the old ducks took him to their house, and made him lie down, and doctored him, and nursed him and fed him. When he was well again, Hawk Chief gave them each a lot of bead money. "Now I am going!" "Thank you, boy! Thank you, boy! But why do you want to go back to that old rascal?"

Now Hawk Chief left the house of the Duck Old Men and went around the world wandering in the dark. Everything had been burnt and destroyed. He couldn't find anybody. He couldn't find his wife, Sun Woman. He was cold, the fire had all been drowned. Hawk Chief went around, looking for somebody.

Grandfather Coyote was wandering around also, looking for his grandson. He was feeling bad and lonesome. He thought; "I ought to have helped him. Maybe he is dead now!"

Hawk Chief came to a creek. He saw a man on the other side. They called across to each other.

"Heh! Who are you?"

"Who are you yourself?"

"But you, who are you? You must be full of magic power to be going around like that when all the world is destroyed!"

"You must have some power yourself, to call at me like that! What's your name anyway?"

"My name is Hawk Chief!"

"Grandchild! Grandchild! Grandchild! You are my grandchild!" cried Coyote Old Man, "Huye-e-e, huye-eee...." and he leaped across and took his grandchild in his arms and carried him home, and made him lie down, and doctored him, and fed him, and took care of him for a long time.

THE REBUILDING OF THE WORLD

1. *The Stealing of the Fire*

H AWK BEGAN GOING AROUND. BUT HE WASN'T HAPPY. HE DIDN'T LIKE the world. He was shivering all the time.

"Grandfather! Why is it so cold? Why don't we have a little fire?"

"But there is no more fire anywhere, boy! The world has been destroyed. Don't you remember? You are too young, you don't understand these things!"

"Grandfather, I want the fire!"

"But how am I going to get it?"

"Oh, you know how! You are a doctor!"

"All right!" said Coyote Old Man, "I'll see what I can do."

Then Coyote Old Man took his stick, and he hung his little buckskin bag around his neck, and he started. He went, *tonno-no-no-nonono*, running along the trail until he came to the house where the two mice lived. He stood outside and called. One of the two brothers called from inside the house: "The door is on the south side! What's the matter with your eyes? Can't you see?" The other mouse scolded his brother: "What's the matter with you? Are you crazy? That's no way to talk. How do you know but it may be somebody important? Look, it's Grandfather Coyote. There must be something wrong for grandfather to be traveling so far!"

(Note: The door of a house should normally face east, west only when certain peculiar conditions make it necessary, but never north or south. People who live in such a queer house must be queer people, with magical powers.)

Coyote Old Man went into the house and sat down against the wall. He didn't say anything. Then he took his little buckskin sack from his neck. He opened it and pulled out a long string of beads. He cut the string and tied the ends. Then he pulled another long length of string out of his little bag, and cut it and tied the ends of that. Then he pulled another long length of shell beads out of the little bag. He pulled four lengths of money out of the little bag. He gave two of the bunches to one of the mice. He gave two of the bunches to the other mouse. Then he said, "That's for you. I want you to help me. I want you to go and get the fire for me. There is no more fire in our place, and my grandson doesn't like it. He is cold all the time. He wants fire." "Where is the fire, grandfather?" "There is fire in the south world. In the south world there is fire. You go and get fire for me!"

"All right, grandfather, we will, we will try our best. We will start tomorrow!"

Then Coyote Old Man trotted back home along the trails, *tonno-nononono....* (Note: The Lake Miwok have an interesting vocabulary for the various sounds that Coyote makes, which are listed at the end of the Lake Miwok dictionary in Appendix I, on page 340.)

The next morning the two mice started for the south world. They arrived at the gate of the south world. The gate opened from the inside and they went through. They went running abreast, the two mice, until they arrived at the house of the South People. Everybody was in the house, asleep. Inside the house they kept two crows. When the crows caw, sparks of fire shoot from their mouths. That's the way the South People kept their fire overnight. The mice had brought along two sticks of rotten punk wood. When the crows said: "cawww..." they held out their sticks and got a spark. Then they started to wend their way out of the house among the sleeping people. But when they got to the door they stumbled over the legs of the two crane watchmen who were sleeping across the doorway. The cranes jumped up: "Wa-a-a-a-ak! Wa-a-a-a-ak!" Everybody got up. "What's the matter? Somebody is stealing our fire! Where are they! It's the mice brothers, those two thieves! Catch them! Kill them! No! Don't kill them! Let's keep them for pets!" In the confusion, the mice escaped under some leaves. "Where are they? They are gone! Why did you let them go? It's all that fellow's fault. I wanted to kill them. He said 'No! Let's keep them for pets....'" The mice were running. When they got to the gate, it opened of itself and let them through.

They ran all the way to Coyote's house. "Here, grandfather, here is the fire." "Thank you, grandchildren. Now your brother will be happy."

2. The Making of Humans and the Departure
of Coyote and His People.

BUT IT WASN'T LONG BEFORE HAWK CHIEF COMPLAINED AGAIN. THIS time he wanted people. "Grandfather, why aren't there people? There ought to be people..."

This time Coyote got mad. "All right," he said, "All right! Now we will go away! Now you have spoiled it!"

So Coyote made people. He went to work and made human people. He shut himself in his house and danced all night. Then he made people. He carved them out of wood. He used all kinds of woods: white oak, redwood, fir, pine, black oak, sugar pine, buckeye, maple, live oak. He made them like sticks and he stuck them in the ground all around the house. He sang and danced all night. "In the morning, you will be people!" The next morning they were people.

Then he gave them names. He said: "You are Bluejay, and you, you are Deer, and you, you are Dog!" Everybody he named like that. But they still didn't talk.

So he made a big dance. He made them dance all night. They were dancing all night. Coyote was singing and singing. "Tomorrow you will talk!"

When they awoke the next morning, the people were all talking together. "The fleas were terrible last night! Those fleas nearly finished us!"

Then Coyote Old Man made a speech. "Good morning," he said. But the people were still talking about the fleas. Then Coyote got mad. "Yes! That's all right!" he said, "but now listen to me. I am going away. My grandson doesn't like it here, so I am going away. We are going away."

Then he said to Frog Old Woman: "Come on, old lady, gather your things and your baskets. Let's go!"

Then he made another speech to the people. He said: "When you die, you are to come to my land. Beyond the ocean I shall be. None but the dead people are to come to my land. Not living people. Dead people only. After four days, they are to come to my land, the dead people."

Then he went away with Frog Old Woman, Hawk Chief and all his people.

APPENDIX III:

Vallejo's Treaty

THE SPANIARDS AND THE MEXICANS MADE NO TREATIES WITH ANY of the Indian tribes because they felt the land was theirs by right of discovery, act of possession and settlement. Between the seizure of California by the Americans in 1846, and California's statehood in 1850, yet another military government (this time American) controlled the land. Many men, especially wealthy landowners whose land was not covered by any of the Mexican grants, sought to legalize their claims by getting written documents from the Indians. When the American rule of California became official, men with written proof of land "ownership" generally kept their property.

In 1848, Mariano Vallejo (who, by this time had no official power or position, but was still an influential man), signed a treaty with 11 Indian chiefs, including many Southern Pomos and Lake Miwok hoypus. The treaty reads:

To Whom It May Concern: Be it known that we the undersigned chiefs of Tribes and Rancherias in and about the Big Lakes of the Sonoma Frontier of Upper California do solemnly affirm and declare that we are friends with good hearts toward the whites our powerful friends and neighbours, that we will make no aggression upon them nor their property and if injured ourselves by anybody, we will apply to the proper authorities of the whites for protection and redress.

Sonoma California, June 1, 1848

Menac X of Alenok[1]	Thayte X of Chiliyomi
Cuyagui X of Tuiiyomi[2]	Shonepoca X of Limaema
Hilali X of Mosliyomi	Namostk X of Tsaysymayomi
Tsapat X of Chitimocmyomi	Tum Tum X of Molgueyacyomu
Calgui X of Holhonpiyomi	Calichem X of Meynimocmayomi
Hutznun X of Lupiyomi[3]	

---

1. These are probably their most formal, most public names. The "X" symbolizes "his mark", a common sight on documents of the time. It is doubtful that any of these men (nor many of their non-Indian contemporaries) could read or write English.

2. Probably Tuleyome.

3. Possibly what is now Middletown.

NOTES ON SOURCES

THE LAND ITSELF

3 "In the vicinity of Harbin Hot Springs..." Lyman L. Palmer, *A History of Napa and Lake Counties*, p. 14. **5** "one yielding water impregnated..." Winslow Anderson, *Mineral Springs and Health Resorts of California*, p. 10. **8** "Of the 600 simple minerals..." Palmer, *Ibid.*, p. 12.

THE FIRST PEOPLE

18 "The Thunder eats people..." told by Salvador Chapo, a Lake Miwok man, to Angulo and Freeland, circa 1947. **22** "Round about the roaring fire..." C.A. Menefee, *A Historical and Descriptive Sketchbook of Napa, Sonoma, Lake and Mendocino Counties*, p. 11.

SETTLING THE WILDERNESS

62 "a connecting link..." C.A. Menefee, Ibid., p. 27. **63** "If, as not infrequently happens..." *Illustrated History and Atlas of Yolo County*, p. 6. **63** "A Digger, perfectly naked..." Menefee, *Ibid., p.* 26. **68** "as the Indians of that section..." Lyman L. Palmer, *Ibid.*, p. 48. **71** "the line that divides..." Edwin Bryant, *What I Saw in California*, p. 24. **73** "The old Indians of this section..." Palmer, *Ibid.*, p. 151. **73** "the waters of the springs..." Menefee, *Ibid.*, p. 242. **76** "He was lying upon his face..." *Daily Alta Californian*, July 10, 1856. **80** "two or three years after the discovery..." Menefee, *Ibid.*, p. 242. **80** "We started for the West..." San Francisco *Examiner*, June 27, 1897. **82** "[I] was with the army..." San Francisco *Examiner*, June 27, 1897. **82** "Sarah Adams and I liked each other..." Ibid. **83** "the howl that went up..." William O. Russell, *History of Yolo County California*, p. 61. **86** "Had there been timber..." Henry Mauldin notebooks, Lake County Museum, p. 984. **86** "When I felt lonely..." S.F. *Examiner*, June 27, 1897. **88** "Here I am content..." *Examiner*, Ibid. **90** "the property with its one log cabin..." Palmer, *Ibid.*, p. 151.

TAKING THE WATERS

91 "Everything north of the Napa..." William H. Brewer, *Up and Down California in 1860-1864*, p. 226. **94** "the road is a very good one..." Bancroft Library scrapbook #1. **95** "Helping to offset the work ethic..." Kevin Starr, *Americans and the California Dream*, p. 175. **97** "first resort of any consequence..." Lakeport *Press and Record*, March 26, 1937. **97** "This is fast becoming..." C.A. Menefee, *Ibid.*, p. 242. **100** "No topic more occupied..." Bruce Haley, *The Healthy Body and Victorian Culture*, p. 3. **102** "The beauty of the situation..." Joseph Wechsburg, *The Lost World of the Great Spas*, p. 180. **103** "When our California springs..." Winslow Anderson, M.D. *Ibid.*, p. xxx. **103** "similar to that of the famous..." *Paulson's Handbook...(1874)*, p. 54. **105** "Immediately in back of..." Lyman L. Palmer, *Ibid.*, p. 151. **105** "Mineral springs are not cure-alls..." Anderson, *Ibid.*, p. 12. **106** "They reach and search..." Anderson, *Ibid.*, p. 19-20. **107** "The visitors this season..." San Francisco *Bulletin*,

June 21, 1876. **108** "The best paying properties..." *Ibid.* **108** "About 4 weeks ago..." Bancroft Library scrapbook, p. 312. **109** "that form of nervo-hysterical..." Anderson, *Ibid.*, p. 64. **110** "One old gentleman ... A mechanic from the Mare Island..." Bancroft Library scrapbook. **110** "to give our readers..." *Paulson's Handbook*, p. 54. **111** "expended upon the property in grading..." Napa *Daily Journal*, June 1, 1875. **112** "over a route affording..." *Lake County California* (1885 pamphlet), p. 78. **113** "summer clothing..." S.F. *Bulletin*, June 21, 1876. **114** "It was a ride..." Gertrude Atherton, *A Daughter of the Vine*, p. 177. **116** "CAUTION: Do not commence..." Anderson, *Ibid.*, p. 60. **116** "The bather undresses..." Anderson, *Ibid.*, p. 41. **118** "the servants are polite..." *Paulson's Handbook*, p. 54. **121** "garden productions from Harbin..." *Pomo Bulletin*, November 1984. **122** "the cottages are genuine..." Palmer, *Ibid.*, p. 150. **124** "A man of great executive..." Lower Lake *Bulletin*, July 8, 1882. **124** "That elegant resort..." Lakeport *Bee-Democrat*, July 7, 1882. **132** "Messrs Hays and Williams..." Lower Lake *Bulletin*, September 20, 1894.

PUGILISTS IN PARADISE

133 "J.H. Ford..." Clear Lake *Press*, November 6, 1894. **133** "large quantities..." Middletown *Independent*, November 17, 1894. **135** "a handsome new hotel..." San Francisco *Call*, April 19, 1896. **136** "the baths are unsurpassed..." Harbin Springs brochure, circa 1900. **137** "A MARVELOUS CURE OF DROPSY..." Ibid. **138** "REMARKABLE CURE OF KIDNEY DISEASE..." Ibid. **139** "Mountain quail..." Ibid. **150** "The resort became a young city..." Henry Mauldin notebooks, Lake County Museum, p. 8101. **151** "The wife of one of Jeff's close friends..." DeWitt Van Court, *The Making of Champions in California*, p. 98. **152** "Fitzsimmons had built a pen..." San Francisco *Chronicle*, July 10, 1903. **154** "As the vehicle drew..." *Chronicle*, July 14, 1903. **156** "While resting in the shade..." unpublished notes of Gary Phillips, boxing historian. **160** "WITNESSED MANY STRIKING CURES..." Harbin brochure, circa 1907. **161** "One of the finest gymnasiums in the state..." Ibid. **171** "now everything is in satisfactory condition..." Margaret Hays petition, in probate file of Jim Hays, Lake County Museum. **171** "Eddie Hays met a consignment..." Lake County *Bee*, June 30, 1910. **178** "It would be inadvisable..." letter in probate file, loc. cit. **172** "The manner in which the books have been kept..." report in Jim Hays probate file, loc. cit. **173** "The Harbin Springs property..." petition in Hays probate file, loc. cit. **173** "Six towels..." ledger, Hays probate file, loc. cit.

A FAMILY RESORT

175 "My earliest recollection..." *Pomo Bulletin*, May 1985. **178** "The bear which for years..." Lake County *Bee*, June, 1916. **178** "The present management..." F.C.S. Saunders, *California As a Health Resort*, p. 48. **181** "Newt Booth is busy..." and "Mrs. Booth with many early..." and "Mr. and Mrs. N.S. Booth..." Lake County *Bee*, various issues, circa 1918-1920. **182** "We had to leave Harbin's..." *Pomo Bulletin*, May 1985. **183** "Lake County was now..." Henry Mauldin notebooks, p. 6078. **184** "The best equipped..." San Francisco *Chronicle*, April 23, 1919. **184** "BOOTHS SPENDING..." Lake County *Bee*, April 10, 1918. **185** "Supplies such as gasoline..." Harbin brochure, circa 1918. **187** "The new Plunge..." and "There are quiet and shady..." and "The location of Harbin..." Harbin Hot Springs brochure, circa 1918.

194 "This famous resort..." Ibid. **195** "narrow roads where dust..." Lake County *Bee*, July 1, 1925. **198** "Music was furnished..." Lake County *Bee*, May 18, 1927. **199** "HARBIN SPRINGS TO HAVE..." Lake County *Bee*, circa 1929. **201** "a location about three miles..." Palmer, *Ibid.*, p. 185. **205** "dress for dinner..." interview with Lucille Goodwin (Harbin waitress, 1922 and 1923), October 1990. **205** "Accommodations to please..." Stuparich Resort brochure, circa 1923. **206** "Turkish baths..." and "climate is dry..." Ibid. **209** "The only dining room in the world..." Ibid. **209** "Meals are the most important..." Ibid. **210** "STUPARICH'S SOLD..." Lake County *Bee*, October 29, 1927. **211** "NEGRO SOCIAL CLUB..." Lake County *Bee*, February 22, 1928. **212** "NEGRO INVASION..." Lake County *Bee*, March 14, 1928. **213** "STUPARICH RESORT DESTROYED..." Lake County *Bee*, October 10, 1928. **217** "In selecting Harbin Springs..." Lake County *Bee*, October 24, 1935. **220** "TRAVEL IS POTENT STIMULANT..." Lake County *Bee*, April 10, 1942. **222** "Priorities to rebuild..." Lake County *Bee*, January 14, 1944. **229** "On the broad verandas..." San Francisco *Chronicle*, August 24, 1952. **231** "BOOTHS WERE HONORED..." Middletown *Times-Star*, May 17, 1957.

FAILED DREAMS

233 "When smart people..." Harbick, "There's a Chieftain in the Highlands," in *Game and Gossip*, May 10, 1972. **234** "Dial telephones..." Middletown *Times-Star*, October 31, 1957. **234** "Lake County's Foremost Fun and Pleasure Resort..." advertisement in San Francisco *Chronicle*, circa 1959. **234** "All is changed..." *Times-Star*, July 11, 1958. **236** "MAIN HOTEL ..." *Times-Star*, October 14, 1960. **237** "Fire hoses..." *Times-Star*, October 14, 1960. **237** "Owner Robert Ramsey..." *Times-Star*, October 14, 1960. **238** "SELLIN' THINGS..." *Times-Star*, January 20, 1961. **239** "At the east end..." *Times Star*, March 10, 1961. **240** "Harbin Springs is reminiscent..." mimeographed promotional letter, circa 1961. **242** "There are still many, many buildings..." *Times-Star*, June 22, 1962. **243** "Complete with six sauna baths..." *Times-Star*, May 15, 1964. **244** "In addition to a chef who sings..." *Lake Times*, Summer 1964. **245** "NEW SPORT..." *Times Star*, July 3, 1964. **246** "HARBIN SPRINGS SOLD..." *Times-Star*, August 20, 1965. **246** "Many of the 'old timers'..." *Times-Star*, September 17, 1965. **247** "The smorgasbord..." *Times-Star*, January 21, 1966. **249** "A new relationship..." *Vector*, May 1968. **251** "Extend the frontiers..." Articles of Incorporation, Frontiers of Science Fellowship, filed with the Secretary of State of California, May 3, 1968. **251** "a huge run-down..." Vassi, *The Stoned Apocalypse*, p. 75. **252** "The group intends to make..." *Times-Star*, September 5, 1968. **253** "Disclose the nature of the forces..." Donald Hamrick in *The Changes*, October 1968. **253** "Hamrick, the executive..." *Times-Star*, August 8, 1968. **254** "a bar of non-conducting..." Gaskin, "The Great Harbinger Bust" in *Amazing Dope Tales*, p. 239. **254** "We did inquire..." *Times-Star*, September 19, 1968. **255** "It was the hippie sacrament..." Jay Stevens, *Storming Heaven*, p. xiv. **256** "give you an IQ test..." Stevens, *Ibid.*, p. 24. **259** "The psychedelic movement..." Stevens, *Ibid.*, p. 355. **260** "The scene at Harbinger..." Vassi, *Ibid.* p. 76. **261** "They started to interest IBM..." Vassi, *Ibid.* **262** "Projections along the perennial trip..." *Harbinger*, circa fall 1968. **263** "They had a hot bath..." Gaskin, *Ibid.* p. 231. **265** "I saw H. lecture..." Gaskin, *Ibid.*, p. 237. **265** "We came charging..." Gaskin, *Ibid.*, p. 233. **267** "The young people..." Vassi, *Ibid.* p. 79. **268** "Numerous violations..." *Times-Star*,

January 30, 1969. **270** "crystal in the center..." *Rolling Stone*, April 5, 1969. **271** "Tim Leary was there..." Gaskin, "The Synapse Dance," in *ADT*, p. 220. **271** "Hamrick's wife..." San Francisco *Chronicle*, April 10, 1969. **272** "Stalwarts from the local constabulary..." Vassi, *Ibid.*, p. 77. **273** "We noted that..." *Times-Star*, March 6, 1969. **274** "Other alternatives..." *Times-Star*, March 6, 1969. **274** "We moved here..." *Times-Star*, March 20, 1969. **274** "abate the nuisance..." Santa Rosa *Press-Democrat*, March 14, 1969. **275** "A temporary restraining order..." Santa Rosa *Press-Democrat*, March 14, 1969. **276** "Do you know how many people..." Donald Hamrick in *Changes*, circa Spring 1969.

RENAISSANCE AND COMMUNITY

280 "When money is available..." Middletown *Times-Star*, January 5, 1972. **281** "I had a dream of community..." Ishvara, unpublished interview, October 1990. **282** "The philosophy of the place..." letter from Bob Hartley to prospective members, circa 1973. **287** "I didn't want to organize Harbin..." Ishvara, interview, September 1989. **291** "We identify ourselves..." Ishvara, *Living the Future*. **291** "The purpose of H.C.C...." Articles of Incorporation, filed with Secretary of State, February 1975. **292** "Sunday is our regular visiting day..." letter from Bob Hartley to prospective visitors, circa 1975. **299** "I fight hard to maintain structure..." Ishvara, unpublished papers, circa 1977. **300** "Most communities were too coercive..." Ishvara, interview, September 1989. **301** "People would come in..." Ishvara, interview, October 1990. **303** "Visitors should respect..." Harbin brochure, circa 1978. **304** "Only highly dedicated..." HCC correspondence, circa 1978. **306** "GRASS GREW TALL..." Lake County *Bee*, October 11, 1978. **308** "A tremendous potential exists..." Ishvara, *Living the Future*. **309** "Allowing people to do what they want..." Ishvara, "Nudity," in *Harbin Hot Springs Quarterly*, Spring 1990. **310** "We decided we were going to build..." Ray Testman, interview, November 1985. **310** "Most attempts to change..." Ishvara, unpublished papers, circa 1980. **312** "In most communities, everyone eats together..." Ishvara, interview, September 1989. **316** "You could order something..." Taliq Adams, interview, circa 1985. **317** "When I first got here..." Roger Windsor, interview, circa 1984. **318** "The idea is that any given individual..." Ishvara, unpublished papers, circa 1985. **319** "We provide a serene..." introduction to Harbin Resident Handbook, 1983. **334** "I don't have any belief how things..." Ishvara, interview, October 1990.

BIBLIOGRAPHY

THE LAND ITSELF

American Journal of Mines and Geology. Vol. 50, No. 2, April, 1954.

Anderson, Winslow, M.D. *Mineral Springs and Health Resorts of California.* San Francisco: The Bancroft Company, 1890.

Palmer, Lyman L. *History of Napa and Lake Counties, California, Comprising Their Geography, Geology, Topography, Climatography, Springs and Timber....* San Francisco: Slocum, Brown & Co., 1881. (Facsimile edition of Lake Co. section only: Fresno: Valley Publishers, 1974.)

White, Anne Terry. *All About Our Changing Rocks.* New York: Random House, 1955.

Zim, Herbert S. and Paul R. Shaffer. *Rocks and Minerals.* New York: Golden Press, 1957.

THE FIRST PEOPLE

Allen, Elsie. *Pomo Basketmaking.* Happy Camp, CA: Naturegraph Publishers, 1972.

Angulo, Jaime de and L. S. Freeland. "Miwok and Pomo Myths," in *Journal of American Folk-Lore,* April-June, 1928.

Auel, Jean M. *The Clan of the Cave Bear.* New York: Bantam Books, Inc., 1980.

Brown, Vinson and Douglas Andrews. *The Pomo Indians of California and Their Neighbors.* Happy Camp, CA: Naturegraph Publishers, 1969.

Callaghan, Catherine A. "Lake Miwok," in *Handbook of North American Indians, Volume 8.* Washington, D.C.: Smithsonian Institution, 1978.

Callaghan, Catherine A. *Lake Miwok Dictionary.* Berkeley: University of California Press, 1965.

Crump, R.W. "Lake County," in *California, As It Is.* San Francsico: Call Pub. Co., 1882.

Erdoes, Richard and Alfonso Ortiz, Editors. *American Indian Myths and Legends.* New York: Pantheon Books, 1984.

Klein, Max. *Boulder Sitting.* San Francisco: Terra Incognita, 1987.

Kroeber, Alfred L. *Handbook of the Indians of California.* New York: Dover Publications, 1976. (Originally published as *Bulletin 78* of the Bureau of American Ethnology, Smithsonian Institution, 1925.)

Mauldin, Henry. *Lake County Indian Lore.* Lakeport, CA: Lake County Historical Society, 1977.

Menefee, C.A. *Historical and Descriptive Sketchbook of Napa, Sonoma, Lake and Mendocino Counites, Comprising Sketches of Their Topography, Productions, History, Scenery and Peculiar Attractions.* Napa City, CA: Reporter Publishing House, 1873.

Merriam, C. Hart. *The Dawn of the World: Myths and Weird Tales Told by the Mewan Indians of California.* Cleveland: Arthur H. Clark Co., 1910.

Nieto, Donna. "The History of Harbin Hot Springs, Part I: The Tuleyomi Indians," in *Harbin Hot Springs Quarterly*, Spring, 1986.

Parker, John. *Archaeological Evaluation of Selected Portions of the Harbin Springs Complex*, (manuscript) 1982.

Sadovsky, Otto J. von. "The Discovery of California: Breaking the Silence of the Siberia-to-America Migrators," in *The Californians*, November/December, 1984.

Sadovsky, Otto J. von. "Siberia's Frozen Mummy and the Genesis of California Indian Culture," in *The Californians*, November/December 1985.

SETTLING THE WILDERNESS

Albertson, Dean. "Dr. Edward Turner Bale, Incorrigible Californio," in *California Historical Society Quarterly*, San Francisco, September, 1949.

Alexander Hardy, et. al. vs. James Harbin, et. al. Supreme Court of the United States, #556, November, 1871.

Atherton, Gertrude. *A Daughter of the Vine*. London: The Bodley Head, 1899.

Bancroft, Hubert H. *History of California, (7 Vols.)* San Francisco: The History Company, 1886. (Facsimile edition Santa Barbara: Wallace Hebberd, 1965.)

Brewer, William H. *Up and Down California in 1860-1864*. Edited by Francis P. Farquhar. Berkeley: University of Califoria Press, 1966.

Bryant, Edwin. *What I Saw in California, Being the Journal of a Tour...in the Years 1846, 1847*. Minneapolis, MN: Ross and Haines, Inc., 1967.

Carpenter, Aurelius O., and Percy H. Millberry. *History of Mendocino and Lake Counties, California*. Los Angeles: Historic Record Co., 1914.

Coy, Owen C. *Guide to the County Archives of California*. Sacramento: California State Printing Office, 1919.

Gregory, Tom. *History of Solano and Napa Counties*. Los Angeles: Historic Record Co., 1912.

Harbin, James Madison. "The King of the Mountain," in *San Francisco Examiner*, June 27, 1897.

Heizer, Robert F. and Thomas Roy Hester. "Some Early Treaties with California Indians," in *Papers on California Ethnography*. Department of Anthropology, UC Berkeley, July, 1970.

Hoffman, Ogden. *Report of Land Cases, U.S. District Court*. San Francisco: Numa Hubert, 1862. (Facsimile ed. Buffalo, NY: Demais and Co., 1966.)

Illustrated History and Atlas of Yolo County, California. San Francisco: DePue and Co., 1879.

Lewis, Ruth, and Cora Benson et. al. *Stories and Legends of Lake County*. Santa Rosa: *Press Democrat*, 1949.

Nava, Julian and Bob Barger. *California: Five Centuries of Cultural Contrasts*. New York: Macmillan Publishing Co., 1976.

Pen Pictures from the Garden of the World: A Memorial and Biographical History of Northern California. Chicago: Lewis Publishing Company, 1891.

Rolle, Andrew F. and John S. Gaines. *The Golden State: A History of California, 2nd edition.* Arlington Heights, IL: Harlan Davidson, Inc., 1979.

Russell, William O., Ed. *History of Yolo County, California.* Woodland, CA: Privately published, 1940.

Stross, Fred, translator. *Ethnographic Observations on the Coast Miwok and Pomo by Contre-Admiral F.P. von Wrangell and P. Kostromitonov of the Russian Colony Ross, 1839.* Department of Anthropology, UC Berkeley, 1974.

Warden, Richard E. and Stanley Howse. "The History of Harbin Hot Springs, Part II: 1835 to 1968," in *Harbin Hot Springs Quarterly,* Summer, 1986.

TAKING THE WATERS

8-County Directory of Humboldt, Marin, Napa, Yolo, Lake, Solano, Mendocino and Sonoma Counties. San Francisco: L.M. McKenney and Co., 1885.

Adams, Ira Clayton. *Memoirs and Anecdotes of Early Days in Calistoga.* Calistoga, CA: Privately published, 1942, 1946.

Bachrach, Walter, et. al. *History of Camptonville.* Camptonville, CA: Privately published, 1966.

Bancroft's Tourist Guide. San Francisco: A.L. Bancroft and Co., 1871

Crook, James K., M.D. *Mineral Waters of the United States and Their Therapeutic Uses.* New York: Lea Brothers and Co., 1899.

A Description of Lake County, California, Showing Its Advantages as a Place of Residence (pamphlet). Lake County, CA: Board of Supervisors and Clear Lake Press, 1888. (Reprint by Lake County Historical Society, 1988.)

Haley, Bruce. *The Healthy Body and Victorian Culture.* Cambridge: Harvard University Press, 1978.

Kotzsch, Ronald E. "Natural Healing with Water," in *East West: The Journal of Natural Health and Living,* Fall 1987.

Lake County, California, Illustrated and Described Showing Its Advantage for Homes (pamphlet). Oakland: W.W. Elliott, 1885.

Starr, Kevin. *Americans and the California Dream, 1850-1915.* New York: Oxford University Press, 1973.

A Trip to the Geysers and Into Lake County, Famous as the Switzerland of America, Quickly and Easily Made, Delightful and Not Expensive (pamphlet). Southern Pacific Co., 1893.

Wechsburg, Joseph. *The Lost World of the Great Spas.* New York: Harper and Row, 1979.

PUGILISTS IN PARADISE

Fleischer, Nat. *The Heavyweight Champions.* New York: B.P. Putnam and Sons, 1949.

Mandell, Richard D. *Sport: A Cultural History.* New York: Columbia University Press, 1984.

Rader, Benjamin G.. *American Sports From the Age of Folk Games to the Age of Spectators*. Englewood Cliffs, NJ: Prentice Hall, 1983.

Sanders, F.C.S., M.D. *California as a Health Resort*. San Francisco: Boltie and Braden, 1916.

Sugar, Bert Randolph. *100 Years of Boxing*. New York: Galley Press, 1982.

Van Court, DeWitt and Walter V. Dobbs. *The Making of Champions in California*. Los Angeles: Premier Printing Co., 1926.

A Family Resort

Bailey, L. Scott, publisher. *The American Car Since 1775*. New York: Automotive Quarterly, Inc., 1971.

Financing an Empire: A History of Banking in California. Chicago: S.J. Clarke Publishing Co., 1927.

Hobson, Doris. "David Lobree," in *Pomo Bulletin*, Lake County Historical Society, May 1985.

Lewis, C. Phil. "Middletown Road Building," in *Pomo Bulletin*, Lake County Historical Society, August, 1970.

Liebs, Chester H. *Main Street to Miracle Mile: American Roadside Architecture*. New York: Little, Brown and Company, 1985.

Margolies, John. *The End of the Road: Vanishing Highway Architecture in America*. New York: Viking Press, 1981.

Mineral Springs of California. Sacramento: California State Chamber of Commerce Travel and Recreation Department, 1939.

Official Guidebook—Golden Gate International Exposition. San Francisco: The Crocker Company, 1939.

Waring, Gerald A. *Springs of California*. Water Supply Paper #338, U.S. Geological Survey. Washington, D.C: U.S. Government Printing Office, 1915.

Failed Dreams

Beardemphl, W.E. "Parries and Thrusts," a column in *Vector*, May 1968.

"Celestial Synapse at the Fillmore," in *Rolling Stone*, April 5, 1969.

Cooper, Patricia and Laurel Cook. *Hot Springs and Spas of California*. San Francisco: 101 Productions, 1978.

Feine, Donald M. *R. Crumb Checklist of Work and Criticism*. Cambridge: Boatner Norton Books, 1981.

Gaskin, Stephen. *Amazing Dope Tales and Haight Street Flashbacks*. Summertown, TN: The Book Publishing Company, 1980.

Gitlin, Todd. *The Sixties: Years of Hope. Days of Rage*. New York: Bantam, 1987.

Hamrick, Donald J. "Cycles, Seasons and Codes," in *Changes*, April, 1969.

Hamrick, Donald J. "Introduction," in *The Changes*, October-November 1968.

Harbick, Lee. "There's a Chieftain in the Highlands," in *Game and Gossip: Today and Yesterday on the Monterey Peninsula*, May 10, 1972.

La Fontaine, Barbara. "Girl Behind a Golden Door," in *Sports Illustrated*, November 2, 1964.

"Middletown Golden Spa," in *Lake Times*, Midsummer, 1964.

Palmer, Cynthia and Michael Horowitz. *Shaman Woman, Mainline Lady: Women's Writings on the Drug Experience*. New York: William Morrow and Co., 1982.

Schwartz, Hillel. *Never Satisfied: A Cultural History of Diets, Fantasies and Fat*. New York: The Free Press, 1986.

Stevens, Jay. *Storming Heaven: LSD and the American Dream*. New York: Harper and Row, 1987.

Vassi, Mario. *The Stoned Apocalypse*. New York: Pocket Books, 1973.

Wolfe, Tom. *The Electric Kool-Aid Acid Test*. New York: Bantam, 1969.

RENAISSANCE AND COMMUNITY

Anderson, Walter Truett. *The Upstart Spring: Esalen and the American Awakening*. Reading, MA: Addison Wesley, 1983.

Ball, John. *Ananda: Where Yoga Lives*. Bowling Green, OH: Bowling Green University Press, 1982.

Connole, Bernadette and Diana Morgan Smith. "The History of Harbin Hot Springs, Part III: Evolution of a Community," in *Harbin Hot Springs Quarterly*, Fall 1986.

Hawken, Paul. *The Magic of Findhorn*. New York: Bantam, 1976.

Hine, Robert V. *California's Utopian Colonies*. New Haven: Yale University Press, 1953, 1966; Berkeley: University of California Press, 1983.

Ishvara. *Living the Future*. Harbin Hot Springs, 1978, 1989.

Ishvara. "Nudity," in *Harbin Hot Springs Quarterly*, Spring 1990.

Melton, J. Gordon. "A History of the New Age Movement," in *Not Necessarily the New Age* (Robert Basil, ed.). Buffalo: Prometheus Books, 1988.

Stern, Jane and Michael Stern. "Decent Exposure," in *The New Yorker*, March 19, 1990.

Wauck, John. "Paganism American Style," in *National Review*, March 19, 1990.

INDEX